IMAGINING WAR AND PEACE IN EIGHTEENTH-CENTURY BRITAIN, 1690–1820

Ranging over political, moral, religious, artistic and literary developments in eighteenth-century Britain, Andrew Lincoln explains in a clear and engaging style how the 'civilizing process' and the rise of humanitarianism, far from inhibiting war, helped to make it acceptable to a modern commercial society. In a close examination of a wide variety of illuminating examples, he shows how criticism of the terrible effects of war could be used to promote the nation's war-making. His study explores how ideas and methods were developed to provide the British public with moral insulation from the overseas violence they read about, and from the dire effects of war they encountered at home. It shows, too, how the first campaigning peace society, while promoting pacifism, drew inspiration from the prospects opened by imperial conquest. This volume is an important and timely call to rethink how we understand the cultural and moral foundations of imperial Britain.

ANDREW LINCOLN is Emeritus Professor of English at Queen Mary, University of London. He has previously published on William Blake, including a 1992 edition of *Songs of Innocence and Experience* and the monograph *Spiritual History* (1996), and on Walter Scott, with his monograph *Walter Scott and Modernity* (2007). His current research focuses on eighteenth-century responses to war and ideas about how to achieve peace.

IMAGINING WAR AND PEACE IN EIGHTEENTH-CENTURY BRITAIN, 1690–1820

ANDREW LINCOLN

Queen Mary University of London

Shaftesbury Road, Cambridge CB2 8EA, United Kingdom

One Liberty Plaza, 20th Floor, New York, NY 10006, USA

477 Williamstown Road, Port Melbourne, VIC 3207, Australia

314–321, 3rd Floor, Plot 3, Splendor Forum, Jasola District Centre, New Delhi – 110025, India

103 Penang Road, #05–06/07, Visioncrest Commercial, Singapore 238467

Cambridge University Press is part of Cambridge University Press & Assessment, a department of the University of Cambridge.

We share the University's mission to contribute to society through the pursuit of education, learning and research at the highest international levels of excellence.

www.cambridge.org
Information on this title: www.cambridge.org/9781009366540

DOI: 10.1017/9781009366519

© Andrew Lincoln 2023

This publication is in copyright. Subject to statutory exception and to the provisions of relevant collective licensing agreements, no reproduction of any part may take place without the written permission of Cambridge University Press & Assessment.

First published 2023

A catalogue record for this publication is available from the British Library

Library of Congress Cataloging-in-Publication Data
NAMES: Lincoln, Andrew, author.
TITLE: Imagining war and peace in eighteenth-century Britain, 1690–1820 / Andrew Lincoln.
DESCRIPTION: Cambridge ; New York, NY : Cambridge University Press, 2023. | Includes bibliographical references and index.
IDENTIFIERS: LCCN 2023002042 (print) | LCCN 2023002043 (ebook) | ISBN 9781009366540 (hardback) | ISBN 9781009366519 (ebook)
SUBJECTS: LCSH: War in literature. | English literature – 18th century – History and criticism. | War and society – Great Britain – History – 18th century. | Public opinion – Great Britain – History – 18th century.
CLASSIFICATION: LCC PR448.W36 L56 2023 (print) | LCC PR448.W36 (ebook) | DDC 820.9/005–dc23/eng/20230313
LC record available at https://lccn.loc.gov/2023002042
LC ebook record available at https://lccn.loc.gov/2023002043

ISBN 978-1-009-36654-0 Hardback

Cambridge University Press & Assessment has no responsibility for the persistence or accuracy of URLs for external or third-party internet websites referred to in this publication and does not guarantee that any content on such websites is, or will remain, accurate or appropriate.

To W.A.L and K.R.L

Contents

List of Figures	*page* ix
Preface	xi
Introduction	1

PART I   DEVELOPING IDEALS

1 The Culture of War and Civil Society, from William III to George I	31
2 War and the Culture of Politeness: The Case of *The Tatler* and *The Spectator*	57
3 Sacrifice: Heroism and Mourning	75
4 Sacrifice: Christian Heroes	100

PART II   DEVELOPING QUESTIONS

5 War and the 'Elevation' of the Novel	123
6 War and the 'Science of Man'	157

PART III   WAR AND PEACE IN AN AGE OF REVOLUTIONS

7 Complicities in the Novel	185
8 Saving Individual Virtue	199
9 Saving Communal Virtue	220
10 Thomas Clarkson and the Ideal of Non-resistance	244

vii

viii   *Contents*

PART IV   THE LANDSCAPE OF CONQUEST

11 A Case Study: Gibraltar   261

Further Reading   281
Index   293

Figures

1 John Sheffield, 1st Duke of Buckingham monument, designed by Denis Plumiere and sculpted by Laurent Delvaux and Peter Scheemakers (1722) [© Westminster Abbey] *page* 92

2 'Tandem Triumphans', 1746. Cumberland leads the British cavalry against the Jacobite infantry. [© British Museum] 102

3 William Woollett, engraved after Benjamin West, *The Death of General Wolfe*, 1770 (1776) [© Ivy Close Images / Alamy] 116

4 John Hall, engraved after Benjamin West, *The Treaty of Penn with the Indians* 1771–1772 (1775). [© Granger Historical Picture Archive / Alamy] 248

5a John William Edy, after George Bulteel Fisher, *Water Port Gate, Gibraltar* (1796) [© British Museum] 277

5b Robert Hyde Colebrook, *South-Western View of Ootra-Durgum* (1793) [© British Library] 277

Preface

There is now a large and growing area of scholarship devoted to the cultural impact of war in the eighteenth century. Much of this work has appeared in the wake of Linda Colley's *Britons: Forging the Nation, 1707–1837* (1992) which examined among other things the role of war in shaping a sense of 'Britishness' in the eighteenth century. Since Colley's book appeared a range of studies has illuminated the social impact of war, the role of women in warfare, the representation of the armed forces in British culture, and the influence of war on poetry, drama, and the novel – work that has run in parallel with, and drawn upon, more specialist studies of the navy, the army, and militia, as well as upon new political histories. As a result of this activity, we now have a much better understanding of just how pervasive the cultural influence of war became in the eighteenth century, and are less likely to see warfare and culture as separate entities. Gillian Russell in *Theatres of War: Performance, Politics and Society 1793–1815* (1995) revealed the close interrelationships between the armed forces and the theatre during the revolutionary and Napoleonic wars, as soldiers and sailors become actors themselves, and plays were performed in the war zone. Margarette Lincoln, in *Representing the Royal Navy: British Sea Power 1750–1815* (2002), showed how the image of British sea power was constructed and deployed in the public sphere through a variety of cultural practices. Simon Bainbridge demonstrated that war was a powerful influence upon British poets during the Revolutionary and Napoleonic wars, in *British Poetry and the Revolutionary and Napoleonic Wars: Visions of Conflict* (2003). Philip Shaw has explored a range of responses to the Battle of Waterloo in *Waterloo and the Romantic Imagination* (2002) and has examined the relationship between sentiment and the representation of suffering in Romantic military art in *Suffering and Sentiment in Romantic Military Art* (2013); I share his interest in the process by which audiences were conditioned to respond to scenes of ruin with revulsion but not to undertake political action against war. A number of studies have

xii   *Preface*

focused on the complex interactions between war, culture, and politics during the Seven Years' War, including John Cardwell's *Arts and Arms* (2004) and a collection of essays edited by Frans De Bruyn and Shaun Regan, *The Culture of the Seven Years' War* (2014).[1] In some studies, literary works have been approached as lenses through which to look at the wider impact of hostilities upon the life of the nation. Carol Watts, for example, in her 2007 book *The Cultural Work of Empire*, argued that the Seven Years' War (1756–63) gave rise to a re-imagining of relations between the individual and the state, a process she approached through a discussion of Laurence Sterne's *Tristram Shandy*. Mary Favret, in *War at a Distance* (2009), took William Cowper's poem *The Task* as a starting point for a complex account of how war impinged upon and shaped the everyday consciousness of civilians. Holger Hoock, in his monumental *Empires of the Imagination* (2010), looked at a century of British history from 1750 to 1850 and included both art works and exhibitions; here culture itself became a site of battle, as Britons engaged in 'culture wars' in the process of legitimating their developing empire and its military aggression. In other works, scholars have focused upon the impact of war on special areas of eighteenth-century culture, including gender and sentiment, or have considered how the study of war contributes to the history of emotions, or how war give rise to new forms of writing, including the military memoir and the military tale.[2]

My own study is indebted to the example of these works, and to some of their findings, although its aim is rather different. The book has grown out of my work on William Blake and Walter Scott, who, in spite of their many differences, share an interest in the processes by which the violence of war is justified in a modern commercial society. I am primarily concerned with the question: how do such societies reconcile themselves to war? I attempt to find some answers by looking at a range of materials – including poems, novels, periodical essays, philosophical studies, sermons, historical writing, paintings, and some plays – selected from the field of British culture in the long eighteenth century.

In writing this book I have incurred many debts. I owe special thanks to the late John Richardson, from whose writing on war I learned a great deal, and to whose generosity as a scholar, and at a more personal level, I am much indebted. I have benefitted from numerous conferences that have been organised to represent the field. The 'Soldiers and Soldiering' network and conferences set up by Kevin Linch and Matthew McCormack, the 'Complicity and Politics of Representation' conference organised at Ruhr-Universität Bochum by Cornelia Wächter, Alex Adams, Robert Werth,

Preface

the Kings College conference on 'War and Peace in the Age of Napoleon' organised by Zac White, and the 'War, Literature and the Arts' at the US Airforce Academy, Colorado Springs (where I learned, among many other things, that the Academy introduces its cadets to anti-war literature in an attempt to make them better warriors) – all of these have played an important role in the development of this book. I owe thanks to the members of a University of Singapore workshop John Richardson organised: Ala Alrysse, Anders Engberg-Pederson, Thomas Keymer, Lynda Mugglestone, Melinda Rabb, and Neil Ramsey, whose knowledge and enthusiasm, as well as their critical insight, proved invaluable. I thank Markman Ellis and Christopher Reid, who read parts of this work in typescript. Parts of this study incorporate material that first appeared in a different form in articles published in *Eighteenth Century Life and Eighteenth-Century Studies*. I am grateful to the editors of these publications for their permission to include the material here. My deepest debt is to Margarette Lincoln, who was a patient and knowledgeable adviser at every stage of this project.

Notes

1 John Cardwell, *Arts and Arms: Literature, Politics and Patriotism during the Seven Years War* (Manchester: Manchester University Press, 2004); Frans De Bruyn and Shaun Regan, eds., *The Culture of the Seven Years' War: Empire, Identity, and the Arts in the Eighteenth-century Atlantic World* (Toronto: University of Toronto Press, 2014).

2 On gender: Margarette Lincoln, *Naval Wives & Mistresses* (London: National Maritime Museum, 2007); Julia Banister in *Masculinity, Militarism and Eighteenth-Century Culture, 1689–1815* (Cambridge: Cambridge University Press, 2018). On the history of emotions: Stephanie Downes, Andrew Lynch, and Katrina O'Loughlin, eds., *Writing War in Britain and France, 1370–1854: A History of Emotions* (London: Routledge, 2018). Neil Ramsey, *The Military Memoir and Romantic Military Culture* (London: Routledge, 2016).

Introduction

How did a people learning to think of themselves as 'civilised' reconcile themselves to war? How did they manage the problems of conscience posed by the terrible effects of warfare? And how did those who tried absolutely to oppose war justify their attempt? These questions relate primarily to moral issues rather than to problems of strategy, fire-power, logistics, or the many other factors that might occupy a historian of war. In this study, such questions are posed in relation to an expanding reading public, some of whom went to war, but most of whom stayed at home.

It was a readership that included growing numbers of women, and that was increasingly influenced by the social and moral concerns of the middling sort. It was often addressed by writers concerned with moral and material improvement – with the improvement of readers, of the poor and, increasingly, of those who lived in distant lands that had come under the power and influence of Britain. War had to be justified in ways compatible with peaceful social ideals, just as morals and manners had to be reformed in the light of those ideals. The glorification of war was always in tension with the promotion of good manners and morals, and in some areas of culture, such as the novel, it was sometimes condemned and contrasted with the peaceful virtues of domestic life – usually represented most clearly by a young heroine. In the later decades of the century, as opposition to particular wars and their consequences becomes more widespread, there are signs of a growing awareness of the ways in which ordinary social life is not only influenced by, but implicated in, the violence of war. By the end of the century the same moderating process that worked to reconcile war with gentler manners had begun to motivate organised opposition to war. Opposition to government policy was sometimes tempered by, or deflected into, a broader concern with changing the public's general attitude to war. This is the point at which the drive for moral reform gives rise to what we now term 'peace education', and to the founding of the first Peace Societies dedicated to a non-resisting pacifism. The ideal

2   Introduction

of peace was often bound up with the prospects of empire, of spreading Christianity and British civilisation abroad.

This book is concerned with attempts to define an appropriate response to war, whether of justification or opposition, in a modern commercial society defended by professional armed forces. It offers a selective survey of examples drawn from across the long eighteenth century as a whole. Many of these examples are works of literature, but in citing such works I am not concerned to give a comprehensive reading of them, nor with their current canonical status. My aim is to show what they can tell us of contemporary attitudes to the morality of war. This means that works like John Breval's Gibraltar poem *Calpe* and Richard Glovers' epic *Leonidas* – which are routinely passed over in literary studies – can receive as much, or more, attention than works that are widely discussed, while many canonical works that might have been cited are not mentioned at all. The field of study is vast, and this survey is necessarily highly selective. I have referred to a few dramatic works in passing, but there is obviously much more to be said about war and the theatre. An adequate treatment of that would require a separate study, one that could do justice to the combination of special factors that condition theatrical performances, including the licensing system, the social composition of the audience, the styles of acting and the technical capacities of the theatre itself. Some fine work has already been done in this area, but there is much more to be done.[1] Many of the examples in this book are from areas of eighteenth-century culture that are not usually considered to be literary: religious, philosophical, historical. They all involve attempts to imagine war, or peace, in moral terms.

In the rest of this Introduction, I shall outline some of the particular concerns of the study: moral dualism, the need to confront violence, the moral situation of the non-combatant and of what we now term the 'pacifist'. I shall consider some of the historical conditions that influenced these issues, define some of the key terms at work, and conclude with a brief chapter plan.

Moral Dualism

In war, the moral codes that normally organise social life begin to lose their purchase. The peaceful operation of society requires murder, plunder, and a host of other violent practices to be outlawed; in war, the same practices are accepted and even promoted. This issue was addressed in a wide range of eighteenth-century writings, from Bernard Mandeville's *Fable of the Bees* (1714) to an anti-war sermon by Anna Barbauld (1793).[2]

Introduction

The twentieth-century sociologist Maurice Davie claimed that societies have two moral codes, 'one for the comrades inside and another for strangers outside'.[3] The moral dualism may not be quite so clearly defined as this suggests, but it certainly gives rise to two general views of war, which for convenience I shall term 'moral' and 'national'. I avoid using the term 'patriotic' here, since this is a notoriously protean term which, while it always signified 'love of country', could be harnessed to quite different causes and be conceived in different ways, as we shall see later. The moral view, seeking to encourage good conduct within society, recoils from the cruelty, suffering and corruption produced by war and by its glorification. The national view, focusing on national interest in relation to 'outside' communities, justifies and celebrates the nation's war-making.

In the eighteenth century, the national war effort was endowed with a vision of historical destiny, hallowed by the authority of royal command, and given a privileged relationship with divinity itself, reinforced by the national Fasts and Thanksgivings, sermons and other religious activities. It was endowed, that is, with a complex mythical framework designed to control its interpretation. In this way, the overriding of moral norms in the collective national interest could be made to seem not only an unfortunate necessity, but inherently good. However, a stream of writings emphasising the moral view of war flowed throughout the eighteenth century, including sermons, educational works, essays and fictions. This view could be inflected in various ways – as what twenty-first-century readers might identify as anti-heroic, anti-imperialistic, or pacifist – but all shared a moral disapproval of war. Some of the most famous works of the century were part of this stream, including Fénelon's modern prose 'epic' *Telemachus*, Swift's satirical fiction *Gulliver's Travels*, Rousseau's *Discourse on the Origin of Inequality* and, with some ambivalence, Tom Paine's *Rights of Man*. Some political theorists, without embracing absolute non-resistance, formulated proposals for establishing political and legal structures that would enable peaceful conflict-resolution. The Abbé de Saint-Pierre's project for a 'Universal Peace' founded on a general alliance of sovereigns appeared in an English translation in 1714, and its aims were echoed and modified by a series of later writers, including Rousseau, Bentham and Kant.[4] For these writers, war was a malign symptom of moral and political failure that required major changes in the approach to government. In Britain, party politicians usually had no such ambitions, but argued for or against particular wars according to the interests at stake, and sometimes, in seeking to discredit a wartime ministry, deplored the destructive effects of a campaign.

4   Introduction

The public at large, while subject to a wide range of national propaganda, was kept well informed about the horrific brutality and suffering generated by war. Although most Britons were spared direct exposure to the terrors of the battlefield, since most of the century's battles were fought overseas, the human costs of war were clearly apparent. Those who had lost fathers, sons, brothers, or husbands in warfare knew these costs only too well. Soldiers and sailors returning home from combat could give first-hand accounts of the violence, while the maimed and wounded were a familiar sight in towns and villages across the country. The setting up of daily newspapers with detailed war reports, the publication of war journals, essays and pamphlets about ongoing campaigns meant that the public had access to unprecedented amounts of information about the conduct of war.

The flow of opinion and information helped to ensure that, despite the vast resources devoted to promoting war, the national view of it had to coexist in an unstable relationship with the moral view. We can see this coexistence in many areas of the culture of eighteenth-century Britain. War is celebrated as a defence of national liberty and condemned as a source of social oppression. It is conceived as a valiant defence of the nation's homes and as a disastrous wrecker of society's domestic fabric. Sailors and soldiers are seen as both heroic defenders of the nation and as a disreputable menace to social order. The dualism was unstable in part because it was subject to ever-changing conditions, including those produced by political rivalries. The popularity of wars could wax and wane. The threat of invasion inevitably boosted the national view, just as the arrival of peace tended to stimulate complaints about war's dire social consequences.

We need to understand that the two views do not necessarily present themselves as alternatives that people can simply choose between. There is abundant evidence that, in the eighteenth century, individual Britons were able to judge war from both a moral point of view and a national one without reconciling them. It is hardly unusual for people to hate war, and complain about its horrors while loyally supporting their nation's own war effort – the famous case of the First World War poet Wilfred Owen, who wrote movingly of the futility of war while recovering in Britain from shell shock, but returned to the war zone to fight, vividly illustrates this possibility. Indeed, it is possible for people to argue for the abolition of war while expressing some pride in their nation's military successes – as we shall see below in the case of the poet William Cowper. The moral view of war and the national view can evidently coexist without cancelling each other out.

Introduction 5

While the unstable relationship between these views of war seemed in practice ineradicable, the appeal to ideas of virtue could provide a form of reconciliation between social and martial values. Social order and war-making depend upon some of the same virtues: not only obedience to authority, but group loyalty, and a willingness to make sacrifices for the common interest. Within the context of nation states they both involve 'love of country'. Official justifications of war usually emphasise this common ground. As we shall see in Chapters 3 and 4, the idea of sacrifice assumes a major importance in pro-war works of the period.

The emergence of humanitarian accounts of human nature, including ideas of benevolence, proved useful in the process of reconciling the public to war (see Chapter 1). Benevolence did not simply involve doing the right thing; it was also an emotional predisposition to do the right thing. By associating goodness with a predisposition of the agent, rather than insisting on the immediate or distant effects of an agent's actions, expressions of compassion could provide a kind of absolution for civilians who were implicated in wars through their consumption, trade or investments, and for the soldiers and sailors who actually did the fighting. The kinds of feeling involved in war therefore began to assume a new importance. Saint Augustine had acknowledged the significance of right intention and feeling in war, arguing that a good man will lament the necessity of just wars, and feel the misery of the evils caused by them.[5] In eighteenth-century Britain, this principle was transformed into an important form of justification. It encouraged a tendency to approach the morality of war as a matter of individual conduct, of individual virtue, rather than a systemic issue; it provided a way of insulating individual combatants, and readers, from the wider moral implications of organised violence. Both the combatant in the war zone and the non-combatant at home had to be imagined in the appropriate way, and endowed with suitably benevolent feelings. As we shall see, the role of benevolence when imagining war was typically to make a virtue of acquiescence.

Confronting Violence

One of the most influential exponents of benevolence, Shaftesbury, argues that war is akin to philanthropy:

> it is strange to imagine that war, which of all things appears the most savage, should be the passion of the most heroic spirits. But it is in war that the knot of fellowship is closest drawn. It is in war that mutual succour is most given, mutual danger run, and common affection most exerted and

6   Introduction

> employed. For heroism and philanthropy are almost one and the same. Yet
> by a small misguidance of the affection, a lover of mankind becomes a rav-
> ager, a hero and deliverer becomes an oppressor and destroyer.[6]

The difference between war as a noble form of philanthropy and war as a
kind of savagery is conceived not as a huge gulf between contrasting methods of fighting, humane and brutal, but as the result of a 'small misguidance of the affection'. Brutality, like humanity, is a matter of feeling. It
follows that, to avoid this 'small misguidance,' affection must be properly
guided, so that virtue can be reinforced.

   Here Shaftesbury is giving eloquent expression to assumptions that
seem to have been widely shared. The rise of humanitarianism produced
writings which criticised the way feelings about war were misdirected by
literature and history. There was a growing discomfort with the martial
values of epic.[7] And there was increasing criticism of the way violent historical conquerors had been represented as admirable heroes in history.
The celebration of Alexander and Caesar, for example, was condemned by
a wide range of writers, including William Temple, Madeleine de Scudéry,
Boileau, Samuel Clarke, Alexander Pope and Henry Fielding.[8] What had
once been hailed as virtues were now condemned as vices. John Locke
in his *Thoughts on Education* ventured a general condemnation of all histories that treat slaughter as heroic.[9] Such criticisms did not necessarily
signal any fundamental disapproval of warfare. Indeed, the demonization
of commanders such as Alexander and Caesar could help to justify the
war effort of one's own nation. After all, Saint Augustine had defined just
wars in contrast to wars driven by aggressive ambition.[10] If these historical figures were judged in personal terms, as compelled by tyrannical and
cruel passions, then condemnation of them could be a sign of one's own
humanitarian feeling and moral virtue. Vilifying them and the destruction
they caused could help to create an alternative, virtuous space for one's
own war effort. Samuel Clarke, for example, in the dedication of his edition of Caesar's *Commentaries*, contrasts Caesar's war-making, which he
sees as driven by an ambition for personal renown, with that of the Duke
of Marlborough, which he claims was a defence of the rights and Liberties
of Europe and of his Country.[11] Marlborough's war-making, he implies,
entailed protective rather than aggressive feelings.

   This co-option of the moral view by the national view served the dual
purpose of simultaneously arousing and pacifying the public. On the one
hand the public must be encouraged to support the nation's own war-
making, and overcome any reluctance to bear the costs of it; but on the
other hand, from a humanitarian point of view, it must be discouraged

Introduction 7

from displaying unseemly bellicosity, and preserve an appropriate sense of moral horror in relation to war. The attempt to reconcile these two apparently conflicting demands was initially the job of writers and artists – but it was soon taken over by combatants themselves.

At the beginning of the eighteenth century, we find dramatists, poets, and essayists attempting this kind of reconciliation – trying to show warriors as at once effective men of war and sensitive men of feeling, reconciling martial and social virtue.[12] The idea of dying for one's country as an admirable form of sacrifice was one of the ways in which war and philanthropy could be reconciled. But there was also a need to idealise the process of inflicting violence on others. As Philip Shaw notes, images of the suffering inflicted by war were produced 'with the express purpose of conditioning audiences to support belligerent activities'.[13] It would be a mistake to regard such fictional, idealised representations as mere fantasies that had no influence upon combatants who had to deal with intractable realities of war. There is some evidence that the way war is imagined by writers – even by those who have no experience of war – can have a significant and even formative influence on the way combatants think about what they are doing when they fight. The work of poets in addressing the moral problems posed by war is sometimes especially revealing, as their use of condensed, idealising forms can bring the problems and their imagined solution into sharp focus.

One of the most influential examples of the attempt to reconcile martial and social virtue was Joseph Addison's poem *The Campaign*, which celebrated the Duke of Marlborough's victory at the Battle of Blenheim (1704). Like other Whig poets who celebrated Marlborough's victory, Addison did not shy away from the brutality of the Blenheim campaign, in which tens of thousands of soldiers died and in which Marlborough ordered a systematic ravaging of the Bavarian countryside, burning and plundering villages. Addison needed to accommodate such brutality in order to show the appropriate emotional response to it. His first readers would have already learned about the battle from newspapers, printed reports, and other sources. The most authoritative would be the eye-witness accounts sent by serving officers, to which no doubt Addison himself referred for some of the details of his poem. Here is an extract from one of these, showing how an Officer who was in the engagement described the burning of Bavarian villages:

> The Elector of Bavaria having return'd evading Answers, to the kind Invitations sent him for an Accommodation: a Party of 4000 Horse was commanded out to burn and lay waste his Country. But the Elector continuing obstinate, and depending much upon the Relief which Mareschal Tallard

was bringing up to him, our Generals resolv'd to attack the Town of Ingol-stadt; and Prince Eugene being advanced as far as Dillengen, we pass'd the Paer, and came to Kiebash the 4th of Aug. Our Left Wing reaching to Aycha, and the right beyond the Castle of Winden, burning all the Villages we had spared before between those two Camps.[14]

This is fairly typical of the way officers reported engagements at this time. It is not eloquent or even particularly clear. But the idea is to give the facts dispassionately, in a matter-of-fact way and to apportion blame to the enemy as clearly as possible. There is no attempt to describe the emotional responses of those involved, which seem completely irrelevant to the Officer's purpose. The account reflects the military ethos of the period – stoical and professional.[15]

This is how Addison describes the destruction of Bavarian villages in his poem *The Campaign*:

> In Vengeance rous'd, the Soldier fills his Hand
> With Sword and Fire, and ravages the Land,
> A Thousand Villages to Ashes turns,
> In crackling Flames a Thousand Harvests burns,
> To the thick Woods the woolly Flocks retreat,
> And mixt with bellowing Herds confus'dly bleat;
> Their trembling Lords the common Shade partake,
> And Cries of Infants sound in ev'ry Brake:
> The list'ning Soldier fixt in Sorrow stands,
> Loth to Obey his Leader's just Commands;
> The Leader grieves, by gen'rous Pity sway'd,
> To see his just Commands so well obey'd.[16]

Addison imagines the event as a sensory and emotional experience – he evokes the various sounds involved, and the disturbance to animals and children. In fact, he makes it seem much more dreadful than the minimal eye-witness report. The dreadfulness is important to his purpose. He is supposedly thinking about the feelings of the combatants here. But of course, his primary interest is in the feelings of his audience. This representation of the soldier's sorrow is clearly designed to allow readers to imagine that all who took part in this atrocity were not motivated by malice or brutality: they showed the appropriate feeling, a conflict between compassion and duty. At the same time, the lines show how readers themselves should respond to such acts of violence: not with sadistic glee, or even with a matter-of-fact stoicism, but with resolute compassion, with humanitarian feeling. Violence requires acquiescence, in the form of pained benevolence. Addison was not condemning Marlborough for this terrible atrocity, but absolving and vindicating him, and so endowing him with a more acceptable kind of glory.

Introduction 9

Historians have identified a range of influences that contributed to the spread of humanitarian feeling in the mid-eighteenth-century Britain: the evangelical revival which promoted a religion of the heart, the rising influence of the professional classes who could exercise power through philanthropic initiatives, the increasing influence of women readers, the influence of conduct books, the development of the novel, the work of the Scottish Enlightenment.[17] It seems clear that comparable developments were taking place in other European countries at this time.[18] Such developments helped to encourage the use of the language of humanity in discussions of war. Whereas at the beginning of the eighteenth century, this language is found primarily in the idealising work of poets like Addison, in heroic dramatists, periodical journalists and other 'literary' contexts, by the time of the Seven Years' War (1756–63) it had become common in eye-witness reports coming from war zones. It appears in reports from French and German officers, in accounts involving Russian forces and elsewhere. This suggests that by the mid-century military officers and commanders, who were sending back reports to the ministry or to newspapers, had generally absorbed this language from their own reading. They used it to guide the sympathies of their readers.

So, the *London Magazine* of March 1758 includes a report from a Hanoverian officer to prince Ferdinand of Brunswick, of an action involving an attack with fixed bayonets. The writer assures us that 'humanity suffered for the slaughter which then happened' (139). Those who inflicted the violence are represented as victims of it. In a report about the siege of Fort William Henry in the *Universal Magazine* in October 1757, the Marquis the Montcalm tells Colonel Monroe 'I am obliged in humanity to require you to surrender your fort' because he is unable to restrain the 'savages' (that is, his native American allies) much longer (183). The language of humanity is used to deliver a threat. In guiding the reader's reactions, it was not unusual to focus on victims in a tableau. We can see this in an 'Impartial Narrative' of a failed British expedition to St Cas on the coast of France in 1758, which describes how British soldiers were left stranded on the beach, exposed to the guns of advancing French forces, with not enough rowing boats to get them to the safety of the ships out at sea. This passage describes the fate of soldiers clinging desperately to the side of the rowing boats:

> the Sailors, lest the Boat should sink, were obliged to cut some of their Hands off [...] It is impossible to describe the Feeling of the Troops, who from the Ships beheld this dreadful Scene, looking on their Fellow Soldiers and Friends, without being able to sustain them.[19]

In this 'dreadful scene' we are invited to think not about the feelings of those struggling in the water having their hands cut off, nor about the feelings of those in the boat trying to save themselves by doing the cutting, but the feelings of the helpless onlookers on the ship. That is how it must be appreciated, as a horror beyond the reach of personal intervention. Here, as in the previous passages, the spectators' compassion is a sign that individual will, and hence moral choice, is being overruled by circumstances.

A final example provides a convenient comparison with Addison's poem. The *Gentleman's Magazine* July 1760 includes a letter from Major General James Murray, writing from Canada. It is written in an apologetic mode that recalls Addison's *Campaign*, and explains his decision to torch much of the village of Sorel (in Canada) to teach its inhabitants a lesson:

> I found the inhabitants of the parish of Sorel had deserted their habitations and were in arms. I was therefore under the cruel necessity of burning the greatest part of these poor unhappy people's houses. I pray God this example may suffice, for my nature revolts when this becomes a necessary part of my duty. (275)

The letter was published under the heading 'The HUMANITY of the Major Murray'. Murray's sister wrote to him about the very warm public reception of this letter in Britain: 'The world does you justice [...] the letter is thought a masterpiece'.[20] The letter could be seen as a masterpiece because, like Addison's poem, it was clearly written with the specific intention of reconciling readers to what was, in fact, a rather commonplace atrocity. Instead of making readers feel terrible about a horrific action done in their name, the reference to humanity could actually make them feel good about it. The feeling is a guarantee that this violence is not the work of 'savages', but of civilised individuals with an appropriate care for human life and private property, who feel an apt moral horror, and are performing their duty in an admirable spirit.

In eighteenth-century Britain, the image of the soldier fighting in a spirit of humanity, a sign of just conduct, was used as a substitute for, and an implicit guarantee of, the justice of the cause. It apparently helped to reconcile readers at home to the horrors of war, and to their own complicity in them, and it helped to reconcile some combatants, apparently, to the violence of their occupation. By mid-century, some writers and artists began to turn from the process of inflicting violence to dealing with the consequences of violence – foreground acts of humanity, such as, relieving the distresses of the besieged, attending to the wounded on the battlefield, rescuing sailors from the sea. But the feelings of the combatant remain

Introduction   11

an important concern and, as we shall see in Chapter 9, by the end of
the eighteenth century the supposed impersonality of the modern professional soldier under strict discipline became a basis for criticism in protests
against government war policy.

The Non-combatant

The term 'civilian' did not begin to acquire its current meaning, 'a non-
military person', until the Romantic period. It apparently took more than
a century for the establishment of professional armed forces to give rise to
the need for such a term. A possible explanation for this lies in the enduring influence of civic humanism. As the work of John Pocock has shown,
in civic humanist tradition, which descends from the work of Machiavelli
in the Italian Renaissance, the (male) citizen's virtue was bound up with
his ownership of land and readiness to bear arms in defence of his community.[21] Martial virtue was an intrinsic part of his masculine identity.

The civic humanist ideal remained influential in eighteenth-
century Britain. It was keenly invoked by advocates of the militia, the
non-professional defence force in which martial virtue could find some kind
of active expression, and which was clearly contrasted with the professional
standing army (often seen as a potential instrument of state repression). But
the ideal was challenged by alternative conceptions of individual identity.
In the realm of philosophy, for example, David Hume and other enlighteners, looking back to the achievements of Isaac Newton and John Locke,
sought to establish what Hume thought of as a 'Science of Man'. Hume
attempts to ground the study of society and morality upon an empirical
epistemology and dispassionate historical enquiry. In an approach that
would now be defined as 'liberal' he treats the male individual as a private
being, one who may choose to take on public responsibilities but whose
freedoms are a personal matter. This modern individual, living in a commercial society, has been released from the kind of feudal dependencies and
duties that once involved military service. He does not have the defining
martial responsibilities of the civic humanist citizen – responsibilities which
had now been assigned to professional combatants.[22] Hume's fellow-Scot,
Adam Smith, bases his philosophical enquiries upon a comparable conception of the individual – an individual that certainly seems 'non-military'.
When Smith describes the behaviour of soldiers in the warzone, he thinks
not of fierce passions but of 'moral sentiments' involving reasonable reflection. In this respect, his combatant seems modelled on the non-combatant
(Chapter 6). Hume and Smith both regard the modern professional army

with its discipline and resources as inevitably superior to the militia, and as capable of fighting in a spirit of 'humanity'.

If the (implicitly male) individual at the centre of these philosophical enquiries was not defined by military responsibilities, in eighteenth-century culture femininity was often conceived in essentially peaceful terms. In Vivienne Jones's account, the eighteenth-century ideal of femininity is mainly a product of 'middle-class discourses' which 'restricted middle-class women to the role of domestic consumers and subjected working-class women to a double repression, erasing them culturally and economically by projecting leisured domesticity as universal'.[23] The characteristics of this ideal femininity included what were usually thought of as the 'softer virtues', such as amiability, sensibility, compassion, sociability, family affection, and refined manners. The virtuous female was usually thought of as, implicitly, 'non-military', and in writings aimed at a polite readership, pacifist sentiments were more likely to be attributed to females than to males. The novel, as it developed in the hands of Samuel Richardson, Henry Fielding and others, became a form in which examples of feminine virtue could be set in contrast to ideas of martial heroism (Chapter 5). Such virtue was not necessarily incompatible with support for war, but it was at odds with the aggression, violence and disorder, produced by war, and an obvious focus for anti-war sentiment. In such novels, the moral view of war tends to prevail over the national view.

If the liberal male subject and the ideal feminine subject did not have the military responsibilities traditionally attributed to the civic humanist male, that did not mean that such non-combatants had no responsibility for war. Hume and Smith both recognise that the non-combatant may be responsible for encouraging wars. They approach collective responses to warfare in psychological terms, and conclude that a public remote from the warzone may be susceptible to a dangerous national partiality that can cloud the judgement and work to promote appallingly destructive and ruinously expensive conflicts. The question of public responsibility for war was addressed in other ways by the Church. Through its Fast and Thanksgiving services it taught that everyone was responsible for the nation's wars, and had an active role to play in a national war effort, if only through prayers. The idea that wars were expressions of divine will, and punishments for sin, helped to make them seem inevitable – beyond the power of mere humans to prevent – while making each individual personally answerable for them.

There were various ways in which non-combatants, both men and women, could voluntarily support the nation's war effort without fighting.

Introduction 13

They could contribute to philanthropic endeavours to help servicemen. Individuals and groups with relevant professional experience could help by offering specialist advice.[24] Celebrations of victories and of the arrival of peace could involve all levels of British society. Such celebrations might be encouraged by both government and oppositions for their own political ends, and they could sometimes lead to violence when, for example, the mob demanded that householders illuminate their windows. But they offered profitable opportunities and social benefits independent of political objectives.[25] For the elite inhabitants of a community, local victory celebrations could be occasions of patronage which reinforced existing hierarchies and communal bonds, and so helped to secure their position and influence in the local community. Local merchants and tradesmen who raised subscriptions for celebrations were able to promote their own reputations and commercial good-will while demonstrating civic spirit. For the shopkeepers, manufacturers, publicans, and others who provided customised goods and services, they boosted profits. For the poorer classes, they often provided free drinks and entertainment. For all participants, a victory celebration was – whatever their political views – a ritualised affirmation of social solidarity. It produced local benefits that could be felt immediately by all concerned, independent of any national or political advantages that might accrue from military success. This does not mean, of course, that everyone was willing to participate. Amelia Opie's poem 'Lines Written at Norwich on the First News of Peace' describes a mother who refuses to take part in a peace celebration because her soldier son has been killed in the war fighting far from home; such a refusal may have been a common reaction.[26] Felicia Hemans's poem 'The Illuminated City', ponders the grief concealed by victory celebrations.[27] Some Britons, like William Hazlitt, refused to participate on principle.[28]

While war brought violence, poverty, loss and misery to some, it also provided careers and commercial opportunities, and it fed into the nation's intellectual and artistic activities at every level. At the beginning of the eighteenth century, the outbreak of the War of the Spanish Succession helped to establish daily newspapers in England. Warfare inspired a stream of other publications – including campaign journals, maps, military dictionaries, memoirs and histories – and when monthly magazines were established in the 1730s, it became a reliable source of material for them. There was a burgeoning commerce in war-related merchandising, including celebratory ballads, prints, ceramics, medals and playing cards.[29] A growing demand for commemorative statues and plaques inside churches and in public spaces made work for sculptors.[30] Military and naval reviews, the launching of warships, parades and other activities drew crowds who might prove profitable to local tradesmen and publicans.[31] The theatre was often patronised by military and naval officers, and celebrated the nation's military successes in prologues and epilogues, while sometimes offering plays on martial and naval themes. There were re-enactments of battles, inside and outside the theatre. Music worked to boost national morale in the form of popular songs and concerts featuring especially composed works.[32] As the market for British painting developed war inevitably became an important subject. War-related paintings appeared in public spaces – including the Foundling Hospital and Vauxhall Gardens in London. In the later decades of the century, the public exhibitions of the Royal Academy and Society of Artists in London included privately commissioned portraits of military officers, naval commanders, and commemorations of naval and land victories. In the 1790s, the British forces engaged in India took artists with them to commemorate their activities and represent territorial acquisitions, while a new kind of visual display, the Panorama, offered immersive spectacles of battles and naval reviews.[33]

Many aspects of British culture in the eighteenth century give the impression of a deep national interest in war – even an enthusiasm for it. Holger Hoock's *Empire of the Imagination*, which looks at relations between politics, war and the arts in the period from 1750 to 1850, throws light on the growing role of state sponsorship in the representation and commemoration of war, and shows how the arts were used to display and glorify Britain's growing imperial power. His work demonstrates how much attention was given to encouraging imaginative participation in the heroics of the war zone, reinforcing the national view of war, while building a sense of communal solidarity. His findings can be cited to support the argument made by Linda Colley, that the development of mass allegiance and a sense of Britishness in the long eighteenth century was related to the experience of 'a succession of wars between Britain and France'. Colley acknowledges that not all Britons supported the nation's wars, and notes the presence of dissenting voices, which grew louder in the later part of the century. But she emphasises the 'far greater numbers of Britons who, for many different reasons, supported these successive war efforts'. She observes: 'Patriotism served as a bandwagon on which different groups and interests leaped so as to steer it in a direction that benefitted them'.[34]

The tendency to equate patriotism with support for war seems irresistible, but is rather misleading, since opposition to war did not necessarily imply lack of patriotism. The Quakers were usually ready, even anxious, to declare their loyalty and love of country. The Peace Societies represented

Introduction 15

themselves as patriotic. Anti-war protesters were often ready to rally to the flag in times of invasion. If we focus too exclusively on official commemorations and works concerned to glorify the nation's wars we may overlook the ways in which the arts and other activities gave expression to the reservations, dilemmas and compromises entailed in the process of coming to terms with war. To vary Colley's metaphor: war was a bandwagon on which all Britons found themselves, whether they like it or not.

In a modern commercial society the sinews of power lay, as John Brewer has demonstrated, in 'a radical increase in taxation, the development of public deficit finance (a national debt) on an unprecedented scale, and the growth of a sizable public administration devoted to organising the fiscal and military activities of the state' (Xvii). These unheroic and bureaucratic activities worked to ensure that even those Britons who disapproved of war and refused to participate in pro-war activities would find it hard to avoid contributing to the nation's wars. In the developing modern economy one could contribute to the funding of war through one's ordinary expenditure.[35] Taxes were applied to a wide range of consumer goods and services, including wines, silks, fine linen, coal, beer, salt, leather, the hiring of Hackney carriages and even to goods sold by hawkers and peddlers. There was some recognition that consumer spending could be a cause of war. In a debate about East India imports during the 1690s, for example, Charles D'Avenant argued that 'the custom of a hundred years' had made spices, silks and calicoes necessities in Europe, and that the forts, castles and garrisons needed to protect merchants could not be supported by a limited trade. Competition between European states ensured there was no way out of this vicious circle.[36] Later in the century, the connection between war and other forms of household spending was kept in the public mind by the patriotic advertising associated with coffee, tea, tobacco, sugar and other products, which sometimes provided visual reminders that the supply of such goods depended on naval and other forms of military power (and in some cases on slavery).[37] The domestic realm, which was conventionally thought of as a peaceful area under female supervision, was deeply implicated in the business of war through its routine expenses, whether or not its menfolk went to war.

In modern society if one disapproved of war one could opt out of celebration and one could, within limits, protest (although both options risked incurring a hostile response from others); but one could not easily avoid contributing to war. The choice was between positive acceptance and acquiescence. And modern war gave rise to economic opportunities that could be hard to resist. The financial tentacles of the 'military-fiscal state' stretched into the remotest corners of the kingdom, taking possession of families, businesses and communities, and generating long-term dependencies through direct patronage (including half-pay officers and pensioners) or indirect opportunities for gain. The financial opportunities generated by war reached into the lives of those with little sympathy for it. Charlotte Smith's novel *The Old Manor House* (1793), written about the American War of Independence, contains a searing indictment of the folly of war, and yet Smith, while she was at work on her novel, helped one of her sons obtain an ensigncy in the army (Chapter 7). The army was not her son's first choice but was regarded as a respectable and honourable career. William Blake, whose visionary poems and visual designs include critical views of war, was persuaded to engrave a drawing of a military monument by his friend John Flaxman; to ensure the topicality of his one man show in 1809 he included spiritual portraits of Nelson, Pitt and Napoleon, which reflected upon the ongoing war with France; and he produced many paintings for his patron Thomas Butts who worked in the military bureaucracy (in the office of the Commissary General of Musters). The Quakers, committed to absolute non-resistance by their 'Peace Testimony', attempted to minimise their engagement by, for example, refusing to undertake militia service and paying fines instead.[38] But all Quakers who actively participated in the British economy inevitably made some indirect contribution to the nation's war-making, and some did so more directly, even trading in 'prize goods', or supplying the armed forces: the Birmingham Quaker Samuel Galton, a gun-maker, sold large quantities of arms to the government and the East India Company.[39] The business of war gave rise, directly, or indirectly, to opportunities that were hard, or impossible, to avoid.

Disapproval of war, then, did not insulate individuals economically or morally from the nation's war-making. But criticism of war became louder in the second half of the century. Britain emerged from the Seven Years' War with a new awareness of itself as a territorial empire, a development that gave rise to debates about the malign effects of imperial power and about the justice of the violence it entailed. There was unease about the use of military force by the East India Company, a monopoly with a high degree of autonomy, and fears that imperial conquest created oppression abroad and corruption at home.[40] The anxieties about territorial empire were intensified by the American War of Independence (1775–1783), which severely divided opinion in Britain and produced sharp criticism of the Church's traditional role of supporting the nation's war-making.[41]

As doubts about the justice and wisdom of the nation's war-making became more widespread and were discussed more openly, the question of

Introduction   17

public responsibility for war became more pressing. There was scope for vocal opposition to wars, in Parliament, in print, and in petitioning, and of course, there were sometimes more violent protests by mobs or organised crowds. But the vast majority of Britons could not vote in Parliamentary elections, and so had little direct influence over government policy. And there are signs of a growing recognition that responsibility for war did not lie simply with governments. During the American war, for example, the pro-American novelist, Samuel Jackson Pratt, drew on Rousseau's speculations about the development of civilisation to suggest (in his sentimental novel *Emma Corbett*) that the middle-class home, the domestic sanctum of feminine virtue, was morally implicated in the horrors of war through its basis in private property (Chapter 7).

Worries about the wisdom or justice of the nation's war not only raise questions about public responsibility but complicate assumptions about loyalty and love of country. One can feel love of country while at the same time disagreeing intensely with the government's policy and hating its wars. One can believe the nation is engaged in an unjust war while still hoping for the safety of its armed forces. One can even have doubts about the justice of a cause while accepting that there is a duty to fight in it. From the period of the American war we begin to find examples of what has been termed the 'domestication of patriotism', a love of country expressed through private attachments, love of landscape and antiquities, cultural heritage, rather than through a direct commitment to the public good conceived in political terms.[42] This understanding of patriotism contrasts strikingly with the military responsibility and public commitment of the civic humanist citizen. It seems appropriate to the non-combatant, to the private individual of what would today be termed liberalism. We find accounts of loyal war service told from a non-combatant's point of view that seem more concerned with the damaging consequences of war than with battles or the political issues at stake, a growing concern with war victims who suffer far from the war zone, and the development of ways of formally insulating those at home from the moral guilt of war (Chapter 8).

Some of these developments seem to blur the boundaries between support for war and opposition to it. And that is perhaps not surprising, since works that encourage support for war, and those seeking to oppose or abolish it, may both be influenced by the movement to improve the manners and morals of society, and the need to maintain peaceful social order – an influence that can moderate both the appeal to martial ardour and the impulse to protest.

When, at the time of the French Revolution, war broke out between Britain and France, there was vigorous anti-war protest which was often joined to claims for political reform. Some protestors bitterly condemned the British public's acquiescence in an unjust war, just as abolitionists had begun to condemn public acquiescence in slavery.[43] But in a society where the government had an effective monopoly of military might, opposition to war had to coexist with compliance with the rule of law. Acquiescence could therefore be seen as both a problem and a duty. There was also, of course, vigorous support for the war. At a time of invasion scares coupled with fears of unrest at home, the twin aims of encouraging martial ardour and encouraging the pacification of society assumed an extreme urgency, and writers attempted to meet them by a variety of measures, such as linking pro-war sentiment with a turn to collective mourning, or recreating the feelings associated with obsolete forms of combat. Such devices could provide a kind of moral insulation by evoking communal or individual responses in terms distanced from divisive social issues and by arousing a melancholy sense of inevitable loss that promoted and justified acquiescence in the burden of war (Chapter 9).

Pacifism

The domestication of patriotism that appears in the later decades of the eighteenth century can be related to the appearance of the 'civilian' as a non-military person, an individual free of the military responsibilities associated with the civic humanist tradition. This development is apparently a precondition of the emergence of what we now term 'pacifism' – the doctrine of absolute non-resistance – from the realm of marginal religious groups such as Baptist and Quakers and from the imagined private realm of the virtuous novel heroine, to play a more prominent role in British culture. It is a transformation made possible by the concept of benevolence which, as we have already seen, could make a virtue of acquiescence. And it was also bound up with the widening prospects of empire.

We can approach these complex issues by considering the influential example of William Cowper. In the wake of the American War Cowper published a long blank-verse poem, *The Task* (1785), which included some reflection upon the role of the nation's acquiescence in enabling wars to be fought. Cowper presented himself as at once a proud supporter of Britain's past military successes and a moralist who suggested that public folly and passivity allowed sovereigns and commanders to engage in war:

Introduction 19

> But war's a game, which were their subjects wise,
> Kings should not play at. Nations would do well
> T'extort their truncheons from the puny hands
> Of heroes, whose infirm and baby minds
> Are gratified with mischief, and who spoil
> Because men suffer it, their toy the world.[44]

Cowper's lines present a recognisably modern view of war. 'Nations' are conceived as fundamentally separate from the military realm of 'heroes' (elsewhere in the poem Cowper denounces the dire moral influence that service in militias has upon the labouring poor – even if it improves their physical posture).[45] Nations have a political option in relation to kings, heroes and war which they do not exercise: essentially passive, and apparently deluded, they allow themselves to be dominated by those who seem superior but who are in fact 'puny'. After the outbreak of the French Revolution, comparable ideas found expression in the writings of radical theorists such as Tom Paine, and in the revolutionary, apocalyptic myth-making of Blake's *The Four Zoas* and Shelley's *Prometheus Unbound*, in which humanity awakens from the delusions of history into a new age of peace and liberty. But Cowper was no revolutionary. He was a disillusioned liberal Whig who was appalled at the corruption he saw permeating all parts of the social order in modern Britain, and an evangelical Christian who regarded the war with America as a disaster, a divine punishment visited upon Britain for its sins. He had retired to the countryside having suffered a mental breakdown at the prospect of taking up a public office.

In *The Task* his attitude to war exhibits in stark form the unreconciled coexistence of the moral and national views: he writes as a moralist who condemns war *and* as a celebrant of war who praises the warlike achievements of the age before the American Revolution. On the one hand, he recoils from the 'mischief' of war and condemns the public acquiescence in its continuation. On the other hand, he celebrates the imperial heroes Chatham and Wolfe, who at the time of the Seven Years' War 'made us many soldiers,' and he laments the effeminacy of those who 'love when they should fight'.[46] These contrasting views simply appear in separate parts of the poem, with no attempt to reconcile them or even acknowledge the conflict between them. The national view of war, however, is associated with the past rather than the present and helps to define the poet's sense of Britain's subsequent moral decline. At various other points in the poem he denounces slavery, the exploitation of India, unjust imprisonment, and other signs of corruption in contemporary Britain. But while

20   Introduction

he condemns imperial oppression he imagines the civilising potential of British rule abroad, which may spread liberty 'through every vein' of the empire.[47] As poetic spokesman he is unlike the independent landowner of civic humanist tradition – as Tim Fulford points out, it was Cowper's landlessness, his distance from the landed interest, 'that kept him independent'.[48] His dedication to a quiet life of 'Friends, books, a garden, and perhaps his pen' allows him to 'suffer' the wars he reads about in the newspapers (wars which, as Mary Favret has shown, permeate his consciousness) while enjoying a comfortable lifestyle and declaring, 'England, with all thy faults, I love thee still'.[49] In this respect he enacts the problem he identifies: in modern Britain denunciation of war appeared to coexist quite easily with acquiescence in war – and even with praise of it.

What then is the function of Cowper's lines about the game of war? In suggesting that war could and should be ended, they evoke the kind of forceful public action for which, as he shows elsewhere, he feels personally disqualified and from which his life of retirement is a refuge ('To shake thy senate [...] was never meant my task').[50] And while he may seek to have some general influence upon public opinion, the virtue he claims is associated not with political action but with benevolent feelings inspired by his observation of natural beauties and his Christian faith.[51] Under the sign of benevolence, his own state of acquiescence becomes not an unwise abnegation of responsibility but a wise and pure communion with Nature 'Where cruel man defeats not her design'.[52] To celebrate and encourage benevolent feelings beyond the world of political power is an adequate commitment to peace, apparently. In this way admirable acquiescence is implicitly distinguished from its culpable counterpart. Benevolence once again makes a virtue of acquiescence.

Cowper's way of imagining his own acquiescence is rooted in his personal circumstances, but may also be the sign of a wider shift in attitude. Fulford notes that the young Romantic poets who followed Cowper were inspired by his location of moral authority neither in politicians nor the landed gentry but in his retired, landless condition.[53] This development presages the full emergence of the civilian as distinct from both the professional man of war and the civic humanist citizen. The position Cowper imagines here would subsequently be recognised as a model for writers who urged opposition to particular wars, or to war in general, but lacked or disclaimed direct political influence. The lines about the game of war were quoted by, among others, Charlotte Smith, Vicesimus Knox, and George Beaumont in anti-war writings; and they appeared repeatedly in the *Herald of Peace*, the journal of the Society for the Promotion of Permanent and Universal Peace.[54]

Introduction 21

The moral conflicts in Cowper's state of benevolent acquiescence are ultimately resigned to the care of providence: his poem ends with a vision in which all human conflict will be banished by the intervention of divine power: 'Where violence shall never lift the sword'.[55] In this way, the quest for peace is pushed into a future of indefinite distance but certain promise. Cowper's reflections on the role of providence in putting an end to war are of their time. In the wake of the American conflict, the idea of establishing a state of permanent peace began to be taken up by writers across a range of opinion.[56] The belief that the kingdom of Christ was now foreseeable and would extend itself over all nations bringing universal peace became the subject of sermons and other works even before the eruption of millenarian hopes inspired by the outbreak of revolution in France.[57] This view, encouraged by the expanding horizons opened up by voyages of discovery, imperial conquest and the increasingly global nature of modern commerce, could be embraced in different ways by both radical and more conservative writers; it allowed writers to imagine war as part of the course of the providential transformation by which it would be abolished, and imperial domination as a civilising influence that could be detached from aggression.[58] In practice, the expansion of British cultural influence through the nineteenth century usually depended upon martial power, since territory had to be secured and 'pacified' before it could be effectively administered. The representation of such territory as a realm approached with sensitivity by a civilised, peace-loving observer, became a significant part of the strategy of conquest, a strategy developed throughout the eighteenth century (see Chapter 11).

The book that follows is concerned to contextualise and elaborate some of the issues raised here about responses to violence, responsibility for war, imperial expansion and peace, in a survey that includes some discussion of individual texts and some general discussion. The structure of the book is broadly chronological, although since I am following issues and trends rather than a sequence of events there is sometimes considerable overlap between the temporal scope of individual chapters, while the final chapter, a case study of Gibraltar, ranges over the eighteenth century as a whole.

Part One: Developing Ideals

This part spans a period from the reign of William III, when what is now termed the 'military-fiscal state' was consolidating, to the end of the Seven Years War, by which time Britain had acquired a large empire. The works considered here are engaged in advocacy, promoting the national view of war by representing war as compatible with social and/or Christian virtue, by offering ideal models of the combatant at war and by illustrating appropriately sensitive responses to violence and loss. Most emerge within contexts of official or party-political patronage; some try to encourage an appropriate response to contemporary crises. Chapter 1 shows how representations of war were used by those who sought to regulate and refine the manners of society, and how attempts to promote gentle manners worked in the service of military aggression. Chapter 2 examines the relationship between politeness and war in the influential periodicals, *The Tatler* and *The Spectator* (produced by the Whig writers, Richard Steele and Joseph Addison) which worked to reconcile readers to the growing human and financial costs of the ongoing War of the Spanish Succession at a time of growing war-weariness.

Chapters 3 and 4 show how, in promoting the national view of war, the ideal of martial sacrifice was reimagined to suit changing conditions. Chapter 3 describes how a heroic, classical ideal of martial sacrifice was developed in the early decades of the century, an ideal that had to be reconciled with a growing interest in the process of personal and then national mourning. The discussion includes Richard Glover's epic poem *Leonidas*, and poems by William Collins. In contrast, Chapter 4 shows how a specifically Christian hero-as-martyr was imagined in the wake of the Jacobite rebellion of 1745–6, and in response to the operations of British forces in North America, a hero whose private virtues are used to justify war as part of a 'civilising' process in the face of 'savage' violence. The discussion includes Philip Doddridge's *Life of Colonel James Gardiner* and responses to the death of General James Wolfe.

Part Two: Developing Questions

This examines works mostly detached from state and political patronage, from traditional heroic ideals and forms of authority, and centred more empirically upon the experience of individuals in society. Chapter 5 considers how the 'elevation' of the novel into moral respectability led novelists to criticise the damaging effects of the celebration of war in literature, to expose the corruption and incompetence associated with the armed forces, and to explore the harmful impact of war on non-combatants and veterans. It includes novels by Daniel Defoe, Samuel Richardson, Henry Fielding, Tobias Smollett and Laurence Sterne. Chapter 6 shows how the attempt of David Hume and Adam Smith to ground the study of society and morality upon an empirical epistemology and dispassionate

Introduction 23

historical enquiry influenced their approach to war. In both writers, a stark contrast emerges between the improving models of behaviour they endorse and the public's aggressive response to destructive and expensive contemporary wars.

Part Three: War and Peace in an Age of Revolutions

This part considers how the divisions stimulated in Britain by the American and French revolutions helped to deepen criticism of the causes and effects of war, complicated the process of reconciling the public to war, and eventually led to the emergence of peace societies. Chapter 7 looks at two novels that explore the social causes of war. Samuel Jackson Pratt's *Emma Corbett* (1780), published during the War of American Independence, describes a young woman's conversion to a position of absolute pacifism, and Charlotte Smith's *The Old Manor House*, which shows how a British soldier fighting loyally against rebels in America is led to question the purpose of war and to see its utter futility. Chapter 8 explores developments that work to insulate non-combatants morally from the horrors of war, including the 'domestication of patriotism', the reinterpretation of the pacific elements of Christian doctrine, and the representation of humanitarian sympathy for domestic victims of war. These issues are examined in a range of writings – moral, polemic, and poetic, concluding with a brief consideration of Jane Austen's fiction. Chapter 9 considers a different kind of insulation, a response to the unusual circumstances created by the Revolutionary and Napoleonic Wars against France, when supporters and opposers of Britain's wars had reason to worry about the outbreak of violence at home. It shows how an interest in communal mourning, in obsolete cultural forms, or in a fashionable despondency could allow audiences to engage with rousing representations of violence while relieving them of the sense that they were being called to action. Chapter 10 discusses the emergence of an absolute, non-resisting pacifism into the mainstreams of British reforming culture during this turbulent period. It places the pacifist writings of Thomas Clarkson in the context of a wider interest in exporting Christianity and in using the opportunities arising from the violent expansion of empire.

Part Four: The Landscape of Conquest

Chapter 11, focused on Gibraltar, spans the eighteenth century as a whole and looks forward to the imperial conquests of the nineteenth century.

24   Introduction

It illustrates how taking territory from others was justified by the idea of civilised custody, registered in responses to the landscape, including its natural features and cultural relicts; how this idea changed in the light of the successful defence of Gibraltar against Spanish forces; and how the bare features of this outcrop came to symbolise the defence of British liberty and civilisation – an icon that could be evoked in the context of other conquered territories.

Notes

1 John Loftis, *The Politics of Drama in Augustan England* (Oxford: Oxford University Press, 1963); Bridget Orr, *Empire on the English Stage 1660–1714* (Cambridge: Cambridge University Press, 2001); *British Enlightenment Theatre* (Cambridge: Cambridge University Press, 2020); Daniel O'Quinn, 'Theatre and Empire', in *The Cambridge Companion to British Theatre, 1730–1830* (Cambridge: Cambridge University Press, 2007), 233–246; *Staging Governance: Theatrical Imperialism in London, 1770–1800* (Baltimore: The Johns Hopkins University Press, 2005); *Entertaining Crisis in the Atlantic Imperium 1770–1790* (Baltimore: The John Hopkins University Press, 2011); Gillian Russell, *The Theatres of War: Performance, Politics, and Society: 1793–1815* (Oxford: Oxford University Press. 1995); David Worrall, 'Theater in the Combat Zone: Military Theatricals at Philadelphia, 1778', in Elizabeth Fay and Leonard von Morzé, eds., *Urban Identity and the Atlantic World* (New York: Palgrave, 2013), 219–235; Georgina Lock and David Worrall, 'Crisis without Anxiety: The Jacobite Moment of Ann Macklin's Benefit Night, 23rd April 1746', *Restoration and Eighteenth-Century Theatre Research*, 32 (2017), 5–28; Joel Schechter. *Eighteenth-century Brechtians: Theatrical Satire in the Age of Walpole* (Exeter: Exeter University Presss, 2015); Dana Van Kooy, *Shelley's Radical Stages: Romatic Drama in Wartime* (London: Routledge, 2016); Susan Valladares, *Staging the Peninsular War: English Theatres 1807–1815* (London: Routledge, 2016).
2 Bernard Mandeville, *The Fable of the Bees* (London, 1714), 192–193; [Anna Barbauld], *Sins of Government, Sins of the Nation* (London, 1793), 25.
3 Maurice R. Davie, *The Evolution of War: A Study of Its Role in Early Societies* (New Haven: Yale University Press, 1929), 18.
4 J. J. Rousseau, *A Project for Perpetual Peace* (London, 1761); Jeremy Bentham, *Plan for a Universal and Perpetual Peace (1786–1789)*, (London: Peace Book Co., 1939); Emanuel Kant, *Project for a Perpetual Peace* (London, 1796).
5 For example, in *The City of God*, Book 19, Section 7.
6 Anthony Ashley Cooper, Earl of Shaftesbury, *Characteristics of Men, Manners, Opinions, Times* (London, 1711), 3 vols., I, 113.
7 For example, John Milton, *Paradise Lost* (1667), Fénelon, *Adventures of Telemachus* (1719).
8 David Nokes, ed., *Henry Fielding, Jonathan Wild* (Harmondsworth: Penguin 1982), Introduction, 7–24, 19.

Introduction 25

9 John Locke, *Some Thoughts Concerning Education*, ed. Ruth W. Grant and Nathan Tarcov (Indianapolis: Hackett Publishing Company, 1996), 90–91.

10 Gregory M. Reichberg, Henrike Syse, and Endre Begby, *The Ethics of War: Classic and Contemporary Readings* (Oxford: Blackwell, 2006), 73.

11 Samuel Clarke, *The Dedication of Dr Clarke's Edition of Caesar's Commentaries* (London, 1712), 9.

12 See John Richardson, 'Nicholas Rowe's Tamerlane and the Martial Ideal', *Modern Language Quarterly*, 69 (2008), 269–289.

13 Philip Shaw, *Sentiment and Suffering in Romantic Military Art* (Farnham: Asghgate, 2013), 4.

14 *A Full and Impartial Relation of the Battle Fought on the 13th of August, 1704. N.S. in the PLAIN of HOCHSTETTE By an Officer who was in the Engagement* (London, 1704), 4.

15 See Sharon Alker, 'The Soldierly Imagination: Narrating Fear in Defoe's Memoirs of a Cavalier', *Eighteenth-Century Fiction*, 19: 4 (2006–7), 1–26.

16 Joseph Addison, *The Campaign, A Poem*, 2nd edn (London, 1705), 11–12.

17 Donna T. Andrew, *Philanthropy and Police: London Charity in the Eighteenth Century* (Princeton: Princeton University Press, 1989); G. J. Barker-Benfield, *The Culture of Sensibility*, (Chicago: University of Chicago Press, 1992); Arthur Herman, *The Scottish Enlightenment* (London: Fourth Estate, 2003); Michael Barnett and Thomas G. Weiss, eds., *Humanitarianism in Question* (Ithaca NY: Cornell University Press, 2008); Karen O'Brien, *Women and Enlightenment in Eighteenth-Century Britain* (Cambridge: Cambridge University Press, 2009); Michael Barnett, *Empire of Humanity: A History of Humanitarianism* (Ithaca NY: Cornell University Press, 2011).

18 See Peter Stamatov, *The Origins of Global Humanitarianism: Religion, Empires and Advocacy* (Cambridge: Cambridge University Press, 2013), 81–96.

19 *An Impartial Narrative Of the Last Expedition to the Coast of France, By an Eye Witness* (London, 1758), 18–19.

20 Major-Gen R. H. Mahon, *The Life of General The Hon., James Murray, a Builder of Canada* (London: John Murray, 1921), 275.

21 J. G. A. Pocock, *The Machiavellian Moment* (Princeton NJ: Princeton University Press, 1975): *Virtue, Commerce and History* (Cambridge: Cambridge University Press, 1985), 48–50.

22 See Frederick G. Whelan, *Hume and Machiavelli: Political Realism and Liberal Thought* (Lanham, Maryland: Lexington Books, 2004), 3.

23 Vivienne Jones, ed., *Women in the Eighteenth Century: Constructions of Femininity* (London: Routledge, 1990), 6–7.

24 Ruth K. McClure, *Coram's Children: The London Foundling Hospital in the Eighteenth Century* (New Haven, CT: Yale University Press: 1981); Linda Colley, *Britons: Forging the Nation 1707–1837*, (New Haven: Yale University Press, 1992), 82–3; Sarah Kinkel, 'Saving Admiral Byng: Imperial Debates, Military Governance and Popular Politics at the Outbreak of the Seven Years War', *Journal for Maritime Research*, 13; 1 (2011), 3–19.

26 Introduction

25 Kathleen Wilson, 'Empire, Trade and Popular Politics in Mid-Hanoverian Britain: The Case of Admiral Vernon,' *Past and Present*, 121 (1988), 74–109; Nicholas Rogers, *Whigs and Cities: Popular Politics in the Age of Walpole and Pitt* (Oxford: Oxford University Press, 1989); Gerald Jordan and Nicholas Rogers, 'Admirals as Heroes: Patriotism and Liberty in Hanoverian England, *Journal of British Studies*, XXVIII: 3 (1989), 201–24; Kathleen Wilson, '"Empire of Virtue": The Imperial Project and Hanoverian Culture, c. 1720–1785'; in Lawrence Stone, ed., *An Imperial State at War. Britain from 1689 to 1815* (London: Routledge, 1993), 128–64; Nicholas Rogers, *Crowds, Culture, and Politics in Georgian Britain* (Oxford: Oxford University Press, 1998).

26 *The European Magazine*, LXII (July 1802), 43–44.

27 *The Monthly Magazine*, 2 (1826), 515.

28 A. C. Grayling notes Hazliit's refusal to join the 1814 celebrations that greeted the abdication of Napoleon, whom Hazlitt 'always' vindicated: *The Quarrel of the Age: The Life and Times of William Hazlitt* (London, Weidenfield and Nicolson, 2000), 172.

29 See John Brewer, 'Commercialization and Politics' in Neil McKendrick, John Brewer and J. H. Plumb, *The Birth of a Consumer Society* (Bloomington: Indiana University Press, 1982), 239–52.

30 Cinzia Sicca and Alison Yarrington, eds, *The Lustrous Trade: Material Culture and the History of Sculpture in England and Italy, c 1700–c 1869* (London: Leicester University Press, 2000).

31 Margarette Lincoln, *Representing the Royal Navy: British Sea Power 1750–1815* (London: Routledge, 2002), 17–19.

32 Susan Wollenberg and Simon McVeigh, *Concert Life in Eighteenth-century Britain* (Farnham, Ashgate, 2004).

33 Hermione de Almeida and George H. Gilpin, *Indian Renaissance: British Romantic Art and the Prospect of India* (Farnham: Ashgate, 2005), 148; Markman Ellis, '"Spectacles within Doors": Panoramas of London in the 1790s', *Romanticism*, 14: 2 (2009), 133–148.

34 *Britons*, pp. 4, 5, 6.

35 Patrick K. O'Brien, 'The Political Economy of British Taxation, 1660–1815', *The Economic History Review*, N.S., 41 (1988), 1–32.

36 Charles D'Avenant, *An Essay on the East-India Trade* (London, 1696), 14, 51.

37 Troy Bickham, 'Eating the Empire: Intersections of Food, Cookery and Imperialism in Eighteenth-Century Britain', *Past and Present*, 198: 1 (2008), 71–109.

38 Margaret E. Hirst, *The Quakers in Peace and War* (New York: Swarthmore Press, 1923), 210–215.

39 Paul Langford, *A Polite and Commercial People* (Oxford: Oxford University Press), 622.

40 Philip Lawson and Jon Phillips, '"Our Execrable Banditti": Perceptions of Nabobs in Mid-Eighteenth-Century Britain', *Albion: A Quarterly Journal Concerned with British Studies*, 16: 3 (1984), 225–241.

Introduction 27

41 James Bradley, *Popular Politics and the American Revolution* (Macon, Ga: Mercer University Press, 1986); Linda Colley, *Britons*, 138–139; Kathleen Wilson, *The Sense of the People: Politics, Culture and Imperialism in England, 1715–1785* (Cambridge: University Press, 1995), 237–284; Troy Bickham, *Making Headlines: The American Revolution as Seen through the British Press* (DeKalb: University of Illinois Press, 2009), 84–85; Roland Bartel, 'The Story of Public Fast Days in England,' *Anglican Theological Review* 37: 3 (1955), 191–93.

42 See Harriet Guest, *Small Change, Women Learning, Patriotism, 1750–1810* (Chicago: Chicago University Press, 2000), 176–192.

43 See J. E. Cookson, *The Friends of Peace: Anti-War Liberalism in England, 1793–1815* (Cambridge: Cambridge University Press, 1982), 54–55.

44 V: 187–192. William Cowper, *The Task and Selected Other Poems*, edited by James Sambrook (Harlow: Longman, 1994), 172.

45 V: 617–58, pp. 160–61.

46 II: 245, 230, p. 92.

47 See Matthew Wyman-McCarthy, 'Rethinking Empire in India and the Atlantic: William Cowper, John Newton, and the Imperial Origins of Evangelical Abolitionism' *Slavery and Abolition*, 35: 2 (2014), 306–327.

48 Tim Fulford, *Landscape, Liberty and Authority* (Cambridge: Cambridge University Press, 1996), 53.

49 III: 355, p. 122. Mary A. Favret, *War at a Distance: Romanticism and the Making of Modern Wartime* (Princeton, NJ, Princeton University Press., 2009).

50 II: 216–18, p. 91.

51 The poet's private lifestyle is not cut off completely from public events; he claims that he still 'serves his country' (VI, 968). See Dustin Griffin, *Patriotism and Poetry in Eighteenth-Century Britain* (Cambridge: Cambridge University Press, 2002), 249–250.

52 VI: 343, p. 207.

53 *Landcape, Liberty and Authority*, 54.

54 Charlotte Smith, *The Old Manor House* (London, 1793), epigraph to Volume III; Vicesimus Knox, *Antipolemus, or the Plea of Reason, Religion and Humanity against War* (London 1794), xvi; George Beaumont, *The Warrior's Looking Glass* (Sheffield, 1808), 154; *The Herald of Peace*, Vol 1 (1819), 135; Vol 2 (1820), 16; Vol 3 (N.S) (1823), 5;, Vol 8 (N.S.) (1831–32), 84, 412.

55 VI: 843, p. 222.

56 See Martin Ceadel, *The Origins of War Prevention: The British Peace Movement and International Relations, 1730–1854* (Oxford: Oxford University Press, 1996), 66.

57 Joseph Cornish, *The Miseries of War, and the Hope of Final and Universal Peace* (Taunton, 1784); Richard Price, *Observations on the Importance of the American Revolution* (London 1784).

58 For a wide ranging discussion of the influence of millenarianism in the Romantic period, see Tim Fulford, ed., *Romanticism and Millenarianism* (Basingstoke: Palgrave, 2002).

PART I

Developing Ideals

CHAPTER I

The Culture of War and Civil Society, from William III to George I

In *The Civilizing Process* Norbert Elias outlines a transformation by which, in modern states, 'drives' such as 'joy in killing and destruction' are systematically repressed, to find socially permitted expression in carefully regulated activities such as sporting contests, in the 'passive, more ordered pleasure of spectating', and in our experience of the arts. In a pacified society 'Physical clashes, wars and feuds, and anything recalling them [… are] banished from view or at least subjected to more and more precise social rules'. Elias argues that 'immense social upheaval and urgency, heightened by carefully concerted propaganda, are needed to awaken and legitimize in large masses of people the socially outlawed drives'. The sequential process envisioned here – of systematic repression followed by periodic awakening and legitimisation – appears to be coloured by the experience of world war and general conscription, the immense upheavals Elias experienced himself in the early twentieth century. He does not pursue the issue of propaganda, since his theory emphasises the compensatory function of the imaginary rather than its formative or conditioning role: he sees 'dreams […] books and pictures' as providing a substitute satisfaction of suppressed drives. And he has little to say about the role of religion, which he claims 'never has in itself a "civilizing" or affect-subduing effect', and whose 'expressions and forms of behaviour' he characterises as 'childish'.[1] Because he separates the processes of suppression from the use of propaganda and the imagining of violence he does not consider the role played by the representation of war in the pacification of society. But there is evidence that war, described by poets as a test of heroism, and represented by the church as the occasion for spiritual purgation, served the interests of those who wanted to regulate and refine the manners of civil society; and that the promotion of gentler manners did not undermine the commitment to military aggression, but worked in the service of it. In this chapter, I will examine this evidence in relation to the era of William III, Queen Anne, and George I, an era which saw both the consolidation of what John

32 Part I: Developing Ideals

Brewer terms the British 'military-fiscal state' and an attempt to establish a culture of politeness.[2]

The separation of war into a professional activity may have contributed to the rise of humanitarian ideas in the later seventeenth century. In the sermons of 'Latitude men' keen to refute Hobbes's war-like image of human nature, in the work of Neoplatonist philosophers, in protests against cruelty to animals, in satirical accounts of brutal masculine habits, and in critical reflections upon the tradition of military heroism, a movement to soften the manners of society began to gather momentum, a movement that emphasised the human capacity for goodness.[3] Some, like the third Earl of Shaftesbury, postulated an inborn, natural benevolence, which was in practice far from universal, being influenced by custom (including religion) and education, and being developed most securely within the civil realm.[4] Some, like John Locke, denied the natural status of benevolence in order to stress the importance of the educational influences needed to cultivate it.[5] While philosophers might disagree about its basis in human nature, the idea of benevolence was taken up by writers, artists, preachers, and political theorists and made to play an important role in the 'civilizing process'.

The growing influence of humanitarianism overlapped with the establishment of a permanent 'standing' army in the face of widespread suspicion and a massive increase of investment in the navy. These developments have origins that precede the Glorious Revolution of 1688, but after the Revolution, the scale of the nation's involvement in war, and of attempts to reconcile the public to this involvement, increased dramatically. The decoration of the new royal hospitals at Chelsea and Greenwich (for veterans of the army and navy respectively) was designed to link war-making with ideas of benevolence. Both hospitals were partly funded by deductions from servicemen's pay, but were represented primarily as acts of philanthropy. They followed the example of Les Invalides, Louis XIV's magnificent hospital for veterans in Paris (1670), but unlike that institution they were not decorated with heroic battle scenes. The murals that adorned their great halls certainly evoked the nation's global ambition but also emphasised a commitment to social virtue. Chelsea was established in the reign of Charles II, but the dining hall mural that depicts Charles was worked on by Antonio Verrio between 1688 and 1692 (and completed by Henry Cooke). Among its allegorical figures, a bare-headed man in a toga pours a libation as he is helped aloft by a female representing the Public Weal: a philanthropic gesture.[6] The sight of hospital inmates dining together before this mural became a visitor attraction.[7] In the Painted

The Culture of War and Civil Society

Hall at Greenwich, the murals by Richard Thornhill depicting William and Mary and the new Hanoverian dynasty of George I not only suggested the power of the royal subjects but also evoked loving family relations between them. The first detailed discussion of this Painted Hall appeared in Richard Steele's periodical *The Lover* (1714), a work aimed at an expanding polite public of both sexes, and concerned to emphasise the importance of 'the softer Affections of the Mind, which being properly raised and awakened, make way for the Operation of all good arts'.[8] The hospitals were the most monumental and expensive examples of a wider trend to suggest the continuity between the nation's war-making and virtues such as 'Humanity, Benignity, Goodness, Generosity, Mercy, Liberality, Magnanimity, and Hospitality' – which were illustrated in separate paintings (now lost) within the Hall at Greenwich.

In a new age of post-Revolutionary party politics, war was a focus of political contention, and the state's investment in the military was subject to close parliamentary scrutiny and sharp criticism. In peacetime, the standing army was liable to be drastically reduced to allay fears of military government. Politicians on both sides of Parliament sometimes adopted the language of 'Country ideology' to defend established rights from the growing state power – of which the army and navy were the most visible examples. The suspicion of standing armies, combined with a policy of hiring foreign mercenaries and subsidising allied forces, kept a check on the expansion of the army, while a preference for investment in naval defence helped keep conflict away from the mainland.[9]

The increasing professionalisation of the armed forces worked to place military activity beyond the range of most gentlemen. The traditional link between the gentleman and military service lived on: guides to the breeding and management of horses routinely combined advice about sports and war, while books on gentlemanly leisure might include military exercises.[10] Increasingly, though, it was assumed that military service would have no necessary place in a gentleman's life, while gentlemanly virtue became associated with a range of other activities, including spiritual introspection, self-management, care of family and dependents, and improving studies.[11]

But as war-making became professionalised, it also penetrated more deeply and widely into the culture of daily life. The increased long-term investment in war meant a huge growth in civilian employment devoted to war, while the creation of the Bank of England (1694), and of means to fund war through public credit, created a new body of investors who drew profits from war, a body that included a significant number of women.[12] The volume of publications devoted exclusively to war, or engaging with it

34 Part I: Developing Ideals

in passing, was considerable by the later seventeenth century and increased sharply after the Revolution of 1688.[13] Beyond the official religious and heroic writings produced under the influence of the church and state, there were many technical studies of the art of war, a widening range of news reports, histories, and memoirs, and even some short-lived periodicals linked to ongoing conflicts.[14] Many publications worked to reconcile readers to war by normalising it. News was supplemented by handy, topical guides which claimed that war endowed places with historical and cultural significance, and motivated improving studies.[15] While pamphlets on trade argued that commerce had to be protected by military investment, debates about taxation addressed the means by which domestic consumption helped to fund such investment.[16] Fears that wars would decimate the male population were countered by political arithmeticians, who considered its human costs in statistical terms.[17] As discussions of the technical, economic, and social implications of war proliferated, reading about war, like paying for it, became an increasingly familiar activity.

Even if much of England continued to enjoy peace during the wars of William, Mary, and Anne, the violence of war was not exactly 'banished from view' as Elias claims. The public had a voracious appetite for war news, and the outbreak of war could give a dramatic boost to newspaper sales, even when England was not directly involved.[18] The lapsing of the licensing laws in 1695 helped to increase the volume of information. The first English daily newspaper appeared at the outbreak of the War of the Spanish Succession, since war made daily news a viable proposition.[19] The public appetite for war news in itself appeared to be helping the print market expand.[20]

The constant presence of war news reminded non-military males of what they were *not* doing. The separation of war-making into a professional activity left them vulnerable to the charge that they had abandoned traditional masculine roles and were becoming corrupt or 'effeminate'. As Emma Clery explains, effeminacy could be understood as 'the sum of a complex of derogatory ideas [...] gendered "feminine", including corruption, weakness, cowardice, luxury, immorality and the unbridled play of passions'. It did not imply homosexuality, but behaviour unfit for the manly responsibilities of the civic role, which could include excessive attachment to women.[21] The outbreak of war could be presented as an opportunity to regain lost honour, as in Addison's 'A Poem to His Majesty' (1695), which praised William's reawakening of military vigour in an English youth grown 'negligent of arms'.[22] In the militia debate of 1697–1702, Country Whigs opposed to the professional 'standing army' claimed that without military training the ordinary citizen would be prone to corruption; one of them, Andrew Fletcher, saw a correlation between the rise of the arts in modern society and the spread of corrupting luxury and represented the professional army as a sign of lost virtue.[23] The development of a rhetoric of moral reformation also worked to set martial virtue against social corruption. The Societies for the Reformation of Manners, which aimed to curb profanity of speech, lewdness, and prostitution among ordinary citizens, argued that in war time such vices could weaken the nation and lead to military defeat. Sermons addressed to Reforming Societies sometimes contrasted the luxury and debauchery of effeminate citizens with traditional ideas of manly virtue that included courage and readiness for war.[24]

If war and martial virtue were elevated against the threat of corruption and effeminacy, the rise of humanitarianism worked to soften the often harsh and violent practices common within eighteenth-century society. This opposition to brutality may seem to conflict with the celebration of war-like, manly virtue, but these movements were not necessarily opposed, and could reinforce each other. Measures for the more humane treatment of servicemen were often promoted under the double sign of benevolence and encouragement to bravery. In an era of increasing political accountability, protests against corruption and internal brutality in the army and navy, which grew after 1690, were often made in the name of encouraging recruitment and valour.[25] Complaints against the brutality of naval commanders appeared alongside complaints of their cowardice (those deemed not sufficiently aggressive against the enemy were liable to be executed).[26]

In literary culture, too, the movement towards gentler manners often coexisted with militarism. The number of women writers publishing and signing their works increased in the 1690s.[27] Some of these authorised themselves by combining feminine softness with a celebration of military courage: Elizabeth Singer came to public attention through a panegyric on William's martial prowess which claimed the poet's voice was 'Too soft [...] the Hero to express'.[28] In the next decade Lady Chudleigh and Elizabeth Elstob both published works that condemned the falseness of military glory, but Chudleigh also recommended writers who promoted such glory, while Elstob praised Queen Anne's military prowess.[29] Carol Barash has noted that Queen Anne functioned as an empowering presence to women writers, who celebrated her as an Amazonian warrior Queen, a figure who united masculine militarism with feminine virtues.[30] Those male authors now most firmly associated with the development of a culture of politeness consistently idealise military courage. As we saw in the Introduction, Shaftesbury, who makes cruelty seem a matter of bad

36 Part I: Developing Ideals

manners, elevates martial heroism into a form of philanthropy.[31] In the *Tatler* and *Spectator*, criticism of brutal sports, of duelling, and of violence on the stage coexists with support for the contemporary war, celebration of the army, and glorification of Marlborough's heroism (see Chapter 2). Addison, Steele, and others, including Daniel Defoe, have been described as working to accommodate 'commerce and the private virtues of "the middle class citizen"' within the discourse of civic humanism.[32] This is to accommodate the demand for gentle manners within a system that associates virtue with martial valour.

The professionalisation of war, then, provides a context for understanding why a movement against brutality coexisted with, and sometimes reinforced, the celebration of martial courage and enthusiastic support for war. These two movements represented moral demands that had to be reconciled within the modern citizen, who must avoid the twin vices of cruelty and effeminacy. We can see this in what was to become the most influential educational work of the eighteenth century, Locke's *Some Thoughts Concerning Education*, which first appeared in 1693. This work was designed to prepare young gentlemen for a future in which military activity, while a possibility, appeared to have no necessary place. Locke describes courage in terms that would be as appropriate to civilian life as to the theatre of war, since 'dangers attack us in other places besides the fields of battle'. For him, courage has nothing to do with physical 'roughness' but entails the calm use of reason and the capacity to act as needed in the presence of fear and danger. While Locke recommends physical exercise, the primary goal is not to develop the child's military skill but to cultivate a defensive 'brawniness and insensibility of mind', to leave the child 'hardened against all sufferings, especially of the body'. This mental brawniness becomes more important than physical prowess and is specifically intended to counteract 'effeminacy of spirit'. But while Locke seeks to 'harden' the child in this sense, at the same time he seeks to *counteract* a tendency to 'harden' children towards cruelty. He refuses to see cruelty as natural, describing it as a 'habit borrowed from custom and conversation', and fostered by histories that treat slaughter as the most heroic of virtues. A good education must nevertheless make use of bellicose history but will seek to preserve the child's natural aversion to cruelty, and encourage 'gentle' manners.[33] This education, then, works to counteract the two spectres that haunt civil society: a mental toughening-up counters effeminacy and provides the basis for self-discipline and courageous self-sacrifice; the avoidance of unnatural cruelty counters brutality.

To conceive of a continuity between the courage of the battlefield and the courage appropriate to social life is to recognise the need for what William James would later call a 'moral equivalent' to martial virtue within civil society – the need to preserve the capacity for self-sacrifice, discipline, public spirit within the realm of peaceful leisure.[34] The soldier's calm adherence to duty in the face of military violence becomes exemplary of the mental toughness civilians must acquire. Non-combatants with gentle manners do not need to inflict violence – but in the military-fiscal state they must be attuned to supporting it and confronting news of it, and if they are 'hardened against all sufferings, especially of the body' they will accept it more readily. At the same time, such mental toughness need not mean any diminution of gentleness to others, or any endorsement of unnecessary cruelty. An exemplary response to the violence of war would elicit, as Locke implies, both hardness and softness at the same time.

The Arts

While Locke's theoretical discussions of courage and gentle manners formulate desired forms of behaviour, they do not engage the reader with the challenge of violence. But key areas of culture within the developing military-fiscal state did attempt to engage non-combatants imaginatively with the violence of war, an engagement that functioned as pro-war propaganda and simultaneously contributed to what Elias would term 'pacification'. The state was able to garner support for its own war effort through its influence over the arts. The example of Louis XIV, who spent huge sums on works to glorify his own military achievements, was both ridiculed and emulated in England, where William III commissioned paintings and tapestries to celebrate his victories, where plays – in theatres dependent on royal patronage – included prologues, epilogues, and other references commending his heroism, and where the system of patronage encouraged a host of aspiring poets to write panegyrics on his campaigns.[35] Beyond these forms, there was a tradition of popular songs and ballads in which battles, military leaders, and the fortunes of ordinary soldiers and sailors were celebrated.[36]

The violence of war was confronted most directly in panegyrics and other poems celebrating battles and campaigns. These shared some aims with the heroic paintings and tapestries ordered by William, Marlborough, and his generals, which glorified the heroic commander and the achievements of his troops. But they also had different aims. The heroic works of court painters like Jan Wyck or Dirk Maas could seem remote from the interests of civilians.[37] The Flemish tapestries based on De Hondt's *Art of War*, which depict the military camp with camp-followers and flowing wine, and show soldiers pillaging peasants, emerge from a courtly tradition not easy to reconcile with the reformation of manners.[38] In representing war for a growing public audience well supplied with war news, poets had to take into account ideas of conduct that increasingly diverged from heroic tradition.

John Richardson argues that an awareness of the incompatibility of heroic conventions with modern war emerged during the War of the Spanish Succession.[39] But this awareness was already present in the Renaissance, while seventeenth-century mock-heroic sometimes exposed the factitious nature of the heroic tradition.[40] Poets were well aware that even in their classical models heroic conventions were not usually applied directly to contemporary conflicts, but to wars far distant in time, that had already acquired a legendary status (Addison claims that Virgil was separated from his subject by 'A Thousand Years').[41] Even Lucan, who was usually regarded as a historian rather than a true heroic poet, wrote about events that occurred a hundred years earlier.[42] The problematic expectation that poets would celebrate in heroic terms events that could be read about in the news – as popular ballad writers did – was a legacy of the panegyric tradition established in the reign of James I.[43] The continuing production of battle poems was stimulated by court patronage. As Abigail Williams reminds us, much of this poetry was produced by poets working under Whig political influence, in an era in which 'state finances, government affairs, court authority and literary culture' were deeply interconnected.[44] But it can also be understood in relation to a contemporary unease with the growing volume of publicly available information about ongoing conflicts.[45] It is notable that John Dennis and Joseph Addison, who both wrote poems celebrating war in violent terms, both satirised the effect of the public obsession with war news, as we shall see. It was not the representation of war in itself that concerned them, apparently, so much as the manner and effect of that representation.

A primary source of information about what happened in military conflicts was eye-witness accounts of participants. Such accounts, whether in letters printed in newspapers, in military autobiographies, or in 'Exact' Journals of campaigns, made clear the destructive power of modern arms and explosives, which could sink ships, decimate battlefield formations, and reduce towns to rubble. But they tended to report violence in a matter-or-fact style, with occasional tributes to courage or laconic reflections upon fear, in ways that reflected contemporary military discipline.[46]

The Culture of War and Civil Society

The dialogic nature of newspapers, in which copy was assembled at speed from a variety of sources, inevitably generated 'Contradictions [...] Doubts, and Wants of Confirmations', as Steele complained.[47] In the absence of professional foreign correspondents, papers translated reports of overseas news verbatim from foreign newspapers, inserted under headings identifying the source – which was often a newspaper representing the enemy's point of view, such as *The Paris Gazette*. Newspapers usually attempted to distinguish English bravery from foreign barbarity, but it was difficult to preserve a consistent moral tone when expressions of editorial outrage about the cruelty of the enemy had to coexist with accounts from conflict zones, reporting in the blunt idiom of combatants, how 'we made a terrible slaughter of them', or how they were 'cut in pieces'.[48] The destructiveness of modern war revealed in the papers did not diminish its fascination to the public. It was even suggested that newspapers exaggerated the casualties of war in order to boost sales. In an early number of *The Tatler*, Addison claims that while 'Prince Eugene has slain his Thousands, Boyer [i.e. Abel Boyer, editor of the *Post Boy* newspaper] has slain his Ten Thousands'.[49]

In an age that was discovering a new concern to promote gentler manners, it appeared that news was feeding a public appetite for violence that was potentially brutalising. John Tutchin's *Observator* addressed this problem directly. Here, avoiding the usual mosaic of verbatim reports, news was presented through a dialogue between Mr Observator, 'a man of learning [...] acquainted with state affairs', and a bluff 'Countryman' with rural manners and a love of 'fighting stories'. The news of Marlborough's victory at Blenheim was characteristically delivered by the Countryman in a display of sheer delight that 20,000 French and Bavarians had apparently been killed, and at the idea of farmland 'finely dunged with the carnage of slain'.[50] His unrestrained enthusiasm for violence, associated with the rough sports of childhood, is at once indulged and quietly reproved by Mr Observator.[51] The dialogue is symptomatic of a growing sense that the public's response to war needs to be schooled if it is to be distinguished from a vulgar response to the violence of the cock-fight and the boxing match.

Apart from fears about its brutalising influence, some writers criticised the public alarm generated by war news. The violence in war news was certainly 'spectatorial' in Elias's sense, but it represented events that were only too real. There were genuine reasons for alarm, including fears of invasion, and anxieties for family members and friends who had gone off to fight. Public credit rose and fell in direct reaction to reports of battles, which,

40   Part I: Developing Ideals

as Addison complained in the *Spectator* paper, were generally cried about the streets of London 'with the same Precipitation as *Fire*'.[52] The concern that the obsession with war news was spreading beyond the elite ranks appears most famously in Addison's portrait of the political upholsterer, who neglected his business to follow news of continental campaigns.[53] But the type of the 'foolish false Politician' was already well established. John Dennis claimed in 1702, at the beginning of the War of the Spanish Succession, that the fixation with war news was posing a problem for dramatists, since it was reducing the variety of contemporary human characters to this single type: 'Go among either the Lame or the Blind, and you shall find them intercepting the Plate Fleet, or sending Forces into Italy. For all men are alarmed by the present posture of affairs, because all men believe they are concerned, which universal alarm has reduced those Characters which were so various before, to a dull uniformity'.[54]

The symptoms of public alarm revealed an absence of mental 'brawniness', just as vengeful patriotism was at odds with the movement to refine brutality from public manners. The challenge to poets who celebrated war was to exemplify an alternative, appropriate response to war, in which a tough acceptance of violence could be combined with humanitarian sympathy and the virtues of sociability. Abigail Williams notes that 'enthusiasm for gory bellicosity was central to the popularity of poetry' in the reigns of William and Anne.[55] Poets often included grisly details of slaughter ('The Shape of Man half bury'd in the Wound'), or insisted on its numerical magnitude (the 'Thousands' slain), and its devastating impact on civilians (as in Addison's description of Marlborough torching Bavarian villages in *The Campaign*).[56] But the hero's courage usually exemplified an ability to remain composed in the presence of such carnage – a model for a public alarmed or excited by the mere representation of violence:

> Above these Storms my Royal Hero bore
> The same clear Mind and settl'd Judgment wore.[57]

In contrast to the serene masculine hero, the public response to war was sometimes represented in terms of feminine emotion. In the 1690s many poems evoke the situation of women left at home during the war, perhaps echoing the situation of Queen Mary. A number of popular ballads of the period focus on soldiers parting from loved ones, sometimes giving voice to a feminine sorrow at the disruptive effect of war, while balancing this with admiration for masculine bravery.[58] In a courtly panegyric, George Stepney represents unstable public emotion in the figure of a loving Britannia whose 'unconstant bre[a]st' is alternately 'swell'd with Rapture,

The Culture of War and Civil Society 41

by Despair deprest' during William's absence at war, while she enjoys 'The Spoils of Conquest and the Charms of Peace' under Queen Mary's 'tutelary Care'.[59] In Charles Montagu's *Epistle to the Right Honourable Charles Earl of Dorset* (1690) Mary's exemplary control of her own anxieties complements William's heroism on the battlefield:

> Dissembling Cares, she smooth'd her Looks with Grace,
> Doubts in her Heart, and Pleasure in her Face. (9)

Poets may evoke the extremities of war – both the violence of the battlefield and the anxieties of the home front – in order to provide models for self-discipline in society. In this era, though, the representation of feminine responses is sometimes ambivalent, as some poems suggest a close relationship between an effeminising weakness which must be moderated, and a feminine gentleness capable of moderating the brutalising potential of war.[60] In Addison's 'A Poem to His Majesty', for example, the poet depicts his own muse as an anxious female waiting for the hero's return, worrying about the hardened soldier's ability to reconnect with a life that requires social virtues:

> but oh! Let us descry
> Mirth in thy brow, and pleasure in thy eye
> Let nothing dreadful in they face be found,
> But for awhile forget the trumpet's sound. (8)

The lines gently suggest political anxieties about the tenor of the king's future reign, while evoking a traditional concern about the potentially hardening effects of war.

In an age when the internal brutality of the armed forces was the subject of protests and scrutiny, the social virtues of military leaders were increasingly celebrated alongside their courage. The rising number of elegies on eminent soldiers and naval officers during the second half of the seventeenth century illustrate this. While a mid-century elegy on Robert Blake (c1657), defines the rough violence of the admiral's 'death-doing' heroism in contrast to the role of husband ('War was his mistress, he did her embrace'), in later decades leaders increasingly had to unite undaunted physical courage with qualities in which the public might find a reflection of the good father, husband, and householder.[61] The process of public mourning was one of the areas in which admiration for military courage could be ceremonially related to the gentler virtues. In the second half of the seventeenth century there were state funerals in Westminster Abbey for General Monck (1670), and for eminent admirals, the Earl of Sandwich

42 Part I: Developing Ideals

(1672), and Sir Edward Spragge (1673); in 1707 there was a state funeral for admiral Cloudesly Shovell. On these occasions, the commander's courage was celebrated alongside his ability to inspire affection.[62] During the public mourning for Queen Mary, William's image as warrior king was deliberately modified in elegies which showed him swooning and succumbing to his 'tender part' in sentimental tableaux.[63] An elegy for William himself endows him with the soft qualities that he had earlier been distinguished from in comparisons with the Stuarts.[64] An elegy on Cloudesly Shovell describes the grief of his consort and children, paying tribute to his qualities as householder, husband and father, as well as to his courage.[65]

A concerted effort to establish Marlborough as a good-natured, sensitive, family man – in the face of growing Tory hostility – appears in newspapers, periodicals, poems, and ballads.[66] The military hero's sociability and sweetness of temper appeared to guarantee that, on the battlefield, he would not act unjustly or with avoidable cruelty, and that he would inspire the loyalty and affection of his troops. In a society torn by the rage of party politics, by suspicion of a 'monied interest' and fears of rebellion, war could be seen as generating the noblest form of sociability, in which soldiers were unified by a common feeling that transcended self-interest. Nicholas Rowe describes Marlborough as animating his 'Social Warriors Arms' with his 'great Example', while Dennis sees a divinely inspired unity emerging within the diverse allied forces under Marlborough's command at Ramillies:

> United as they were one Nation all,
> One Family, Relations all, and Friends …
> And greatly each resolves to Die for all.[67]

The relevance of such idealisations for contemporary members of society was clear enough. But the attempt to reconcile military heroism with the needs of a modern society was always problematic. It was not difficult for poets to represent sociability and aggression as complementary qualities by focusing on the character of the hero in stylised, paradoxical compliments, as in this portrait of William III:

> His cheerful Looks a gayer dress put on,
> His eyes with decent fury shone:
> Dangers but serv'd to heighten every Grace,
> And add an awful Terrour to the Hero's Face.[68]

But there was an inherent conflict between the calm hero and the language of terror used to describe the effects of his violence.[69] And when poets attempted to depict the destructive capacity of modern war more directly, the significance of the hero's exemplary qualities could be implicitly called into question, as in Henry Denne's *A Poem on the Taking of Namur* (London 1695):

> The Signal giv'n up flies a fiery Bomb,
> Hizzing amidst the Clouds, and brings the Doom
> Of Squadrons: Now another seen from far
> Glares like a Meteor, while it burns the Air.
> Again another, and another now;
> Hundreds at once fly in a dreadful Row,
> And scatter Ruine on the Town and Foe [...].
> Triumphant Fate away mean Wretches bears,
> And falling Nobles mourn unfinisht years.
> Urgd by success the Engineers apply
> Dismissive Flame, and Legions upwards fly. (4-5)

Denne foregrounds the extraordinary relationship between cause and effect that can arise in modern war: the application of the 'Dismissive Flame' to gunpowder can initiate a wholesale slaughter without any further human intervention or personal aggression, a ruin that may fall indiscriminately 'on the Town', on soldiers and non-combatants alike. Where is the lesson in either courage or gentleness, one might ask, when nobles, legions, and townspeople may be at the mercy of the engineer? The firepower unleashed in land and sea battles might pose the same question. Addison may want to celebrate William's war-making as a humanitarian response to 'The Cries of Orphans, and the Widdows Tears', but his imagination is drawn to the indiscriminate nature of destruction in modern war, to William's obliteration of fleets at sea in which 'Planks, and Arms, and Men, promiscuously flow'd', or to the power of his bombardment which can transform a 'thousand Turrets' and their 'gilded Spires' into 'An undistinguished heap of Dust'.[70] The 'promiscuous' nature of such destruction can make it seem like the negation rather than the defence of human values.

Poets, then, while attempting to render war compatible with emergent ideas of sociable conduct, were beginning to expose a gap between the hero as moral agent and the destructive effects of his orders. In some battle poems, victims die as if struck by an impersonal fate, or by what John Philips terms 'unhostile Wounds', the random effects of having entered a chaotic theatre of war.[71] The terror of war appeared to break free of its human agents. The calm acceptance of such effects is not in itself a moral justification of them. A different kind of justification was needed.

The Church

The church had no difficulty in providing such a justification, since it could attribute the devastating effects of war ultimately to the transcendent power of God. And in this period, the established church remained the state's most powerful means of encouraging support for war. National fasts and thanksgivings were familiar responses to war in the seventeenth century, but as Tony Claydon has shown, in the 1690s their use was extended and modified. Building on a recognised tradition, '[Gilbert] Burnet and his circle advanced a "Hebraic" view of their nation which described it as a body united by its peculiar relationship with God', in order to 'nationalize' King William and the war effort.[72] The pattern established here was adopted in Queen Anne's reign and provided the basis for the church's practice throughout the eighteenth century.[73]

The prayer services represented violence as normal both in the human and divine sphere, seeing it as an aspect of fallen human nature, rooted in the lusts of the body, and also as typical of divine retribution. Wars were seen as punishments drawn down upon the whole nation by its 'crying sins'. But individuals were accountable for their own sins and so ultimately the battle between sovereign states was subsumed within another battle – the ongoing war within each individual against sin and corruption. This implied that everyone shared a direct responsibility for war as a punishment and should strive to suppress his or her unruly drives. But it also implied that everyone had a role to play in the war effort. Published versions of sermons that accompanied the prayers sometimes elaborate on this theme. William Fleetwood assured the Lord Mayor and Court of Aldermen at St Mary le Bow in 1692 that '*We* are the Body, of which *they* [the soldiers] are the Hands to defend us'.[74] John Worth told his congregation at Marlborough in 1704 that in the battle against sin, all could be 'private soldiers in this sense'.[75] The personal battle could have a direct influence on the national war effort, since prayer and repentance were conceived as armaments in a struggle for divine favour. Deuel Pead urged his listeners at Clerkenwell in 1695 to 'muster up Legions of Devout, Humble and Fervent Prayers' in the battle against 'Proud *Sennacherib's* Army'.[76] John Griffith announced to his congregation at Edensor in 1704: 'every holy ejaculation, when our lives are amended, may give new courage to the drooping soldier, every sigh fill our victorious canvas with prosperous gales'.[77] All individuals, through the sincerity of their humiliation or praise, could hope to influence an outcome which lay ultimately not in military tactics, bravery, or the sinews of national power, but in the hands of a higher being.

The Culture of War and Civil Society 45

Fasts were still proclaimed in response to natural disasters – great snows and frosts, plague, fire, as well as to wars, which were all seen as signs of God's displeasure. The biblical rhetoric of the chosen psalms, lessons, and epistles often focused on the violence of the elements – of the God who moves the storms and winds, lightning, and pestilence, who can melt the hills 'like wax' (Psalm 97) and make 'desolation' across the earth (Psalm 46).[78] The language appealed insistently to the senses and emotions, representing states of extreme terror or blissful relief. Thanksgiving lessons sometimes included Isaiah 26, 1–12, a song celebrating God's power to bring 'the lofty city [...] even to the dust'.[79] In an age when the destructive power of military technology was steadily increasing, that power was made to seem feeble in relation to the devastating might of the Lord. Sermons sometimes elaborated this theme. John Griffin, enumerating the shattering loss of naval and merchant ships in the storm of 1703, observed that English fleets had beaten the Spanish Armada 'without half the ruin'. It just took 'one puff, one blast from heaven' to 'purge our hearts' of pride.[80] The ostensible purpose of emphasising the dwarfing magnitude and cleansing effect of God's destructive power, was to diminish human pride; but by endowing extreme violence with a positive moral significance the comparison also offered a precedent and justification for resorting to the destructive methods of war. Sometimes texts were chosen for their relevance to specific incidents from the wars. The Thanksgiving service for Blenheim included Judges 5: 1–22, Deborah and Barak's song of thanksgiving, clearly chosen for the parallel not only with Queen Anne and Marlborough but also with the gruesome deaths of thousands of French cavalry in the Danube: 'The river of Kishon swept them away [...] Then were the horse-hoofs broken by the means of the prancings'.[81]

The language of the prayer services, then, encouraged an imaginative participation in violence. At the same time, though, it found means to dissociate that violence from human aggression. Psalm 144, which appears in some Fast Day and Thanksgiving services, begins with David's cry: 'Blessed be the Lord my strength, which teacheth my hands to war, and my fingers to fight'. This sanctifying of bodily aggression is quickly followed by a resignation to the superior power of the Lord, which allows the urge for destruction to be indulged in an acceptable form: 'Bow thy heavens, O Lord, and come down [...] Cast forth lightning, and scatter them: shoot out thine arrows, and destroy them. Send thine hand from above'.[82] The liturgies often select biblical passages in which divine wrath is unleashed in terrifying form on behalf of the Israelites, who are positioned as passive beneficiaries rather than as aggressors. And chosen texts often show how peaceful acts of collective worship could be instrumental in gaining – and sanctioning – military victory.

Both Fast Day and Thanksgiving services sometimes included 2 Chronicles 20 to v 31, which describes the defeat of the Moabites and Ammonites by Jehoshaphat, who sought the Lord's aid and proclaimed a fast throughout all Judah; as a result of the fast, Jehoshaphat's enemies destroyed each other, leaving him and his people to strip the slain of their riches.[83] In its context, the story illustrates the desire that motivates all aspects of the prayer service, to represent those who live in obedient and devout peacefulness as worthy beneficiaries of a violence that occurs elsewhere. The story of Jehoshaphat usefully connected plunder with providence and so provided a sanctified precedent for the violent appropriations that occur in war. This was a connection that Thanksgiving sermons often made, when they identified signs of God's approval rather than his displeasure. The case of the naval plan to assault Cadiz in 1702 was a favoured example: the assault had failed because the fleet was obstructed by an adverse wind – but this failure allowed the fleet to stumble unexpectedly upon treasure ships at Vigo. The triumphant taking of this plunder was seen as a visible sign of God's particular providence, one that illustrated the difference between fallible human plans and a benevolent divine purpose, and that provided concrete evidence to refute the claim that God's providence is manifest only in the general laws of motion.[84]

In these occasions, either of imagined communal abasement or of stylised acts of praise, congregations would participate in what a modern anthropologist terms a public 'acceptance': a visible act of conformity, a momentary performance of unification that transcends doubt, diversity of interest, and differences in rank and opinion.[85] Acceptance was enacted physically, since one was expected to join in the answers at the prescribed moments. These events provide a stark contrast with the kind of national imagining Benedict Anderson associates with newspapers, which address a readership unified by its cultural interests, and its procession through 'homogenous empty time'.[86] Through these collective acts of worship, war was imaginatively embedded directly and continually in the daily life, both public and private, of the individual. In acts that were repeated simultaneously up and down the entire kingdom, the congregation was invited to see itself in relation to its forebears and posterity, sharing responsibility for past and future, and for an unfolding national history. It was invited to look momentarily beyond the world of newspapers, war reports, taxes, and levies, a world in which policy decisions, party politics, trade, commerce, and technology might be seen as genuine determinants of military outcomes. As subjects, its members were ultimately responsible for the success or failure of the war effort. The church therefore worked to close the gap between the non-combatant and the war zone in the realm of spiritual struggle, while at the same time placing personal meekness and unrestrained divine violence in a complementary relationship.

The Sublime

The sinful soul with war in its members, which the church emphasised, was easier to connect with the *passions* of war than the sociable self which was, by definition, in control of its passions, moderate and even good humoured. And mass destruction could be justified more consistently in terms of sin and divine punishment than in terms of sweet-tempered courage. The religious service, with its recourse to the wrath and irresistible power of the vengeful god, was able to evoke the violence of war with fewer problems than the poets. It is perhaps not surprising that some who wrote bellicose poems turned to Christian tradition as a source of the sublime.[87] Critics have rightly emphasised the connection between the sublime and political liberty in the poetry of the period.[88] But the sublime also provided an aesthetic rationale for the confrontation with the violence of war.

This can be seen most clearly in the work of John Dennis. Critics have noted the originality of Dennis's insistence on terror as an attribute of the sublime, and of his justification of violent religious machinery in heroic poetry in terms of its sublime effect.[89] His understanding of the sublime is usually discussed in literary or political contexts, but it can also be understood in relation to the contemporary Fast Day and Thanksgiving services. For while a variety of influences shaped Dennis's views of the sublime, including Longinus, neo-classical critics, and his own experience of landscape, the biblical heroics of his sublime battle poems followed the Church in linking the violence of contemporary war to the divine wrath evoked in the Old Testament. Indeed, Dennis claimed that his poetic celebration of Blenheim, *Britannia Triumphans* (1704), was prompted by the Thanksgiving for that victory.[90] In his theoretical discourse, *The Advancement of Modern Poetry* (1701), Dennis argues that sublime astonishment derives from something that 'is very Terrible, and likely to hurt', and he finds the highest, most terrible form of sublimity in the bible, citing the description of divine wrath in Psalm 18 (a Psalm used in a Thanksgiving service).[91]

In some respects, Dennis's emphasis on reactions to violence can be compared with Locke's understanding of courage and 'brawniness' of

48   Part I: Developing Ideals

mind. Some of Dennis's examples of sublimity – from Horace (the brave man unmoved by the threat of destruction) and Milton (Satan, battle-scarred but unbowed) – illustrate an undaunted reaction to overwhelming destruction. But Dennis assigns to the reader a powerful emotional reaction quite unlike the unmoved courage of the exemplary hero. The emotional effect of this confrontation is itself now said to be potentially restorative, for man's unfallen condition was one of both 'lofty ravishing passions' and 'habitual charity' (147). Dennis argues that poetry, like religion, should aim to re-establish the original harmony of the human powers (131, 162, 168).[92] He developed his views in *The Grounds of Criticism in Poetry* 1704), arguing that enthusiastic passion could be moved by 'Ideas occurring in Contemplation' and that terror could be transformed into 'Joy' through reflection.[93] By relating passion and terror to the realm of reason, he attempted to clarify the process by which violence – whether represented or actual – could give rise to an elevating experience that transcended its brutal origin. In this way he provides an aesthetic justification for the aggressive preoccupations of poets keen to celebrate war. While he retains a concern with religious obedience and poetic justice, his concept of the sublime attributes to the arts a power independent of ethical injunctions and allows readers to appreciate the effects of violence independent of its justice. At the same time, the sublime breaks the link between bodily exercise and mental conditioning that Locke had retained. While militia advocates represented military training as a necessary defence against corruption, Dennis endows the aesthetic experience of violence with a comparable function: it can strengthen us emotionally by reconciling us with the experience of terror; it can develop our sensitivity by restoring our disordered passions to something like their pre-lapsarian harmony and habitual charity. Implicitly, it works against both brutality and effeminacy and can bridge the gap between the rage and horror of the battlefield and the peaceful experience of the sociable civilian.

This conception of the sublime provided a theoretical justification for Dennis's own biblical heroic poems in celebration of Marlborough's victories, which attempted to accommodate the overwhelming violence of the Old Testament 'God of great Revenge, true God of War', while presenting the heroic Marlborough as a model of sociability, 'always mild, attractive, bright, serene'.[94] It also influenced the thinking of Addison and Steele, who adopted a secularised version of this sublime in order to reconcile their military interests with their advocacy of polite manners. In the *Spectator*, for example, Steele argues that true courage in war, such as great commanders have, is derived from thought and reflection and

The Culture of War and Civil Society 49

appears when 'The Force of Reason gives a certain Beauty, mixed with the Conscience of Well-doing, to all which was before terrible and ghastly to the Imagination'.[95] In this way courage is aestheticised: the experience of the warrior who has learned to accept the possibility of death resembles the sublime experience of the reader who knows how to appreciate terror in works of art.

The cultural response to war in the reigns of William and Anne inevitably included propaganda in support of the war effort, propaganda which sometimes invited an imaginative participation in violence. Much of this was designed, in Elias's terms, to 'awaken and legitimize' a martial spirit in the public, and at the same time to regulate that spirit, to render it compatible with social discipline and the cultivation of gentler manners. Elias is right to emphasise the regulation of drives in a modern state. But we need to recognise that in the military-fiscal state, the urge to war and the urge to pacification may exist in a complementary relationship and can reinforce each other. The separation of war-making into a professionalised activity may create the illusion that war is an alien interruption to the normal processes of civilian life, but there is evidence that it played a formative role in the development of the ideals of civil conduct and aesthetic ideas of a 'pacified' society.

Notes

1 Norbert Elias, *The Civilizing Process*, tr. Edmund Jephcott, ed. Eric Dunning, Johan Goudsblom, Stephen Mennell, rev edn. (Oxford: Blackwell, 2000), 170, 375, 169.

2 John Brewer, *The Sinews of Power: War, Money and the English State 1688–1783* (London: Routledge, 1789), xx.

3 Isabel Rivers, *Reason, Grace, and Sentiment, Vol I, Whichcote to Wesley* (Cambridge: Cambridge University Press, 1991), 77–80; Keith Thomas, *Man and the Natural World: Changing Attitudes in England 1500–1800* (London: Allen Lane, 1983), 154, 166; [Lady Chudleigh], *The Ladies Defence* (London, 1701), 3, 20; [Elizabeth Elstob, tr.], *An Essay upon Glory.[.] Written by Mademoiselle de Scudery* (London: J. Morphew, 1708); G. J. Barker-Benfield, *The Culture of Sensibility* (Chicago: University of Chicago Press, 1992).

4 Lawrence E. Klein, ed., *Shaftesbury: Characteristics of Men, Manners, Opinions, Times* (Cambridge: Cambridge University Press, 1999), 320, 327.

5 The difference between Locke and Shaftesbury is explored in Daniel Carey, *Locke, Shaftesbury and Hutcheson* (Cambridge: Cambridge University Press, 2006), 98–149.

6 This female reappears in the Painted Hall at Greenwich Hospital, where the artist James Thornhill identifies her as 'the Publick Weal'.

50   Part I: Developing Ideals

7 John Chamberlayne, *Angliae notitia: Or, the Present State of England* (London, 1704), 421.

8 *The Lover*, Feb 25, 1714, 1.

9 Brewer, *Sinews of Power*, 157, 29–33.

10 See, e.g., *The Gentleman's Jockey* (London, 1672); *The Gentleman's New Jockey* (London, 1687); R. H., *The School of Recreation, or a Guide to the Most Ingenious Exercises* (London, 1696).

11 George C. Brauer, *The Education of a Gentleman* (New York: Bookman, 1959), 13–19; Steven Chapin, *A Social History of Truth* (Chicago: University of Chicago Press, 1994), 63; Lisa Smith, 'The Relative Duties of a Man: Domestic Medicine in England and France, 1685–1740', *Journal of Family History* 31 (2006), 247; W. R. Owens and P. N. Furbank, general eds., *Religious and Didactic Writings of Daniel Defoe*, vol. 10, *The Compleat English Gentleman and of Royal Education*, ed. W. R. Owens (London: Pickering and Chatto, 2007), 48–65.

12 P. G. M. Dickson, *The Financial Revolution in England* (London: Macmillan, 1967), 256–260.

13 In the *English Short Title Catalogue*, the number of titles relating to 'war' increases sharply in 1688 and thereafter remains at a level significantly higher than before this year.

14 The Nine Years' War gave rise to two such periodicals: *The Weekly Memorial or Political Observations on England's Benefits by the War with France* (London, 1692); *The Gentleman's Journal for the War* (London, 1693, 1694).

15 E.g. Laurence Eachard's *The Gazetteer's or Newsman's Interpreter* (London, 1693) and Abel Boyers' *The Martial Field of Europe* (London, 1694).

16 See Brewer, *The Sinews of Power*, 191–217, and Patrick K. O'Brien, 'The Political Economy of British Taxation, 1660–1815', *Economic History Review* 2nd ser. XLI(1) (1988), 1–32.

17 John Graunt's studies of Bills of Mortality suggested that the number of males exceeded females by one thirteenth – a difference that compensated for war deaths. Graunt claimed that labour markets depleted by war soon recovered. John Graunt, *Natural and Political Observations [...] upon the Bills of Mortality* (London, 1672), 48–49. William Petty conceded that war losses, like those through natural disasters, were 'Terrible at the Times and Places where they happen' but were 'no great matter in the whole Nation' since the population doubled every 360 years in spite of all of the temporary decimations. *An Essay Concerning the Multiplication of Mankind* (London, 1686), 18.

18 The 1683 siege of Vienna by Turks created abnormal demand for *The London Gazette*. P. M. Handover attributes this in part to the special interests of traders and shipowners, *A History of the London Gazette 1665–1965* (London: HMSO, 1965), 22.

19 *The Daily Courant* was launched on March 11 1702 as the War of the Spanish Succession was beginning. The first issue was dominated by war reports.

20 Mr Spectator sees himself as trying to capture the new readership brought into being by the rage for war news, *The Spectator* 452 (8 August 1712), 4: 90–94.

The Culture of War and Civil Society   51

21 E. J. Clery, *The Feminization Debate in Eighteenth-Century England: Literature, Commerce and Luxury* (Basingstoke: Palgrave, 2004); 10. Carolyn Williams, *Pope, Homer and Manliness: Some Aspects of Eighteenth-Century Classical Learning* (London: Routledge, 1993), 36–37.

22 Joseph Addison, *A Poem to His Majesty: Presented to the Lord Keeper* (London, 1695), 3.

23 Andrew Fletcher, *A Discourse of Concerning Militias and Standing Armies* (Edinburgh, 1698), 7–9.

24 Stephen H. Gregg, '"A Truly Christian Hero": Religion, Effeminacy, and Nation in the Writings of the Societies for Reformation of Manners', *Eighteenth-Century Life* 25(1) (2001), 18–19. Edward Stillingfleet, *Reformation of Manners [...] In a Sermon Preach'd at White-hall* (London, 1700); Thomas Emlyn, *A sermon preach'd before the Societies for the Reformation of Manners in Dublin October 4th 1698* (Dublin, 1698); William Ward, *A Sermon Preached for Reformation of Manners, at Portsmouth Nov 24th 1699* (London, 1700); Christopher Wyvill, *A Sermon Preach'd in the Collegiate Church of Ripon 22nd September 1695* (London, 1695); William Bisset, *More Plain English in Two Sermons Preach'd for the Reformation of Manners in the Year 1701* (London, 1704).

25 George St Lo, *England's Safety* (London, 1693); William Hodges, *Humble Proposals for the Relief, Encouragement, Security and Happiness of the Loyal, Courageous Seamen of England* (London, 1695); William Hodges, *Ruin to Ruin, after Misery to Misery* (London, 1699); Robert Crosfeild, *England's Glory Reviv'd* (London, 1693); D. C., *A Letter to a Member of Parliament, on Behalf of the Army in General; the Non-commissioned Officer, Soldier, and House-keeper in Particular* (London, 1701); *A Short Method Propos'd to Prevent the Desertion of Soldiers for the Future* (London, 1710).

26 John Tutchin, in *Remarks upon the Navy. The Second Part* (London, 1700) claimed that 'Cruelty and Cowardice are things inseparable' (22); Robert E. Glass notes that 'Courage and conduct' were often linked in pamphlets condemning the behaviour of gentlemen captains, 'The Image of the Sea Officer in English Literature 1660–1710', *Albion* 26(4) (1994), 589. See also N. A. M. Rodger, *The Command of the Ocean: A Naval History of Britain, 1649–1815* (London: Allen Lane, 2004), 202.

27 Carol Barash, *English Women's Poetry 1649–1714* (Oxford: Oxford University Press, 1996), 216.

28 *Poems on Several Occasions Written by Philomela* (London, 1696), 31, 32.

29 Lady Chudleigh, wrote: 'The bloody Masters of the martial Trade/ Are prais'd for Mischiefs, and for Murders pay'd', *The Ladies Defence* (London, 1701), 20; but Virgil and Plutarch appear among the authors she recommends to female readers: *The Poems and Prose of Mary, Lady Chudleigh* ed. Margaret J. M. Ezell (Oxford: Oxford University Press, 1993), xxvii. Mme Scudéry's *Essay on Glory* condemns the glory of conquerors while praising Louis XIV's victories; in her anonymous translation of 1708, Elstob transfers the praise to Queen Anne.

30 *English Women's Poetry*, 222–232.

52   Part I: Developing Ideals

31 Anthony Ashley Cooper, Third Earl of Shaftesbury, *Characteristics of Man, Manners, Opinions, Times*, ed. Lawrence E. Klein (Cambridge: Cambridge University Press, 1999), 52.

32 John Barrell, *The Political History of Painting from Reynolds to Hazlitt* (New Haven: Yale University Press, 1986), 9.

33 John Locke, *Some Thoughts Concerning Education and of the Conduct of the Understanding*, ed. Ruth W. Grant and Nathan Tarcov (Indianopolis: Hackett Publishing Company, 1996), 86, 84, 90–91.

34 William James, 'The moral equivalent of war', in *War: Studies from Psychology, Sociology Anthropology*, ed. Leon Bramson and George W. Goethals (New York: Basic Books, 1954), 21–31.

35 Peter Harrington, *British Artists and War: The Face of Battle in Paintings and Prints, 1700–1914* (London: Greenhill Books, 1993), 15; Alan Wace, *The Marlborough Tapestries at Blenheim Palace and Their Relations to Other Military Tapestries of the War of the Spanish Succession* (London: Phaidon, 1968); Jeri Bapsola, *Threads of History: the Tapestries at Blenheim Palace* (Oxford: Alden, 2005). John Loftis, *The Politics of Drama in Augustan England* (Oxford: Oxford University Press, 1963), 27. Abigail Williams, *Poetry and the Creation of a Whig Culture 1681–1714* (Oxford: Oxford University Press, 2005), 204–246. For ridicule of Louis, see Charles Montagu's *Epistle to the Right Honourable Charles Earl of Dorset* (London: Francis Saunders, 1690), 8–9.

36 C. H. Firth, *Naval Songs and Ballads* (London: Navy Records Society, 1908); John Marshall Carter, *The Military and Social Significance of Ballad Singing in the English Civil War, 1642–1649* (Kansas: Kansas State University, 1980).

37 Steele argues 'to fill a Room full of Battle-Pieces, pompous Histories of Sieges, and a tall Hero alone in a Crowd of insignificant Figures about him, is of no Consequence to private Men', *The Tatler* 209, 10 August 1710, 3: 107.

38 Jeri Bapsola, *Threads of History*, 44–59.

39 John Richardson, 'Modern Warfare in Early-Eighteenth-Century Poetry' *SEL Studies in English Literature 1500–1900*, 45:3 (2005), 557–577.

40 Michael West notes the use of anachronistic chivalric conventions in Renaissance epics and identifies 'deliberate burlesque' in Spenser who recognised the absurdity of the chivalric narrative in an age of siege warfare. 'Spenser's Art of War: Chivalric Allegory, Military Technology, and the Elizabethan Mock-Heroic Sensibility' *Renaissance Quarterly*, 41: 4 (1988), 654–704, p. 703. Richard Terry, *Mock-Heroic from Butler to Cowper: An English Genre and Discourse* (Farnham: Ashgate, 2005), 39–41.

41 'A Thousand Years in full Succession ran/ E'er *Virgil* rais'd his Voice, and sung the Man'. *A Poem to His Majesty*, 2.

42 *Pharsalia*, describing the war between Julius Caesar and Pompey of 48 BC, was begun c61 CE.

43 Arthur S. Williams, 'Panegyric Decorum in the Reigns of William III and Anne', *The Journal of British Studies*, 21:1 (1981), 56.

44 Abigail Williams gives an excellent account of the systems of Whig patronage in *Poetry and the Creation of a Whig Literary Culture*, 204–240.

The Culture of War and Civil Society   53

45 Shaftesbury, uneasy at the proliferation of voices in modern print culture, declared 'It will be in vain for our Alexanders to give orders that none besides a Lysippus should make their statue', *Characteristics*, 102.

46 The emphasis on facts rather than emotions is characteristic of military memoirs of the renaissance and seventeenth century. Yuval Noah Harari, *Renaissance Military Memoir, War, History and Identity, 1450–1600* (Woodbridge: Boydell Press, 2004); Paul Delany, *British Autobiography in the Seventeenth Century* (London: Routledge and Kegan Paul, 1969).

47 *The Tatler* 178 (30 May 1710), 2: 471.

48 Both phrases are from reports on Blenheim from *The Post Man* 12–15 August 1704.

49 *The Tatler* 18 (21 May 1709), 1: 149.

50 *The Observator* (12 August 1704).

51 When Mr Observator himself recommends violence he does so without excitement, as if accepting the grim necessity of adjusting means to ends: 'If the French besiege Maastricht, it gives the confederate armies an opportunity of ravaging and laying under contribution those provinces they have evacuated and left defenceless', 13 May 1702.

52 *The Spectator* 251 (18 December 1711), 2: 476. *An Essay towards the History of the Last Ministry and Parliament* (London, 1710) noted that credit rose on news of the first Allied Victory in Spain, on confirmation of the victory at Saragossa, and again with the expectation of Peace at Gertruydenberg, and fell when peace talks were broken off (70–71).

53 This figure's appearances in *The Tatler* 155 (6 April 1710), 160 (18 April 1710) and 178 (30 May 1710) are all concerned with war news.

54 Epistle Dedicatory, *The Comical Gallant* (London, 1702): n.p. 'For all the great and numerous originals [that were written about in the age of Charles II] are reduced to one single Coxcomb, and that is the "foolish false Politician"'.

55 *Poetry and the Creation of a Whig Literary Culture*, 6.

56 'A Poem on the Seat of War in Flanders, chiefly in relation to Sieges: With the Praise of Peace and Retirement, written in 1710', in William Broome, *Poems on Several Occasions*, 2nd edn (London, 1739), 65; R. Clare, *The English Hero: or The Duke of Marlborough* (London, 1704), 2; Joseph Addison, *The Campaign, a Poem to His Grace the Duke of Marlborough*, 2nd edn (London, 1705), 12.

57 Charles Whitworth, *Albion Rediviva: In a Poem to His Majesty on His Happy Success* (London, 1695), 12.

58 The Bagford Ballads include several examples associated with William III and his wars which focus on the disruptive effect of war on family life, the conflict between war and family, and the plight of those left behind – usually including a tribute to military courage. *The Bagford Ballads*, ed. Joseph Woodfall (Hertford: Ebsworth Ballad Society, 1878, 2 vols. In volume 1: 'The Weeping Lady' (178); 'The Protestant Commander' (305); 'The Soldier's Return' (335): 'The Souldier's Departure from his Love' (355); 'The Courageous English Boys of Several Trades and Callings' (381). In volume 2: 'A Dialogue between a Souldier and his Love' (547). C. H. Firth, *Naval Songs and Ballads* includes

54   Part I: Developing Ideals

some comparable naval ballads from the same period: 'The Undaunted Seaman' (99–101); 'The Sea-Man's Adieu to His Dear' (101–104); 'The Seamen's Wives' Vindication' (145–146).

59 *An Epistle to Charles Montagu Esq., on His Majesty's voyage to Holland* (London, 1691), 4, 5.

60 This is especially noticeable in elegies, such as Samuel Cobb, *A Pindarique Ode Humbly Offer'd to the Ever-blessed Memory of our Late Generous Sovereign Lady Queen Mary* (London, 1695) or *An ode occasion'd by the Death of Her Sacred Majesty By a Young Lady* (London, 1695).

61 George Harrison, *An Elegie on the Death of the Right Honourable Robert Blake, Esq.* (London, 1657), Firth, *Naval Songs and Ballads*, 48–52.

62 Peter Reese, *The Life of General George Monck: For King and Country* (Barnsley: Pen And Sword Military, 2008), 184; Simon Harris, *Sir Cloudesley Shovell: Stuart Admiral* (Staplehurst: Spellmount, 2001), 376. John Rowland, *Great Britain's Bitter Lamentation over the Death of Their Most Valiant, and Most Puissant General George Lord Monck* (London, 1670), praises Monck for his combination of boldness and modesty: 'Moses for Meekness, and in setting forth/ The mildest Esteemer of his own worth'. See also E. M., *An achrostickal epitaph on Sir Edward Sprague* (London, 1673). Other elegies attempt to balance sympathy for grief with warlike sentiments. Anon., *An Elegy on the Much Lamented Death of William Duke of Devonshire* (London, 1707), describes how the Duke 'Did wondrous Things in Fields, and seas of Blood', and how in 'Emasculating Sighs', all people are now 'in Floods of Sorrow drown'd'. Anon., *A New Elegy upon the Much Lamented Death of That Valiant and Victorious General and Soldier, the Lord Cuts* (London, 1707), describes the dead hero as 'one flush'd in Seas of Blood', while empathising with the grief of English soldiers and 'The Royal Mistress'.

63 Alex Garganigo, 'William without Mary: Mourning Sensibility in the Public Sphere', *The Seventeenth Century*, 23:1 (2008), 120. Garganigo argues that 'Mary's death provided an opening for the discourse of sensibility to enter the public sphere, that William had to be "refurbished" after her death, and that elegies worked to make him "less forbidding, more lovable"' (120, 123).

64 Anon., *The Mournfull [sic] Muse, an Elegy on the Much Lamented Death of King William IIId* (London, 1702). William, compared to the arrogance of the French king, is celebrated as 'So meek and humble on his splendid throne', a 'Royal Beggar' for the 'distressed Poor'.

65 William Pittis, *A Funeral Poem, Sacred to the Immortal Memory of the Deceas'd Sir Cloudesly Shovel, Kt.* (London, 1708).

66 The first official news of Blenheim derived from the famous letter from Marlborough, published in the *Gazette* August 12 1704. Written in pencil to his wife, it included a brief account of the battle with news of his own bother General Churchill. A later issue of the *Gazette* says the letter was sent at 7 o'clock in the evening, after Marlborough had been sixteen hours in the saddle. This account was also published by itself as a Gazette Extraordinary. It presents Marlborough as a family man, who offers a brief account of the

The Culture of War and Civil Society

action shaped for a female reader. Robert D. Horn's *Marlborough: A Survey* (Folkestone: Dawson, 1975) gives an indication of the extraordinary flood of praise (and blame) of Marlborough that arose after Blenheim. A contemporary ballad 'The Fight near Audenarde' shows how the heroic aspects of the hero were softened. It tells the tale of the French king's young heirs, found abandoned in a wood after the French retreat:

> At this the Duke was inly mov'd
> His Breast soft Pity beat,
> And so he straightway ordered
> His Men for to retreat.   *Bagford Ballads*, I: 396.

67 N. Rowe, *A Poem upon the Late Glorious Success of Her Majesty's Army &c* (London, 1707), 11; John Dennis, *The Battle of Ramillia: Or, the Power of Union a Poem in Five Books* (London, 1706), 131.

68 Thomas Yalden, *On the Conquest of Namur a Pindarique Ode* (London, 1695), 9.

69 In *A Congratulatory Poem to His Grace the Duke of Marlborough, &c.* (London, 1704), for example, while the hero is 'Sedate' and controlling, his violence is described in quite different terms: 'As when some Lion raging for his Prey,/ Through the wide Desarts bounding tears his Way', 8.

70 *A Poem to His Majesty*: 4, 5. While celebrating Marlborough's achievements at Blenheim, Addison imagines similar devastation:

> Whole Nations trampl'd into Dirt, and bruis'd, In one promiscuous Carnage lye confus'd. (*The Campaign*, 8)

71 *Blenheim, a Poem* (London, 1705), 8.

72 Tony Claydon, *William III and the Godly Revolution* (Cambridge: Cambridge University Press, 1996), 127.

73 H. Bartel, 'The Story of Public Fast Days in England', *Anglican Theological Review*, 37: 3 (1955), 190–200.

74 William Fleetwood, *A Sermon Preach'd before the Right Honourable The Lord Mayor and Court of Aldermen at St Mary le Bow 11th APRIL 1692* (London, 1692), 27.

75 John Worth, *The Lord our Banner, or true valour protected and prospered from heaven. In a sermon preached at Marlborough Sept 7th 1704* (London, 1705), 24.

76 Deuel Pead, *A Word in Season: being a sermon preach'd in the parish-church of St James Clarkenwell [sic] Wednesday the 11th of December, 1695* (London, 1695), 4.

77 John Griffith, *A sermon preach'd on Jan. 19, 1703/4, being the day appointed for the fast, occasioned by the storm and tempest, November 26, 27* (London, 1704), 21.

78 Fast Days 12 March 1689, 10 May 1693.

79 For example, Thanksgivings 6 and 20 November 1691, 12 November 1702.

80 John Griffith, *A sermon preach'd*, 19.

81 *A Form of Prayer and Thanksgiving [...] Thursday 7th September* (London, 1704).

82 For example, Fast Day 29 April 1691; Thanksgiving 8 April 1692, 7 September 1704.

83 Fast Day 12 March and 5 June 1689, 29 April 1691, and was still in use on 28 March 1711.

Part I: Developing Ideals

84 Jonathan Trelawney, *A Sermon Preach'd before the Queen and Both Houses of Parliament at St Pauls, November 12 1702* (London, 1702); Richard Chapman, *The Providence of God Asserted and Maintained December 3rd 1702* (London, 1703); Edward Smith, *A Sermon Preached before Their Excellencies the Lords Justices at Christ Church, Dublin 3rd December 1702* (Dublin, 1703); Thomas Wise, *A Sermon Preach'd at the Church of Richmond in Surrey 3rd December 1702* (London, 1703). Thomas Wise used the example of Vigo against the view of a French Philosopher (probably Descartes) that 'God established some general laws of motion' and has 'stood ever since as an idle spectator', 7.

85 Roy A. Rappaport, 'Enactments of Meaning', Michael Lambeck, ed., *A Reader in the Anthropology of Religion* (Oxford: Blackwell, 2002), 446–467, 454.

86 Benedict Anderson, *Imagined Communities* (London: Verso, 1991), 24.

87 Elizabeth Singer, for example, paraphrased violent biblical passages. Addison and Dennis both saw Christian tradition as the highest source of the sublime. David B. Morris, *The Religious Sublime* (Kentucky: University of Kentucky Press, 1972), 104–154; Abigail Williams, *Poetry and the Creation of a Whig Culture*, 182–183.

88 David Norbrook, *Writing the English Republic: Poetry, Rhetoric and Politics, 1627–1660* (Cambridge: Cambridge University Press, 1999), 137–139; Abigail Williams, *Poetry and the Creation of a Whig Culture*, 175ff.

89 Samuel H. Monk, *The Sublime: A Study of Critical Theories in Eighteenth-Century England* (New York: Modern Language Association, 1935), 54; Patricia Meyer Spacks, *The Insistence of Horror*, (Cambridge Mass.: Harvard University Press, 1962), 43–44; David B. Morris, *The Religious Sublime*, 73–74.

90 John Dennis, *Dedication to Britannia Triumphans* (London, 1704).

91 John Dennis, *The Advancement of Modern Poetry* (London, 1701), 36, 184. *A form of prayer and solemn thanksgiving to Almighty God for the wonderful preservation of His Majesties person, and his good success towards the reducing of Ireland* (London, 1690), 2.

92 Critical of the church as a divisive presence in contemporary politics, he implies in *An Essay upon Publick Spirit* (London, 1711) that the poet must take on its traditional role as reforming influence (v).

93 John Dennis, *The Grounds of Criticism in Poetry* (London, 1704), 19–20, 86.

94 *Britannia Triumphans*: 1, 23. See also *The Battle of Ramillia* (1706). See Dustin D. Stewart, 'Angel Bodies to Whig Souls: Blank Verse after Blenheim', in Blair Hoxby and Ann Baines Coiro, eds., *Milton in the Long Restoration* (Oxford Scholarship Online, September 2016).

95 *The Spectator* 152, (24 August 1711) 2: 97–98.

CHAPTER 2

War and the Culture of Politeness
The Case of The Tatler and The Spectator

In Chapter 1, we surveyed some of the ways in which the promotion of gentle manners could work to support a commitment to war during a period when the British military-fiscal state was consolidating; in this chapter, we take a closer look at a key example of the relationship between war and politeness in two of the most influential periodicals to be published in the eighteenth century. The influence of *The Tatler* and *The Spectator* on the development of a polite culture in Britain has long been recognised.[1] Scholars have shown how in these periodicals Addison and Steele encourage politeness in an attempt to imagine a cultural middle ground between the landed and commercial interests and to modify the acceptable norms of gentlemanly behaviour 'from a primarily courtly and aristocratic code, given to the display of power and wealth, to a more bourgeois, commercial and feminised code, given to the display of benevolence, and sensibility'.[2] At the same time, it is well known that, as Whigs, Addison and Steele were active in support of the contemporary wars against Louis XIV.[3] They participated in a Whig culture in which, as Abigail Williams has reminded us, an 'enthusiasm for gory bellicosity' was common.[4] But the relationship between their commitment to gentler civil manners on the one hand, and support for military aggression on the other, needs to be clarified. In this chapter, I am concerned with how these two interests are related in the periodicals. I will argue that one function of Addison's and Steele's attempt to promote politeness was to reconcile readers to a massive increase in military activity, by providing them with fictionalised alternatives to the unsettling realities of war represented in the newspapers.

As we have already seen, during the last decades of the seventeenth century and the first decades of the eighteenth, transformations in the financing and organisation of the military allowed England, and then Britain, to wage war abroad on an unprecedented scale.[5] The campaign to curb the power of Louis XIV, begun in 1689, required not only heavy

57

expenditure on foreign troops but also a huge increase in the size of the national navy and army. It fuelled traditional fears about the presence of a standing army, suspicion of the growing power of a 'monied interest', and discontent about rising costs. In the face of such difficulties, many writers worked to influence public opinion about the aims and conduct of the war, during the Nine Years' War of 1688–97 and then during the War of the Spanish Succession, 1701–1714. Addison and Steele, before they began work on these periodicals, had already served the second of these war efforts on behalf of the Whig administration.[6] When he launched *The Tatler*, Captain Richard Steele, one-time member of the 34th Regiment of Foot, was editor of the *London Gazette*, the official government newspaper and the primary source of war news in England.[7] Addison was at this time Secretary to the Earl of Wharton, Lord Lieutenant of Ireland. In 1704, he had written what was to become the most admired poetic celebration of Marlborough's victory at Blenheim, *The Campaign*, and in 1707 had published an anonymous pamphlet urging a massive increase in the levy of English soldiers to crush Louis XIV and protect British commercial interests.[8] In their periodicals, Addison and Steele remained committed to promoting the war effort.

The *Tatler* (1709–10) appeared when peace was in prospect but tantalisingly out of reach, and when the Whig administration needed to attune the public to the continuation of an expensive campaign.[9] *The Spectator* was launched at the beginning of 1711, some months after a Tory election victory had removed Addison's and Steele's patrons from office. The debate that followed the Tory election victory of 1710, which centred on Britain's continued participation in the War of the Spanish Succession, and was conducted in pamphlets, periodical essays, newspapers, broadsides and sermons, has been called 'the first example in England of a public debate of a great national issue with full media participation'.[10] The Tories, determined to secure peace, worked hard to turn public opinion against Britain's former allies but had to maintain British troops in the field until terms had finally been agreed.[11] This means that both *The Tatler* and *The Spectator* appeared during years of deep crisis, in which public discontent with the war was fuelled by high taxes, enforced recruitment, losses sustained in battle, government concessions to the allies, and party propaganda.[12] At a time of growing war-weariness, both periodicals attempted to reconcile the public to the human and financial costs of war, and to counter negative impressions of the army. The revived *Spectator* appeared from June to December 1714, when peace had arrived and Britain was struggling to cope with the return of disbanded soldiers.

It worked to counteract the effect on public opinion of this problem. In the hands of Addison, Steele and their collaborators, the periodical essay emerged as an important alternative to the newspaper in shaping public opinion about war.

War News

In a nation where most men were not combatants, war generated an ever-increasing volume of reading materials to satisfy a growing demand. *The Tatler* and *The Spectator* show a keen awareness of this development and seek to influence it. Both publications satirise the contemporary appetite for war news, and the willingness of newspapers to gratify it. Brian Cowan has usefully considered *The Tatler* and *The Spectator* in relation to a seventeenth-century tradition of hostility to 'the inordinate appetite of the English public for news'.[13] But while Cowan considers this issue primarily in relation to the Sacheverell crisis of late 1709 and early 1710, and the setting up of the news-free *Spectator*, the critique of news begins in *The Tatler* months before the Sacheverell affair. The issue is complicated, since for the first few months of its life, *The Tatler* not only included news but, as Robert Achurch has shown, by appearing tri-weekly it could sometimes pre-empt the twice-weekly *Gazette*, also under Steele's editorship.[14] *The Tatler* began to drop its news only after the *Gazette* also became a tri-weekly publication – but it continued to report military victories, and when news of Malplaquet was received critically, Steele represented discussion of the battle by eager coffee house news readers as a sign of public spirit.[15] Nevertheless, the realisation that *The Tatler* could survive without news was probably welcome and set a precedent for *The Spectator*. In both periodicals, the criticism of news is primarily directed against the enormous contemporary popularity of war news.

It is no accident that the advent of the first daily newspapers in England coincided with the beginning of the War of the Spanish Succession, since the interest generated by war helped to make daily news a viable proposition.[16] But the criticisms of news in both *The Tatler* and *The Spectator* suggest that war presented a special problem both to the writer and reader of news. In Chapter 1, we mentioned the uncertainties and ambiguities that characterised a news industry that had no professional foreign correspondents, and that included reports taken from foreign newspapers (often giving the enemy's point of view). The intriguing uncertainty generated by this kind of news was one of the effects criticised in both *The Tatler* and *The Spectator*. Since the war was a focus of bitter party rivalry, war news was particularly liable to be spun according to party views. In addition, reports of war were often laced with technical terms, some newly imported from France, creating a distinctive military discourse which could be confusing to the uninitiated.[17] Perhaps the most disturbing criticism made by Addison and Steele is the suggestion that newspapers commodified and exaggerated war deaths since the sensational impact of such deaths helped to sell newspapers (see Chapter 1).[18]

Lennard Davis has argued that during the late sixteenth and early seventeenth centuries it was an extremely unusual, if not impossible thing, for a reader to consider a narrative as being purely factual or actually recent.[19] The advent of daily news created a new kind of expectation, which helped to transform war into a kind of soap opera, with new forms of regular suspense and sensational climaxes. It generated intense anxiety, relief or jubilation, and provided a basis for gossip that could be justified as unquestionably public-spirited. In the new age of public finance, there was cause to be concerned about its economic impact. Since the 1690s, the funding of war had become increasingly dependent upon credit, much of it raised through the Bank of England, and there was a growing awareness of the relationship between credit and public opinion. The *Spectator* first appeared on 1 March 1711, during a period of deep financial crisis caused by government borrowing.[20] In its third issue, Public Credit, personified as a valetudinarian young virgin, receives news 'from all Parts of the World [...] perpetually', according to which she displays symptoms of health or sickness.[21] In fact, public credit rose and fell in direct reaction to reports of battles, which, as Addison complained in another *Spectator* paper, were generally cried about the streets of London 'with the same Precipitation as *Fire*'.[22]

If the obsessive interest generated by war news was seen as a special problem, it also came to be seen in *The Spectator* as offering a special opportunity. In a paper written by Addison with Pope when the war was drawing to a close, Mr Spectator sees himself as attempting to capture a new readership brought into being by the rage for news of war: 'This general Curiosity has been raised and inflamed by our late Wars, and, if rightly directed, might be of good Use to a Person who has such a Thirst awakened in him'. He argues that the news reader might be encouraged to 'apply himself to History, Travels', and other improving writings.[23] In this view, war has helped to provide the conditions for the development of a polite culture. But if readers must be 'rightly directed' away from unsettling war news, in the periodical they were also directed towards a view of war more compatible with a culture of politeness.

War and Polite Society

In addressing contemporary manners, *The Tatler* and *The Spectator* were participating in, and attempting to transform, the interest in the reformation of manners that had grown during the last decades of the seventeenth century.[24] But in these periodicals, the movement for moral reformation becomes a movement for refinement. Their understanding of politeness can be aligned with what E.J. Clery terms a 'discourse of feminization' that developed partly in response to the influence of female readers.[25] 'Feminization' refers to the development of qualities that are conventionally gendered as 'feminine', and involves a positive ideal of 'femininity', and the idea that females can have a beneficial influence upon men – who are improved by acquiring or displaying 'feminine' qualities such as sociability and domestic affection. The periodicals seek to work against the more aggressive or brutal aspects of contemporary society, from the divisive effects of party rage to the degrading appetite for cruel sports. But Addison and Steele's interest in gentler, refined manners had to be seen as compatible with manly courage and readiness for war. If refinement worked against brutality, it had also to avoid the dangers of effeminacy.

Markku Peltonnen has reminded us that politeness was not an exclusively Whig concept and that debates about it did not follow party lines.[26] But that does not mean that it could not be used to promote specific political aims. In practice, Addison and Steele's cultural programme is carefully distinguished from the Whig political programme it advances, and this is particularly apparent in their treatment of war. In these periodicals, war is detached from specific political or economic objectives, such as the aggressive pursuit of commercial advantage that Addison had recommended in his pamphlet of 1707. It is discussed in terms of manners and morals, in terms of principles that can be regarded as 'natural' and 'universal'. When the causes of war are discussed, they are assigned to the personal ambition of Louis XIV, and described in terms of a corrupted taste and judgment.[27] In accord with this cultural project, the periodicals have to suggest that modern war does not negate the values of polite society, but reinforces them; that a modern urban world, in which the better-off have more leisure to spend in 'Clubs and Assemblies, at Tea-Tables and in Coffee-Houses', can resist the corruptions of luxury and sustain the moral fortitude necessary to meet the increasing demands of war; and that a modern professional army can operate without brutalising its soldiers.

One of the most difficult problems to be contained – apart from the sheer financial burden of the war – was the cost of suffering. During the

62 Part I: Developing Ideals

publication of *The Tatler* important battles occurred in France and Spain, including the deadly victory at Malplaquet. The periodical had to encourage an appropriate response to the fate of those killed in battle, those widowed or orphaned, maimed, or displaced. Strategically positioned references show how such effects of war, which might lower morale or stir discontent, can instead strengthen public spirit by giving private individuals at home scope for acts of benevolence. After noting the successful launch of a new lottery to support the war effort, the fictional author of *The Tatler*, Isaac Bickerstaff, announces that he has settled an annual pension on a family of Palatine war-refugees (whose presence in London was decried in Tory publications).[28] When then public is absorbed with the Sacheverell case, he cites the case of two war-orphans whose education is to be maintained through an act of charity.[29] Sometimes, the losses of war are addressed in overtly fictional narratives written in a sentimental or gently comic mode. Their uncomplicated outlines and clear moral focus represent the antithesis of the bewildering war report. One paper presents the contrasting letters of two love rivals (Jack Careless and Colonel Constant) written before they were killed at the battle of Almanzar.[30] Another describes the deaths of a Corporal and a Private at the Siege of Namur and shows how their animosity is overcome as the extremities of the battlefield call out a selfless comradeship.[31] This kind of fiction not only personalised the losses of warfare but also allowed some account to be given of those who were normally below the horizon of public attention since only high-ranking officers were likely to be mentioned in dispatches or listed as casualties.

The attempt to imagine soldiers who were usually beyond the range of public notice had a political purpose. A long tradition of hostility to the professional army had recently been given new life by Tory pamphleteers, including Ned Ward, who claimed that regiments were sinks of corruption filled with vicious criminals.[32] At the same time, Marlborough was attacked by Tories as a monopoliser of glory.[33] *The Tatler* praises the singular heroism of Marlborough, but supplements this praise with tales of ordinary heroism. In the wake of Malplaquet, Bickerstaff is asked pointedly by Mr Kidney (a waiter at St James's coffee- house) to explain 'how the same Actions are but mere Acts of Duty in some, and Instances of the most Heroick Virtue in others'.[34] Paper 87, which appeared a month later, imagines the unsung virtue of the lower ranks: it includes a letter supposedly from a sergeant of the foot guards, serving at Mons, to a sergeant in the Coldstream Regiment 'at the Red-Lettice in the Butcher Row'. The writer reports his own head wound and the death of common friends, including one for whose widow he has gathered money. Bickerstaff considers it an

War and the Culture of Politeness 63

'honest Representation' of the typical poor soldier's 'chearful heart', and of the Gallantry of those in the 'Heap' of an army – who have the same regard to fame as those above them, if their fame exists in the eyes of a different, smaller public. The paper ends with an imaginary scheme for proportioning the glory of a battle among a whole army, dividing it into shares after the method of the million lottery.[35] This fantasy ignores the brutal treatment soldiers actually experienced in the army. It is no surprise that Steele did not approve of the portrait of Sergeant Kite in Farquhar's *The Recruiting Officer*, which made audiences laugh at the horrifying realities of army recruitment.[36] It is not that Steele cannot acknowledge harsh realities – but those that are acknowledged must be reconciled with the attempt to improve manners and promote public spirit. That is, they must be seen as issues of personal conduct, rather than of systemic brutality.

In both *The Tatler* and *The Spectator*, idealised views of the soldier coexist with an unsatisfactory reality in need of reform. *The Tatler* refers to the soldier who may defraud his country in his muster roll, *The Spectator* has passing references to the immodest talk of soldiers about the town, their loud and overbearing manners, and their tendency to corruption.[37] In *The Tatler*, Isaac Bickerstaff (himself an old soldier) is the antithesis of the ill-mannered, loud-mouthed soldier of popular concern. He refers to other soldiers who exemplify his belief that 'Good Sense is the great Requisite in a Soldier', such as the lieutenant of marines at his sister's wedding feast, who discomforts an 'ill-bred coxcomb'.[38] *The Spectator* takes the idealisation of the soldier further. The Spectator club includes among its members the gentlemanly Captain Sentry – courageous, modest, thoughtful, sensitive, and apparently well read.[39] Through this figure, the conventional idea that the experience of war renders soldiers unfit for ordinary social life is inverted: war emerges as the field in which manners and morals receive their most rigorous test, and their most effective improvement. Indeed, in *The Spectator*, as in Shaftesbury's *Characteristics* (published in 1711), war begins to emerge as an activity in which characteristics associated with disinterested sociability – such as good manners, good conversation, an open disposition, and a sympathetic concern for others – are most clearly revealed.[40] Showing gentler manners to be typical of the courageous soldier allows them to be seen as compatible with the noblest form of masculinity, and so as distinct from effeminacy. It also makes the soldier seem an asset within polite society. As Julia Banister shows, at times both Addison and Steele suggest that professional military service can inculcate qualities 'that can only be impolite'.[41] But I would argue that this is not the dominant impression given by either periodical. In the *Spectator*, the compatibility of

64 Part I: Developing Ideals

war service and politeness was given particular emphasis as the war came to an end, and Britain faced the prospect of soldiers returning. In *Spectator* 544 (published as the ceasefire was beginning in 1712), Sentry celebrates those soldiers who, having passed through the dangers and hardships of warfare, have preserved their modesty and humanity. In his view, these are 'the most valuable of men', and he plans to invite Gentlemen who have served their Country in the army, to join him at Coverley Hall in what sounds like a military alternative to the Spectator club.[42] By Christmas 1712, many British regiments had already been disbanded, and more were discharged on the signing of the peace in May 1713. Special legislation was passed to encourage the readmission of soldiers to the trades and apprenticeships they had left when enlisting, but soldiers were also encouraged to serve in the colonies, or as Fortescue puts it, 'to go into perpetual exile'.[43] *Spectator* 566, issued after the end of the war in 1714, encourages a more welcoming attitude. It includes a letter from a soldier which represents the army as a kind of finishing school, where patience and courage are exercised, and a unique 'Freedom of behaviour' is allowed. The correspondent concedes that the army may turn a coxcomb into a public nuisance, but insists that it will improve a man of sense; he quotes with approval Rochefoucault's dictum that 'A Man, who has been bred up wholly to Business, can never get the Air of a Courtier at Court, but will immediately catch it in the Camp'.[44] The manners of the soldier, it seems, will be more polished than those of the man of business. While Clery points out that in these periodicals the 'topic of women is almost invariably put forward in the framework of their necessary influence on men and on society generally' (45), the topic of the soldier introduces a competing idea – that the manners of men can be improved most effectively beyond the influence of women, in the homo-social environment of the army.

If the need to counteract negative views motivated this elevation of the soldier above the non-combatant, the periodicals also needed to counteract the arguments of militia advocates, who associated virtue with military training. During the 'paper war' or standing army controversy of 1698–1702, Country Whigs such as John Toland and Andrew Fletcher argued that without military training, the ordinary citizen would be prone to corruption. Fletcher, adopting what J. G. A. Pocock defines as a 'neo-Harringtonian' perspective, argued that only a militia could preserve public liberty and declared that 'the whole free people of any nation ought to be exercised to arms'.[45] John Toland offered more detailed plans for a militia led by local landowners that would engage in regular competitive military exercises to foster health, self-discipline, and community spirit.[46]

In contrast to such claims, *The Tatler* and *The Spectator* suggest that in the modern urban world, in which the arts flourish, citizens can preserve the virtues of self-discipline, fortitude in the face of hardship, and a willingness to make sacrifices for the public good, without such arduous physical training. One *Spectator* paper (by Budgell) evokes a tight-knit rural English community in which health and social spirit are maintained in strenuous and even brutal customary sports involving people of all ages and both sexes. Mr Spectator relates these sports to classical precedents, and to the old English statute for exercising the long bow, which once gave us 'all the real Advantages, without the Inconvenience of a standing Army'.[47] His reflections echo the arguments of pro-militia writers, but their nostalgic tone also indicates the distance between such communal activities and the polite urban world he actually inhabits, in which participation in rough, combative sports is no longer desirable (elsewhere Mr Spectator recommends riding as a healthy pastime and admits to exercising every morning with a dumb-bell).[48] Implicitly rejecting the arguments of the militia advocates, *The Tatler* and *The Spectator* both ridicule the amateurism of the 'Trained-bands', the militia maintained for the defence of the City.[49] They seek to accommodate what Pocock has described as 'a civic morality of investment and exchange' and to suggest that, in a world increasingly shaped by commerce, the arts can defeat luxury and effeminacy and promote virtue.[50] But they also address a potential problem in this assumption.

War and Cultural Heritage

The growing influence of humanitarian views in the later seventeenth century threatened to expose a gap between the moral goals of education and its traditional – often brutal – resources. When Locke, in *Some Thoughts on Education* (1693), defined cruelty as unnatural, a 'habit borrowed from custom and conversation', he concluded that historical discourse was a major source of corruption. History promoted cruelty and glorified slaughter because of its focus on, and valuation of, war: 'All the entertainment and talk of history is nothing almost but fighting and killing'.[51] But, of course, history retained a centrally important place in Locke's educational programme – including works that focused on fighting and killing.[52] The contradiction that Locke exposed here was one that haunted many contemporary writers concerned with the reformation of manners: it was not only the work of historians that glorified fighting and killing, but the arts more widely, in an age when the heroic poem was still considered the

66   Part I: Developing Ideals

highest form of poetry, when the English stage was notorious for its representations of violence, and when state-sponsored military painting was 'at its zenith'.[53] Since European cultural heritage – both courtly and popular – was steeped in what increasingly appeared barbaric values, and since this heritage – like war itself – could not simply be rejected, educational practices and forms of criticism would need to be developed that would allow the past to be approached through appropriately critical attitudes.

Both periodicals negotiate with cultural heritage in order to regulate its savage aspect. They condemn unreservedly the aristocratic commitment to duelling, as well as the violent popular entertainments of the bear-garden. But cultural manifestations of violence, both popular and aristocratic, that relate to war, are subject to careful critical appraisal. Drawing on and helping to popularise neo-classical and newer forms of criticism, they work to secure the moral usefulness of the bellicose content of the arts, distancing it from aristocratic codes of honour and from sensational barbarism.

The problem of the violence of Homeric epic is addressed directly in a *Spectator* paper by Budgell. Here a correspondent argues that while Alexander the Great's capacity for barbarous actions is 'generally ascribed to his Passion for Homer', it is more plausibly attributed to his faulty education, which encouraged him to admire Achilles, and 'think it glorious to imitate this Piece of Cruelty and Extravagance'.[54] Instead of being urged to emulate such models, the paper argues, boys should be encouraged to reflect critically upon them. *The Tatler* suggests that very young children can derive salutary lessons in good conduct from violent stories: Bickerstaff admires the accomplishments of his little Godson, who studies 'the Lives and Adventures of Don Bellianis of Greece, Guy of Warwick, the Seven Champions'. The boy is not corrupted by chapbooks that delight in violence: by reading critically, he is preparing himself for a life of resilient self-discipline and patriotic duty. 'He would tell you of the Mismanagements of John Hickathrift, find Fault with the passionate temper in Bevis of Southampton, and loved Saint George for being the Champion of England; and by this Means, had his Thoughts insensibly moulded into the Notions of Discretion, Virtue and Honour'.[55]

The Tatler suggests that heroic art must transcend its cultural origin. At a time when English military painting had become established after William III had commissioned Jan Wyck and Dirk Maas to celebrate his own victories, Steele implies that courtly heroic art can be limited by its very insistence on the elevated nature of its action and character: 'to fill a Room full of Battle-Pieces, pompous Histories of Sieges, and a tall Hero alone in a Crowd of insignificant Figures about him, is of no Consequence

War and the Culture of Politeness   67

to private Men'. To attain such consequence, 'great and illustrious Men' must be shown in circumstances in which we can empathise with them 'meerly as they were Men'.[56] The tall hero and his violent circumstances become, in their very distinctiveness, examples of alienating specialisation. Art must meet us upon common ground, where meaningful equivalences can be established between imagined conflict and the experience of the polite non-combatant.

In practice, the assumption that 'There is a Propriety in all things' allows both periodicals to suggest an equivalence between the experience of war and other kinds of experience.[57] *Spectator* paper 350, which features Captain Sentry, exemplifies the tendency to move between, and align, different frames of reference – military, social, moral, and aesthetic – in order to suggest that ideas of manliness, courage, social decorum, and artistic expression can all be judged in the same terms. A letter to Captain Sentry contains the story of a little English corn vessel attacked by a French privateer. The singular bravery of the English captain inspires an 'unmanly' desire for vengeance in the French Commander who takes him prisoner. The English prisoner is beaten, bound, and starved – against the humanitarian inclinations of the French crew and to the disgust of the governor of Calais. Humanity is seen as a natural sign of manliness, and so as transcending barriers of nation and rank, while inhumanity is localised in the corrupt French Commander. As Captain Sentry moves to consider the manners of the 'Town', the situation is reversed, since here the man of true gallantry is likely to be despised, while the impudence of youths is admired in the eyes of little people. While moral vision assumes clarity in the extremities of war, it becomes clouded in the social life of the Town and its assemblies. At this point, Captain Sentry suggests that judicious literary criticism will help to counteract the malign influence of urban life. Just as criticism can help us to distinguish between the true and the false sublime, so it can help us to distinguish between true and false courage, as the French Critic Le Bossu shows in his comparison between the ostentation of Virgil's Turnus, and the quieter, defensive courage of Aeneas. In this paper, then, the violence of war is accommodated within a system of equivalences: a proper appreciation of martial courage is equivalent to a proper discrimination of the sublime and to a proper estimation of manners. War is judged as if brutality arises from the moral disposition of the mean individual, and one can choose to oblige one's enemies.[58]

The discussions of heroic poetry in *The Tatler* and *The Spectator* tend to play down the specifically military aspects of the poems in order to consider other features. Adopting and popularising neoclassical criteria, they

68 Part I: Developing Ideals

consider Homer's and Virgil's 'common sense', their moral precepts, their use of epithets, dreams, allegories and mythical fables, while the 'lack of delicacy' in Homer's sentiments is attributed to his times. But elsewhere the periodicals work to validate representations of the violence of war. The newly psychologised sublime, as theorised by John Dennis, proved useful here as it allowed equivalences to be found between emotional responses to art and to war itself. As we saw in Chapter 1, Dennis argued that enthusiastic passion could be moved by 'Ideas occurring in Contemplation' and that terror, the most transporting experience, could be transformed into 'Joy' through reflection.[59] This transferring of terror from the realm of libidinous sensation to the realm of reason allowed the violence of war – whether represented or actual – to transcend brutality and produce an elevating experience. For example, *The Tatler* comments admiringly on an image from Charles Lu Brun's series of paintings on the life of Alexander the Great commissioned by Louis XIV. Steele singles out a detail which shows an Indian Prince falling wounded with looks that move both 'Horrour' and 'Pity'.[60] We are directed away from the formal purpose of the painting – a flattering allusion to the military conquests of Louis XIV – towards the skill of the artist in moving us to a sublime experience. The principle of aesthetic reflection is invoked in the most elaborate account of courage in *The Spectator* (no. 152, which we discussed in Chapter 1). Here, Steele contradicts his earlier attempt in *The Tatler* to attribute heroic virtue to the 'Heap' of an army, since he wants to emphasise the link between virtue and politeness. What looks like courage in the mass of soldiers is downgraded to a mere 'mechanical' habit. The courage of great commanders, on the other hand, endows the 'terrible and ghastly' with 'a certain beauty' derived from thought and reflection. The horrors of war are aestheticised and resemble the experience of readers who can appreciate terror as sublime.[61]

The conflict between the need to ground courage in the cultivated reason of the educated, and the need to ground it in the experience of 'ordinary' men, arises from an ideological programme that conceives its values as both socially specific and natural. War is an area where the conflict arises acutely, because of the need to suggest that the superior values of a refined public are defended by a unified and inclusive national effort. The conflict is resolved in Addison's *Spectator* papers on the popular ballad of 'Chevy Chase' (or 'The Hunting of the Cheviot'). The ballad is introduced through a discussion that validates popular tradition as both national and universal, since 'Human nature is the same in all reasonable Creatures'.[62] The tale of slaughter that follows might be seen as revelling in sensational bloodshed, as Percy, Douglas and their respective followers engage in deadly combat motivated by an ancient feud. But on the one hand, Addison shows how Le Bossu's criteria for epic can be used to read the poem for lessons in political unity, patriotism, and generosity to enemies.[63] And on the other, he shows how the poem's language, in capturing the violence and pity of war, can be read as offering an elevating experience, in its 'majestick Simplicity', its 'Force and Spirit', and its 'Beauty'.[64] As Steve Newman points out, Addison, who rejects the ideal of poetic justice, indicates that 'The horror of war must be fully pictured in the death of the virtuous'.[65] Addison's approach implies that the poem's beauty reconciles the reader to the terrible sacrifices exacted by war. The polite reader's acceptance is identified as 'common', natural, in line with English tradition, and shared with those who have no access to polite education. The reading implicitly endows art with a dual potential: it can offer an imaginative preparation for the hardships generated by war, and at the same time, it can help to cultivate an emotional and aesthetic sensitivity that will work against the enjoyment of violence or cruelty to others. The sympathetic stories about the recent victims of war in these periodicals serve a comparable function.

In various ways, then, the periodicals work to represent war as an activity that does not conflict with benevolent principles of polite society but promotes those principles. Just as the casualties of war are shown to provide opportunities for polite non-combatants to demonstrate their resilience, philanthropy and public spirit, so its terrors and duties are seen to shape the disinterested character of the soldier and polish his manners. In the extremities of war, as in the refinements of art, moral vision is clarified, and virtue appears in exemplary form. The informal mode and supposedly disinterested stance of the periodical essay helped the development of this ideological project, since it offered a generic freedom, an ability to move easily between different frames of reference and different points of view, to mix fact with fiction, the serious and trivial, comedy and pathos, and to accommodate contradictions without resolving or even acknowledging them. The project is developed more fully in *The Spectator*, where the Club allowed different value systems to coexist as if on easy terms. Here the commercial interests of modern Britain, represented by the idealised figure of the Whig merchant, Sir Andrew Freeport, can be shown to exist in relative harmony with the alternative values of the Tory landowner, Sir Roger De Coverley. Commerce is carefully divorced from the violence of empire and seen as essentially peaceful, promoting a 'mutual Intercourse' among mankind.[66] And while the professional army was often criticised by landowners whose taxes helped to sustain it, Captain Sentry is the heir of

70 Part I: Developing Ideals

Sir Roger, whose estate he inherits. This symbolic reconciliation between a traditional virtue grounded in landownership, and the tried and tested virtue of the professional soldier indicates the place of war within the periodical's system of values. The soldier is not aligned with the enlightened self-interest of the merchant but represents an alternative to it.

As Donald Bonds notes, the evidence suggests that the readership of *The Spectator* was diverse, and the great popularity of the work suggests its success at reaching across party lines and differences of opinion – an outcome its fictional 'Club' was clearly designed to promote. But Bonds also shows that many of those who subscribed to the collected volumes of *The Spectator* came from the financial and mercantile world of London: the subscription lists includes directors of the Bank of England, goldsmiths, private bankers, speculators, East India Company directors. Many of these 'had made money supplying stores of clothing and food to the armed forcers, both in the time of William III and during the War of the Spanish Succession'.[67] The largest group are secretaries, commissioners, clerks, and agents, many in the military branches of government, responsible for managing the war effort, including paymasters of the marine regiments. Many, in other words, were people who in one sense profited from war.

The Spectator's reforming message was carefully directed to such readers. Newman notes that while Addison and Steele attempt to represent and shape a culture that 'is increasingly separate from the Court', they don't believe that the commercial interests associated with the Royal Exchange 'can shoulder the burden of legitimating polite culture'.[68] I would put this rather differently. Commercial interests are shown to be compatible with the virtues of benevolence and philanthropy in civil society; but the soldier, whose character has been developed and tested in a field remote from the material comforts and economic pursuits of modern society, and who has faced the ultimate test of public spirit – being prepared to die for his country – is shown as best qualified to illustrate Mr Spectator's belief that 'the Preservation of Life should be only a secondary Concern, and the Direction of it our Principal'.[69] In the periodicals' idealisations of the soldier, we can glimpse a 'military dream of society' different from the one identified by Foucault (which emphasised 'permanent coercions', rather than the shaping of polite identity).[70] The army emerges as a realm in which 'feminine' characteristics such as compassion and civility can be acquired without the influence of women. It is a realm that fosters sociability in its noblest form, an alternative to the Clubs, Assemblies, Tea-Tables, and Coffee-Houses that most readers know. As such, it is a seductive fiction, which like the other fictions of war the periodicals consider, is offered as a focus for moral instruction and emulation, and as a reassuring alternative to the unsettling realities of war represented in the newspapers.

Notes

1 See for example Richard P. Bond, *The Tatler: The Making of a Literary Journal* (Cambridge Mass.: Harvard University Press, 1971); Terry Eagleton, *The Function of Criticism: From The Spectator to Post-Structuralism* (London: Verso, 1984); Stephen Copley, 'Commerce, Conversation and Politeness in the Early Eighteenth-Century Periodical', *British Journal for Eighteenth-Century Studies*, 18 (1995), 63–77; John Brewer, *The Pleasures of the Imagination* (London: HarperCollins, 1997); Erin Mackie, *Market à la Mode: Fashion, Commodity, and Gender in The Tatler and The Spectator* (Baltimore, MD; Johns Hopkins University, 1997); Markman Ellis, *The Coffee House: A Cultural History* (London: Weidenfeld and Nicolson, 2004).

2 Markman Ellis, *The Coffee House*, 188.

3 Charles A. Knight, *A Political Biography of Richard Steele* (London: Pickering and Chatto, 2009); Peter Smithers, *The Life of Joseph Addison* (Oxford: Oxford University Press, 1968).

4 *Poetry and the Creation of a Whig Literary Culture 1681–1714* (Oxford: Oxford University Press, 2005), 6. Hannah Smith has argued that 'the Protestant soldierly ideal' remained important to perceptions of monarchy throughout the eighteenth century: *Georgian Monarchy: Politics and Culture, 1714–1760* (Cambridge: Cambridge University Press, 2006), 22.

5 The best account of this transformation is John Brewer's *The Sinews of Power: War, Money and the English State, 1688–1783* (London: Unwin Hyman, 1989).

6 The classic account of the political context of the war is G. M. Trevellyan's *England Under Queen Anne* (3 vols) (London: Longman, 1930). See also John B. Hattendorf, *England in the War of the Spanish Succession* (New York: Garland, 1987); David Francis, *The First Peninsular War, 1702–1713* (London: Benn, 1975).

7 He worked under the Earl of Sutherland, Secretary of State for the Southern Department in the Whig administration.

8 *The State of the War and the Necessity of an Augmentation, Consider'd* (London, 1708).

9 The *Tatler* was launched in March 1709 when peace negotiations were beginning.

10 Heinze-Joachim Müllenbrock, *The Culture of Contention: A Rhetorical Analysis of the Public Controversy about the Ending of the War of the Spanish Succession* (München: Fink, 1997), 11.

11 Preliminary agreements with France were signed on October 8 1711, but the terms were not accepted in Britain until the Queen had created more Tory peers in January 1712, while agreement at the Congress of Powers was not finalized until the spring of 1713. Swift's pamphlet, *The Conduct of the Allies*, published in November 1711, was designed to prepare public opinion for Britain's desertion of its allies.

72 Part I: Developing Ideals

12 For accounts of the effects of war in these years, see G. M. Trevellyan, *The Peace and the Protestant Succession* (London: Longman, 1934), and Hattendorf, *England in the War of the Spanish Succession.*

13 Brian Cowan, 'Mr. Spectator and the Coffeehouse Public Sphere', *Eighteenth-Century Studies*, 37:3 (2004), 345–366.

14 Robert Waller Achurch, 'Richard Steele, Gazetteer and Bickerstaff', in *Studies in the Early Periodical*, ed. Richmond P. Bond (Chapel Hill, University of North Carolina, 1957), 50–72.

15 *The Tatler* 69 (September 17, 1709), in *The Tatler*, ed. Donald F. Bond, 3 vols. (Oxford: Oxford University Press, 1987), 1: 481. All subsequent citations refer to this edition.

16 *The Daily Courant*, the first regular daily newspaper published in England, was launched on March 11 1702 as the War of the Spanish Succession was beginning. The first issue was dominated by war reports.

17 This 'Modern Military Eloquence' is satirized in *The Spectator* 165 (8 September 1711), 2: 151.

18 *The Tatler* 18 (21 May 1709), 1: 149.

19 Lennard J. Davis, *Factual Fictions: The Origins of the English Novel* (New York: Columbia University Press, 1983), 70.

20 Larry Neal, *The Rise of Financial Capitalism* (Cambridge: Cambridge University Press, 1990), 47.

21 *The Spectator* 3 (3 March 1711), in *The Spectator*, ed. Donald F. Bond, 5 vols. (Oxford: Oxford University Press, 1965), 1: 16.

22 *An Essay towards the History of the Last Ministry and Parliament* (London, 1710), noted that credit rose on news of the first Allied Victory in Spain, on confirmation of the victory at Saragossa, and again with the expectation of Peace at Gertruydenberg, and fell when peace talks were broken off (70–71). *The Spectator* 251 (18 December 1711), 2: 476.

23 *The Spectator* 452 (8 August 1712), 4: 90–94.

24 Abigail Williams notes that a rhetoric of moral reformation appears in a range of texts in the late 1680s, including some in support of James II (*Poetry and the Creation of a Whig Literary Culture*, 85–92).

25 E. J. Clery, *The Feminization Debate in Eighteenth-Century England: Literature, Commerce and Luxury* (Basingstoke: Palgrave, 2004), 3.

26 Markku Peltonen, 'Politeness and Whiggism, 1688–1732', *The Historical Journal*, 48: 2 (2005), 391. Peltonen qualifies Klein's view of politeness as an aspect of Whig cultural ideology; see, for example, Lawrence E. Klein, ed., *Shaftesbury: Characteristics of Men, Manners, Opinions, Times* (Cambridge: Cambridge University Press, 1999), xvii.

27 See Bickerstaff's Letter to Louis XIV *The Tatler* 23 (2 June 1709), 1: 182–184.

28 *The Tatler* 124 (24 January 1710), 2: 231.

29 *The Tatler* 140 (2 March 1710), 2: 302–303.

30 *The Tatler* 30 (18 June 1709), 1: 227–8.

31 *The Tatler* 5 (21 April 1709), 1: 51–53.

War and the Culture of Politeness

32 'A Regiment is a Corporation which consists of Individuals, detach'd from Bridewell, the Queen's Bench, Fleet, Newgate and the Compters'. Ned Ward, *Mars Stripped of his Armour* (London, 1709), 2.

33 For example, Swift in *The Examiner* 16 (23 November) 1710. *The Examiner and Other Pieces Written in 1710–11 by Jonathan Swift*, ed. Herbert Davis (Oxford: Blackwell, 1957), 23.

34 *The Tatler* 69 (17 September 1709), 1: 481.

35 *The Tatler* 87 (29 October 1709), 2: 49–50.

36 'There is not [...] the Humour hit in *Sergeant Kite*'. *The Tatler* 20 (26 May 1709), 159.

37 *The Tatler* 183 (10 June 1710), 2: 492; *The Spectator* 37 (12 April 1711), 1: 153; 132 (1 August 1711), 2: 22–25; 298 (11 February 1712), 3: 65; (16 April 1712), 3: 322; 533 (11 November 1712), 4: 402–3; 544 (24 November 1712), 4: 447.

38 *The Tatler* 191 (29 June 1710), 3: 36; 79 (11 October 1709), 2: 7.

39 He is introduced in *The Spectator* 2 (2 March 1711), 1: 11.

40 According to Shaftesbury, 'it is in war that the knot of fellowship is closest drawn.' *Characteristics of Man, Manners, Opinions, Times*, ed. Lawrence E. Klein (Cambridge: Cambridge University Press, 1999), 52.

41 Banister, 32.

42 24 November 1712, 4: 447.

43 J. W. Fortescue, *A History of the British Army* (London: Macmillan, 1899), vol. 2, 3.

44 566 (12 July 1714), 4: 533–536.

45 J. G. A. Pocock, *The Machiavellian Moment* (Princeton: Princeton University Press, 1975), 416; Andrew Fletcher, *A Discourse of Government with Relation to Militias* (Edinburgh, 1698), 7–9.

46 John Toland, *The Militia Reformed* (London, 1698), 26–27.

47 *The Spectator* 161 (4 September 1711), 2: 131–33. The games, intended to gain the approbation of onlookers, include cudgel players, wrestlers, and young ladies competing at 'pitch a Bar'.

48 *The Spectator* 115 (12 July 1711).

49 For the Trained-Bands, see e.g. *The Tatler* 28 (14 June 1709), 1: 213–4; *The Spectator* 43 (19 April 1711), 1: 183, 376 (12 May 1712), 3: 415.

50 Pocock, *Machiavellian Moment*, 440.

51 *The Educational Writings of John Locke*, ed. James L. Axtell (Cambridge: Cambridge University, 1968), 225–227, 226–227. He returned to this problem in his manuscript essay 'Of Study': 'looking on Alexander and Caesar and such like heroes as the highest instances of human greatness [...] we are apt to make butchery and rapine the chief marks and very essence of human greatness'. Axtell, 410.

52 For introductory Latin Locke recommends Justin (whose history begins with the imperial conquests of the Assyrian king Ninus), Eutropius (whose history begins with the conquests of Romulus), and Quintius Curtius (the historian of Alexander the Great).

74 Part I: Developing Ideals

53 Peter Harrington, *British Artists and War: The Face of Battle in Paintings and Prints, 1700–1914* (London: Greenhill Books, 1993), 15. James William Johnson discusses some attempts to 'de-emphasize' the traditional emphasis on military conquest in 'England, 1660–1800: An Age without a Hero?', *The English Hero 1660–1800*, ed. Robert Folkenflik (Newark: University of Delaware, 1982), 25–34. Ulrich Broich considers the effects of 'increasing skepticism towards the world views' of classical epics in *The Eighteenth-Century Mock-Heroic Poem* (Cambridge: Cambridge University Press, 1990), 4.

54 *The Spectator* 337 (27 March 1712), 3: 247.

55 *The Tatler* 95 (15–17 November 1709) 2: 92–3.

56 *The Tatler* 209, 10 August 1710, 3: 107.

57 *The Spectator* 350 (11 April 1712), 3: 303 [by Steele],

58 *The Spectator* 350 (11 April 1712), 3: 303–4.

59 John Dennis, *The Grounds of Criticism in Poetry* (London, 1704), 19–20, 86.

60 *The Tatler* 8 (28 April 1709) 1: 73–74.

61 *The Spectator* 152 (24 August 1711) 2: 97–8.

62 *The Spectator* 70 (21 may 1711) 1: 297–303.

63 Donald F. Bond notes that Addison is following Le Bossu's *Trait du poem epique* (1675), I, vii, which describes epic poetry as moral instruction disguised under the allegory of an action, 1: 298n.

64 *The Spectator* 74 (25 May 1711) 1: 315–321.

65 Steve Newman, *Ballad Collection, Lyric, and the Canon* (Philadelphia: University of Pennsylvania Press, 2007), 28.

66 *The Spectator* 69 (19 May 1711) 1: 294.

67 *The Spectator*, 1: lxxxvi–xcii.

68 Steve Newman, *Ballad Collection*, 58–62.

69 *The Spectator* 25 (29 March 1711) 1: 108.

70 Michel Foucault, *Discipline and Punish: The Birth of the Prison* (London: Penguin, 1991), 169.

CHAPTER 3

Sacrifice
Heroism and Mourning

In Mr Spectator's belief that 'the Preservation of Life should be only a secondary Concern', we glimpse Addison's understanding that public spirit may entail sacrifice. The first half of the eighteenth century has been described as 'a depressingly materialistic time', with 'no great causes, no spirit of heroic self-sacrifice'.[1] In Britain, there was certainly a growing preoccupation with the rise of domestic consumption, with the spread of luxury and effeminacy, and with the role of self-interest in a modern commercial society. But the idea that there was no interest in self-sacrifice seems too simple. The perceived need to counter the corrupting effects of self-interest helps to explain the continuing vogue for heroic drama, in which virtuous individuals willingly sacrifice themselves or their loved ones for the public good or to preserve their own integrity.[2] And, as we shall see, the bellicose ethos of classical epic could be modified and made more acceptable to a modern audience by placing an emphasis on self-sacrifice. The series of wars fought during the period also helped to keep 'the spirit of heroic self-sacrifice' firmly in the public mind.

While moralists who condemned war saw the deaths it caused as the most compelling argument against it, writers and artists used the fact of death as a justification for war. The idea of sacrifice could be invoked to counterbalance a devastating victory or turn a crushing defeat into a moral triumph. However, the personal bereavement arising from death in war was potentially in conflict with such justifications: it was a private matter, often figured in feminine terms, and since the female might be a widow who was expected to remain faithful to her dead spouse, bereavement might be represented as inconsolable loss and unrelieved isolation. One task of artists and writers who engaged with war was to bring private loss into a satisfactory relationship with public justification. This task became more important as the process of mourning assumed a new significance in eighteenth-century culture.

76 Part I: Developing Ideals

Justification and Victory

When war is in progress, the public is usually relieved when its own losses are light and outraged when its own losses seem excessive. This proposition seems self-evident, although the effect of losses on public opinion is now subject to detailed statistical analysis.[3] The so-called 'casualties hypothesis', which predicts that the public will turn against their nation's war effort as losses mount, has been developed in an age of wide media coverage of war, but it seems generally relevant to the very different public of eighteenth-century Britain. The cost of the Duke of Marlborough's victory at Malplaquet (1709), for example, in which his forces sustained almost twice as many casualties as his French enemy did, was widely regarded as far too high. And since the battle was part of a war conducted by a Whig ministry, such an imbalance inevitably gave ammunition to the Tory opposition in the ongoing struggle to influence the public.[4]

Opinion was, and is, less sensitive to the losses we inflict upon our enemies. Indeed, it may at first seem that in the eighteenth century there was no point at which the enemy losses would be met with any reaction other than open satisfaction. A crushing national victory, such as Marlborough's triumph at the battle of Blenheim, was generally welcomed, even by the Opposition. Here is Matthew Prior – at this time a Tory – confronting the poet Boileau with the French and Bavarian losses at Blenheim:

> In one great Day on HOCHSTET'S fatal Plain
> FRENCH and BAVARIANS Twenty Thousand slain;
> Push'd thro' the DANUBE to the Shoars of STYX
> Squadrons Eighteen, Battalians Twenty Six: […]
> Tell me, is this to reckon or rehearse?
> A Commissary's List, or Poet's Verse?[5]

Prior is writing for a public that is well supplied with such casualty statistics – numbers which make the keeping of a scorecard a simple matter. His lines refer to the most violent incident at Blenheim, in which Marlborough drove thousands of French cavalrymen to their deaths in the Danube. It was an incident that could hardly be ignored by those who welcomed the victory. Preachers assigned the violence to providence, Biblical precedents were found, while some observers engaged in gloating.[6]

But in an age when ideals of benevolence and politeness were gaining ground, it seems likely that heavy losses inflicted on the enemy sometimes cause not only xenophobic jubilation but also a certain discomfort. Indeed, Prior's lines above are usually seen as a parody of Boileau's poetic jingoism registering his own unease at poetic gloating over war casualties.[7]

Bernard Mandeville alluded to the Danube incident when he claimed that those who spoke of pity for distant casualties of war were to be believed in the same manner as when they said they were 'our humble servants'; but he assumed that expressions of sympathy were appropriate in such a case, even if he doubted their sincerity.[8] Britain's wars on the mainland of Europe were usually fought in the interests of maintaining the 'balance of power', not to destroy other powers. The increasing professionalisation of European war was helping to promote the view that moderation between the contending sides was fitting, a development reinforced by the evolving 'law of nations'. Most battles fought between European nation-states in the eighteenth century would now be classified as examples of 'symmetrical warfare', in which combatants on both sides are assumed to have equal rights.[9] In such circumstances, massively unequal casualties inflicted upon an enemy could, without a suitable framing, begin to look like wilful brutality rather than honourable warfare – at least to those learning to think of themselves as good-natured and compassionate citizens.

The Whig John Dennis claimed that his battle poem about Blenheim, *Britannia Triumphans* (1704), was influenced by 'Her Majesty's Proclamation of a General Thanksgiving' for the victory. One function of the Thanksgiving service was to chasten pride and jubilation by attributing the victory to God. Dennis used the religious framework to license a display of national pride; the victory belonged to God, but there was plenty of room to celebrate the courage of His human agents. Dennis generally shows much interest in the violent terrors of battle, but no special interest in those who die. There is a passing reference to British heroes' willingness to die, but the heroes he names are those who survived the battle. As soon as he has described the violence of the Danube incident, however, he enters into an oddly formal process of accounting, in which he implies that individual glory achieved through the death of others requires some personal loss or atonement to become fully acceptable in the realm of civil society:

> O Conqu'ring Death, like Sampson, blind tho' strong,
> Hadst thou the glorious Hecatombs foreseen,
> Which noble Marlborough was ordain'd by Fate
> To offer up to thy insatiate Pow'r
> Thou surely then hadst sav'd one Godlike Youth,
> And to th' Heroick Father giv'n the Son.
> But Blandford in his early Bloom was snatch'd
> To make the Glory of the Sire compleat.[10] p. 69

The previous death (from smallpox) of Marlborough's own teenage son, the Marquis of Blandford, turns out to be a loss which secures Marlborough's

78 Part I: Developing Ideals

personal glory (since the General cannot be accused by 'Th'Invidious World' of fighting to benefit his heir). In a comparable way, the glory accruing to Queen Anne has, we learn, been paid for by the previous death of *her* son, the Duke of Gloucester, a death which has 'raised her Glory to the Stars'. In this view, the eminent principals are the ones who really count, while the other fatalities are merely the 'glorious Hecatombs' offered up by Marlborough (so that the nation's dead seem taken in the gross with the enemy's). The kudos won collectively by the British on the battlefield is, at the end of the poem, offered as a sacrifice to 'Th'Almighty God of War, the God of Great Revenge' – before whom the surviving heroes engage in a death-like prostration, as 'equal to the Worm'.[11] This final gesture of abasement is apparently an act of purification, a guarantee that these men are ready to be reabsorbed safely within the peaceful realms of civil society. They have performed brutal acts, but they have not been brutalised.

For Dennis, then, the terrible violence of the battlefield is atoned for by sacrifices in the realm of civil society – by the death of loved ones, specifically the loved ones of those eminent individuals who carry the most responsibility for the war (the Queen's mourning for her son, joined by the female Britannia, is the only mourning directly cited in the poem), or by ritual acts of abasement by the other commanders. These deaths are represented as forms of what Moshe Halbertal defines as 'sacrificing to', which involves substitution and atonement.[12] Glory is secured by loss and renunciation, in a gruesome system of accounting supposedly appropriate to a Christian understanding of sinfulness and retribution. Such accounting has some parallels with that projected in the Fast and Thanksgiving services organised by the church in time of war, in which the population at home was implicated in the progress or outcome of battles abroad by its presumed sinfulness and need for repentance, while there were prayers for the safety and wellbeing of members of the royal family. But in Dennis's poem, God, Death and public opinion all have to be appeased, and in much the same way.

The model of the official thanksgiving was to prove inadequate to the developing needs of the public, in part because it took so little account of the personal bereavement suffered by those whose loved ones died among the unnamed 'hecatombs'. Nevertheless, the kind of understanding found in Dennis – that in order to satisfy public opinion the violence we do to others must be paid for, or counterbalanced, by some loss on our side – becomes important in eighteenth-century representations of war. (In the following year, John Philips repeated this connection between the death of the French cavalry and of the heirs of Anne and Marlborough in his own poem on Blenheim – although here the French deaths are also said to lay to rest the unquiet ghosts of Britons slain on Landen plains fields. The unquiet dead are avenged).[13] Elsewhere the idea is transformed in order to meet the requirements of a public for whom benevolence is becoming a key social virtue, and for whom the process of mourning, and the reverential commemoration of death in war, is becoming more important.

We can see this kind of transformation in Joseph Addison's poetic celebration of the battle of Blenheim, *The Campaign* (1704). We have already noted that in this poem Addison has a special interest in showing how the violence of war can be reconciled with compassionate good nature. Death poses a special problem. Addison gestures towards a providential interpretation of the Blenheim victory, seeing Marlborough as an agent of divine power; but his model is epic rather than biblical, which frees him from an emphasis on sinfulness and from the official rituals of the church. The famous comparison of Marlborough to an angel enacting divine punishment is a heroic simile used to dignify the action.[14] Vengeance remains important, but the presentation of violence is governed more clearly than in Dennis by a defensive protocol: the poet generally refers to deaths inflicted by the enemy *before* he describes deaths inflicted by Britannia's men. Accordingly, the first victims to be specified are those who have already died at the hands of 'the perjur'd Gaul' in an unsuccessful defence of their Moselle homeland:

> The discontented Shades of slaughter'd Hosts
> That wander'd on her Banks, her Heroes Ghosts
> Hop'd, when they saw *Britannia*'s Arms appear,
> The Vengeance due to their great Deaths was near. (4)

As we shall see, the unquiet ghosts of those who have died unsatisfactory deaths in war – modelled on the troubled, ghostly warriors that haunt classical epics – will become a recurring device in eighteenth-century poetry, where they are sometimes used to represent the demand, and justification, for violent revenge. When Addison gets to the horrific Danube incident, he prefaces it with this account of a British death:

> O Dormer, how can I behold thy fate,
> And not the wonders of thy youth relate!
> How can I see the gay, the brave, the young,
> Fall in the cloud of war, and lie unsung!
> In joys of conquest he resigns his breath,
> And, fill'd with England's glory, smiles in death. (15)

Addison emphasises explicitly the willingness to die that is normally assumed when death in battle is seen as sacrifice. But he has moved beyond the religious context that shapes the conventional elegy for the dead. Death is not a terrifying affair in which the individual must prepare for divine judgement. Life is freely given – not grimly taken as it is in Dennis. Dormer's joyful resignation of life in battle contrasts dramatically with the intimations of sorrow in the poet's response. At an earlier point, the poet laments the 'fatal love of fame!' that drives so many 'generous' young Britons to their deaths at Blenheim (8), but here there is no sense that the young man dies in the expectation of any personal recognition. It is enough for Dormer himself that he is 'fill'd with England's glory' (15). The death is conceived as, in Halbertal's terms, 'sacrificing for', or on behalf of the nation, a form of self-transcendence.[15]

The passage helps to qualify the effect of the Danube episode that follows: not only is death robbed of some of its terrors, but we see that the French deaths have been counterbalanced, or paid for, by such English deaths. The connection is not made formally as Dennis might make it; here it is a matter of directing the reader's sympathy. The sorrow we feel for our own dead functions to cover the aggression we feel towards our enemies. The traditional religious framework may have been superseded, but structurally this death still functions as a form of atonement.

In Addison's poem, unlike Dennis's, the physical sacrifices of the victors are all made upon the battlefield, rather than in the realm of civil society (the heat of battle is 'Only destructive to the brave and great!', 8). The contrast between Dormer's joy and the poet's sorrow is an indication of the distance between the world of heroic action and the civil world of the poet, for whom war is an imagined spectacle. This helps to insulate the poet's own good-natured responses from the aggression he observes, and to remind us that death in battle is actually disconnected from the usual processes of mourning. The normal fate of the victims is undignified obscurity, to 'Fall in the Cloud of War, and lye unsung!' (15). While a few eminent officers who died in battle, like Wolfe and Nelson, might have their bodies carefully repatriated for proper burial, and have elaborate public commemorations, most who died would be cast into unmarked mass graves or dropped into the sea. The bereaved might discover the fate of their loved-ones days, weeks or months after the event, or not at all, while the dead might have no public recognition. We are not told if Dormer leaves a grieving widow or children or other dependents: such possibilities belong to the private realm and so are beyond the scope of this essentially public work. What matters here is that in making his tribute the poet rescues the victim from relative obscurity. Dormer was not a mighty commander: readers would have to scan contemporary casualty lists to discover that he was a Lieutenant-Colonel of the Guards.[16] It is the poet's act of personal commemoration that transforms the random death into a nationally significant sacrifice.

The heroic form of *The Campaign* works to exclude any reference to Britain's commercial interests in the war it describes, although Addison addressed such interests anonymously in a pamphlet.[17] The idea that patriotic sacrifice is motivated by a heroic purpose distinct from the specific material interests actually at stake in war is an important part of its symbolic usefulness.

Sacrifice and the Case for War

Addison's poem can be related to a wider movement to establish a modern culture less dependent upon the traditional authority of the church and the court. This movement helped to develop a secular conception of sacrifice that acquired a significant role in political writing and thinking about war. Sacrifice had played little part in the influential accounts of the origins of social order in Hobbes and Locke, while John Milton's *Paradise Lost* had challenged the tradition of military heroism celebrated in classical epics by associating it with Satan, in opposition to 'the better fortitude / Of Patience and Heroic Martyrdom', Christ's willing self-sacrifice on behalf of humanity (IX: 31–32).[18] But heroic sacrifice assumed a noteworthy role in the highly influential ethics of the third Earl of Shaftesbury, which were first unfolded in the *Inquiry Concerning Virtue or Merit* (1699) and elaborated in a series of later works culminating in the *Characteristics* (1711). Shaftesbury, a Whig, adopted a 'neo-Harringtonian', civic humanist perspective which, as John Pocock explains, harked back to the increasingly obsolete 'farmer-warrior world of ancient citizenship'.[19] In attempting to reconcile the stern virtues of Sparta with gentlemanly good nature, Shaftesbury detaches patriotic sacrifice from the sanction and rituals of the church, from the expectation of future rewards and punishments, and from the world of sordid material interests and political advantage. He aligns it instead with natural sociability and disinterested virtue. The (implicitly aristocratic) patriot who dies for his country does it not for any personal glory: Shaftesbury proclaims, with a glance at an Ode by Horace, that for the true patriot 'DULCE ET DECORUM EST ['Sweet and proper it is'] was his sole reason'.[20] He ascribes a 'noble enthusiasm' to heroes in his *Letter Concerning Enthusiasm* (1708), and elaborates this

82   Part I: Developing Ideals

in *Characteristics* (1711): 'He who yields his life a Sacrifice to his Prince or Country' is like those amorous and religious martyrs who draw their views 'whether visionary or real' from a 'Pattern and Exemplar of Divinity'.[21] The analogy, which leaves the status of the inspiration open to question, lifts the sacrifice into the realm of the universal and the sacred. In this way, the military hero's patriotic death can be thought of as akin to Christ's sacrifice. Shaftesbury provides a kind of answer to Milton.

While Shaftesbury associates sacrifice with the impulse of the disinterested individual, the 'Patriot' ideology developed in the 1720s connected this ideal firmly with the political and material interests of the nation. The idea of death in war became an inspiring focus for political commitment among those who had no intention of putting themselves personally at risk on the battlefield. In the wake of the South Sea Bubble of 1720, many commentators – in newspapers, pamphlets, and literary satires – wrote of a decline of moral standards in contemporary life, sometimes associated with the rise of public credit and stock-jobbers, and with the Whig ministry of Robert Walpole, who became prime minister in 1721. When an effective Parliamentary opposition emerged, led by Lord Bolingbroke (once a Jacobite and Tory) and William Pulteney (as a dissident Whig), it claimed to be motivated by patriotic virtue. 'Patriot' thinking was, like Shaftesbury's, informed by the 'neo-Harringtonian' perspective in which a landowner's readiness to bear arms in defence of the public good is a sign of virtue. However, since in the modern world responsibility for fighting had already been transferred to the military professional, the Patriot's virtue had to be expressed as a *readiness* for war. Christine Gerrard points out that the Patriot actively opposed to Walpole 'was now less likely to be a rural squire than a tradesman living in London, Manchester, or Bristol, one who defines his patriotism through defence of a "national interest" in which Britain's commercial enterprise and potential colonial expansion played a central role'.[22] The Patriots saw themselves as engaged in an embattled defence of 'Liberty' against two complementary threats: pusillanimous corruption inside the state (especially the Walpole ministry) and insulting violence outside (the imperial ambitions of the absolutist monarchs of Spain and France). Both threats occasioned a call to resist, and both were thought to require a willingness to make personal sacrifices that could draw inspiration from the bloody sacrifices of war.

In the *Craftsman*, the periodical which became the opposition's mouthpiece, Bolingbroke attacked Walpole's character by using analogical portraits of corrupt figures from earlier ages, and condemned Walpole's cautious handling of a developing conflict with Spain, calling for a more robust war effort. The Patriots were suspicious of military engagements in continental Europe, which laid a tax burden on landowners and appeared to profit the financiers. They favoured a naval 'blue-water' policy instead, focused on developing Britain's commerce overseas and with the colonies. The Patriots' war strategy was driven in part by pressure from merchants for the right to trade in Spanish America, in defiance of treaty obligations. They made clear the commercial interests at stake, but represented their position in defensive terms, as a response to unjustified Spanish aggression upon British merchants – to Spanish 'depredations'. The idea of sacrifice was used to strengthen and purify their position.

In contrast to Shaftesbury's voluntaristic conception of sacrifice, in the *Craftsman* Bolingbroke's ideal of sacrifice is motivated by a demanding sense of duty originating not in the pattern of divinity but in history. Patriot ideology looks back to idealised models of public virtue in ancient Greece and Republican Rome, and to an ancient English constitution supposedly based upon libertarian principles and maintained through subsequent ages by blood sacrifice. Bolingbroke's 'Remarks on the History of England' (1730–31), for example, develops a secular national history, shaped by the spirit of Liberty, in which the 'whole Fabrick' of the constitution, raised upon the solid foundations laid by the Saxons, has been 'cemented by the Blood of our Fathers'.[23] The theme is repeated in later essays, in one of which the constitution appears as a mighty tree cultivated with blood.[24] We find a comparable history in James Thomson's Patriot poems, *Britannia* (1729) and *Liberty* (1730), and a similar insistence on the need for sacrificial heroes who are 'prodigal of Blood' in his *Castle of Indolence* (1748).[25] In some of Bolingbroke's *Craftsman* essays, the highest duty is not to the deity or the monarchy, but to the nation – conceived as a single, continuously unfolding entity upheld and hallowed by the transmission of patriotic obligation rooted in sacrifice. In *Letters on the Spirit of Patriotism*, (written in 1736, published 1749) Bolingbroke insists that those who join the struggle to defend national liberty should not think of themselves simply as 'volunteers' but as 'listed in the service'. It is no surprise that for Bolingbroke, Cato, the hero celebrated by Addison in a famous heroic tragedy, cannot be the most appropriate model of patriotic virtue. Cato took his own life rather than surrender himself to Julius Caesar. Bolingbroke declared that Cato 'would have died I think with a better grace at Munda than at Utica' – that is, fighting against Caesar on the battlefield, rather than taking his own life at home.[26]

The Patriot conception of sacrifice, framed in terms of public virtue, and concerned with specific material interests, encouraged a more openly

84 Part I: Developing Ideals

belligerent attitude than Shaftesbury had done, and celebrated war-like monarchs – Alfred, Edward III, Henry V, Elizabeth I – and naval heroes who had fought against Spain, such as Sir Francis Drake and Sir Walter Raleigh.[27] Their belligerence did not sit easily with the attempts of reformers to school the public in the gentler virtues appropriate to polite society. Bolingbroke and other Patriots do sometimes formally embrace the virtues of compassion and benevolence, which were currently acquiring a new philosophical underpinning in the works of Frances Hutcheson; but they implied that the true Patriot might have to sacrifice such virtues in the cause of Liberty. Their conception of sacrifice – political, masculine, and warlike – was necessarily in tension with the sense of personal loss caused by war deaths, traditionally associated with feminine experience. This tension emerges with particular clarity in the most ambitious patriot poem of the period, Richard Glover's blank verse epic *Leonidas*.

The Last Epic Hero: *Leonidas*

Richard Glover was a representative of London's upwardly mobile, gentrifying commercial ranks. A Hamburg merchant in the City of London, he mixed with 'Patriot' Whig circles led by George Lyttleton and patronised by Frederick, Prince of Wales. Schooled in classical literature, when Glover wrote about martial virtue, he did so initially in a heroic form modelled on classical epic, a mode that demonstrated his own cultural credentials, while distancing him from the realms of modern commerce to which he belonged. He worked on *Leonidas* in the 1730s, and when this long blank verse poem appeared in 1737, he inscribed it to Lord Cobham, by this time an influential Opposition figure. The poem is based on historical accounts of the Grecians' war with Xerxes, but Glover's use of history, like Bolingbroke's, is analogical: ancient Greece in its struggle against the Persian empire functions as an analogue for the Patriot struggle against the despotic forces of corruption both inside the state (Walpole) and abroad (the aggressive imperialism of absolutist France and Spain). The hero's willing sacrifice to preserve the liberty of his country is offered as a stern exemplum of patriotic virtue, and as a purifying justification for violence. The treatment of death provides a chilling illustration of the counterbalancing principle we encountered earlier: a readiness for self-sacrifice validates the 'sacrifice' of one's enemies. And while the actions of the hero show that personal feeling must be subordinated to public good, Glover also includes a subplot in which personal feeling becomes the dominant motive for action, and we are led to consider the personal loss and mourning that arise in the aftermath of violence. The structure of the poem thus forms a kind of dialogue between a stern neo-Harringtonian commitment to public virtue, and a growing awareness of the claims of sympathy, compassion, and private virtue.

While the poem's analogical patterns may be complex, this is not an obscure poem as is sometimes claimed. It is an attempt to draw the reader into an archaic world of heroic action familiar from classical epic, in a simple, at times monosyllabic, and often prosaic blank verse that shuns Miltonic inversions and complex imagery. It is adapted to the needs of a modern readership that may not have a classical education, one that is used to the relatively uncomplicated language of contemporary periodicals and prose tales. A review in the *Gentleman's Magazine* claimed that its language was 'softer and more harmonious than that of Milton'.[28] The historian Henry Winder thought that the poem would encourage female readers to engage with classical epic.[29] The narrative has no divine intervention, and no impropriety, while its abundant violence co-exists with modern humanitarian sentiment. The result is certainly not great poetry, but a narrative that endows a range of connected modern issues with an idealised classical ancestry. Its immediate success indicates that Glover accurately judged the interests of his readership. The poem was reprinted twice in the first year of publication and was soon translated into French. According to Ian McGregor Morris, it was later translated four times into German (1748, 1756, 1778, 1842) and into Danish (in 1786).[30] It inspired several history paintings, including a study by Jacques-Louis David. In Britain it continued to be excerpted, and anthologised, for the next one hundred years.

Glover's attitude to military activity reflects the neo-Harringtonian perspective shared with other Patriots, and so differs in some respects from Addison's. The Patriots deplored the government's hiring of thousands of Hessians to defend George II's Electorate in Hanover, and sometimes linked the Electorate with 'Oriental' despotism.[31] They wrote of the modern professional or 'standing' army as a sign of corruption, favouring instead a militia rooted directly in, and organised for the defence of, local communities.[32] Their criticism of George II intensified with the emergence of his estranged son, Prince Frederick, as a patron of the Patriots. Bolingbroke's *Idea of Patriot King*, which circulated in manuscript at this time, is sometimes seen as a compliment to Frederick. Its vision of 'a free people, governed by a Patriot King' as 'a patriarchal family, where the head and all the members are united by one common interest, and animated by one common spirit' is an ideal embodied in Glover's account of Leonidas's reign.[33]

86   Part I: Developing Ideals

The central theme of the poem – heroic self-sacrifice – is the implicit justification for its extreme violence. Glover writes for a society haunted by fears of luxury, effeminacy, cowardice, a public that, he supposes, needs to be inspired with the courage and fierce warlike spirit – and the acceptance of violence – that animated earlier ages. That spirit is assumed to be missing from those who fight only for money. The central figure, Leonidas, is a hero designed for a modern age that has become aware of its distance from the martial ethos of the classical epic. He is not a wily Odysseus, nor an aggressive Achilles, nor a pious Aeneas on an imperial mission – although he has qualities of all of these. He is closer to Hector – the hero who dies in defence of his own people. (His parting from his wife and child in Book I is clearly based upon the famous episode of Hector's departure from Andromache in the *Iliad* book VI, although the tone is more sentimental). Leonidas is presented as a compelling orator, a skilful strategist, a courageous fighter, a charismatic leader – all qualities appropriate to his kingly status. But his most important attribute is his willingness to die, which is triumphantly consummated in battle. Following Shaftesbury, Glover offers an answer to Milton's critique of martial heroism in *Paradise Lost.* Like Milton's Christ, Glover's Leonidas goes knowingly and willingly to his death. Glover insists that the hero and his companions, who at the end of the poem die in defending their country against overwhelming numbers, 'obtain'd more glory in their fall than others from the brightest victories'.[34] The hero shares this assessment:

> To live with fame
> The Gods allow to many: but to die
> With equal lustre, is a blessing, Heav'n
> Selects from all the choicest boons of fate,
> And with a sparing hand on few bestows (I, 139–145, p. 11)

At Thermopylae, as the last of his group to die, Leonidas views his 'beauteous wounds' with 'serenest joy' (IX, 704, 706, p 334). Virtue transforms defeat into moral victory; his death is presented as an exemplum that, through the work of historian and poet, will inspire future generations.

Glover's 'confederate' Greece is a collection of independent city states and overseas colonies, defended by 'assiduous fleets' (I, 45, p. 5). It is analogous to a 'blue water' conception of Britain with its notionally separate nations and with colonies to defend in the West Indies and in North America. As a federation of autonomous states, it is contrasted with the Persian empire ruled under the supreme authority of a central power, analogous to the absolutist regimes of Spain and France (and to the Hanoverian

Sacrifice: Heroism and Mourning 87

conception of Britain with its continental commitments).[35] The Persian Xerxes, master of wealth and luxury, dreams of 'universal empire' as his forces invade Greece. Like Milton's Satan, he appears enthroned at the beginning of the third book. His military campaign depends upon professional and mercenary forces, unlike the Grecians, who fight in militias for their own communities.

The thematic contrast between the virtuous Greek militias fighting courageously for their homeland, and the servile, cowardly mercenaries on the Persian side, who fight merely for plunder, ensures that the Greeks are repeatedly shown slaughtering opponents who offer little or no effective resistance. Although the noble Persian commanders fight courageously, and there are scenes of man-to-man combat between individuals who seem more evenly and honourably matched, much of the violence entails one-sided killing of the cowardly Persian rank and file. One such scene would appear familiar to anyone who had read accounts of Blenheim: at the end of Book V, a company of Persians retreat to the shore where, surrounded by the Greeks, they are driven to their deaths in the sea, and 'devoted hecatombs to Mars' (V: 766–781, 770, pp. 201–202). The sacrificial reference here is more than an aside: it indicates the interpretive assumption that operates throughout the poem. The Greeks' willingness to sacrifice themselves justifies their 'sacrifice' of others.

This is made explicit by Glover's inclusion of a scene of ritual sacrifice like those found in Homer and Virgil. In the eighth book – the prelude to the climax of violence – a ceremonial arming is followed by a religious ceremony at which a consecrated ox is sacrificed to the Muses. The ritual, in which both ox and heroes are decked in laurel, and the ox flesh is committed to the flames on an altar, is a defining moment, which marks off the corrupt, treacherous Thebans (who withdraw without participating) from the patriotic Spartans. It foreshadows both the coming sacrifice of the battle, and the banquet the heroes expect to receive in blest abodes. During this pagan Last Supper (their 'last repast') Leonidas assures his men:

> All conspires
> To this great sacrifice, where thousands soon
> Shall only wake to die. (VIII, 280–282, p.282)

The great sacrifice implicitly includes *all* those who will die – both the Grecians who will sacrifice themselves for their homeland, and the Persians they will slaughter in the process – a sacrifice to liberty. As the warriors share the flesh of the sacrificial victim, they prefigure all these deaths in a

88   Part I: Developing Ideals

joyful ritualisation of the fellowship of war. In an age when clerics were vigorously debating the meaning of the Anglican Communion, partly in response to falling attendances, Glover describes a pagan alternative as a symbol and agent of visceral communal bonding.[36]

The account of the ritual indicates how the sequence which follows is to be read. This is an account of the Grecians' night-time attack on the Persian camp – an event that does not appear in Herodotus but was added by later historians, and which allows Glover to show the Greeks in an invasive rather than defensive mode, and triumphing in an orgy of killing. Glover has already told this story in the words of Diodorus Siculus, which he translates in the Preface. Diodorus describes how, in the confusion of the surprise attack, the Persians 'destroy'd each other without distinction' (xi). In Glover's poem, the episode is fundamentally transformed: the Grecians make 'A sacrifice to Freedom', plunging their swords into the breasts of ten thousand 'naked, pale, unarm'd' Persians as flames consume the camp (58, p. 296; 30, p. 294). Here the Persians are not even cowardly soldiers, but mere defenceless victims. Modern commentators on ancient sacrificial rituals note how the sacrificial victim has to be 'innocent' or 'relatively indifferent' in order to be 'sacrificeable', since the offering must be pure in order to be acceptable.[37] The episode, with its blood and flames, recalls the sacrifice of the ox which immediately precedes it. We are to conclude, apparently, that the idea of sacrifice licenses and purifies what might otherwise be mere atrocity. These deaths will be paid for by the heroes' deaths; there will be an appropriate atonement. The reader is being challenged to accept such horrific brutality as, in the circumstances, not only a military necessity, but right and proper. Sacrifice is a form of hedging, since it makes victory and defeat interchangeable – the death of the hero is always a moral victory, which counterbalances both our losses and the enemy's.

As a contribution to the anti-Walpole drive for a war against the Spanish, the poem's anti-imperial, self-sacrificial celebration of defeat seems remote from the pursuit of commercial interests that Glover actually supports, and that he champions directly in his next significant poem, *London: or the Progress of Commerce* (1739). The epic genre of *Leonidas* allows heroic virtue to be imagined with an ideal purity, as in the heroic drama of the period. But an alternative agenda does leak out in the eighth book, where Leonidas recounts a dream which includes a mountain-top vision of the future (corresponding to Adam's in book ten of *Paradise Lost*), a vision in which carnage gives way to peace and plenty. The sage Megistas interprets this as an omen that Greece will be 'Enrich'd with conquest, and Barbarian spoils'

Sacrifice: Heroism and Mourning

(95–96, p. 271). In spite of all of the indications that Greek patriotism is purely defensive and disinterested, at this point the prospect of a material reward appears, mirroring Xerxes's imperial drive for conquest and spoils. The repressed returns – in the interpretation of a dream.

Mourning

The structure of Glover's poem is designed to represent heroic sacrifice as a deliberate moral decision: the ritual precedes and anticipates the hero's death. Glover does not want to show the immediate aftermath of Leonidas's death – the fate of his body, and the sorrow and mourning that must follow. Such consequences are not part of the 'public' significance with which the death is to be endowed. They belong to the realm of private feeling which the hero himself has sacrificed in serving his country, and which the poet has largely suppressed in his account of violence. In order to conclude with the impression of death as an unqualified triumph, such considerations are displaced from the end of the poem into the story of Teribazus and Ariana, which appears in books V and VI. Here the theme of sacrifice is developed in terms of personal feeling, which replaces patriotic duty as the main cause of action. Teribazus is a Persian whose wealth consists not in land but in his wide-ranging education. This has given him an admiration for Greek culture that determines even his choice of armour. He secretly aspires to, and unknowingly wins, the affections of Darius's daughter Ariana; assuming his love can never be reciprocated, he seeks to escape his dilemma through an honourable death in battle. He fights not to serve Xerxes, but for personal fame. When he is killed fighting heroically against the Greeks, Ariana makes her way to the Greek camp at night, where Leonidas allows her to look for his body (like Priam looking for Hector's body in the *Iliad*). It is found, still with its armour, 'beneath a mass of Persians slain' (VI, 113, p. 211). Ariana embraces the body and kills herself over it. The lovers' bodies are eventually sent back to Xerxes, so that he too can mourn.

In this episode, Glover begins to expose the difference between the emotionally gratifying forms in which we prefer to commemorate those who die in war, and the inglorious realities that make such commemoration necessary. The recovery of Teribizus's body allows us to glimpse the more usual aftermath of battle: the unreclaimed Persian bodies lying, unburied, in a heap on the battlefield. Those familiar with Herodotus's account of Leonidas's death would know its undignified aftermath: when Xerxes found Leonidas's body he ordered the head to be cut off and stuck

90   Part I: Developing Ideals

on a pole.[38] Ariana, an unmarried woman, stands in a complementary relationship with Leonidas's wife, who is to be widowed: Leonidas sees in her an image of his own wife's sorrow. By placing Ariana on the battlefield, confronting directly the horror of wounds and blood, Glover attempts to accommodate the terror and distress of the bereaved in a form that provides tragic closure. The woman looking for her dead lover on the battlefield would become a recurrent theme in poetry published later in the century, one that recognised the anxiety faced by many relatives who simply did not know what had happened to the remains of menfolk lost in battle.[39] The episode exposes the isolating despair that may arise from death in war, the opposite of the inspirational and socially unifying effects attributed to it in the main plot; the heroic masculine sacrifice on the battlefield finds its pathetic, opposing counterpart in the feminine sacrifice of the bereaved. This opposition between the private feeling attributed to the female and the martial glory attributed to the male anticipates a contrast that would soon assume a rather different form in the novel, as we shall see in Chapter 5.

While Glover's poem worked to establish the figure of Leonidas as a popular icon of Liberty among other writers, the increasing emphasis on humanitarian sympathy in eighteenth-century culture worked to make this kind of violent epic hero seem outdated.[40] The descriptions of ferocious hand-to-hand fighting have their precedents in classical epics, and may have been intended to stiffen the martial resolve of a society susceptible to luxury; but they represent a suspension or denial of compassion for the victims of war, and they seem oddly in excess of the moral example offered by the hero's self-sacrifice. As a moral value, sacrifice in war has no necessary connection with martial prowess. It is not the hero's ability to kill others, but his willingness to give up his life for others that provides a model of admirable self-transcendence, in opposition to mean self-interest, apathy, or cowardice. The rise of humanitarianism meant that writers and artists would increasingly need to show martial sacrifice in terms that appealed to the compassion of the audience. The growing vogue for works that evoked sympathy and pathos helps to explain why the Ariana episode in *Leonidas* had a life apart from the rest of the poem during the eighteenth century (it sometimes appeared as an excerpt).[41]

The interest in this episode is symptomatic of the growing importance of the perspective of the bereaved. Ariana, in her distress over the dead body of Teribazus, is said to resemble 'a marble form/ Fix'd on the solemn sepulchre' (VI 145), an allusion to contemporary funeral monuments, which sometimes included the figure of a mourning widow, seated or standing by the sarcophagus – separated from the main part of the monument. While bereavement was formally feminised and set apart in this way, Glover was writing in a period when there was, as Esther Schor puts it, a 'shift toward the masculine gendering of mourning' accompanied by 'a strengthening conviction of [its] public significance'.[42] The emergence of the professional undertakers during the 1720s and 1730s, the increasing importance of money and personal choice (as opposed to position in social hierarchy) in the conduct of funerals, the publication of obituary notices – such developments were accompanied by the appearance in periodicals of elegies and odes to the dead and the rising popularity of epitaphs.[43]

This shift can be seen in the contemporary commemoration of soldiers and sailors. Addison had complained in the *Spectator* (1710) about Grinling Gibbons's memorial to the Admiral Cloudesly Shovell, erected at Queen Anne's command in Westminster Abbey. The monument had no naval motifs and in Addison's view made the admiral, who is shown resting on cushions and wearing a voluminous wig, look like a 'beau'.[44] To make matters worse, the inscription emphasised the accidental nature of the admiral's death in a shipwreck, instead of his glorious actions as a naval commander. Addison does not mention that more than 1400 sailors died along with Shovell in the same disaster, or that they featured only as anonymous and uncounted 'others' on this memorial. At this point in time, it seems, the one must stand for the many. But Addison's criticisms anticipate future developments. He treats the style of commemoration as a matter of national concern. Naval motives are called for, and the fulsome wig is not, because the national significance of the figure outweighs merely social connotations, just as its role in promoting the myth of sacrifice – and the national view of war – outweighs mere historical fact.

Addison's comments herald a new era in the commemoration of eminent members of the army and navy. Following the example of the monument to the Duke of Buckingham in Westminster Abbey, installed in the 1720s, in funeral monuments to eminent soldiers or sailors, sculptors began to place the recumbent figure, clothed in classical armour or robes, within a scene that might suggest death in battle (rather than simply prayer or the contemplation of resurrection) whatever the circumstances of the subject's death (Figure 1).

Even if the figure was a simple bust, the accompanying imagery might still suggest death in battle, as in the case of Roubiliac's memorial to Admiral Warren in Westminster Abbey. David Bindman and Malcolm Baker point out that 'All but two of the soldiers and sailors commemorated

Figure 1   John Sheffield, 1st Duke of Buckingham monument, designed by Denis Plumiere and sculpted by Laurent Delvaux and Peter Scheemakers (1722)
[© Westminster Abbey]

by Roubiliac in substantial monuments (in the 1740s and 1750s) died comfortably in their beds, mostly at an advanced age after lucrative rather than glorious careers; yet in almost all of them the imagery suggests that they died heroically in battle'.[45] Westminster Abbey, in particular, was becoming a national pantheon for military and naval figures, having been opened for the burial of any client who could afford the fees.[46] A guide book helped visitors to Westminster Abbey identify the monuments and the people they commemorated.

Benedict Anderson suggests that the tomb of the unknown soldier and the empty cenotaph, established in the wake of the First World War, have no true precedents in earlier times.[47] But such twentieth-century memorials, where the spectator must supply in imagination and feeling what the empty monument withholds, are the logical conclusion of that change of emphasis desired by Addison, from the mere facts of the case – the veritable history and identity of the hero – to what Anderson terms the 'national

Sacrifice: Heroism and Mourning

imaginings' of the spectator. The eighteenth-century commemorative tombs that evoked patriotic sacrifice were well adapted to facilitate this change. The visitor was placed for a while in a role which resembled that of a mourner but which required the enactment of national rather than private feelings:

> Briton, behold, if Patriot Worth be dear,
> A Shrine that claims thy tributary Tear[48]

On some tombs, the figure of the mourning female had allegorical attributes which suggested a merging of public and private grief.[49] The momentary sorrow supposed to felt by the grateful and reverential public did not depend upon personal knowledge of the deceased (the guidebook might be needed); but it did depend upon an understanding of the moral type that was represented, and of the appropriate response to it. In this situation, mourning that was figured as isolating, even paralysing, could be thought of as drawing the spectator into unity with the imagined feelings of the nation as a whole, and as inspiring future sacrifice. Commemoration could become a point at which virtue was transmitted.

The poet Mark Akenside imagines commemoration in such terms in his 'British Philippic', a passionate call to arms against Spain published in *The Gentleman's Magazine* in 1738. The poet invokes the 'great spirits' of Britain's martial past – 'Ca'endish, Rawleigh, Blake' – and those of 'later name' in terms that resemble the idiom of 'Patriot' poets. But when he turns to the process of commemoration, 'a lower, yet a noble scene', he evokes a moral type rather than an historical personage. The poet insists that a warrior who welcomes death for the benefit of others will be treated as a god-like figure:

> Paint the just honours to his reliques paid,
> Shew grateful millions weeping o'er his grave;
> While his fair fame in each progressive age
> For ever brightens; and the wise and good
> Of every land in universal choir
> With filial richest incense of undying praise
> His urn encircle, to the wondering world
> His num'rous triumphs blazon; [50]

In this fantastic vision, the self-sacrificing patriot takes the place of the saint in modern society, as an object of quasi-religious veneration. Mourning is unifying and inspiring, part of the process by which virtue is diffused. The universalising of fame does not undermine the honour to the nation, but amplifies it.

94 Part I: Developing Ideals

Since in the realm of national imaginings, myth trumps history, the great funereal monuments which sought to perpetuate the memory of eminent individuals were a means by which it became possible to imagine a more inclusive commemoration, extended to those who could in fact have no such respectful treatment. We can see this process in two of the Odes of William Collins.

His 'Ode to a Lady' was apparently a response to the devastating defeat of British forces at the battle of Fontenoy, 11th May 1745, details of which Collins gathered directly from his uncle, who had fought in the battle. The full title identifies Colonel Ross as the subject and, as Howard Weinbrot notes, 'Ross was known to be part of the anti-Hanoverian opposition'. The name may therefore signal Collins's own misgivings about the war on the continental mainland. However, in the poem itself, the fallen soldier is nameless and in Collins's collected odes Ross's Christian name and the date of composition were omitted.[51] Weinbrot suggests a possible connection here with contemporary French responses to the battle, in which poets were criticised for naming some of those who died while excluding others (he notes that Voltaire added a generalised tribute to *La Poëme de Fontenoy* in the face of such criticisms 33–34).[52] But it is not simply the full name that is withheld: the soldier's personal characteristics and even his actions in battle have all become irrelevant to the poet's purpose. All that matters here are the imagined feelings of those who respond to his death. And the sentiments seem relevant to any youth who died in the battle:

3

By rapid Scheldt's descending wave
His country's vows shall bless the grave,
   Where'er the youth is laid:
That sacred spot the village hind
With every sweetest turf shall bind,
   And Peace protect the shade.

4

Blest youth, regardful of thy doom,
Aerial hands shall build thy tomb,
   With shadowy trophies crowned:
Whilst *Honour* bathed in tears shall rove
To sigh thy name through every grove,
   And call his heroes round.[53]

The fate of the body is uncertain – 'Where'er the youth is laid' – and the funeral rites associated with it are, quite obviously, compensatory fantasies.

Sacrifice: Heroism and Mourning 95

The burial of combatants who died on campaign was usually a hasty business: on land, as Richard Holmes observes, bodies were commonly 'tumbled half naked into graves whose sites are rarely marked', while at sea they were customarily shrouded in a sail or hammock, weighted, and dropped overboard.[54] In Collins's Ode the tomb crowned with trophies, the familiar public memorial, exists only in imagination. At a time when burial was still associated with consecrated ground in or near a church, Collins encourages his readers to think of the corner of some foreign field as holy.

In the fullest version of the work, the poet moves between death as a unifying national event and as an isolating personal loss: the public myth and the private grief ultimately remain separate and in conflict. On the one hand, the victim joins the masculine national pantheon of the warlike dead, 'Old Edward's sons', who are collectively filled with feelings of revenge. On the other hand, the poet acknowledges the unnamed lady's personal and even inconsolable sense of loss:

9.

If, weak to sooth so soft an heart,
These pictured glories nought impart
  To dry thy constant tear;
If yet, in Sorrow's distant eye,
Exposed and pale thou see'st him lie,
  Wild War insulting near:

10.

Where'er from time thou court'st relief.
The Muse shall still, with social grief,
  Her gentlest promise keep:
Ev'n humble Harting's cottaged vale
Shall learn the sad repeated tale,
  And bid her shepherds weep.[55]

The dead soldier is, as it were, exhumed in the mourner's imagination from his fictional grave and seen lying 'Exposed and pale' with 'Wild war insulting near'. This fate is the brutal probability that the poet has initially tried to mask. It is not only the fictiveness of the 'pictured glories' that is at issue, but their ineffectiveness. The poem actually suggests that there may be no adequate closure for this death: 'repeated' reading of the poem is a substitute ritual that may not work. Part of its effect lies in the recognition that the monuments to the eminent dead provide those who mourn less fortunate victims with a model for imagining what *should* have taken place, but hasn't. Ultimately, historical experience remains stubbornly resistant here to the consolations of national myth.

96   Part I: Developing Ideals

In Collins's poem 'How Sleep the Brave', however, myth predominates.

ODE,
Written in the beginning of the Year 1746.

1.
How sleep the brave, who sink to rest,
By all their country's wishes blest!
When Spring, with dewy fingers cold,
Returns to deck their hallowed mould,
She there shall dress a sweeter sod,
Than Fancy's feet have ever trod.

2.
By fairy hands their knell is rung,
By forms unseen their dirge is sung;
There Honour comes, a pilgrim grey,
To bless the turf that wraps their clay,
And Freedom shall a-while repair
To dwell a weeping hermit there!

The 'brave' are not identified or distinguished by anything beyond the fact that they 'sink to rest', so that bravery is associated with dying rather than with action. The claim that each brave victim of battle is individually blest by 'all their country's wishes' and will receive the equivalent of traditional funeral rites and be the subject of an annual remembrance is manifestly a fantasy. The poem actually indicates what will not happen in fact: the knell, dirge, and individually honoured grave can be supplied only in imagination. The poem may have been written in response to another defeat for the British army, this time at the hands of Jacobite rebels at Falkirk, at the beginning of 1746. But the emphasis on the rituals and feelings associated with mourning, and on the reverence paid to martyrs, makes the outcome of the battle seem irrelevant.

In this Ode, then, Collins shows how the most obscure deaths in war – indeed, the deaths of unknown soldiers – could be imagined as nationally significant sacrifices; how the absence of care for the individual victim could be imagined as the presence of such care, how bodies disposed of in the gross could be imagined as the individual focus of cultic reverence. In this way, the idea of sacrifice could be universalised, turning defeat into a kind of moral victory.

In 1753, the poem was inserted at the end of Act II of *Alfred the Great* (an opera version of a Patriot drama by James Thomson and David Mallett). This gives some indication of how it was seen by contemporaries. The Act

Sacrifice: Heroism and Mourning 97

presents near its beginning the lament of a nymph Edith for her shepherd Damon, slain in 'cruel War' on a 'Detested, bloody Field'.[56] In this context, Collins's poem allows the idea of celebration to displace feminine despair, converts the 'Detested' field of war into holy ground, and turns cruel loss into an incentive to fight (in the drama we soon learn that King Alfred's forces have defeated the Danes who threaten his kingdom).

In the Thanksgiving service that had served John Dennis as a starting point for celebrating victory, praise is a sacrifice to the Lord. The nation is instructed to mortify its own corrupt affections and proclaim its own unworthiness. The idea of patriotic sacrifice offered a less demeaning response to war. It united the moral ideal of self-abnegation with admiration for human worth, accommodated both the solitary grief of bereavement and the collective sorrow of the nation, and combined humanitarian sympathy with an element of national pride, powerfully reinforcing the national view of war. When it found a focus in commemorative monuments, it united these functions with the appeal of celebrity and tourism, allowing them to acquire a serious moral purpose and a sacred aura. The Church's official involvement in orchestrating the public response to war would come under increasing critical scrutiny during the final decades of the century, but it is perhaps not surprising that the idea of heroic sacrifice, and the commemoration of the deaths of war heroes gained a firmer hold on the public imagination.

Notes

1 Stephen C. Neff, *War and the Law of Nations: A General History* (Cambridge: Cambridge University Press, 2005), 91.

2 Brett D. Wilson, *A Race of Female Patriots: Women and Public Spirit on the British Stage 1688–1745* (Lewisburg: Bucknell University Press, 2012).

3 See for example, Teresa A. Myers and Andrew F. Hayes, 'Reframing the Casualties Hypothesis: (Mis)Perceptions of Troop Loss and Public Opinion about War', *International Journal of Public Opinion Research*, 22:2 (2010), 256–275.

4 Anne Somerset, *Queen Anne; the Politics of Passion* (London: HarperCollins, 2012), 386–387.

5 *A Letter to Monsieur Boileau Depreux: Occasioned by the Victory at Blenheim, 1704* (London, 1704), 4.

6 John Grant, *A Sermon Preach'd at the Cathedral Church of Rochester* (London, 1704); Samuel Bromesgrove, *A Sermon Preach'd at the Tabernacle in Spittle-Fields* (London, 1704); John James Caesar, *God's Inevitable Judgement on Perjur'd Princes* (London, 1704); Nathaniel Hough, *Success, When the Signs of Divine Favour* (London, 1704); Joseph Stennett, *A Sermon Preach'd on 7th September, 1704* (London, 1704).

98 Part I: Developing Ideals

7 John Richardson, 'War, the Poetry of War, and Pope's Early Career,' *Journal of English and Germanic Philology*, 102: 4 (2003), 486–505, 491; Claude Rawson. 'War and the Epic Mania in England and France: Milton, Boileau, Prior and the English Mock-Heroic', *Review of English Studies*, 64: 265 (2012), 433–453, 448–49.

8 Bernard Mandeville, *The Fable of the Bees*, 6th edn. (London, 1729), 205–206.

9 Michael L. Gross, *Moral Dilemmas of Modern War: Torture, Assassination, and Blackmail in an Age of Asymmetric Conflict* (Cambridge: Cambridge University Press, 2010); Shannon E. French, *The Code of the Warrior: Exploring Warrior Values Past and Present* (Lanham: Rowman & Littlefield, 2003).

10 John Dennis, *Britannia Triumphans* (London, 1704), 69.

11 *Britannia Triumphans*, 69–70, 1, 72.

12 Moshe Halbertal, *On Sacrifice* (Princeton, NJ: Princeton University Press, 2012), 2.

13 *Blenheim, A Poem*, 3rd edn., (London, 1705), 13–14.

14 Joseph Addison, *The Campaign, A Poem* (London, 1704), 14.

15 *On Sacrifice*, 4.

16 The death is recorded in the *Post Man and Historical Account*, September 2-September 5, 1704, and in Francis Hare, *An Exact Journal of the Campaign in Germany for the Year 1704* (London, 1704), 46.

17 *The state of the war and the necessity of an augmentation, consider'd* (London, 1708).

18 On Hobbes and Locke see Halbertal, *On Sacrifice*, 104.

19 J. G. A. Pocock, *Virtue, Commerce and History* (Cambridge: Cambridge University Press, 1985), 48.

20 *Characteristicks of Men, Manners, Opinions, Times*, 3 vols. (London, 1711), I, 102.

21 *A Letter Concerning Enthusiasm* (London, 1708), 82; *Characteristicks*, III, 34.

22 Christine Gerrard, *The Patriot Opposition to Walpole: Politics, Poetry and National Myth, 1725–1742* (Oxford: Oxford University Press, 1994), 11.

23 The 'Remarks' first appeared as essays in *The Craftsman. Remarks on the History of England* (London, 1743), 55.

24 *Craftsman* 26 January, 1734, Letter X, 395; *A Dissertation upon Parties, in Several Letters to Caleb D'Anvers* (London, 1735), Letter XVI, 194.

25 James Thomson, *Liberty, The Castle of Indolence*, ed. James Sambrook (Oxford: Oxford University Press, 1986), 110, 214–15.

26 *Letters on the Spirit of Patriotism: On the Idea of a Patriot King, on the State of the Parties* (London, 1749), 26, 36.

27 See Gerrard, *The Patriot Opposition*, chapter 6.

28 *Gentleman's Magazine*, VII (1737), 224.

29 Henry Winder, *A Critical and Chronological History of the Rise, Progress, Declension and Revival of Knowledge Chiefly Religious* (London, 1741) (2 vols), II, 155–156.

30 Ian McGregor Morris, *The Legend of Thermopylae in British Political Culture, 1737–1831*, University of Manchester, PhD thesis (2000), 20.

31 For example, George Lyttleton, *Letters from a Persian in England to His Friend at Ispahan* (London, 1735), which appeared anonymously.

32 See Isaac Kramnick, *Bolingbroke and His Circle: The Politics of Nostalgia in the Age of Walpole* (Ithaca, NY: Cornell University Press, 1968), 72–73.

Sacrifice: Heroism and Mourning 99

33 Bolingbroke, *Letters on the Spirit of Patriotism*, 148.

34 Richard Glover, *Leonidas* (London, 1737), xiii.

35 See David Armitage, 'The Cromwellian Protectorate and the Languages of Empire', *The Historical Journal*, 35: 3 (1992), 531–555, 552.

36 Susan Rutherford, 'Benjamin Hoadly: Sacramental Tests and Eucharistic Thought in Early Eighteenth-century England,' *Anglican and Episcopal History*, LXXI (2002), 473–497.

37 Halbertal, *On Sacrifice*, 32–33; René Girard, *Violence and the Sacred*, translated by Patrick Gregory (Baltimore: Johns Hopkins University Press, 1977), 4.

38 Herodotus, *The Histories*, VII, CCXXXVIII.

39 Later taken up by, among others, Thomas Penrose in 'The Field of Battle'. See John Richardson, 'Literature and War in the Eighteenth Century,' *Oxford Handbooks Online*, July 2014, tiny.one/5n76hdam.

40 Leonidas is celebrated, for example, in Jane Brereton's 'A Vision' (1744/5), George Splitimber's 'On Public Virtue,' addressed to Henry Pelham (1745), in James Thomson's 'Winter' (1746).

41 Oliver Goldsmith, *Poems for Young Ladies* (London, 1785), 163–180; *The Muses' Bower* (London, 1809), 2 vols, II, 97–118; Thomas Campbell, *Specimens of the British Poets* (1844) 594–597. The episode is quoted generously in a glowing review of *Leonidas* in Smollett's *Critical Review* 30 (1770), 378–385.

42 Elizabeth Schor, *Bearing the Dead: The British Culture of Mourning from the Enlightenment to Victoria* (Princeton, NJ: Princeton University Press, 1994), 19.

43 Ralph Houlbrooke, *Death, Religion and the Family in England* (Oxford: Oxford University Press, 1998), 286, 293, 319, 357.

44 Joseph Addison, *The Spectator* 26 (30 March, 1711).

45 David Bindman, Malcolm Baker, *Roubiliac and the Eighteenth-Century Monument Sculpture as Theatre* (New Haven: Yale University Press), 147.

46 Ingrid Roscoe, *Peter Scheemakers, 'The Famous Statuary' 1691–1781* (Leeds: Henry Moore Institute, 1996), 3.

47 Benedict Anderson, *Imagined Communities: Reflections on the Origin and Spread of Nationalism* (London: Verso, 1983), 200, 9.

48 Lines on the memorial to John Duke of Argyle and Greenwich (erected 1749).

49 Bindman and Baker, 166.

50 *Gentleman's Magazine*, VIII (1738), 427–428.

51 Roger Lonsdale, ed., *The Poems of Gray, Collins, and Goldsmith* (London: Longman, 1969), 455.

52 Howard D. Weinbrot, *Britannia's Issue: The Rise of British Literature from Dryden to Ossian* (Cambridge: Cambridge University Press, 1995), 19, 33–34.

53 *The Poems of Thomas Gray, William Collins, Oliver Goldsmith*, ed. Roger Lonsdale (London: Longman, 1992), 458–59.

54 Richard Holmes, *Redcoat: The British Soldier in the Age of Sword and Musket* (London: Harper Collins, 2001), 419.

55 Lonsdale, 437.

56 *Alfred The Great: A Drama for Music* (London, 1753), 14.

CHAPTER 4

Sacrifice
Christian Heroes

With hindsight, we can see that the classical hero Glover tried to revive would soon become outdated. His nobility and his paganism, along with his unchecked ferocity on the battlefield, would make him seem increasingly remote from the concerns of the expanding modern public as they reacted to Britain's warfare. A new kind of hero, less socially elevated, gentler, and representing Protestant Christianity, would come to seem more relevant to the needs of a nation fighting in areas remote from the battlefields of continental Europe.

The mid-1740s were a key period in the development of ideas about the role of Britain's military forces. The nation's activity in the wars on the continent during the War of the Austrian Succession (1740–1748) continued to be promoted as a struggle in defence of liberty and against imperialism and absolutist ambition. But in the wake of the Jacobite rebellion of 1745, and the capture of Cape Breton in Canada from the French in the same year, a different conception of Britain's martial activities began to assume more importance. The rebellion, which ended in defeat at Culloden in 1746, initiated a new phase in the transformation of the Scottish Highlands: a systematic attempt to dismantle the traditional clan system and renewed efforts to introduce Protestant education, in the interests of absorbing the Highlanders within the political structures and culture of modern Britain.[1] The capture of Cape Breton, as Brendan Simms notes, 'moved the New World from the margins of strategic debate closer to the centre of attention' in Britain.[2] The Cape was handed back to France during the peace negotiations at Aix la Chappelle, but the prospect of a major contest with the French in North America loomed into view – a contest in which both sides would seek alliances with, and fight against, Native American forces.

The Civilised and the Savage

The conflicts against Scottish Highlanders and against Native Americans were widely represented as the struggle of Protestant civilising forces against

Sacrifice: Christian Heroes

uncivilised enemies. But while propaganda against these peoples had long represented them as backward and 'savage', some Highland regiments fought on the government side during the Jacobite rebellion, while Native Americans fought in alliance with British forces in America.[3] Attempts to distinguish between 'civilized' and 'savage' forms of violence were fraught with difficulties. Such problems could be circumvented by moving attention away from the business of wounding and killing the enemy to focus more closely on areas in which Christian ideals and humanitarian concerns could be represented more securely. In these circumstances, the death of the hero assumed a new significance.

As Thomas Keymer points out, from the standpoint of the Whig-Hanoverian establishment, the Jacobite 'rebellion' of 1745 had to be described in terms that kept at bay any potentially legitimising suggestion of civil war.[4] The conflict gave rise to two quite different kinds of hero, both of whom served this purpose: one who acquired earthly glory by a crushing victory, the other who rose to heavenly glory in a humiliating defeat. George II's youngest son the Duke of Cumberland, who led the British forces which finally put down the rebellion at the Battle of Culloden (1746), was hailed by a relieved public as a triumphant conquering hero. Like Admiral Vernon, the hero of the raid on Portobello of 1739, he was widely celebrated in poems and commemorative merchandise (medals, prints, fans, teapots etc). Unlike Vernon (who was used by the political Opposition to attack the Hanoverian Succession and the power of Robert Walpole), Cumberland was promoted as a princely hero by Hanoverian propagandists to support the Succession. Even though, as Danielle Thom notes, some prints tried to place him in a dual role as both 'everyman and prince', Cumberland was inevitably elevated by his royalty and his rank as a military commander and took much of the credit for having rescued Britain from Popery and savagery.[5]

In poems, he was hailed as a masterful warrior who had pursued and 'crushed' the rebels as if they were 'Beasts of Prey', or who fought like a lion who leaves 'many a Carcase' strewn 'on the reeking Plain', or who drove the rebels like 'trembling Hares' before his 'eager Dogs'.[6] In visual representations, he was sometimes physically elevated, as a warrior on horseback on the battlefield or before an emblematic battle. Sometimes, he was represented in allegorical form, as a lion or as Hercules, to signify his courage and power.[7] However, in view of the violent reprisals Cumberland had inflicted on the Highlanders in the wake of the battle, Tory sympathizers soon began to develop a counterimage of him as a 'Butcher'.[8] The heavy price paid by the rebels and by those associated with them

Figure 2 'Tandem Triumphans', 1746. Cumberland leads the British cavalry against the Jacobite infantry. Tandem Triumphans, 'Triumphant at Last', was inscribed on Prince Charles's standard when he landed in Britain [© British Museum]

was acknowledged even by Cumberland's supporters (a print celebrating his victory at Culloden 'Tandem Triumphans', 1746, showed his forces attacking unarmed women; Figure 2).

As more details about the violence used in the Highlands became public knowledge – dispossessions, burnings, executions, and violations – the idea that Cumberland was defending the kingdom against savagery came under pressure. Tobias Smollett's song, *The Tears of Scotland* (1746?), invited its audience to sympathise with the sufferings of innocent Highland victims of British cruelty, including a dying mother and her helpless orphans. The success of Smollett's song, which was twice set to music, indicates the difficulty of sustaining an image of triumphant violence in a culture that was increasingly attuned to the appeal of sensibility, benevolence, and humanitarian compassion. While the plight of Cumberland's desolate victims could be shown in terms that attracted sympathy, Cumberland himself was in a sense isolated by his very elevation. As Steele had complained in

Sacrifice: Christian Heroes

the *Spectator*: 'a tall Hero alone in a Crowd of insignificant Figures about him, is of no Consequence to private Men'. To attain such consequence, Steele argued, 'great and illustrious Men' must be shown in circumstances in which we can empathise with them 'meerly as they were Men'.[9] For Steele and others who worked to soften the bellicose responses of the British public, empathy had a greater appeal than admiration for rank and martial prowess. The hero must be brought down to earth.

This recommendation was amply fulfilled by another hero who emerged from the Jacobite rebellion, one who would help to change the army's public image at a time when some of Cumberland's officers were patrolling in colonial postings overseas.[10] Colonel James Gardiner came to public attention as the victim of a shameful defeat: he was killed when the British army was overwhelmed by charging Highlanders at the Battle of Prestonpans (21 September 1745). Gardiner had fallen while urging on the remnant of his men, most of whom fled in the face of the Highlanders' onslaught. He had lain wounded upon the field of battle for two hours, during which time he was stripped by the rebels of his valuables, boots, and upper garments. He was then conveyed by an attendant to a nearby minister's house, where he died in bed. A report of Gardiner's death appeared in several newspapers a few weeks after the battle. At a time of fear and panic, when there was an urgent drive to recruit men to resist the rebels, and when Protestant unity was being emphasised in the face of a Catholic threat, the story of Gardiner's heroic, defensive stand – near his own home – had a particular resonance. 'Brave Col. Gardiner is killed; a Man that feared to Sin, but not to Fight' the *General Evening Post* announced. 'He died on his own Estate', and when the News came to his Lady, 'tis said, that she died immediately'.[11] The news of his widow's demise proved inaccurate, but she remained a significant presence in later retellings of the story.

Gardiner was a modern, polite, spiritually reformed Scottish Presbyterian, a good family man, an image of modern patriotism in striking contrast to the popular British idea of the savage Highland rebel, a more homely figure of patriotic sacrifice than an ancient, pagan king like Leonidas, and a figure quite unlike the victorious Duke of Cumberland. His death provided a way of deriving a moral victory from a disgraceful setback, and an occasion for urging retribution. The story featured in several contemporary sermons, which showed none of Shaftesbury's aversion to linking sacrifice with the prospect of an eternal reward.[12] The inspirational potential of Gardiner's death was developed most fully by the dissenter Phillip Doddridge, who was actively engaged in the military defence of the kingdom during the rebellion, helping to raise a volunteer

104 Part I: Developing Ideals

force with his patron the Earl of Halifax. As the victorious Jacobite army made its way south, Doddridge preached a sermon about Gardiner to the congregation of his Castle Hill meeting house in Northampton, which Gardiner had attended as a member of Lord Cadogan's regiment. In the Sermon, a call to arms, Gardiner is described as a Christian martyr: 'For what is *Martyrdom*, but voluntarily to meet Death, for the Honour of God, and the Testimony of a good Conscience?' While sympathising with Gardiner's widow, Doddridge finds death in battle a source of joy and a form of conquest, since the victims will reap 'the celestial and immortal Fruits, of that last great Victory'.[13]

When the sermon was published Doddridge was already thinking of writing a more extended account of Gardiner's life, a spiritual biography outlining a progress through sin, conversion, and pious advance towards heroic death. But this account did not appear until 1747, by which time Cumberland had defeated the rebels at Culloden and accounts of the grisly vengeance enacted upon them had already appeared in print, as had protests against them.[14] As Lord Kilkerran had noted in a letter to Doddridge, Cumberland's 'very name seems to have brought terror along with it'.[15] In this context, the Gardiner story acquired more than one function. For many readers, Gardiner's experience of conversion was undoubtedly the key part of the work – the vision of Christ on the cross that came to him one night while he was waiting to liaise with someone else's wife.[16] But this was not Doddridge's only concern. He also worked to counterbalance any sense that the post-Culloden pacification of the Highlands entailed unwarranted violence. Gardiner, no longer used as a call to arms, could provide a justification for the consequences of victory.

In the new account, we are never allowed to forget the brutality of the rebels, which now extends from the battlefield into Gardiner's home, and is seen to have affected even the process of writing. Doddridge attributes his delay in publication to the sad condition of Gardiner's widow, who had possession of Gardiner's papers, and to the disorder in which the rebels had left them. The physical cruelty of the rebels is said to be 'dreadfully legible on the Countenances of many who survived it'.[17] It is a threat to domestic order and to the intellectual order upon which civilisation rests.

The spiritual biography, in which Gardiner's frankly acknowledged sinfulness is followed by his conversion and life of piety, guarantees that the hero who died shared none of the coarseness and brutality often attributed to soldiers. Unlike Cumberland, who never married and had many mistresses, Gardiner becomes a loving husband and father.[18] Since he has an impeccable record of military service, his manliness and warrior credentials

Sacrifice: Christian Heroes

are not in question, and Doddridge is free to develop his spiritual side and show his 'tenderness' (99). This is ultimately a devotional work, not a record of heroic aggression or martial adventure. It is a book that Richardson's Clarissa, who shuns tales of 'battles fought and enemies overcome', could read with approval, since it emphasises the pursuit of truth and holiness in the face of difficulty. The vision that redeems him is of Christ 'pierced for my transgressions' (32). His life illustrates the escape from unbelief and sinfulness to Christian devotion, and the practical benefits that result. Achieving self-command allows Gardiner to become an effective commander of others, one who shows exemplary care for the physical and moral well-being of his men, and recommends preferments strictly on merit.

Doddridge, having established the reformed Gardiner's ideal character, goes on to supply a detailed account of his death, the climax of the whole, replete with last words reminiscent of Fulke Greville's account of Sir Philip Sidney's death (which appeared in the 1724 edition of Sidney's works). Historians have noted that as the printing of funeral sermons declined in the first part of the eighteenth century, a range of other devotional writings took on the role of teaching the Christian reader how to face death – including 'graveyard literature', elegies, and odes.[19] The account of Gardiner's death in the *Life* was probably influenced by Doddridge's own prose work, *The Rise and Progress of Religion in the Soul* (1745), which explains that in dying the Christian should 'exercise Patience under bodily Pains and Sorrows', 'bear an honourable Testimony to Religion', give 'a solemn Charge to surviving Friends, especially recommending Faith in Christ', 'keep the Promises of GOD in view', and 'commit the departing Spirit to GOD'.[20] Doddridge's Gardiner fulfils most of these requirements.

He is exonerated from responsibility for the defeat (having been overruled in some of his recommendations for the coming actions), but anticipates it, and declares his readiness to die 'for my Country's Safety' (179–180). Before the battle, he dismisses three of his servants with 'most affectionate Christian Advice', and 'solemn Charges relating to the Performance of their Duty and the Care of their Souls'. (183). He spends the remainder of his time before battle, Doddridge supposes, in 'devout Exercises of Soul' (184). He fights bravely, encouraging his troops, who nevertheless flee, and when he is fatally wounded, he advises his remaining servant to 'Take care of yourself'. Lying in his wounded state, Gardiner tells a Highland enemy '"You are fighting for an Earthly Crown, I am going to receive an Heavenly one"; or something to that effect' (187).

In dying, then, Gardiner is shown as an exemplary Christian; but more than this, he is also seen as a Christ-like martyr. Doddridge's friend James

106 Part I: Developing Ideals

Hervey, in his *Meditations among the Tombs* (1746), had criticised the elaborate funeral monuments designed to glorify contemporary military men; he contrasted the death of a noble warrior in battle with the death of Christ and emphasised Christ's willing embrace of humiliation and protracted suffering.[21] Doddridge attempts to distance his own soldier-hero from conventional military glory by showing the undignified distress Gardiner has to endure. The plundering and ignominy the dying hero suffers at enemy hands after his own troops have fled, and the attention he subsequently receives from his servant and a Minister, are carefully noted. He is honourably buried in his local church, attended by 'some Persons of Distinction' (191). The mixture of protracted suffering, violation, and desertion on the one hand, with faithful attendance and care on the other, give this death a Christ-like resonance. And just as Christ exerted an influence upon some of those who crucified him, some of the rebels spoke honourably of Gardiner and lamented his fall. Death has 'embalmed' Gardiner's virtues so they can be 'transmitted to the most remote Posterity' (193).

One aim of this idealising narrative is to justify the vengeance that has now fallen upon the rebels. This is made particularly clear in the appendices added to the narrative. Two poems composed by dissenting minister friends of Doddridge both celebrate Gardiner as someone whose death joined 'the *Hero* to the *Saint*', and present the subsequent punishment of the Highlanders as a divine reckoning (199, 215–217). But the final appendix shows that what is at issue is not only a matter of divine justice but also of civilisation. This tells the story of three Munro brothers who were all killed by the rebels. These are imagined, like Gardiner, as 'with Pleasure pouring forth their Lives in Blood' for their country.[22] But each of the brothers represents a civilising influence capable of transforming the Highlands from a state of idleness and superstition into a state of economic efficiency and Protestantism. Sir Robert Munro was involved in the sale of estates forfeited by rebels after the 1715 rising – helping to establish parishes and presbyteries in rebel countries where Protestantism had no footing. He was Lieutenant Colonel of a Highland regiment that gave distinguished service at the battle of Fontenoy, an early example of the successful assimilation of Highlanders into the British army. His brother Dr Munro, who died along with his servant and the Surgeon of the Regiment attempting to save Sir Robert when he was wounded at the battle of Falkirk, represents a range of improving activities. Devoted to both medicine and spiritual subjects, he spent time in the East Indies as an observer of native customs and of local commodities. The third brother, Captain George Munro of Culcairn, a veteran of the 1715 rebellion, was employed in disarming the rebels after Culloden, and in spite of his 'humanity' was assassinated 'on the Lord's Day' by one of them while passing by a wood in August 1746 (the assassin concealed himself behind trees and rocks, 257). Like the others, George Munro was a man of God (he was well acquainted with ecclesiastical history). Doddridge's narrative has become a reflection upon the violence associated with resistance to cultural and economic 'improvement' in an age of empire. It shows how honourable beacons of Protestant civilisation fall victim to the savage violence of those they would civilise.

The civilised response to death in battle (exemplified in the selfless concern of those who try to save the wounded Sir Robert) is contrasted with the shocking violence of the rebels: when Sir Robert's body is sought on the day after the battle, his face was 'so cut and mangled by these Savages [...] that it could scarce be known'. Readers are assured that Sir Robert received a Christian burial since the 'principal Persons' among the rebellious Macdonalds are said to ensure that the body is 'buried Honourably' in the Falkirk Churchyard (244). This detail assumes a particular importance in a work intended to show that these brothers have been translated to 'the Regions of endless Peace and triumphant Joy' (257). Readers are of course assumed to participate in the civilised response to death: the cowardly murder of Captain George Munro was 'not to be mentioned without the tenderest Sensibility' and deepest regret by 'all who loved the Publick' (258). The tone of the work as a whole is predominantly one of sympathetic concern and sorrow rather than vengeful anger. Sacrifice puts a compassionate Christian gloss upon the process by which the Highlanders are violently suppressed.

The Gardiner narrative was a milestone in the domestication of military heroism, and in sanctifying the national view of war. Gardiner was not like other recent British heroes: not a mighty aristocrat like Marlborough, nor a well-connected MP and rallying point for the Opposition like Admiral Vernon, nor a member of the royal family like the Duke of Cumberland. He was a country gentleman exalted primarily by his religious conversion and his service to the nation. He became famous not as the hero of a great victory, but as the victim of a defeat. In him, the traditional contrast between the professional soldier who fights for pay and the militia man who fights in defence of his own community was dissolved: Gardiner died close to his own home, seeking to repel a 'savage' invading force. Doddridge's account of Gardiner's life, published in 1747, was reprinted many times – and remained popular long after the appeal of Cumberland had declined. As Isabel Rivers notes, new editions appeared 'every few

108   Part I: Developing Ideals

years, and sometimes annually, up to the later nineteenth century'.[23] When Walter Scott included the death of Gardiner as an incident in the climax of his novel *Waverley*, first published in 1814, he took for granted that his readers would be familiar with the story. Doddridge's description of Gardiner's death – unarmed, disabled, in the care of friends, and distanced from the scene of battle, provided a precedent for the celebration of the hero's death that was to flourish in the second half of the century, and assumed an important place in the public memory through the work of history painters.

Death Without Closure

The ending of Gardiner's story, with a conventional funeral near his home, provided closure to the Christian tale of his suffering; Christian burial rites were usually considered a prerequisite for admission to heaven. The element of closure, however it is imagined, is an integral part of the process of sacrifice because, as Halbertal explains, sacrifice is 'a form of exchange'. The sacrifice has to be acceptable, to God and to public opinion, which in practice means that it must be capable of inspiring reverence and satisfaction, and so of putting the public's mind at rest. A closer look at the grisly fate of many who died in war would make such reverence impossible – which is why William Collins reimagines the fate of war victims in some of his Odes. Concern about these aspects of war is deeply embedded in Western culture, as the epic poetry of Greece and Rome shows. In the *Iliad*, for example, the respectful treatment and the grotesque violation of war dead are famously brought together in a sequence which describes Achilles's elaborate funeral arrangements for his friend Patroclus and his desecration of Hector's corpse (by dragging it around the walls of Troy). The Elysian fields of classical mythology, in which heroes live a happy afterlife, are only reached by an exalted few. In Homer and Virgil, the underworld is haunted by the unquiet ghosts of those whose bodies have not received a proper burial.

At a time of growing public concern about the treatment of the sick and wounded in the army and navy, and about the treatment of prisoners of war, the decision to send British troops to fight in America in the 1750s had the effect of increasing public concern about the treatment of those who died in battle. War in America would of course be directed against the traditional enemy, Roman Catholic France, but it also would entail conflict with Native Americans, who were regarded as savages and had a reputation for scalping and mutilating the dead. The Native Americans'

Sacrifice: Christian Heroes 109

treatment of the dead became a significant index of their savagery and helped to sustain belief in the moral superiority of civilised Europeans. But this belief was always under pressure. The British, like the French, fought with Native American allies. As the conflict developed British readers encountered many horrific reports of Native Americans scalping British colonists, including women and children – actions that were bitterly condemned as evidence of savagery, and that were said to be encouraged and even practiced by the French. But readers also encountered reports of the bounties offered by British colonial governments for the scalps of Native American men, women, and children, and of the work of Native American allies in scalping French soldiers.[24]

Concern about the treatment of the dead was stimulated in a spectacular way by one of the earliest setbacks of the campaign in North America, which occurred even before war with France had been officially declared – the resounding defeat of General Braddock's forces on an expedition to Fort Duquesne, in the summer of 1755. The defeat did not arise from a confrontation between two armies on a battlefield: instead, British and colonial regular soldiers with militia companies were surprised in woods by French and Indian forces.[25] In the confusion, British forces apparently came under fire from their own side. Their losses were very high, especially among the officers (Braddock himself was fatally wounded and died not long after the battle). Losses on the other side, mostly native Americans, were comparatively light. A hasty retreat meant that many British casualties, including officers, were left unburied where they fell.

Comparisons were inevitably made between Braddock's defeat and the defeat at Prestonpans (Braddock's company included troops from the 44th regiment that had fought with Colonel Gardiner at Prestonpans, as well as from the 48th regiment that had fought against the Jacobites at Falkirk Muir and Culloden). Reflections were made on the 'cowardice' of the troops on both occasions, and the fate of Gardiner was remembered.[26] But whereas Gardiner's story had become known primarily through Doddridge's idealising account, Braddock's story reached the public through a range of channels representing conflicting views and was widely debated. Unlike Gardiner, Braddock was the primary commander of the defeated troops, and bore immediate responsibility for the calamity. He was criticised as incompetent, as lacking experience in an unfamiliar kind of warfare, unwilling to take advice, and haughty towards Native Americans (Braddock's attempts to find allies among Indians were largely unsuccessful).[27]

In writings about this incident, readers were repeatedly reminded that the abandoned dead, including some of high rank, lay exposed in an alien and untamed landscape. Braddock had in fact been hastily buried in an unmarked grave, but this was not widely reported. Those who wrote about the deaths usually made no attempt to evoke imaginary funerary rites of the kind Collins had described for the dead soldiers in his Odes. Instead, they emphasised the victims' horrible vulnerability and the possibility that they had suffered some gruesome mutilation. Some writers attempted to see the dead as sacrificial victims, but it was not easy to idealise them in this way, since their condition was manifestly inglorious and offered no closure.

Their situation was unlike that of the unfortunate war-dead who appear in some well-known earlier writings. Patriot poets had made use of the unquiet ghosts of the dead to call for vengeance when urging war against Spain (for example, James Thomson in *Britannia*, 1729; and Richard Glover in *Admiral Hosier's Ghost*, 1740). But in these cases, the 'ghosts' were unquiet because they had died of disease while impatient for action, not because they remained unburied. Their deaths could therefore be adequately revenged and requited by military action. But failure to bury the dead was the neglect of a fundamental Christian duty, capable of inspiring deep disgust in an age of increasing refinement, when the use of professional undertakers and embalming was on the rise. As David Houlbrooke reminds us, the prolonged exposure of a corpse was a mark of ignominy.[28]

Writers used this unhappy situation to support their assumptions about the campaign. When James Oglethorpe described the bodies he imagined their mutilation, but was careful to avoid implicating either the French or the Native Americans; instead, he described the victims being 'torn by Wolves, or eaten up by Bears'. Oglethorpe opposed the Ohio expedition, was against war with France, and admired Native Americans. For him, moral responsibility for this horror lay with the clamour of the British public for war in America which, he insisted, was being whipped up by the press merely on behalf of projectors who had invested in grants of land in the Ohio region.[29]

But unlike Oglethorpe, most who mentioned the bodies were keen to imagine Indian and French atrocities. By treating the dead as victims of an atrocity rather than simply of a defeat, they could deflect blame and suggest a moral distinction between the British forces and their enemies. This allowed Protestant divines to insist on the sinfulness of their own congregations while assuming the moral high ground in relation to the enemy and calling for reprisals. Samuel Davies, for example, leader of the Virginia Presbyterians, in a sermon that was twice reprinted in Britain, imagined the victims 'rolling in their own blood' and scalped by 'merciless Indians'. He tried to present them in sacrificial terms, seeing this grim outcome as a form of atonement and substitution ('they suffer for our sins'). But he also insisted that the only acceptable sacrifice was that of the Lamb of God, and he used the deaths primarily in order to justify a call for revenge.[30] William Smith, in a sermon first addressed to troops about to set out on an expedition against Fort Dusquesne in 1757, and published more than once in London, invited his audience to imagine themselves treading 'gently' among the 'uncoffin'd bones' and to weep over the scattered ashes of the dead as this would give vigour and ardour to their fight against 'Popish Perfidy, French Tyranny, and Savage Barbarity, leagued in triple combination'. Smith was sure the Lord God of Justice would help them to 'extirpate perfidy and cruelty from the earth'.[31]

Poets sometimes presented the violated dead as objects of pathos, which helped to illustrate the difference between the sensitive 'civilized' consciousness and the unfeeling savagery of the enemy. But descriptions of the plight of the unburied dead inevitably left the impression that military revenge would not in itself produce the closure required by this outrage. There was unfinished business here; a duty to take possession of the territory so that the victims could be properly buried. This is made explicit in a poem about Braddock that appeared in *Gentleman's Magazine*, where the poet (punning on 'Braddock' and 'broad oak') imagined the discovery of the general's remains in these terms:

> Beneath some Indian shrub, if chance you spy
> The brave remains of murdered Braddock lie [...]
> Possess the hero's bones of hostile ground.
> And plant the English oak that gave his name[32]

At a time when Britain still saw itself as an empire of the seas rather than as empire of territorial conquest, this unfinished business could make possession of alien territory seem a moral imperative, a matter of simple human decency, as well as of material improvement. Taking care of the victim's body is explicitly identified with transforming the hostile landscape: both actions become part of the same improving process. The English oak, traditionally associated with the Navy, suggests a resurgence of British power rooted in an act of piety and cultivation.

The fate of Braddock's company haunted magazine poems about later defeats (of Abercrombie at Tricoderoga, of Howe at Carillon), about Indian massacres of women and children which 'Strew'd human bones where golden harvests stood', and even about British victory (Amherst at Montreal).[33] While the references to Braddock were used to encourage support for the war, they also kept the unburied dead in the public memory.

112   Part I: Developing Ideals

When the British finally took Fort Duquesne in November 1758, the unfinished business was soon addressed. A detachment which included soldiers, rangers, and Indians was sent from the Fort to the site of Braddock's defeat in order to bury the remains of his company. As recounted in John Galt's *Life of West*, the brother of the painter Benjamin West was in the search party that found the bones; so was Major Sir Peter Halket, whose father and brother were slain in the battle. The remains of Halket's father and brother were found lying across each other and, having been recognised by a grief-stricken Sir Peter, were buried with customary honours. Galt's account evokes fears of 'atrocious rites', but includes 'naked and simple Indians' helping to bury the dead, indicative of civilising British influence.[34] We know from later accounts that not all the dead were buried at this time, since bones remained visible at the site years later.[35] Nevertheless, the French failure to bury the dead fed into Anglo-American propaganda. It helped to justify placing the French in the same category as the 'savage' Native American.

The Death of Wolfe

In contrast to the deaths of Braddock and his men, the death of James Wolfe during his conquest of Quebec lent itself readily to the idea of heroic sacrifice. Wolfe was not the victim of a defeat for which compensation was needed; instead, the death worked to counterbalance the violence inflicted by Wolfe's forces upon their enemies. Wolfe had served in Scotland under Cumberland during the Jacobite rebellion and had been present at the battle of Culloden. He was one a group of officers who had taken up colonial postings in the wake of that event and who, as Geoffrey Plank notes, 'shared a belief that the army could operate as an agent for reform in uncivilised, rebellious, or contested lands'.[36] We now know much more about the practice of Wolfe and other British army officers in North America than contemporary British readers did. Wolfe had a conflicted view of scalping fairly typical of his time – he regarded it as an inhuman practice *and* as a military necessity; like other British officers in North America, he paid bounties for scalps. During his campaign to take Quebec, he often burnt villages and sometimes took women and children as hostages. The villagers who paid the price of war were not incidental victims of a dynastic power-game (as the Bavarian villagers in Addison's *The Campaign* had been) but foreigners whose very presence on the land was being discussed in terms of 'extirpation'.[37] Although much of this activity was not reported as news, some of it was. Here is part of a report of an officer engaged in

Sacrifice: Christian Heroes 113

the siege of Quebec, published in Britain shortly before news of Wolfe's victory was announced:

> We have been so successful as scarce to leave a house in the place that is not battered down by our guns or burnt to ashes by our mortars [...] I am most sure we shall take the place; if not, all France can't save them from ruin and destruction; for we shall burn their houses, destroy their corn, and eat their cattle, which are brought into camp by our parties, 3 or 400 at a time, and killed for the use of the English army. [...] the houses in the lower parts of the town are almost reduced to ashes, and near 300 houses in the upper town demolished, with the Cathedral and the magazine there blown up.

Although most of the people had vacated the city, some had been taken prisoner and were said to be used as human shields:

> it was given out, that the prisoners taken ashore, men, women and children were put on board two large ships, and were put in the first of the Range, that if any more rafts came down they would first meet with them.[38]

In contrast to such events, the battle in which Quebec was finally captured could be seen as an honourable contest between two modern armies on an open field (a small British force against a more numerous French one). It proved an ideal setting for the creation of a national hero. There would be no difficulty in finding closure in Wolfe's death: his body was repatriated, and he was buried at Greenwich in a private funeral.

Soon after news of Wolfe's death arrived in Britain, it was reported that George II proposed to fund a monument to him in Westminster Abbey. A few weeks later, the Prime Minister William Pitt in the House of Commons called for a national monument. But the monument that emerged from this process, sculpted by Joseph Wilton, was not unveiled until more than a dozen years had passed, in 1772[39]. Wilton had made two portraits of Wolfe around 1760, which showed him as an ancient Roman; but a series of paintings that helped the public to visualise Wolfe's death in modern terms did not begin to appear until 1763. In the meantime, a key contributor to the shaping of Wolfe's public image as hero was the Scottish physician, James Pringle. Pringle's *Life of General James Wolfe* (dated 1760, but reviewed by December 1759) has sometimes been dismissed by modern historians, partly on account of Pringle's attempt to endow his narrative with an elevated biblical resonance (an attempt which also deterred early reviewers).[40] But Pringle's account of Wolfe is symptomatic of wider cultural changes and, as the first biographical outline to appear at a time when the public was consumed with Wolfe's victory and death, it set a precedent that proved influential.

114   Part I: Developing Ideals

Pringle was representative of the Scottish Enlightenment's practical contribution to the reformation of British culture. Having trained as a physician in Leiden, he had become Professor of Pneumatics and Moral Philosophy at the University of Edinburgh in the 1730s, at a time when the influence of Frances Hutcheson's work on the moral sense and benevolence was being felt across Scottish intellectual life (when Pringle left Edinburgh to seek a career in the army his chair was offered to Hutcheson, who declined it). Pringle subsequently rose to become physician-general of the army under Cumberland and had played a major role in helping to improve the general welfare of troops and the treatment of the sick and wounded in war. He knew Cumberland well, had served as his personal physician and, like Wolfe, had been present at the Battle of Culloden. By the time of Wolfe's death, Cumberland was already deeply unpopular. After a series of military defeats, he had fallen out of favour with his father and retired from public life. Pringle's life of Wolfe effectively dissociates the hero of Quebec and his operations from the discredited Cumberland, making no mention of Wolfe's own presence at the Battle of Culloden. The kind of military ruthlessness that led Cumberland to be dubbed 'the Butcher' was to be completely overshadowed in Pringle's account of Wolfe by the idea of virtuous Christian self-sacrifice of the kind celebrated in Gardiner. Like Doddridge, Pringle treats his hero within a Christian framework, endows him with an exemplary benevolence and places emphasis less on fighting, more on the manner of Wolfe's death, how he faces it, and the care he receives.

From the outset, Pringle attributes the victory at Quebec to God and his Providential favour towards the British nation. The elevated, often declamatory rhetoric he employed, which has many echoes of biblical prophecy, was clearly intended to keep the sublime religious and moral significance of Wolfe's achievement in mind. Like Gardiner, Wolfe is celebrated as a pattern of Christian virtue, whose courage is inspired by his sense of religion. He embodies an 'Extensive Spirit of Benevolence [...] to promote the universal Good of Mankind'.[41] He is a man who has risen by merit, a commander loved by his men, a loving son who leaves behind a heartbroken fiancé. The *Life* has clearly been written in the light of traditional moral criticisms of martial ambition and of the dazzling pomp associated with military triumphs – criticisms that had recently assumed new form in novels by Fielding, Richardson, and Smollett. Pringle's Wolfe is the anti-type of ambitious commanders who build their reputations brutally upon the killing of others. He is, we are assured, without personal ambition, and has no avarice 'or any other Vice' (19). Although at Minden

Wolfe overthrew the Enemy 'with great Slaughter' (8), this was not the work of personal ambition or aggressive passion, but of the 'Regularity and Exactness of Discipline' (23) he had infused into his men. In Pringle's Wolfe, careful professionalism is combined with the feminine attributes of modesty and gentleness (14). There were alternative accounts of Wolfe's death in circulation, including one that had him smiling with pleasure on hearing the news of his victory.[42] And there were of course heroic precedents for death in victory, including the death of Epaminondas, the ancient Theban, who had died after hearing news of his defeat of Sparta at Mantinea, and who resisted the sorrowful responses of his friends. Pringle notes the parallel with Epaminondas, but in his account of Wolfe's death there is neither joy nor heroic defiance. Instead, pathos predominates: the mighty commander who has captured a huge territory for Britain is shown with the vulnerability and passivity of a Christian martyr as, with head 'drooping' or 'gently reclining', he is subject to the 'mournful ministry of a few soldiers'. On hearing news of his victory, he resigns his mortal life to God and inspires a tribute of tears.

In the wider public response to Wolfe's death, the process of commemoration itself became part of what was celebrated, as Britain became preoccupied with its own acts of collective mourning and remembering. The most celebrated visual representations of Wolfe's death focus not on the battle itself, nor on the moment of his 'fall', but on the reassuringly sympathetic attention he received in dying. In the case of Wolfe, this pattern was established in the earliest painting of the event, by George Romney, and repeated in the paintings by Edward Penny (1764), Benjamin West (1772), and James Barry (1776), and in the memorial to Wolfe sculpted by Joseph Wilton (1772). All show Wolfe dying away from the action of the battle, attended by others. The commander's pose puts him on a lower level than his subordinates, who may lean over him. Penny, who followed Romney, included a figure who is sometimes identified as a surgeon's assistant, an apt representative of the 'civilized' approach to death (Figure 3).

Benjamin West's famous painting of *The Death of Wolfe* was exhibited in 1772 at the newly formed Royal Academy, an institution committed to promoting public history painting. West's expanded group includes a doctor and, among others, a Native American warrior, whose muscular presence suggests the distance between an older tradition of warrior prowess, and the modern, slightly feminised British warrior. The Native American's inclusion within the group of soldiers, and his thoughtful attitude, testifies to the civilising influence of the British presence in North America. The Christian precedents of Wolfe's death are clearly emphasised.

Figure 3   William Woollett, engraved after Benjamin West, *The Death of General Wolfe*, 1770 (1776) [© Ivy Close Images / Alamy]

As Robert C. Alberts explains, West 'placed Wolfe in the centre group, stretched out on the ground as in a seventeenth-century Pieta, his body in the pose of any traditional Lamentation or Deposition of Christ'.[43] The pose suggests an element of atonement in Wolfe's death.

When West created companion pieces for the picture, to hang in the Warm Room of Buckingham House, he chose to depict *The Death of Chevalier Bayard* (1772) and *The Death of Epaminondas* (1773). Bayard, like Gardiner, is an example of a Christian triumph in defeat: the Chevalier, mortally wounded and left behind by his own troops, holds his sword up like a crucifix while he is greeted respectfully by his enemies. As a set, the paintings all privilege the manner of dying over the business of fighting. To the Earl of Grosvenor West proposed a different companion piece for his *Death of Wolfe*, a picture of the 'discovery of the bones of Braddock's men'. As described by Galt, the scene would include 'the gloom of the vast forest, the naked and simple Indians supporting the skeletons, the grief of the son [Halket] on recognising the relics of his father, the subdued melancholy of the spectators and the picturesque garb of the Pennsylvanian sharpshooters'. The idea was rejected by Grosvenor on the grounds that the subject had not been 'recorded by any historian'.[44] But West clearly saw an imaginative connection between this incident and his painting of the death of Wolfe. The subject must inevitably have evoked the sorry beginning of the British campaign in America, in terms that showed the eventual victorious finishing of a notoriously unfinished business. It would have allowed us to see the occupation of an alien territory as the fulfilment of a Christian obligation to the dead, as an act of piety that, since it involved the co-operation of Native Americans, demonstrated emphatically the triumph of Christian civilisation over savagery. The dead, now in the care of sympathetic guardians, could finally be seen as acceptable sacrifices, rather than as objects of shame. And the burial could confer a sacred connection with the land itself. The anthropologist Robert Pogue Harrison observes that 'the surest way to take possession of a place and secure it as one's own is to bury one's dead in it'.[45]

The violent aftermath of Culloden was a foretaste of the conflicts that would accompany attempts to impose British 'civilization' and power upon territories inhabited by peoples who were often seen as, at best, an inconvenience, or as savages. The sometimes-lurid accounts of North American expulsions, unfortunate severities, and terrible destructions appearing both before and after Wolfe's death, made familiar reading for Britons in the eighteenth century. To represent Wolfe as a frail, harmless, ebbing, martyr-like figure was, like the image of Colonel Gardiner established by Doddridge, an attempt to counterbalance the violence that fell upon the victims, both armed and unarmed, of British power, and to suggest the triumph of sympathy over aggression. To see the hero's death in this way no doubt made it easier for the British public to keep reading.

Notes

1 Peter Womak, *Improvement and Romance: Constructing the Myth of the Highlands* (London: Palgrave, 1988).
2 Brendan Simms, *Three Victories and a Defeat* (London: Penguin, 2007), 334.
3 Murray Pittock, *The Myth of the Jacobite Clans* (Edinburgh: Edinburgh University Press, 2009).
4 Thomas Keymer, 'Civil Rage: Poetry and War in the 1740s', *Eighteenth-Century Life*, 44: 3 (2020), 8–29.
5 Danielle Thom, '"William, the Princely Youth": The Duke of Cumberland and Anti-Jacobite Visual Strategy, 1745–46', *Visual Culture in Britain*, 16:3 (2015), 249–266, 252.

Part I: Developing Ideals

6 *The Fourth Ode of the Fourth Book of Horace Imitated and Applied to His Royal Highness the Duke of Cumberland* (London, 1746), 5; *An Ode Sacred to the Victorious Return of his Royal Highness the Duke of Cumberland from Scotland* (London, 1746), 5; George Masters, *A Poem Humbly Inscrib'd to His Royal Highness The Duke of Cumberland on His Defeat of the Rebels at Culloden, April 16th 1746* (London, 1747), 6; *The Battle of Culloden: A Poem on the Late Victory* (London, 1746).

7 Danielle Thom, 250.

8 W. A. Speck, *The Butcher: The Duke of Cumberland and the Suppression of the 45* (Caernarfon: Welsh Academic Press, 1995), 162.

9 *The Tatler* 209 (10 August 1710), 3: 107.

10 Geoffrey Plank, *Rebellion and Savagery : The Jacobite Rising of 1745 and the British Empire* (Philadelphia: University of Pennsylvania Press, 2006), 5–7.

11 *General Evening Post, October 5 to October 8, 1745*, 1.

12 E.g. W. Weston, *Three Sermons Preached before the University of Cambridge at Saint Mary's Church During the Progress of the Rebellion* (Cambridge, 1746?).

13 Philip Doddridge, *The Christian Warrior Animated and Crowned: A Sermon Occasioned by the Heroick Death of the Honourable Col James Gardiner* (London, 1746), 30, 23.

14 *The Tears of Scotland* (Edinburgh?, 1746?); *The Groans of Scotland* (London, 1746); Michael Hughes, *A Plain Narrative and Authentic Journal of the Late Rebellion, begun in 1745*, 2nd edn. (London, 1747), 52, 54–55; John Marchant, *The History of the Late Rebellion in Great Britain* (London, 1747), 369; *London Gazette*, 1746; John Anderson, *The Book of the Chronicles of His Royal Highness William Duke of Cumberland* (Edinburgh, 1746), 23.

15 5 February 174[5/]6, Geoffrey F. Nuttall, ed., *Calendar of the Correspondence of Philip Doddridge DD (1702–1751)* (London: Her Majesty's Stationary Office 1979), 288.

16 Isabel Rivers, *Reason, Grace ad Sentiment, vol 1 A Study of the Language of Religion and Ethics in England, 160–1780* (Cambridge: Cambridge University Press, 1991), 199–203.

17 Philip Doddridge, *Some Remarkable Passages in the Life of the Hon. Colonel James Gardiner* (Edinburgh, 1747), 2, 189.

18 This is how it is seen by Christopher D. Johnson, in 'Artful Instruction: Philip Doddridge's *Life of Colonel James Gardiner'*, *Beyond Sense and Sensibility: Literature, Thought & Culture 1650–1850*, ed. Peggy Thompson (Lewisburg: Bucknell University Press, 2015), 63–77.

19 E.g. Ralph Houlbrooke, *Death, Religion and the Family in England* (Oxford: Oxford University Press, 1998), 325; Eric Parisot, 'Piety, Poetry, and the Funeral Sermon: Reading Graveyard Poetry in the Eighteenth Century', *English Studies*, 92: 2 (2011), 174–192.

20 Philip Doddridge, *The Rise and Progress of the Religion of the Soul* (London, 1745), 297.

21 James Hervey, *Meditations among the Tombs* (London, 1746), 40–41.

22 The quotation comes from the 'Dedication' (which has no page numbers).

Sacrifice: Christian Heroes 119

23 Isabel Rivers, *Vanity Fair and the Celestial City: Dissenting, Methodist, and Evangelical Literary Culture in England, 1720–1800* (Oxford: Oxford University Press, 2018), 325–326.

24 See *The Scots Magazine*, September 1755, 447, 454; October 1755, 496–498; *Universal Magazine*, January 1756, 38; *Newcastle General Magazine*, September 1757, 536. See also Alan McNairn, *Behold the Hero: General Wolfe and the Arts in the Eighteenth Century* (Liverpool: Liverpool University Press, 1997), 169.

25 David Dixon, *Never Come to Peace Again: Pontiac's Uprising and the Fate of the British Empire in North America* (Norman: University of Oklahoma Press, 2005), 16.

26 For example, *Gentleman's Magazine*, XXV, 1755, 380; *Whitehall Evening Post*, August 30, 1755, 315; *Public Advertiser*, August 27, 1755. See also N. Darnell Davis, 'British Newspaper Reports of Braddock's Defeat', *The Pennsylvania Magazine of History and Biography*, (23) 1899, 310–328.

27 Paul E. Kopperman, *Braddock at the Monongahela* (Pittsburgh, PA: University of Pittsburgh Press, 1973).

28 *Death, Religion and the Family*, 331.

29 James Oglethorpe, *The Naked Truth*, No. 1, Fifth Edition (London, 1755), 30.

30 Samuel Davies, *Two Discourses, Occasioned by the Severe Drought in Sundry Parts of the Country; and the Defeat of General Braddock* (Glasgow, 1756), 7.

31 William Smith, *Discourses on Several Public Occasions during the War in America* (London, 1759), 118 121–122.

32 *Gentleman's Magazine*, XXV (August, 1755), 383.

33 'On the defeat at Triconderoga, or Carilon, by a Lady in America', *The Edinburgh Magazine*, 3 Feb (1759), 77; 'Horace, Book I, Ode IV, Paraphrased', Samuel Rogers, *Poems on Several Occasions* (London, 1764), 115; *The Patriot Muse by an American Gentleman* (London, 1764), 13, 58; 'On the Taking of Montreal by General Amherst', *Newcastle General Magazine*, October 1760, 524–525.

34 John Galt, *The Life, Studies, and Works of Benjamin West, Esq* (London, 1820), 66–67.

35 Thomas A. Chambers, *Memories of War: Visiting Battlegrounds and Bonefields in the Early American Republic* (Ithaca, NY: Cornell University Press, 2012) 21–24.

36 Geoffrey Plank, *Rebellion and Savagery*, 5. 7.

37 Plank, 162.

38 'Extract of a Letter from an Officer, dated K. George's Battery at Point Levee, near Quebec, Aug 13', *London Chronicle*, October 13–16, 1759.

39 Joan Coutu and John McAleer, '"The Immortal Wolfe"? Monuments, Memory, and the Battle of Quebec', in *Remembering 1759: the conquest of Canada on historical memory*, ed. Phillip Buckner and John G Reid (Toronto: University of Toronto Press, 2012), 29–57, 32–33; Joan Coutu, *Persuasion and Propaganda: Monuments and the Eighteenth-Century British Empire* (Montreal: McGill-Queens University Press, 2006), 103–146. Douglas Fordham, 'Scalping: Social Rites at Westminster Abbey', Tim Barringer, Geoff Quilley, Douglas

120 Part I: Developing Ideals

Fordham, eds., *Art and the British Empire* (Manchester: Manchester University Press, 2007), 99–119, 102–106. Nicholas Rogers, 'Brave Wolfe: The Making of a Hero', in *A New Imperial History, Culture, Identity and Modernity in Britain and the Empire 1660–1840*, ed. Kathleen Wilson (Cambridge: Cambridge University Press, 2004), 239–259, 253–255; David Solkin, *Painting for Money: Visual Arts and the Public Sphere in Eighteenth-century England* (New Haven: Yale University Press, 1993), 209–210.

40 A review in the *London Magazine*, 28, (December, 1759), 688, thought it 'fitted to a preachment rather than an oration'; Tobias Smollett in *The British Magazine* thought it a 'very florid (not to call it fustian) eulogium', I, February, 1760, 96.

41 James Pringle, *The Life of General James Wolfe, Conqueror of Canada* (London, 1760), 5.

42 *Gentleman's Magazine*, 29 (1759), 556.

43 Robert C. Alberts, *Benjamin West: A Biography* (Boston, Houghton Mifflin, 1978), 105.

44 John Galt, *Benjamin West*, 67, 68.

45 Robert Pogue Harrison, *The Dominion of the Dead* (Chicago: University Press, 2003), 24.

PART II

Developing Questions

The advocacy of war entails tacit or explicit endorsement of the national view, and the presentation of figures who can legitimize the national war effort, from heroes on the battlefield to humbler counterparts like Captain Sentry of the Spectator Club. Much of the advocacy we considered in Part I emerged from contexts of official or party-political patronage, or in the case of Doddridge's Gardiner, from a specifically religious context. I now turn to forms of writing published without patronage, that distance themselves from some of the traditional assumptions normally invoked to justify war. The novel, as it emerged in the wake of Samuel Richardson's *Pamela*, and the philosophy of the Scottish Enlightenment, as it appeared in the work of David Hume and Adam Smith, were distinctive and influential developments in eighteenth-century writing, and both made significant contributions to eighteenth-century views of war. They are often less concerned with advocacy than with questioning the damaging influence of war upon society.

CHAPTER 5

War and the 'Elevation' of the Novel

The eighteenth-century novel became a form that focused more readily on the dire social consequences of war than on its national glories. Maximilian Novak, observing that eighteenth-century novelists produced nothing like Scott's *Waverley* (1814), let alone Tolstoy's *War and Peace* (1867), cites in explanation 'an anti-heroic impulse' that was 'dominant among writers during a large part of the century'.[1] But what is 'dominant' in any complex culture varies according to context, and is determined in part by the requirements and expectations of particular audiences. Samuel Johnson, whom Novak cites for 'typical' evidence of anti-heroic opinion, began his professional writing career producing biographies of British naval heroes for *The Gentleman's Magazine*.[2] Poems celebrating the nation's war heroes and victories continued to appear throughout the century, while the theatre, frequented by army and navy men, often resounded with pro-war rhetoric and heroic battle scenes.[3] A number of novelists who presented critical views of war in their novels actively contributed to and benefitted from the nation's war-making in other areas of their work: the financial opportunities associated with support for war were too important to ignore. But whatever their economic and professional relationship to war might be, novelists with literary ambitions rarely encouraged support for ongoing wars in their novels – at least not until the era of the French Revolution. Henry Fielding's disruption of the chronology of *Tom Jones*, in order to allow his hero to volunteer against the Jacobite rebellion of 1745, is an exception that helps to define the rule.[4] The national view of war is generally excluded, while the moral view predominates, the latter often taking a distinctly anti-heroic form.

The explanation for this tendency may reside less in a general anti-heroic 'impulse' than in the wider conditions that influenced simultaneously both attitudes to novels and to war. Some of the factors evoked by modern literary and cultural historians to explain the emergence of new forms of prose fiction in the eighteenth century also help to account for the incidence of anti-heroic discourse in the period. These factors include the challenge to 'received authorities and a priori traditions' by an empiricist epistemology; the post-Reformation elevation of individual experience; the typographical revolution which gave readers an opportunity to compare different accounts of the same event; the decline of literary patronage by the nobility and the court; and the increasing sway of the middling sort, including many women, in the growing market for books.[5] All of these developments tended to challenge the status of heroic visions of warfare. They ensured that readers who did not go to war might have potential access to a plethora of first-hand, matter-of-fact reports of modern combat appearing in newspapers, military journals, secular histories, and other publications, sometimes written by comparatively obscure or even unnamed participants. The gulf between what readers found in such reports and the accounts of war found in epics and prose romances was only too obvious. The proliferation of first-hand information about recent and ongoing conflicts inevitably worked to generate criticism of war and war-makers. A variety of war-related issues became subjects of vigorous debate and frequent censure, including the patronage system that governed promotions, the bureaucracy responsible for the administration of pay and pensions, and the terrible conditions endured by men on active service.

Anti-heroic discourse, which gathered momentum in the later seventeenth century, condemned the glorification of war as both false and morally inappropriate. Moral and educational writings criticised the martial ethos of classical epics or deplored the praising of brutal commanders in historical works.[6] The emergence of mock-heroic poetry indicated a growing awareness of the distance between the values of the ancients and of the modern world.[7] Cervantes' ironical treatment of chivalric idealism in *Don Quixote* became highly influential.[8] The status of the French heroic prose romances (by de Scudéry, D'Urfé, and La Calprenède) that had been fashionable in the seventeenth century, and of their English imitators (such as Roger Boyle's *Parthenissa* or John Barclay's *Argenis*), inevitably suffered more than the status of classical epics.[9] As the publication of Pope's translations of Homer showed, the classics had influential champions and could claim an aesthetic value that transcended historical shifts in manners. But 'Romance' became a by-word for fanciful exaggeration. The treatment of martial heroism in romances – the astounding feats of arms they often described – contributed to their reputation for hyperbole and irresponsible falsehood.

There were incentives, therefore, for writers of prose fiction to distance themselves from heroic romances and the fanciful descriptions of war they contained. However, more empirical approaches to war also entailed problems. The narrative technique developed by Daniel Defoe in his prose fictions of the 1720s might seem well adapted to deal with the moral problems associated with war: these fictions are presented as memoirs grounded exclusively in individual experience, with retrospective moral judgements upon the errors of the past. As Michael Warner points out, this approach allows Defoe's narrators to 'indulge what they censure, repeat what they proscribe'.[10] But when Defoe turns to war, the problems of conscience arising from a direct involvement in battle violence cannot be localised in the individual. The writer is no longer dealing with the personal errors and sins of a fallible castaway, rogue, or harlot, but with a group practice of a kind that is routinely endorsed by monarchs and officially celebrated. As well shall see, the experiential authenticity claimed by such novels does not necessarily make the representation of war more acceptable than the fantasy of heroic romance, but can make it problematic in a different way.

What Warner and others see as the programmatic 'elevation' of the novel by Samuel Richardson and Henry Fielding in the 1740s involved, among other things, a general avoidance of the battlefield, and a preference for the moral view of war, even though they were writing at a time when public interest in war was at a height and they profited from this interest in other areas of their work. In the preface to *Joseph Andrews* (1742) Fielding compares his own novel to Fénelon's modern prose 'epic' *Telemachus* – in which war is repeatedly denounced – while dismissing a range of French romances ('Clelia, Cleopatra, Astraea, Cassandra, the Grand Cyrus') all of which contain heroic battle scenes. *Joseph Andrews* is not without scenes of violence, but these are in a mock-heroic mode. Richardson's *Clarissa* (1748) sets itself clearly against the martial ethos of heroic romance, as the virtuous heroine disdains to read 'subjects of heroism [...] battles fought and enemies overcome, 4 or 500 hundred by the prowess of one single hero' (209).[11] These writers' younger contemporary, Tobias Smollett, who had been a surgeon's apprentice on a British warship, did describe war directly in some of his fiction, but in a decidedly unheroic mode. These novelists began to evoke war as a pervasive and disruptive influence within society – something that permeated cultural practices, or that exerted a malign influence through the career opportunities and financial dependencies it created, and that threatened the security and happiness of families and individuals caught up in its demands. In a period when many voices were raised against the practice of reading novels, the treatment of war became an issue that helped to establish the moral and critical respectability of the form.

126   Part II: Developing Questions

The Regrettable Necessities of War: Daniel Defoe

The novels of Defoe illustrate the kind of problems that later novelists tend to avoid in their fiction. While Defoe treats warfare quite directly in some of his fictions, his preference for adventuring heroes tends to keep the national view of war at bay, while the moral view never quite comes into steady focus. Defoe had some personal experience of war since, as a Dissenter, he had joined the Duke of Monmouth's rebellion in 1685 and fought at the battle of Sedgemoor. In his multifaceted career as a writer, he moved between writing directed to political issues, in which he sometimes expressed a national view of war, and writing devoted to literary and moral issues, in which he sometimes adopted a moral view. He praised the art of war in his *Essay on Projects* (1697), and celebrated Marlborough's victory at Blenheim in a poem, *The Double Welcome* (1705).[12] But he also expressed concern for the suffering caused by warfare, and in his *Essay on Literature* he adopted a conventional anti-heroic stance, complaining of the way 'Scoundrels are made Heroes' in the ancient literature.[13]

His approach to war in his novels looks unflinchingly direct in its treatment of violence, at least when compared with the work of later writers. *Memoirs of a Cavalier* (1720) and *Colonel Jack* (1722), his novels that treat war most closely, have adventuring soldier-heroes who engage personally in the violent actualities of warfare; in these works, brutality is sometimes treated with a casualness that later novelists would avoid. While they are closely focused upon individual experience, and include some reflection upon the moral horrors of war, in practice such reflection does not become a dominant issue that shapes the narratives as a whole. The heroes are mostly seen beyond the realm of domesticity that would become important in many later novels. The Cavalier is from the beginning in flight from the prospect of a settled married life, while none of the four women Jack marries can function as a feminine ideal (he is cuckolded by his first three wives, while the fourth wife, described as 'virtuous', has had a bastard child in her youth). The claims of home have to be minimised or given the slip in order to make room for the hero's amoral adventuring in the realm of war. There is no thematic conflict here between masculine violence and an ideal feminine virtue – a conflict that became important in some novels later in the century. And the martial service of these adventurers is hardly framed in national terms: their loyalties are superficial and changeable and usually shaped by chance rather than by national identity.

Colonel Jack is influenced by the genre of the rogue narrative, while both novels adopt and adapt the modes of contemporary history writing

War and the 'Elevation' of the Novel   127

and news reports. Arthur W. Secord claims that *Memoirs of a Cavalier* was 'almost entirely fabricated from published works' – biographies, memoirs, and histories produced by seventeenth-century eye witnesses, including Clarendon's *History*, Ludlow's *Memoirs*, and Whitelock's *Memorials*.[14] Such sources, in common with much military reporting of the time, often treat violence in a stoical, dispassionate manner.[15] This stoical approach was compatible with Defoe's conception of the hero, which descended from the picaresque novel. The physical dangers of war do not seriously impede the hero's progress and may assist it. Both Jack and the Cavalier are wounded in battle, but escape disabling injuries. When Jack is knocked down in conflict by a giant-like German soldier, the incident saves his life: it allows him to be treated by the enemy's surgeons and rapidly paroled. When he is captured in battle, this turns out to be another stroke of luck, as he is soon able to take his captor as a prisoner. The Cavalier and Jack are both self-centred individualists who, for the most part, do not have strong ideological commitments. The episodic nature of their narratives, in which the hero moves through different locations, different sets of relationships and sometimes even different identities, means that normal conditions of soldiering (the need for collective effort, strict discipline, hierarchical command structures) are not allowed to become enduring constraints. Dependence upon elite patronage for promotion, which is treated by some later novelists as a humiliating source of corruption, in Defoe simply works in the hero's favour. When the Cavalier arrives in Germany to observe a war between Spanish and Swedish forces, he glides effortlessly from the margins of power to the centre through the influence of family and personal connections, receiving special favour from the Swedish King, Gustavus Adolphus. Back in England during the civil wars he is quickly admitted to King Charles's company and war Councils on the strength of his family ties. The hero of *Colonel Jack*, even without such connections to help him, soon wins the favour of the French king, and later, of the Chevalier. The element of romance in Defoe's narratives often ensures an easy passage through obstacles, rather than a serious consideration of their usual consequences.

In his other writings, Defoe is sometimes concerned with corruption in contemporary Britain – in the legal system, for example, or in the church, or as manifest in the incivility and bad manners of his contemporaries.[16] But in these novels, he uses first-person narrators who lack his own keen interest in social problems. He can therefore touch upon areas of public concern – such as the treatment of prisoners and wounded veterans, or the damaging economic effects of war – without the urgency of a reformer.

128   Part II: Developing Questions

Jack notes the terrible conditions endured by ordinary servicemen, which cause many to die of disease. But since he himself survives unscathed, he describes these conditions with little sense of personal outrage.

Defoe was writing at a time of crisis. There had been a succession of public disturbances in London: the Sacheverell riots, followed by a disorderly election campaign in 1710, conflict between Hanoverian and Jacobite groups around the time of the Jacobite rebellion of 1715, unrest caused by food shortages during the hard winter of 1715–16, and anti-Jacobite demonstrations when George I returned to London in January 1717.[17] Defoe was highly critical of such disorder. In the Preface to his *Hymn to the Mob* (1715), he declared 'Tumult of ev'ry Kind is Rebellion' and that 'whoever is for this MOBBING and Rabbling, must be a Friend to the Pretender'.[18] Concern about the Jacobite threat was intensified by the outbreak of War with Spain in 1718, and the rising of 1719. Defoe's approach to war in his fictions can be understood in relation to this turbulent context. He writes as a moderate. Early on in *Memoirs of a Cavalier* we see how war affects the people of Lyons. They have been 'oppressed in Taxes', and the war in Italy has been 'pinching their trade'.[19] Crowds take to the street, some armed, calling for peace, reviling the French king, plundering the houses of tax collectors, demonstrating against the price of bread. Defoe's Cavalier can express horror and regret for the terrible consequence of war, but cannot endorse this kind of popular protest, which was an all-too-familiar feature of life in Defoe's London. Instead, the Cavalier has special praise for the French Queen Mother's skilful defusing of the situation, and declares that this mob action gave him a permanent aversion to popular tumult that would, of itself, have made him support the king's side when the English Civil Wars began (43).

Defoe's supposedly non-ideological heroes are used to encourage moderation in the face of deep political and religious divisions. In *Memoirs*, while the Cavalier exposes the errors, intolerance and zeal on both sides that give rise to the Civil Wars in England, his most outspoken social criticism is directed at Roman Catholic Italy (home to the Pretender since 1717). The wayward hero of *Captain Jack*, encouraged by a Romish Priest, and posing as a French officer, momentarily joins the Jacobite rebels in 1715 before they enter Preston, but simply abandons them before they are surrounded by the royal cavalry. In this context, Jack's desertion merely suggests that he has come to his senses and contributes to the impression of the futility of the Jacobite cause.

Jack is not forced to reflect upon his own complicity in violence in the way the hero of *Memoirs* does. Critics have noted a change in Defoe's

Cavalier in the Civil War section of the *Memoirs*: the emergence of a self-critical humanitarian conscience. Early on the Cavalier wonders if the experience of Germany hardened him 'against the natural Tenderness' which he 'afterwards found return' upon him (119). N. H. Keeble argues that the Cavalier becomes, as he himself claims, 'a melancholly Observator of the Misfortunes of the Times'.[20] But the hero is not only an observer; he remains an active and sometimes brutal participant. And while he does show signs of regret for the cruelties each side inflicts on its compatriots, this regret does not become a guiding light that exerts significant control on his own actions in the conflict. How could it? The actual practice of war, as Defoe continues to show, entails and legitimises horrific violence. When in the heat of conflict the Cavalier's troops temporarily refuse quarter to their enemies, or when they kill all the inhabitants of a house 'without Distinction' after they have been attacked from windows and rooftops by women and others, he can only invoke the customs and rules of war, which license such responses (204). Until the end, he remains deeply implicated in martial brutality. Defoe's realism provides uncomfortable illustrations of the difference between social morality and the amoral 'necessities' of war.[21] It exposes, without resolving, the moral difficulties that later novelists will usually seek to avoid.

Virtue and the Culture of War: Samuel Richardson and Henry Fielding

The publication of Samuel Richardson's epistolary novel *Pamela* in 1740 is usually seen as a milestone in the elevation of the novel genre into moral respectability, even though the novel occasioned much controversy.[22] Richardson began writing *Pamela* in November 1739, just as the 'War of Jenkins's Ear' was beginning. In March 1740 while he was at work on the novel, news arrived that Admiral Vernon had taken Portobello. There was great public rejoicing across Britain, Vernon was hailed as a hero and his victory was celebrated in plays, ceramics, medals, prints, ballads, pamphlets, and other tributes. Richardson's novel appeared on 6 November 1740, 6 days before the first public celebration of Admiral Vernon's birthday on 12 November. This context helps to define by contrast the nature of Richardson's project. The central character of *Pamela* is a young servant girl whose virtue is displayed primarily in her determined resistance to the sexual advances of her employer (Mr B., who eventually marries her). Pamela's virtue could hardly be more remote from martial virtue or the heroism of war. The domestic concerns and moral example of a relatively humble female servant could now be regarded as more relevant to the growing novel readership than either the racy adventures of some earlier novel heroines or the activities of a martial hero. Under Pamela's influence Mr B., a figure corrupted by wealth and rank who once killed man in a duel, is reformed into a reliable husband with a concern for well-ordered domesticity. Richardson's novel helped to establish in fiction a domestic heroism directed to essentially peaceful ends. As Emma Clery notes, this model women who functions as an agent of moral improvement embodies the values of commercial virtue, as opposed to civic humanist with its martial traditions.[23]

Fielding satirised *Pamela* in two novels, *Shamela* (1741) and *Joseph Andrews* (1742), suggesting that the heroine used her 'virtue' as an instrument of social advancement. But in his next novel, *Jonathan Wild* (1743), a comparable virtue, exemplified in the good-natured Mr and Mrs Heartfree, is set in explicit opposition to the glorification of war. The eponymous hero is a notorious criminal who justifies his own immoral behaviour by citing the veneration of war in literature and history. Fielding's decision to portray this praise of war as a malign, corrupting influence in society appears to conflict with other aspects of his writing career, in which he profited by promoting war. Soon after war with Spain had been declared in October 1739, he began to write for *The Champion*, a journal run as a commercial enterprise on what Alan Downie identifies as 'radical Whig' lines, in support of the Opposition to the ministry of Prime Minister Robert Walpole.[24] In *The Champion* Fielding denounced the tameness of Walpole's war effort, praised the bellicose poet Richard Glover, joined the celebrations which greeted the news of Vernon's capture of Portobello, and urged more military action against the Spanish.[25] In this role, Fielding could be aligned with 'Patriot' writers who used support for war with Spain as a means of undermining Walpole. However, in his pro-war stance, Fielding was notably less blood-thirsty than some of his contemporaries, who rejoiced that the anticipated horrors – the fire, plunder, death, and wounds – had actually befallen the Spanish. A poem by an Oxford undergraduate, for example, imagined Vernon ministering 'Constant Supplies to Sharks of human Food'.[26] A comic song celebrated Vernon's conquest as a kind of rape.[27] Such sentiments do not seem out of step with a public that had rushed to see the first infliction of picketing as a military punishment in 1739.[28] Fielding distanced himself from such brutality where he could. On 7 January 1741, for example, he published as a pamphlet the poem *Of True Greatness*, which sought to distinguish between the conqueror as beast of prey and the warrior who fought, as

Marlborough had supposedly done, 'to save, and not to slay, mankind' (this poem was later included in the first volume of the *Miscellanies* – the third volume of which contained *Jonathan Wild*).[29] Two weeks later, on January 22 1741, he published a mock-heroic poem *The Vernoniad*, which attacked Walpole and praised Vernon, but avoided describing battles and included an ironical note on 'the honours in all ages paid to conquerors (*alias* robbers)'.[30]

In *Jonathan Wild*, Fielding distances himself as much as possible from the bellicose role he had adopted in *The Champion*. In the novel, Britain is seen to be at war with France, but there is no attempt to justify or even explain the British war effort. And while there are scenes of conflict at sea, Fielding carefully plays down the potential for violence and avoids any appeal to patriotic feeling. The national view of war is carefully excluded. He sends the virtuous Mrs Heartfree into the theatre of war, rather than her husband Mr Heartfree. As a virtuous woman Mrs Heartfree is removed from the possibility of fighting, and placed continually on the defensive, having her chastity to protect. As Scott Black points out, this part of the novel is written 'in the mode of romance'; but, as in *Pamela*, virtue is exemplified in the woman's power of resistance to masculine desire.[31] This understanding of virtue determines how war is depicted: Mrs Heartfree's virtue must survive its exposure to the perils of battle. The clashes between combatants at sea are quickly defused: the meetings between a French privateer and merchant ship, and between the privateer and man of war, lead to surrenders without a shot being fired. Attention is directed instead to issues of personal conduct. The captain of the English man of war is a brute: Mrs Heartfree finds him 'much rougher and less gallant than the *Frenchman* [the captain of a privateer] had been' (Book IV, ch vii, 144). His ill-treatment of his officers is judged in social terms: it is 'little better than a Man of no great Good-Breeding would exert to his meanest Servant' (145). Mrs Heartfree (and, during the captain's delirious fits, the ship itself) is protected by a lower officer: 'a virtuous and a brave Fellow, who had been twenty-five Years in that Post without being able to obtain a Ship, and had seen several Boys, the Bastards of Noblemen, put over his Head' (147). In the wake of the celebrations of Vernon as a great naval hero, Fielding shows the British navy as giving power to brutal individuals while neglecting genuine merit.

The difference between Fielding's pro-war work for *The Champion* and his critical stance in *Jonathan Wild* is the difference between a political discourse in which martial virtue and patriotic sentiment must be endorsed and promoted, and a moral discourse in which social virtue and individual

132 Part II: Developing Questions

conduct take precedence over other interests. In the novel, the moral view of war is decisively elevated over the national view. This difference sets the novel apart from, and in effective opposition to, public enthusiasm for war and military heroes. This is not to say, of course, that the novel could not have a political purpose. *Jonathan Wild* is usually seen as an ironical attack on Robert Walpole. But the attack is conceived primarily in moral terms, as a critique of moral corruption. The ostensible purpose of the novel is to encourage honesty, good nature, and good sense, and so to moderate chauvinistic attitudes, rather than to encourage patriotic support for the ongoing conflict.

Jonathan Wild draws on some of the same models as Daniel Defoe had used in his novels – the rogue narrative genre that influences *Colonel Jack*, and military histories, such as those by Clarendon and Whitelock, that inform *Memoirs of a Cavalier*.[32] But Fielding's use of such precedents is quite unlike Defoe's: his ironic mode entails a critical questioning of histories. In this, he aligns himself with educationalists and moralists who attack the glorification of war. From the beginning, the narrator poses as an enlightener who aims to dispel the 'Errors of Opinion' inherited from past writers, expose their 'Disingenuity', 'obsolete Doctrines', and their endeavour 'to confound the Ideas of Greatness and Goodness' (he singles out for condemnation, as other writers had done, the histories of Alexander and Caesar) (Book I, ch i, 8).[33] The difference between moral and political values is continually at issue in Fielding's novel, as a source of irony and satirical judgement. This helps to explain why the glorification of military figures is a recurrent issue even though the 'hero', Wild, is not a military figure and Robert Walpole, the apparent target of much of Fielding's irony, was reviled for his peace policy, not for his martial aggression. War is an activity in which the difference between moral and political values can be exposed with particular clarity: in this context, Fielding the moralist works to emphasise their difference rather than to reconcile them. It is Wild who unscrupulously tries to unify them: he notes that 'Honour' can mean 'good-nature and humanity' but can also be applied to 'the Sackers of Towns, the Plunderers of Provinces, and the Conquerors of Kingdoms'. (Book I, ch xiii, 39). Wild notes in self-justification that the *Iliad* provides models of extortion and plunder ('priggism'), while the history of Charles XII of Sweden has parallels with that of Alexander (Book I, ch iii, 14). The irony here is relevant to its context, but gives no direct indication of Fielding's own position: he himself had recently worked on a translated history of Charles XII.

War and the 'Elevation' of the Novel 133

Richardson would adopt a comparable moralistic view of the glorification of war in his next novel *Clarissa* (1748). As in the case of Fielding, such a view (which also appears in his private correspondence) did not stop him from working in the service of war in other parts of his professional life. As a printer Richardson found war good for business, and he was in no position formally to oppose government war policy. He printed pro-war poems (James Thomson's *Britannia*, 1729, Aaron Hill's *The Fanciad* and *The Impartial*, 1743), anti-French propaganda, and John Montcrieff's dialogues in support of strengthening the navy, *Camillus* and *Galba* (1748). He was deeply engaged in government business, having become the first official printer to the House of Commons in 1733 and from 1742 printer of the House of Commons *Journal*.[34] He was apparently involved in printing the *Daily Gazetteer* (1735–1746), a paper whose links with the government after the fall of Walpole are unclear, but which (for example) published upbeat accounts of a British triumph at the battle of Dettingen (1743) at a time when some other publications were more sceptical. None of this suggests a conscientious antipathy to war. But as several critics have noted, Richardson's *Clarissa*, abounds with negative references to war.[35]

Clarissa began to appear on 1 December 1747, during the War of the Austrian Succession (which had followed from the War of Jenkins's Ear in 1740). Throughout the work, Richardson uses references to war in order to expose characters' moral failings. Like Fielding, he adopts the conventional view that the glorification of war in history and literature has a corrupting influence on the morals of society. The moral view of war helps to establish the thematic contrasts at work in the novel. The rakish Lovelace when describing his pursuit of Clarissa repeatedly uses the language of siege warfare and compares himself to famous military commanders (including Caesar and Alexander, Cromwell, Ariosto's Rinaldo, and Hannibal). He invokes such examples to authorise and normalise his own predatory activities, but they also help to define the embattled psychology that he and some of the other characters display. Lovelace compares Clarissa herself to Alexander, and thinks of her as a conqueror, since he thinks of marriage as a state of offence as well as defence, (at one point he declares that he has fortified his recreant heart against her).[36] Other characters also use military language in this way. Even Anna Howe, in pressing her best friend Clarissa about her feelings for Lovelace, invokes a military precedent to justify her tactics: 'Hannibal we read always advised to attack the Romans upon their own territories' (70). The novel does not appear to be set in time of war (its setting may be around 1732) but, as John Cardwell has shown, some of its military references apparently allude to specific

134 Part II: Developing Questions

contemporary events in the ongoing War of the Austrian Succession (such as the publication of Frederick's 'Manifesto' attempting to justify his invasion of Silesia).[37] In the novel, they contribute to Richardson's picture of a corrupt society that is coarsened by reading about military violence. Cardwell suggests that Colonel Morden, who eventually kills Lovelace in a duel, 'personifies military virtue legitimately exerted in defence of king and country, or to avenge betrayed innocence in the case of his cousin and ward Clarissa' (179). But Colonel Morden illustrates the unacceptable rule rather than the exception. In avenging Clarissa, he ignores her injunction not to exact violent revenge, and conforms instead to the expectations associated with his martial background. In later editions, Richardson went out of his way to discourage the idea that this vengeance was justified. Morden, for all his admirable qualities, is yet another man of reprehensible violence. Richardson's next novel, Sir Charles Grandison, would portray an ideal masculine hero, '*a man of TRUE HONOUR*' who is resolutely opposed to duelling.[38]

The anti-war content of *Clarissa* is determined primarily by Richardson's conception of virtue, as manifest in his heroine, a model of feminine conduct. Clarissa's feminine virtue, like Pamela's, is displayed most powerfully in passive resistance. It is essentially peaceful, grounded in her Christian faith and sensibility, which lead her to retreat from the corruption and violence of the world at large. Her virtue is shaped in part by her reading, which consists of 'devout books' (sermons and devotional books) and 'lighter' (but genteel and improving) works of literature. As an exemplary reader she does not read 'inflaming novels and idle romances' (1279–1280). At the end of the book, Richardson writes defensively of those who look upon his work 'as a mere *novel* or *romance*' (1498). The novel's antimilitaristic gestures help to distinguish it from the supposedly corrupting works against which Richardson defines his own novel. It is because the novel takes its conception of Christian virtue so seriously and imagines it in such uncompromising terms, that it must avoid the compromise entailed in any formal endorsement of war. Raymond Williams see *Clarissa* as 'an important sign of that separation of virtue from any practically available world which is a feature of the later phases of Puritanism'. [39] Emma Clery, noting that Clarissa is powerless to reform the rake, argues that in this novel 'Feminization, the promise of reform through the example of female virtue, is violently detached from worldly expectations'; the heroine illustrates Richardson's 'opposition to the civic humanist ethic'.[40] The novel certainly requires the moral view of war to be clearly uncoupled from the national view in order to maintain thematic consistency. In this conception of feminine virtue, there is the potential for a principled opposition to war in general, rather than opposition to this or that war on the grounds of justice. There is, that is, the potential for a form of pacifism. As we shall see, some other novelists clearly recognised and made use of this potential. This does not mean, of course, that any depiction of such feminine virtue implied opposition to war – the wider significance of such virtue was determined in part by its context. Other novelists were able to reconcile peaceful feminine virtue with patriotic support for war – indeed, as we shall see in Chapters 9 and 10, some writers emphasised the supportive role of the virtuous female in wartime. But this latter position seems to have taken some time to become established, and it appears to have involved the emergence of a domesticated patriotism.

Critical Interventions: Smollett and Fielding

The novels of Richardson and Fielding examined so far, then, privilege the moral view of war and evoke the glorification of warfare as a harmful influence upon the culture of civil society. But in practice, British society was not simply passive in relation to the nation's war-making. As historians have shown, during the eighteenth century, the armed forces became increasingly subject to the active influence of the public. This influence took a variety of forms: indirect assistance from charitable foundations (one aim of London's Foundling Hospital of 1739 was to help the future supply of recruits for the armed forces); direct voluntary assistance (for example, the goods and volunteer forces provided during the Jacobite rebellion of 1745); professional advice and assistance from individuals or groups with useful expertise; published criticism from interested individuals.[41] A wide range of issues become matters of discussion in print, not only the conduct of particular campaigns and battles (which were often subjects of fierce contention), but also matters of administration and justice (the distribution of prize money, the conduct of particular courts martial, the system of promotion, bureaucratic inefficiency and corruption), welfare concerns (such as the ventilation of warships, the medical treatment of casualties, the treatment of prisoners of war), and methods of recruitment (especially the controversial practices of crimping and impressment).[42] Criticism did not necessarily imply any disapproval of war in itself and could be conceived as an expression of patriotism. It was part of the wider movement to reform and improve society. One could make an independent contribution to the nation's ability to wage war in terms directed to saving and protecting life.

136   Part II: Developing Questions

The professional armed forces, then, increasingly depended upon the specialised advice and services of non-combatants. The army and navy became important sources of patronage for those with the right expertise or qualifications. Many Scots took advantage of the opportunities opened up to them in this area by the Union of 1707: during the War of the Austrian Succession, for example, David Hume and James Pringle served in the army (as Secretary and physician respectively), while Tobias Smollett served in the navy (as surgeon's apprentice). As a result of this kind of arrangement, the working practices of the armed forces, and specific military operations, became subject to the close scrutiny of well-educated non-combatants. Medical men tended to see their role as to address the often dire conditions in which war was fought rather than to improve the means of destruction. They had a close-up view of the effects of military campaigns and a clear incentive to write about them. Pringle, Richard Mead, John Huxham, and Thomas Trotter are among the medical men who published works about conditions in the army or the navy in the 1740s and 1750s.[43]

Tobias Smollett's first novel, *Roderick Random*, can be understood in relation to this context. The hero Roderick is an adventuring figure of a kind that descends from the picaresque novel, a youth whose sometimes impetuous amorality will eventually be reformed by Narcissa, a model of feminine virtue. His wide-ranging experiences in the contemporary world include some involvement in war zones on sea and land. Smollett's satirical treatment of naval warfare in the novel drew on his own personal experience as surgeon's apprentice on Vernon's Cartagena expedition. The novel appeared in January 1748, before the War of the Austrian Succession had come to an end. It was a new development in the fictional representation of warfare, since it included a non-combatant's deeply critical, eyewitness perspective on the ongoing conflict. The moral view of war is here grounded in first-hand experience.

Smollett depicts the navy not only as a fighting force but also as an establishment within society with its own bureaucracy, methods of recruitment, and processes of public accountability – all subject to the kinds of abuses found in the rest of society. Roderick's attempts to procure work as a ship's surgeon through the Navy Office are foiled by a culture of bribery, fee-taking, and high-handed obstruction. He eventually enters the navy unintentionally through another naval institution, the press gang – and, as surgeon's third mate, gets caught up in the ill-fated Cartagena attack (1741) led by Vernon in the wake of his Portobello triumph. Roderick's experiences form a catalogue of horrors: the tyranny of an abusive captain; the terrors of a storm at sea; deaths and injuries sustained even before a violent engagement; the callous incompetence of the ship's surgeon; arbitrary imprisonment; the terrible dismembering of bodies in battle; the appalling conditions of the so-called hospital ships; and bodies unceremoniously thrown overboard without ballast or winding sheet. The naval historian N. A. M. Rodger rightly considers Smollett's novel as an 'over-rich' substitute for documentary evidence.[44] But if Smollett's fictionalised account entails exaggeration, it draws attention to the on-board conditions of naval warfare which are usually kept out of sight in patriotic celebrations designed to rouse or reassure the public – such as the maritime paintings of Peter Monomy, installed in the supper boxes of Vauxhall pleasure gardens in 1740, one of which gave a distant, orderly view of Portobello being stormed by British forces.[45]

The novel was published in the wake of a public dispute about the failure at Cartagena, and was, among many other things, a reaction to that discussion. Allies of Admiral Vernon published accounts attributing blame to the army under the leadership of General Wentworth; other publications blamed Vernon or claimed to redress the balance.[46] In the event, Vernon emerged with his reputation in tact as a hugely popular patriotic hero.[47] The dispute naturally centred on the views of the officers and commanders and involved records of the Councils of War. But Smollett's novel, launched upon the market, could offer an alternative view. As a poet, he had already sought to expose injustices concealed by the army's official accounts of its campaigns, in the Popean satires *Advice* (1746) and *Reproof* (1747), and in *The Tears of Scotland* (1746?) – a lament for the terrible revenge suffered by highlanders in the wake of the '45 rebellion. *Roderick Random* performs a comparable function. While the published dispute presented the views of those at the top, the novel represented voices of the lower ranks. The tar Jack Rattlin gives a damning assessment of Vernon's naval strategy in the assault on Bocca Chica. Roderick himself is just as critical of Vernon, and of his harmful disputes with Wentworth (who does not escape blame). He assures us that 'all the wits, either in the army or the navy' speculate about Vernon's policy and that 'the most numerous' part of them think the admiral should have 'sacrificed private pique' in a situation 'where the lives of so many brave fellow-citizens were concerned'. He notes with some irony the ease with which Vernon was able to justify his conduct to the 'upright and discerning' ministry on his return to England.[48] Smollett creates the impression of a yawning gap between the well-established public view of Vernon as hero, and the views of those who served and suffered under him. The novel was an instant success, soon selling 6,500 copies. By 1770, its eighth London edition had appeared.[49]

138   Part II: Developing Questions

The popular success of *Roderick Random,* as of Smollett's poem 'The Tears of Scotland' (which was twice set to music), suggests that readers could readily accept works that appealed to their conscience and sympathy concerning the horrors of ongoing wars. This does not mean, of course, that they refused to accept the necessity of such wars, or to join in patriotic celebrations. Nor can we assume that Smollett himself was a pacifist. Jennifer Thorn has emphasised the influence of violent chapbook romance upon *Roderick Random:* while the novel 'denigrates plebeian culture' and celebrates 'literary politeness', it also accommodates the pleasures of adventure and fighting characteristic of chapbooks.[50] In Smollett's *Complete History of England,* we find a dire assessment of the outcome of the wars of 1739 to 1748, and sharp criticism of the some actions and commanders, alongside praise for some actions and tributes to 'gallant' or successful commanders (such as general Sir John Ligonier at the battle of Roucoux, or rear-admiral Anson in a victorious action off Galicia in 1746) which are sometimes accompanied by engraved portraits.[51] The coexistence of such praise and criticism was part of the process of holding the army and navy to account.

The public's influence upon the management of the armed forces became particularly significant as the War of the Austrian Succession came to a close, and the problems caused by demobilisation loomed into view. There was much more public discussion of these problems in 1748–50 than there had been in 1713–14, at the close of the War of the Spanish Succession. This was inevitably so, because the volume of print and the range of publications had increased considerably, as had the size of the reading public. Proposals for resettling or finding employment for discharged servicemen were printed in newspapers and magazines, along with complaints about the terrible hardships they and their families had to endure.[52] There were also reports of dangerous unrest and soaring levels of crime in London and across the country – much of it involving those home from the wars.[53] In this febrile atmosphere, publications appeared that claimed to represent the collective voice of ordinary servicemen. The *Address of Daniel Dettingen* (1749), for example, presents the complaints of the disbanded soldiers and sailors 'of these kingdoms'. Among its patriotic and deferential gestures an implicit threat appears, since it evokes the 'glorious Spirit of Liberty' which had been asserted 'by Men of the lowest Class' from big cities like London and Dublin to towns like Newcastle and Derby – all places where there had been food riots during the war.[54] In a comparable spirit, a 'Petition from British Mariners' published in *the London Evening Post* (19 January 1751) seeks the assistance of 'every

War and the 'Elevation' of the Novel 139

individual in the Kingdom' for payment of the 'long and large arrears' which have reduced them to poverty. Its list of abuses is a shocking indictment of an unjust system that has appalling consequences for ordinary servicemen and their families: discounted tickets, exhausting journeys, contemptuous treatment, debtors' prison, wives and daughters driven to prostitution – and death on the gallows. Historians have argued that in both the army and the navy of eighteenth-century Britain, signs of a 'class consciousness' appeared through their collective experience in conditions that approximate to the 'proletarianization' of labour.[55] These direct appeals, voiced as if from a nationally collectivised group to a national readership, would provide some support for such arguments. They request assistance not as charity but as a right.

Fielding's *Amelia*, first published in December 1751, emerges from this time of post-war disorder. It has been described as 'the first novel of social protest and reform in English'.[56] The war had provided Fielding with more career opportunities: during the Jacobite rebellion of 1745, he was enlisted by the government to produce anti-Jacobite pamphlets and a weekly periodical, *The True Patriot*, which carried plans for the National Militia, reports of the progress of British troops under the Duke of Cumberland, and other items in support of the government. He had apparently changed the plan of *Tom Jones* in order to allow the hero to join a company of soldiers marching against the rebellious Jacobites. He had been rewarded for his loyal service with the office of magistrate, in which capacity he addressed the problem of crime and disorder in the capital. His official *Enquiry into the Causes of the Late Increase of Robbers etc.* (which appeared in January 1751) called for a strengthening of the criminal code as a deterrent, and better regulation of the morals of the poor by curbing luxury. It identified poverty as a cause of crime, but skirted around the problem of demobilisation. *Amelia* was, among other things, an attempt to address the problem. Here the moral view of war produces a searing indictment of social corruption.

Fielding could only explore this issue within carefully maintained limits. The events of the novel are discreetly distanced from the present crisis by being set in 1733, during the era of Walpole, four years after the end of the Anglo-Spanish War of 1727–29. The novel treats war primarily as it impinges on the domestic life and the ambitions of the lower-ranking officer class. The fate of the mass of ordinary servicemen had to be approached more obliquely and in a suitably non-threatening form. Collective protest only appears towards the end of the novel, in a menacing but quickly diffused mob reaction to crime.

140 Part II: Developing Questions

The problems of the post-war veteran are treated chiefly in relation to the fallible army captain, William Booth. He has fought in Gibraltar and been wounded twice but, having been put on half-pay at the end of the war, is unable to get a new, more profitable commission. Those with influence make false offers of help in the hope of seducing his wife, Amelia. Booth's difficulties are made to seem typical of a wider problem through parallels. At the beginning of the novel, imprisoned on false testimony, he encounters among the grotesque inmates of Newgate another veteran of Gibraltar, a man who, having lost a leg and received other wounds, has become a 'Wretch almost naked' who carries signs of 'Honesty, the Marks of Poverty, Hunger and Disease'. Having failed to get into Chelsea hospital, he has been arrested on suspicion of stealing 'three Herrings' and, on acquittal, has been detained indefinitely 'for his Fees' (35). This figure – destitute, solitary, pathetic, without a voice – stands in place of the multitude of impoverished veterans whose collectivised protests had recently been represented in print. Later in the novel, Booth meets another counterpart, Bob Bounds, an 'old Brother-Officer' and veteran of Gibraltar who has been discharged on half-pay (448). Bounds has left the army with a broken heart, since in thirty-five years of loyal service, he has risen only to the rank of lieutenant, 'having had several Boys put over his Head' (450). His sister, the widow of a naval officer, has had her pension delayed by at least two years, which leaves the family at the mercy of loan sharks. Fielding typically represents such hardships in relation to good natured, respectable, vulnerable individuals – not in relation to challenging groups.

In this way, Fielding helps to establish the figure that other novelists will examine – the veteran adjusting, or failing to adjust, to civilian life. The negative effects of war are shown to extend far beyond the war zone. A victorious campaign, we see, may wreak havoc not only upon the defeated: it can blight the lives of victorious survivors and their families. It can impinge heavily upon the life of women beyond the battle zone, as shown in the pregnant Amelia's overwhelming anxiety when her husband Booth is called to war, and in the dire effect on her health as she nurses him when he has been wounded. Those who have made personal sacrifices in the name of King and Country are routinely dishonoured by their corrupt compatriots.

The novel therefore calls into question the interests served by war, and the traditional ideas of heroism that support it. In *Amelia,* Fielding creates parallels with the plot of Virgil's *Aeneid,* inviting critical comparisons with that heroic model and with classical epic more generally. If Virgil presents a revaluation of heroism, a move away from the martial ethics of

War and the 'Elevation' of the Novel 141

Homer towards the more reflective heroism of 'pious' Aeneas, Fielding makes another move, by focusing on the fallible and initially unbelieving hero Booth who learns Christian piety, but finds his own society to be the enemy of virtue. In the process, Fielding redefines heroism in ways that separate it as much as possible from martial aggression. The violence of war is shown as suffered rather than inflicted, and wounds become a sign of good nature rather than of humiliation in battle. Booth conspicuously lacks the ardent bellicosity that patriot poets had tried to inspire in the British public. When his regiment is posted to Gibraltar, he does not rush to war in a fervour to avenge British honour on the Spaniards. Instead, he struggles with the conflict between his love for his wife Amelia (who is expecting their first child) and his military duty. At this point, the national view of war is placed directly against the moral view.

Booth's account of his parting from Amelia not only evokes Aeneas's parting from Creusa in the *Aeneid* book II, but also, and more revealingly, Hector's parting from Andromache in the *Iliad* book VI. When Andromache pleads with Hector not to return to the dangers of the battlefield he – a man born and bred to war – imagines his loss of honour in relation to the malice of his enemies, the victorious Greeks. In the modern world of Fielding's novel, the soldier's reputation is threatened primarily by the malice of the public at home. It is a medical man, the enlightened Dr Harrison, who advises Booth that he must go to Gibraltar. His advice contrasts strikingly with the passionate arguments and fiery rhetoric used by some contemporary patriotic writers to urge their compatriots to war: 'Your Duty to your King and Country, whose Bread you have eaten, requires it'. This 'Duty' is thought of as a personal debt rather than an obligation arising from the justice of the cause. The doctor adds that Booth would lose his 'Character' if he did not go, since the 'World' would not treat him fairly, but would stigmatise him 'as a Coward' (100). Maintaining one's honour, for someone of Booth's rank, does not mean sustaining a glorious military reputation as it did for Hector, but the humbler business of avoiding the censure of those who do not fight.

Here we see a key problem emerging. While it may be prudent to maintain one's character in a society that is pervaded by hypocrisy, virtue can be conceived in terms that demand a rejection of prudential compromise, and so a refusal to participate in war. Faced with the prospect of losing her husband to the call of war, Amelia cries 'Where is the Dishonour, *Billy*? or if there be any, will it reach our Ears in our little Hutt? Are Glory and Fame, and not his *Amelia*, the Happiness of my Husband?' (102). Amelia's questions represent a conception of feminine virtue of the kind

142 Part II: Developing Questions

that Richardson had explored in *Clarissa*, whose heroine eventually withdraws from a corrupt world into virtuous isolation. When, in *Amelia*, this virtue is tested against the claims of patriotic duty, the heroine's reaction suggests a complete rejection of such claims – that is, a withdrawal into a private form of pacifism. Fielding can sympathise with this personal reaction, but cannot formally endorse it. At this point, a gender hierarchy is reasserted: masculine prudence must guide a feminine virtue of the heart; a weak and emotional Amelia will submit to the authority and judgement of her husband. Public duty, as Dr Harrison describes it, is a reality, and the possibility of 'dishonour' cannot be disregarded. Nevertheless, Fielding's uncertainties about the conflict of values here are suggested elsewhere in the novel. Soon afterwards (book III chapter IV) Booth admits that, during a storm at sea, he wished he had taken Amelia's advice, while at a later point (book XII chapter 3), when Amelia worries that Booth will lose his honour if he does not fight a duel, Dr Harrison asks 'What is the Opinion of the World opposed to Religion and Virtue?' and cites Andromache dissuading Hector from danger as an example of an amiable weakness 'becoming the true feminine Character' (504). As traditional conceptions of 'honour' are hollowed out by criticisms of pervasive social corruption, so the claims of patriotic duty begin to seem questionable when set against the values of 'the true feminine character'. The moral view of war undermines the national view.

Where Defoe had accommodated war in his novels by focusing on self-centred, adventuring soldier-heroes who live mostly beyond the settled realms of civil society, Richardson and Fielding make social life the centre of their work and treat the glorification of war as a threat to its moral order. Fielding and Smollett use their professional experience, as magistrate and navy surgeon's second mate respectively, to highlight the horrifying consequences of war for combatants and their families. The novel, aimed at a readership that was dominated by the middling sort, and that included many women, had begun to present a view of war quite unlike that offered in the heroic battle paintings, celebratory poems, musical celebrations, and commemorative merchandise that sustained the official face of war as a glorious national endeavour. This development occurred in a period when the elevation of warriors such as Admiral Vernon and the Duke of Cumberland into national heroes was being promoted by an unprecedented range of cultural practices, and when Westminster Abbey was becoming a national pantheon for military and naval figures. The novel was assuming a form that counterbalanced the emotional appeal of such patriotic activities and allowed some critical questioning of the nation's war-making.

War and the 'Elevation' of the Novel   143

A Warlike Nation?

The emergence of this questioning approach to war in the novel was clearly related to the growing size and influence of a non-combatant readership. There were apparent dangers within this social development. The widespread celebrations of army and naval victories might give the impression that modern Britain was a truly warlike nation, but the panic that broke out in response to the Jacobite March to Derby during the rebellion of 1745 gave a quite different impression. The Treaty of Aix la Chappell (1748), which concluded the War of the Austrian Succession, had left none of the main parties satisfied and was soon followed by a renewed drift to conflict, but the signs of a reviving public appetite for war were not accompanied by a corresponding willingness to fight. In Britain during this period, anti-French sentiments were fed by press reports of France's military and naval activities, and publications stressing the vulnerability of British interests in North America to French ambition.[57] The defeat of American and British troops by the French in the conflicts within the Ohio valley in 1754–1755 made matters worse.[58] There was an urgent drive to increase the size of the army – which, as usual, had been drastically reduced on the conclusion of peace. But the expression of anti-French sentiments was not accompanied by a readiness to do the business of fighting: few volunteers joined up, and the government had to introduce a temporary measure to conscript the able-bodied unemployed.[59] Modern Britain might be able to finance ever more expensive wars, but as John Brown pointed out in his widely read *Estimate of Manners* (1757–58), the 'capital question' was 'Not who shall *Pay*, but who shall *Fight?*'[60] He saw the nation as sunk in 'effeminacy' and 'corruption'. In a modern commercial society, a national preoccupation with war was evidently not a measure of its martial virtue.

The relationship between the modern interest in war and martial virtue was addressed in two novels published in the era of the Seven Years' War. *The Life and Memoirs of Mr Ephraim Tristram Bates, Commonly Called Corporal Bates, a broken-hearted Soldier* (1756) – referred to hereafter as *Tristram Bates* – shows how a soldier's ambition to serve his country is both inspired and undermined in eighteenth-century Britain. This anonymous work has long been recognised as a possible influence upon Laurence Sterne's novel *The Life and Opinions of Tristram Shandy, Gentleman* (1759–67) – or *Tristram Shandy*.[61] Sterne's novel shows, among other things, the reimagining of war by ex-soldiers far from the scene of warfare, a process in which martial virtue is associated with refined moral sentiments and with self-destructive expense rather than with fighting. In both works, the focus

144 Part II: Developing Questions

on martial interests leads to the exclusion of the kind of feminine virtue that featured in the novels of Richardson, Fielding and Smollett.

The Defeat of Martial Virtue: *Tristram Bates*

After a lengthy period of anticipation, Britain declared war on France in May 1756. In the following month the French captured Minora from the British. *Tristram Bates* appeared in the wake of this defeat, giving a brisk, satirical expression to the growing sense of malaise in Britain. Like Fielding and Smollett, its author shows the British war establishment as mired in corruption, and specifically as failing to reward merit. But this novel is unusual, in that it does seek to arouse support for an ongoing conflict, and so it endorses the national view of war. The hero Bates is fired with a disinterested patriotism, which is fed by the volume and variety of information about war in modern Britain. He has the potential and ambition to become a fine soldier, but is thwarted by a British military that – unlike its French counterpart – is seen as amateurish and wasteful. Just before news arrives of the first French attacks in America, Bates has a nightmare that seems to presage national ruin (217). The subsequent news of Minorca breaks the heart of this would-be military hero, and so kills him. The message of the novel could not be clearer: Britain is fatally ill-prepared for another war with France; it will be defeated by enemies at home.

To distinguish Bates's dedicated patriotism from the surrounding corruption his disinterestedness must be clearly established. Early in the novel, therefore, he is disinherited as a result of joining the army (his family having been influenced by clergymen, who insist that soldiers are whore-mongers, thieves and murderers – but who hope to be defended by foreign mercenaries). Bates subsequently refuses to be released from his enlistment, voluntarily giving up an estate worth £80 per year. The estate would have made Bates a freeholder, but here the traditional civic humanist link between martial virtue and landownership is formally broken: the professional virtues of discipline, hard work and technical skill take precedence, while Bates's estate-owning family seems thoroughly unpatriotic.[62] The novel's pro-war message requires the nation's corruption to be distinguished from its capacity to inspire martial endeavour. Bates lives in a society which encourages dreams of military glory in many ways. As a pupil he avidly reads martial histories, lives of heroes, Caesar's *Commentaries* and comparable works. He is inspired by stories of Marlborough's victories, by London print shops which display flattering prints of Generals, by martial songs like 'To Arms, to Arms', and 'Britons Strike Home' which circulate

War and the 'Elevation' of the Novel   145

freely, by county journals which report local military news. He is moved by the vision of noble death in Collins's 'Ode to Colonel Ross'. He reads in the newspapers of how officers abroad are rewarded from the royal hand with a sword set with jewels or a star of some order (51). He meets with old officers on park benches who tell him they were 'rais'd from even private Men' (147). The celebration of war that permeates all aspects of contemporary British culture is seen in generally positive terms, as encouraging Bates to develop his natural talent and appetite for soldiering. In this respect, the national view of war seems vindicated.

But Bates appears to be an exception to the general rule, since despite finding in modern Britain many encouragements to martial virtue, the nation as a whole seems sunk in corruption. The hero's disinterested professionalism sets him apart not only from any concern with property, but also from the venality he encounters among both non-combatants and the army establishment. The reference to Bates developing his shooting skills on a bowling green rather than on a firing range (34) – an idea that apparently influenced *Tristram Shandy* – distances him both from the sociable leisure of non-combatant life and from his less ardent compatriots in the army. Evidence mounts of corruption in every part of the military, including neglect of merit and the disgraceful treatment of wounded veterans. Bates, after a frustrating spell in the Life Guards, fails to get a commission in a new regiment because he has given his family vote to a Colonel in the 'Country Interest' (it is not made clear how the disinherited Bates retains a 'Family Vote', 186). He is thwarted despite his obvious merit, expertise, and ambition, and despite his readiness to fight in America. His defeat, like the fall of Minorca, seems to portend disaster for the nation.

This simple fable has an unmistakable message to the contemporary public and tends to dodge issues that might confuse that message. Not only does it avoid involving its good-natured hero in the violence of battle, it also avoids exposing him directly to any examples of feminine virtue of the kind Richardson, Fielding and Smollett had depicted (although it briefly exposes him to the temptation of less virtuous females). As we have seen, the ideal of feminine virtue placed at the centre of the novel by Richardson was essentially peaceful; such an ideal was potentially at odds with Bates's martial ambitions.[63] However, the novel does not completely exclude references to the domestic realm, and these raise significant questions that remain unanswered. The work is introduced by a brief, comic note supposedly from the hero's widow, which mentions his family of seven children, and it concludes with his farewell letter to her. But Bates is never seen with his wife or children. There is a good reason for this, since

146   Part II: Developing Questions

the British army in the eighteenth century tried to discourage and regulate marriage.[64] At the end we learn that in order to protect his military prospects, Bates has been forced to keep his marriage secret, but that he planned to declare it once he had secured the pension that would come with his promotion. The secrecy means that his wife's feelings about her husband's profession and its dangers are not represented. We do know that he was keen to avoid being asked 'but what will Mrs Bates do, if you are called away?' (235).

The final revelations about the hero's wife and family show that Bates is not, after all, completely free from ulterior interests: the promotion he wants would bring a pension which could support his wife and children. The man who has voluntarily given up the prospect of an estate dies leaving vulnerable dependents. Military service that supposedly protects the home in practice undermines it. The military virtues of the hero are no match for the injustices arising from the unequal distribution of power and opportunity in contemporary Britain. The conclusion of this pro-war novel therefore exposes a variety of problems that remain unexplored.

This novel does not make use of anti-heroic discourse or show any concern with the horrors of the warzone; its critique of corruption in the army is explicitly linked to support for the contemporary war effort. But while it seems unusual in this respect, it illustrates the characteristic effects of a novel form increasingly devoted to the interests and values of the middling sort, to the merits and career ambitions of those who try to make their way in the world against the obstacles imposed by powerful established interests. While this overtly pro-war novel does accommodate the national view of war with some sympathy, it does so not in terms of church doctrine, historical destiny, sovereign authority, or any top-down mythical framework, but as a matter of individual commitment. And while it commends a dedicated and professional martial virtue, it shows that such virtue may be defeated long before it reaches the warzone, within a society that readily proclaims its own interest in war.

Martial Virtue and Sentiment: *Tristram Shandy*

Sterne apparently began work on his narrative in January 1759. By this time, Britain had already lived through the nightmare of humiliation in war presaged in *Tristram Bates*, and had begun to emerge from it. The first two volumes of *Tristram Shandy* were completed at a time when public confidence was buoyed by news of successive victories, and thoughts were beginning to turn towards the terms of peace with France. The next four

War and the 'Elevation' of the Novel 147

volumes were composed when the nation was divided between those, like Pitt, who wanted to press for complete victory, and those, like the Prime Minister Lord Bute, who were concerned to finalise the Peace of Paris in 1763. Thomas Keymer suggests that 'Toby and Trim parody in miniature the profligacy of the war party, while Walter's objections have a discernibly Butite ring'.[65] The novel is conciliatory, offering a mirror in which those appalled by the losses of the war and those ardently supportive of the fighting could, within its parodic gestures and whimsical game-playing, find a comforting reflection of their hopes and fears.[66] Sterne was well aware of the destructive consequences of the war, and not indifferent to the issue of corruption: in letters written during the conflict, he comments indignantly on officers returning from the war zone in the hope of being 'put unfairly over the heads of those who were left risking their lives', and notes George III's determination 'to stop the torrent of corruption and laziness'.[67] But his dedication of the first volume of *Tristram Shandy* to William Pitt, who was then guiding the national war-effort, indicated that he was not going to engage directly in the kind of damning satire found in *Tristram Bates*. In this novel, disturbing questions about contemporary attitudes to war are approached in other ways.

Although Corporal Trim has been protected by the endearing patronage of Uncle Toby, such patronage of low-ranking old soldiers was far from the norm as Sterne and his first readers well knew. As we have already seen, the aftermath of wars brought acute problems of demobilisation, as large numbers of returning servicemen found themselves without jobs or prospects, and effectively surplus to requirement. The ending of the War of the Austrian Succession had led to a dramatic increase in crime and a wave of popular disturbances across the nation, made worse by the disorder brought by the contemporary gin craze and the violence of smuggling gangs.[68] The relationship between Trim and Toby is a sentimental alternative to the harsh realities of neglect and conflict, one which might remind readers of what the novel turns away from. As critics have noted, Toby's concern with war is linked with wider views of society.[69] When arguing with Walter about the purpose of war, he declares that it has 'no object but to shorten the strides of AMBITION, and to intrench the lives and fortunes of the *few*, from the plunderings of the *many*'. He sees a link between war and inequality; but while moralists traditionally attribute war to the ambitions of a powerful few, Toby sees war as a defence against 'the *many*'.

Toby's siege mentality, which generates his obsessive re-enactments of historical sieges, is of course attributable to his traumatic war experience,

148   Part II: Developing Questions

but it sets him in an ironical relationship to the social authority and cus-
todial responsibility traditionally attributed to the freeholder. His military
hobby-horse has been made possible his uncle's gift of 'a little neat country
house' with 'a small estate of about one hundred pounds a year'. (vol ii,
chap v, 96). Where *Tristram Bates* breaks the link between martial virtue
and property, *Tristram Shandy* establishes that link in comic terms. The
ideal virtues of the freeholder, like those of the monarch, were related
to the custody of land. The effective management of estates and kingdoms required independence, integrity, self-discipline, and sound moral
judgement.[70] Toby's patronage of Trim supports a retreat from immediate social problems into a world of private obsessions rationalised as 'in
the national interest'. While Bates uses a bowling green to practice the
arts of gunnery in the hope that he will see active service in future wars,
Sterne's Toby and Trim, who saw service in the Nine Years' Wars (1690s),
use Toby's bowling green to recreate events from the War of the Spanish
Succession (1702–1713), which ended over forty-six years before *Tristram
Shandy* began to appear. The novel's temporal distance from the wars
of Sterne's own time (much greater than the time lapses in *Clarissa* or
Amelia) allowed his readers to engage with issues raised by current events
through a softening process of reminiscence. The national view of war is
evoked, but in terms that divorce it from the ongoing hostilities. This strategy allows Sterne to accomplish in ironic form that reconciliation between
the man of war and the man of feeling that poets and dramatists had
imagined, and that contemporary war reports had begun to suggest. Toby
and Trim are soldiers-as-non-combatants. In their mindset, the distinction between public and private values is dissolved, as war is absorbed into
private actions and private sentiments, and Sterne's readers are offered an
image of warfare that can be judged by the norms of ordinary domestic
life. Toby's situation parodies that of modern, gentlemanly, pro-war non-
combatants more generally, for whom war is a kind of soap opera enjoyed
far from the actual experience of human suffering, and for whom patriotism has become largely a matter of sentiment, paying taxes, and reading
about – and trying to imagine – what has already happened elsewhere. As
John Richardson notes, Toby 'imagines sieges as without people or pain'.[71]
Sterne's emphasis falls on the self-destructive expense of the obsession –
the ironic counterpart of a national obsession. Looking back on the War
of the Austrian Succession David Hume expressed dismay at the spectacle
of 'princes and states fighting and quarrelling, amidst their debts, funds
and public mortgages', which brought to mind 'a match of cudgel playing
fought in a china shop'. To Hume, this madness appeared to be shared

War and the 'Elevation' of the Novel 149

by the wider British nation who, once engaged in war, seemed to lose 'all concern' for themselves and their posterity.[72] Such prodigality was remote from the ideal virtues of the freeholder. Toby epitomises such a lack of concern: his house, garden, and finances are all adversely affected by the war games, as is the future of the Shandy family, when Tristram falls victim to a vandalised sash window.

Sterne's fundamentally ironic approach allows him to give closer attention than previous novelists did to the physical and emotional effects of war upon those who fight it. The war-wound, already established as a sign of virtue in earlier novels, here acquires an unusual prominence. Sterne's Uncle Toby is English fiction's first 'trauma hero'. As Jonathan Lamb observes, Toby's obsessive, chaotic re-visiting of past events 'is entirely faithful to the radical disorganisation of mind and matter caused by war'.[73] His injury generates a great deal of the narrative, as Sterne describes in detail the pain, mental anguish, physical inconvenience, medical treatment, domestic arrangements, and curiosity associated with it, as well as Toby's elaborate personal coping strategies. Such potentially harrowing details can be accommodated here because they are not part of a tale of poverty, neglect or abuse, but are softened by comfortable surroundings, family affection, professional expertise and sociable visits, by Toby's ability to pursue his beguiling hobby-horse – and by the sentimentalism of Toby and Trim, who are represented as men of feeling.

The responses of these feminised characters illustrate two of the distinctive characteristics of eighteenth-century sensibility: sympathy for passive and vulnerable individuals rather than for more menacing or numerous victims; and the assumption that exercising the ability to feel for others is in itself an improving activity. In Sterne, the process of evoking the hardships of individual victims of war repeatedly inspires Toby and Trim to voice admirably sympathetic sentiments. Their sentiments may be a source of irony since they entail a claim on the reader's credence and clearly work to bolster the speakers' own sense of self-esteem. But they also entail a genuine claim on the reader's sympathy. The terrible conditions endured by ordinary servicemen on active duty, for example, which Smollett had described with bitter satire in *Roderick Random*, are evoked rather differently by Sterne's Trim as he assures parson Yorick's curate that a soldier prays as heartily as a cleric does:

> But when a soldier, said I, an' please your reverence, has been standing for twelve hours together in the trenches, up to his knees in cold water,--or engaged, said I, for months together in long and dangerous marches;--harassed, perhaps, in his rear to-day;--harassing others

150   Part II: Developing Questions

to-morrow;--detached here;--countermanded there;--resting this night out upon his arms;--beat up in his shirt the next;--benumbed in his joints;--perhaps without straw in his tent to kneel on;--must say his prayers how and when he can. (ii 505–506)[74]

As we saw in earlier in this chapter, physicians had begun to publish accounts of the privations routinely suffered by large numbers of soldiers and sailors on active service, accounts intended to encourage commanders and ministers to give more attention to the welfare of their forces.[75] James Pringle's *Observations on the Diseases of the Army* (London, 1752), for example, contains harrowing descriptions of troops' continued exposure to cold and wet (21–22). However, Trim's account narrows the focus, to evoke the dogged endurance of 'a soldier' – an individual deserving of compassion and respect – rather than the neglectful attitude of those higher up who routinely expose thousands of soldiers to such hardships. The severe conditions are mentioned as reassuring evidence of piety, rather than as the subject of outraged protest. The sentimental technique confronts readers with an example of good nature that can be read as naivety, while inviting them to see the possibility of an alternative, more critical interpretation.

The most brutal aspects of army life and discipline are similarly evoked in terms that produce displays of sentiment rather than angry condemnation. When Toby recalls how a 'poor grenadier was so unmercifully whipp'd at Bruges about the ducats', Trim responds with tearful pity for the 'innocent' victim; later, he declares he would be 'picquetted to death' before allowing any woman to come to harm.[76] The story of Le Fever, which became highly popular as an extract, has the makings of a grim cautionary tale, but is presented instead as a sentimental one. The younger Le Fever, adopted by Uncle Toby when his father dies, is inspired to take his father's sword to war, but eventually loses 'his time, his services, his health, and, in short, every thing but his sword'.[77] The narrative mode invites us to share Toby's own sentimental valuation of the sword, the father's legacy; a critical reading might conclude that the son is doomed by this legacy.

With their gentle manners and capacity for sympathy, Toby and Trim are the antithesis of the rough, dissolute soldiers that sometimes appear in Fielding's fiction. Sterne's feminisation of these characters allows him to displace feminine virtue of the kind that in Richardson and Fielding threatens simply to negate martial values, just as the author of *Ephraim Tristram Bates* displaces it. Such a model of feminine virtue would stand apart from, and be directly opposed to, Toby's playful destruction of domestic order; it would unsettle Sterne's carefully maintained ambivalence. At various points, the novel implies that war is destructive to sexual relations (Toby's hobby horse is consistently associated with sexual displacement, the war games damage Tristram's manhood, Le Fever's wife is killed by a musket shot as she lies in his arms in an army tent). The novel as a whole entails a devaluation of the female, not only in its presentation of female characters such as Mrs Shandy and the Widow Wadman, but in its attitude to readers. As Barbara Benedict has noted, in narrating his 'Life and Opinions', Tristram segregates his readers by gender: 'whereas the term "Sir" solicits a sympathetic reader, "Madame" evokes a bad one', a device that associates 'debased modern culture, both literary and by implication political, with female values and audiences'. [78] This devaluation of the female is a precondition of the novel's artful reconciliation of military ardour with tender feeling.

Both of these novels reflect upon the waning influence of the traditional link between landownership and martial virtue in a modern world that generates a great deal of interest in war, but that seems self-destructive either despite or because of that interest. In both novels, martial virtue seems anomalous and enclosing, whether it appears as a dedicated professionalism ready for active service, or in the memory of old soldiers who once risked life and limb for their country. The anomalous nature of this dedication to war arises ultimately from the professionalisation of the armed forces in a modern commercial society, which on the one hand (as *Tristram Bates* shows) gives rise to opportunities for patronage and corruption within the professions and on the other (as *Tristram Shandy* shows) embeds war within the non-combatant realm as an object of moralising and historical reconstruction, to which ideas of personal worth and 'national interest' become attached – ideas which, arising from individual sentiments rather than from public responsibilities, may be providing amusement and personal gratification while working to undermine the interests of those involved. In Sterne's Uncle Toby, the fascination with war helps to inspire a destructive private hobby-horse, which seems at once absurdly idiosyncratic and disturbingly representative of the wider nation's preoccupation with war. Sterne's gently ironical portrait of the destructive war games played upon Uncle Toby's estate seems calculated to inspire affection rather than moral horror. If we are amused by this sentimentalised account of a man damaged by and obsessed with war, we are implicated in the moral problem Sterne addresses.

Part II: Developing Questions

Notes

1 Maximillian E. Novak, 'Warfare and Its Discontents in Eighteenth-Century Fiction: Or, Why Eighteenth-Century Fiction Failed to Produce a *War and Peace*,' *Eighteenth-Century Fiction*, 4: 3 (1992), 185–206. 188.
2 For Johnson's complex attitude to war, see H. R. Kilbourne, 'Dr. Johnson and War,' *ELH*, 12: 2 (1945), 130–143.
3 See Bridget Orr, *Empire on the English Stage 1660–1714* (Cambridge: Cambridge University Press, 2001).
4 Thomas Cleary, 'Jacobitism in *Tom Jones*: The Basis for an Hypothesis,' *Philological Quarterly*, 52: 2 (1973), 239–251.
5 Michael McKeon, 'Generic Transformation and Social Change: Rethinking the Rise of the Novel', in *Theory of the Novel: An Historical Approach*, (Baltimore: Johns Hopkins University Press, 2000), 382–399, 384–387.
6 For example, John Milton's *Paradise Lost* (1667); John Locke's *Some Thoughts Concerning Education* (1693); Fénelon's *Telemachus* (1699); Richard Steele's, *The Christian Hero* (1701).
7 See Brean Hammond, *Professional Imaginative Writing in England, 1670–1740* (Oxford: Oxford University Press, 1997), 106, 124–126.
8 Ronald Paulson, *Don Quixote in England: The Aesthetics of Laughter* (Baltimore: Johns Hopkins University Press, 1998).
9 Thomas Philip Haviland, *The Roman de Longue Haleine on English Soil* (Philadelphia: Philadelphia University Press, 1931).
10 William B. Warner, *Licensing Entertainment: The Elevation of Novel Reading in Britain, 1684–1750*, (Berkeley: University of California Press, 1998), 151.
11 Warner, 582.
12 Daniel Defoe, *An Essay on Projects* (London 1697), 252; *The Double Welcome: A Poem to the Duke of Marlbro* (London, 1705).
13 [Daniel Defoe], *An Essay upon* Literature, 115. See Maximillian E. Novak, 'Defoe and the Art of War,' *Philological Quarterly*, 75: 2 (1996), 197–213.
14 Arthur W. Secord, *Robert Drury's Journal and Other Studies* (Urbana: University of Illinois Press, 1961), 79.
15 Sharon Alker, 'The Soldierly Imagination: Narrating Fear in Defoe's *Memoirs of a Cavalier*,' *Eighteenth-Century Fiction*, 19: 1 & 2 (2006), 43–68.
16 See Ashley Marshall, 'Defoe as Satirist,' *Huntington Library Quarterly*, 70: 4 (2007), 553–576.
17 John Stevenson *Popular Disturbances in England 1700–1870* (London: Routledge, 1992), 18–23; Ian Gilmour, *Riot, Risings and Revolution* (London: Hutchinson, 1992), 71–73.
18 [Daniel Defoe], *Hymn to the Mob* (London, 1715), ii, iii.
19 *The Novels of Daniel Defoe*, General Editors W. R. Owens, and P. N. Furbank, vol 4, *Memoirs of a Cavalier* (1720), ed. N. H. Keeble (London: Pickering and Chatto, 2008), 42.
20 *Memoirs of a Cavalier*, 24, 148.

War and the 'Elevation' of the Novel   153

21 Sharon Alker argues that *Memoirs of a Cavalier* 'exposes the cracks in the stoic early modern military memoir and highlights the fragility of narrative that seek to contain the violence of war' (*Soldierly Imagination*, 68).

22 See John Mullan, 'High-Meriting, Low-Descended,' *The London Review of Books*, 24 (2003), 24.

23 E. J. Clery, *The Feminization Debate in Eighteenth-Century England* (Basingstoke: Palgrave, 2004), 95.

24 James Alan Downie, *A Political Biography of Henry Fielding* (London: Pickering and Chatto, 2009), 89.

25 The 13 December 1739 issue has a dream vision apparently by Fielding which places Richard Glover, as author of the violent pro-war epic *Leonidas*, on top of Parnassus, to which he was introduced by Homer and Milton (67–8).

26 *Io Triumphe: A Poem upon Admiral Vernon* (London, 1741), 6.

27 'The Gossips-Toast,' in *Vernon's Glory, a Collection of Songs Occasioned by the Taking of Porto Bello and Fort Chagre* (London, 1740), 19–22.

28 See *The Daily Post*, 9th July 1739.

29 Henry Fielding, *Of True Greatness. An Epistle to the Right Honourable George Dodington, Esq.*, (London, 1741).

30 *The Vernon-iad* (London, 1741), 10, n. 25.

31 Scott Black, 'Henry Fielding and the Progress of Romance', in *The Oxford Handbook of the Eighteenth-Century Novel*, ed. J. A. Downie (Oxford: Oxford University Press, 2016), 237–251, 240.

32 F. Holmes Dudden, *Henry Fielding: His Life, Works and Times* (Oxford: Oxford University Press, 1952), 2 vols., I, 473.

33 *The History of the Life of the Late Mr Jonathan Wild the Great* (London, Dent, 1973),

34 Keith Maslen, *Samuel Richardson of London, Printer* (Christchurch N.Z., University of Otago, 2001), 22–31.

35 See especially M. John Cardwell, 'The Rake as Military Strategist: Clarissa and Eighteenth-Century Warfare,' *Eighteenth-Century Fiction* 19: 1 2006, 153–180. Also John Carroll. 'Lovelace as Tragic Hero,' *University of Toronto Quarterly* 42 (1972), 14–25; Penelope Biggs, 'Hunt, Conquest, Trial: Lovelace and the Metaphor of the Rake,' *Studies in Eighteenth-Century Culture* 11 (1982), 473–502; Margaret Anne Doody, 'Disguise and Personality in Richardson's Clarissa, *Eighteenth-Century Life* 12 (1988), 18–39.

36 Samuel Richardson, *Clarissa: The History of a Young Lady*, ed. Angus Ross (London, Penguin: 1985), 866, 602.

37 Cardwell, 173.

38 Samuel Richardson, *The History of Sir Charles Grandison*, ed. Jocelyn Harris (Oxford: Oxford University Press, 1986), 1: 4.

39 Raymond Williams, *The Country and the City*, (Oxford: Oxford University Press, 1975), 65.

40 E. J. Clery, *The Feminization Debate*, 96, 100, 109, 111.

41 Ruth K. McCLure, *Coram's Children: The London Foundling Hospital in the Eighteenth Century* (New Haven: Yale University Press: 1981); Linda Colley,

154   Part II: Developing Questions

Britons: Forging the Nation 1707–1837, (New Haven: Yale University Press, 1992), 82–3; Sarah Kinkel, 'Saving Admiral Byng: Imperial Debates, Military Governance and Popular Politics at the Outbreak of the Seven Years War', *Journal for Maritime Research*, 13: 1 (2011), 3–19.

42 Arnold Zucherman, 'Scurvy and the Ventilation of Warships in the Royal Navy: Samuel Sutton's Contribution'; *Eighteenth-Century Studies*, 10: 2 (1976–77), 222–234.

43 See Margarette Lincoln, *Representing the Royal Navy: British Sea Power, 1750–1815* (Farnham: Ashgate, 2002), 161–183.

44 N. A. M. Roger, *The Wooden World: An Anatomy of the Georgian Navy* (Glasgow: Collins, 1986), 14.

45 David Coke and Alan Borg, *Vauxhall Gardens: A History* (New Haven: Yale University Press, 2011), 120.

46 Pro-Vernon accounts: *The Conduct of Admiral Vernon Examin'd and Vindicated* (London, 1741); Sir Charles Knowles, *A Journal of the Expedition to Carthagena*, (London, 1744); *Original Papers Relating to the Expedition to Carthagena* (London, 1744). Pro-Wentworth: George Faulkener, *A Journal of the Expedition to Carthagena* (London, 1744). Claiming to Redress the Balance: *Authentic Papers Relating to the Expedition Against Carthagena* (London, 1744).

47 Kathleen Wilson, 'Empire, Trade and Popular Politics in Mid-Hanoverian Britain: The Case of Admiral Vernon', *Past and Present*, 121 (1988), 201–224; Gerald Jordan and Nicholas Rogers, 'Admirals as Heroes: Patriotism and Liberty in Hanoverian England', *Journal of British Studies*, 28: 3 (1989), 201–224.

48 Tobias Smollett, *The Adventures of Roderick Random*, edited with an Introduction by Paul-Gabriel Boucé (Oxford: Oxford University Press, 1979), 188.

49 *Roderick Random*, xxiv.

50 Jennifer Thorn, '*Roderick Random*, Literacy, and the Appropriation of Plebeian Culture', *Eighteenth-Century Fiction*, 24:4 (2012), 687–710, 694.

51 *A Complete History of England, from the Descent of Julius Caesar to the Treaty of Aix La Chappelle, 1748*, 3rd edn. (London, 1760) vol 11, 253, 285, 299, 304.

52 *The Daily Advertiser*, July 1748, argued that tens of thousands of sailors, marines and privateers who were about to be discharged and turned adrift should be settled in the Highlands and the Northern Isles of Scotland, and employed in fisheries. *The Gentleman's Magazine*, outlined a comparable scheme in the same month.

53 Nicholas Rogers, *Mayhem: Post-War Crime and Violence in Britain, 1748–53* (New Haven: Yale University Press, 2012), 108–109.

54 *To the Good People of Great Britain and Ireland. The humble address of Daniel Dettingen [...] In behalf of himself and the rest of the disbanded solders and cashiered sailors of these kingdoms* (Dublin, 1749), 3.

55 Peter Way, 'Class and the Common Soldier in the Seven Years' War', *Labour History*, 44: 4 (2003), 455–481, 458. Marcus Rediker, *Between the Devil and the*

Deep Blue Sea: Merchant Seamen, Pirates, and the Anglo-American Maritime World 1700–1750 (New York: Cambridge University Press, 1987), 291.

56 Henry Fielding, *Amelia*, ed. Martin C. Battestin (Oxford: Oxford University Press, 1983), Xv.

57 Gerald Newman, *The Rise of English Nationalism: A Cultural History* (London: Weidenfeld and Nicolson, 1987), 68 ff.

58 Kathleen Wilson, *The Sense of the People: Politics, Culture, and Imperialism in England, 1715–1785* (Cambridge: Cambridge University Press, 1995), 178–180.

59 Richard Middleton, 'The Recruitment of the British Army, 1755–1752', *Journal of the Society for Army Research*, 67:272 (1989), 226–238, p. 227.

60 John Brown, *An Estimate of the Manners and Principle of the Times* (Belfast, 1758), 35.

61 Helen Sard Hughes, 'A Precursor of Tristram Shandy', *The Journal of English and Germanic Philology*, 17: 2 (1919), 227–251.

62 See Adam James Smith, 'Property, Patriotism and Independence: The Figure of the "Freeholder" in Eighteenth-Century Partisan Print', *Journal for Eighteenth-Century Studies*, 40:3 (2017), 345–362. Smith notes that a property worth 40 shillings (£2) a year qualified the owner to vote in country elections, 346.

63 See G. J. Barker-Benfield, *The Culture of Sensibility* (Chicago: Chicago University Press, 1992), 251.

64 Barton C. Hacker, 'Women and Military Institutions in Early Modern Europe: A Reconnaissance', *Signs*, 6 (1981), 643–671.

65 Thomas Keymer, *Sterne, the Moderns, and the Novel* (Oxford: Oxford University Press, 2002), 190, 199.

66 Keymer notes: 'the evidence of his subscription lists is that he succeeded in finding patronage that was politically much more plural than might have been expected', 190.

67 Letters to Stephen Croft, Christmas Day 1760, and Tuesday March 17, 1761?, *The Florida Edition of the Works of Laurence Sterne Vol VII, The Letters, Part I: 1739–1764*, ed. Melvyn New and Peter de Voogd (Gainesville: University Press of Florida, 2009), 178, 189.

68 Nicholas Rogers, *Mayhem*, 109–122.

69 Howard Anderson, 'A Version of Pastoral: Class and Society in *Tristram Shandy*', *Studies in English Literature, 1500–1900*, 7: 3 (1967), 509–529. Melvyn New, *Tristram Shandy: A Book for Free Spirits* (New York: Twayne, 1994), 87; Carol Watts, *The Cultural Work of Empire: The Seven Years' War and the Imagining of the Shandean State* (Toronto: Toronto University Press, 2007), 80; Andrea Speltz, 'War and Sentimentalism: Irony in Voltaire's *Candide*, Sterne's *Tristram Shandy*, and Lessing's *Minna von Barnhelm*' *Canadian Review of Comparative Literature*, 44: 2 (2017), 282–297, 288; Samuel Weber, 'Militarizing Feeling: What Does It Mean to Fight a *"War on Terror"?*' *Boundary* 2, 44: 4 (2017), 33–55.

70 See Adam James Smith, 'Property, Patriotism and Independence', 346.

156 Part II: Developing Questions

71 John Richardson, 'Tristram Shandy and War Representation,' *Eighteenth-Century Life*, 44: 1 (2020), 27–48, 34.

72 David Hume, *Essays: Moral, Political and Literary*, ed. Eugene F. Miller (Indianapolis: Liberty Classics, 1987): 'Of Public Credit', 137; 'Of the Balance of Power', 110–111.

73 Jonathan Lamb, 'Shandeism and the Shame of War', in *Tracing War in British Enlightenment and Romantic Culture*, ed. Neil Ramsey and Gillian Russell (Basingstoke: Palgrave Macmillan, 2015), 16–36.

74 Laurence Sterne, *The Life and Opinions of Tristram Shandy, Gentleman* (San Francisco: Arion Press, 1988), Vol VI, ch vii, 400.

75 Margarette Lincoln, *Representing the Royal Navy*, 161–183.

76 Vol II, chap iv, 261; Vol V, ch xxi, 360.

77 Vol VI, ch xiii, 410.

78 Barbara M. Benedict, '"Dear Madam": Rhetoric, Cultural Politics and the Female Reader in Sterne's Tristram Shandy', *Studies in Philology* 89: 4 (1992), 485–498, 485.

CHAPTER 6

War and the 'Science of Man'

Some of the factors that help to explain transformations in the realm of novel writing, such as the challenge to traditional authorities by empiricist epistemology, and the increasing interest in the experience of the individual, also influenced key developments in the realm of philosophy. David Hume's attempt to dignify his own philosophical investigations as a 'Science of Man' reflected his conviction that the study of society and morality could be based upon a dispassionate historical and psychological approach to human experience – an approach shared by other writers of the Enlightenment, including his fellow-Scot Adam Smith. The (usually male) individual at the heart of Hume's and Smith's investigations is not approached in the light of the traditional sanctions and obligations prescribed by religion, nor in relation to the roles and duties promoted by civic humanist and other ideologies. His actions, shaped by individual and social experience, are ideally motivated by enlightened self-interest – enlightened implying that it is shaped by reason in conjunction with 'sympathy' or 'sentiment'. He is, in the words of John Pocock, 'a private being, pursuing goals and safeguarding freedoms which are his own and looking to government mainly to preserve and protect his individual activity'.[1] This conception of the individual would now be identified as 'liberal'.

Hume and Smith shared an interest in the idea of progress, and in what Norbert Elias terms the 'civilizing process'. They usually argued that modern war was fought with more humanity than the wars of earlier eras, and they promoted the idea that modern commerce would lead to improved relations between nations, and so would, or at least could, enhance the prospects for peace – an idea now termed 'commercial pacifism'.[2] They were reformers who offered improving models of behaviour, but they also thought of themselves as dispassionate men of science who worked to strip away illusions. Sometimes they wrote and published during wartime when their moral concerns led them to support the national view of war in terms suitable to their reforming agenda. But at other times, they

157

emphasised that war clouded the judgement of the public and of states-men. War was not only an important subject in their work, but a condi-tioning context that influenced both what they said and how they said it. They shared an understanding that in Britain, with its constitutional monarchy and a relatively free press, there was a growing potential for the mutual influence of war and public opinion to shape national destiny. The public they considered was not a mass public, but it had unprecedented access to information about war supplied by daily newspapers, magazines, prints, and pamphlets, and it had an increasing power to influence politics. As their work developed, both writers found that their assessment of the public's response to war threatened to undermine the central claims of their moral theories.

The importance of war in the thought of the Scottish Enlightenment has long been recognised. Military power was seen as essential to state security in much eighteenth-century political theory. This view influenced Scottish theories of progress and underpinned the arguments of Hume and Smith for reserving 'prerogative powers' to the state.[3] It informed the mid-eighteenth-century 'militia debate' between those Scots (like Adam Ferguson) who favoured a Scottish militia, and those (including Hume and Smith) who stressed the superiority of a professional standing army.[4] If Hume and Smith, like others, emphasised the modern state's need to be ready for warfare, they also came to deplore the military course taken by Britain – whose wars, financed by public credit, seemed driven by 'Jealously of Trade'.[5] But, as I shall argue, the problem for Hume and Smith was not only the policies that the governments of Britain and other European pow-ers seemed determined to pursue, but also – and more fundamentally – the public's apparent willingness to tolerate the dire consequences of war. Both writers tried to develop a theory of morality on a psychological basis, distanced from theological ideas of reason and religious institutions. By foregrounding the role of the passions, sentiment, sympathy, and making impartiality a touchstone of enlightened judgement, they inevitably made war a problem, since war was the focus of national partiality. In their work, the national view of war becomes deeply problematic.

David Hume

In the introduction to his *Treatise of Human Nature,* David Hume (1711–1776) conceived the 'Science of Man' to be 'the only solid foundation for the other sciences'. As a 'scientist' Hume intended to draw principles 'as universal as possible' from observation of 'the common course of the world', in particular from 'men's behaviour in company, in affairs, and in their pleasures'.[6] This suggests that his conclusions would be based primarily upon, and relevant to, the experience of the modern non-combatant, who was defended by professional military forces and who stood in implicit contrast to the classical ideal of the 'citizen warrior'.[7] Hume was therefore concerned with society's response to the anomalous pressures of war. As a 'scientist', his view of war was necessarily ambivalent. In that role he had to exemplify, in order to recommend, two rather different aspects of modernity: the enlarged humanity which the refinement, cultivation and sociability of the modern world supposedly promoted; and the objective reasoning made possible by the modern writer's ability to draw upon an unprecedented range of evidence from different periods and cultures. These two requirements did not necessarily support each other, especially when the subject was war. As a humanitarian, Hume was an idealist who imagined 'progress' as extending the moral norms of civil society to international relations, including the conduct of war; as objective reasoner he was a political realist who insisted that in war such norms were relaxed or suspended.

Much of the *Treatise* was completed in France, in a period of peace between 1734 and 1737, where Hume could feel distanced from the immediate pressures and alarms of a nation at war. The work was to be published anonymously, and independently, without a patron or subscribers. This situation may have made it easier to write dispassionately about common responses to war's brutalities. Politically, his major concern was the problem of party conflict, which threatened to destabilise British society. Faced with the divisive, idealistic theories of contemporary Whigs and Tories, he turned to the hard facts of war in order to give lessons in political necessity. In the *Treatise,* he rejects Tory notions of the sovereign's divine right, and the Whig theory that political authority derived from a contract between rulers and ruled. Instead, he traces the origin of virtually all dynasties and forms of commonwealth to acts of 'usurpation and rebellion', which acquire authority through long possession or through the 'right of conquest'. He derives the very idea of political subordination from warfare between primitive communities, and from the realisation that effective war-making requires subordination under 'authority in a single person'. The primitive warlord becomes the forerunner of all magistrates and princes, since military 'Camps are the true mothers of cities' (II, pp. 279, 281, 286). The reign of peace and justice descends from the right of might.

When Hume describes the process of acquiescence in the brutal necessities of war, he usually makes it seem a reasonable response founded upon

160 Part II: Developing Questions

an easily determined self-interest. But he is also aware that war, like other emergencies, generates strong collective passions that may cloud reasonable judgement. This is a problem that will come to haunt his work. In Book 2 of the *Treatise,* his theory of morals takes the passions as its starting point and depends upon the principle of 'sympathy' – the means by which we 'receive by communication' the sentiments of others (II, p. 72). Sympathy has a 'natural' influence on others and is influenced by the passions of those closest to us (II, p. 300). It therefore makes us susceptible to the narrowing influence of partiality. Hume maintains that experience and reflection allow us to overcome partiality, to 'overlook our own interests', to disregard whether we are dealing with 'our acquaintance or strangers, countrymen or foreigners', and to 'correct those sentiments of blame, which so naturally arise upon any opposition' (II, p. 302). But war dramatically illustrates the difference between the 'impartial conduct' that 'reason requires' and the natural course of our passion:

> When our own nation is at war with any other, we detest them under the character of cruel, perfidious, unjust and violent: But always esteem ourselves and allies equitable, moderate, and merciful. If the general of our enemies be successful, 'tis with difficulty we allow him the figure and character of a man. [...] But if the success be on our side, our commander has all the opposite good qualities, and is a pattern of virtue, as well as of courage and conduct. His treachery we call policy: His cruelty is an evil inseparable from war. In short, every one of his faults we either endeavour to extenuate, or dignify it with the name of that virtue, which approaches it. 'Tis evident the same method of thinking runs thro' common life (II: p. 99).

Here, the 'opposition' generated by war makes impartial judgement impossible, producing instead grossly perverted, immoderate, manifestly self-serving views. The narrowing effect of sympathy reinforces immediate self-interest but would prevent a more enlightened perception of self-interest based on a dispassionate appraisal of the enemy. In Book III of the *Treatise,* when Hume returns to confront the distorted judgements produced by war, he claims that 'a man of temper and judgement may preserve himself from these illusions' – but he concedes that this 'seldom happens' (II, p. 206). The national view, stripped of its mythical framework, becomes a problematic national partiality that undermines morality.

This way of characterising a collective response to conflict allows Hume to illustrate an uncomfortable truth about the natural partiality of our judgements in 'common life'. But it proves unhelpful to his view of progress, which depends upon the claim that we can overcome this kind of

War and the 'Science of Man'   161

partiality even when oppositions arise, and so achieve the 'impartial judgement' that 'reason requires'. In Book 3, Hume explains that historically,
members of a society enter into a convention – 'a general sense of common interest' – to bestow stability on the possession of external goods
(II, pp. 221, 220). During this process ideas of justice, property, right, and
obligation arise, which allow commerce to develop. Narrow self-interest is
moderated by the realisation that self-interest and the interests of society
are both served by justice, not only at home, but internationally:

> Where possession has no stability, there must be perpetual war. Where
> property is not transferr'd by consent, there can be no commerce. Where
> promises are not observ'd, there can be no leagues nor alliances. The advan-
> tages, therefore, of peace, commerce, and mutual succour, make us extend
> to different kingdoms the same notions of justice, which take place among
> individuals. (II, p. 289)

Here, commerce plays a key role in moderating international relations, by
helping to generate a common sense of interest between nations. When at
this point Hume refers to the self-interested reactions that arise in response
to international conflict, he does so not in terms of illusory judgement,
but in terms of acquiescence. He concedes that, when conflicts arise, there
may be 'a relaxation of the morality' which can 'reconcile us more easily to
the transgression of justice among princes and republics' (II, pp. 290–291).
This sounds like a process to which individuals of 'reason and judgement'
could reconcile themselves, one which is not necessarily incompatible with
the moderating influence of enlightened self-interest.

Hume's moral theory therefore presents two rather different views of
how 'we' respond to conflict with other nations, both involving a compromising of moral standards – one through a gross distortion of judgement
and one through reasonable adjustment or acquiescence. The second is
more useful to the commercial pacifism that had already begun to take
shape in his work.

Between his return to London in 1737, and the publication of the
Treatise in 1739–40, Hume would have been able to experience at first-
hand public responses to war, both in the press and in the streets, as
a dispute about the Spanish right to inspect British merchant ships in
Spanish American waters set in motion a public clamour that led to war
with Spain, a conflict (the War of Jenkins's Ear, 1739–42) that was quickly
overtaken by a larger war involving other European powers (the War of
the Austrian Succession, 1740–1748). The influence of national partiality
was amply illustrated in the press campaign against Spanish 'depredations'
(joined by a number of eminent writers), in the rapturous celebration of

162   Part II: Developing Questions

Admiral Vernon's victory at Portobello (1740), and in the widespread outrage at Britain's defeat at Cartegena (June 1741).[8]

In the essays published during the ongoing war, Hume's critical view of national partiality was carefully suppressed. The *Treatise* had not sold well, so Hume attempted to reach a larger audience, including female readers, through a series of essays like those of Addison's *The Spectator* or Bolingbroke's *The Craftsman*. In doing so he no doubt wished to distance himself from the 'selfish' school of philosophy with which early reviews of the *Treatise* had linked him.[9] And in a time of war he would have good reason to present himself as a 'public spirited' writer. At the end of 1741, when the war was going badly and the government was in crisis, Hume published the fifteen essays, *Essays Moral, Political and Literary*, which were soon followed, early in 1742 by a second volume containing twelve essays. These essays have rightly been seen as a response to the divisive party politics of Walpolean Britain, and an attempt to promote cultural reform; but in the context of war, they also represent a diplomatic response to the immediate crisis.[10] Instead of insisting on the gross partiality of the moral judgements naturally generated by war, Hume vindicates the national view by representing it in gentler terms. The essay 'Of Moral Prejudices' criticises contemporary raillery against everything previously held sacred by mankind: 'And even public Spirit, and a Regard to our Country, are treated as chimerical and romantic'. National partiality is now defended alongside 'The virtuous and tender Sentiments, or Prejudices, if you will'.[11] In this context, it seems quite distinct from the unpatriotic opportunism of writers who seize upon war as a pretext to oppose government policy whether it is for or against war (writers who are condemned in 'On the Liberty of the Press', p. 9). In other essays, Hume's appeals to the example of 'female softness and modesty' (p. 134) and to delicacy of taste which 'renders the mind incapable of all the rougher, more boisterous emotions' (p. 6) direct his readers away from the passionate bellicose nationalism displayed in contemporary wartime Britain. Hume explicitly distances his own science from violent conflict, arguing that 'the gradual revolutions of a state must be a more proper subject of reasoning and observation, than the foreign and violent, which are commonly produced by single persons, and are more influenced by whim, folly, or caprice, than by general passions and interests' (p. 112). Treating the causes of war as distinct from the general development of society makes it easier for him to claim that 'our modern education and customs instil more humanity and moderation than the ancient' (p. 94).

With the outbreak of war, and with the adoption of a more popular form of writing for his 'scientific' message, there was an advantage in representing national partiality in terms of virtuous sentiment, rather than in terms of illusory judgement. Hume's new emphasis on humanity, tender sentiments, and delicacy of taste is clearly in tension with the politics of necessity, but this tension reflects the difference between civilised social life and the emergencies that may threaten it, a difference that Hume is able to exploit in his explanation of principles of government. In his essay 'Of Passive Obedience' (1748) when he considers the kind of extremity in which rebellion might be justified, he cites examples of tactical violence of the type he himself had witnessed, and that his readers would be familiar with from newspaper reports: 'What governor of a town makes any scruple of burning the suburbs, when they facilitate the approaches of the enemy? Or what general abstains from plundering a neutral country, when the necessities of war require it, and he cannot otherwise subsist his army?' (p. 489). His argument requires readers to recognise and accept as a matter of course that local interests, and the interests of other nations, might be reasonably violated in war, and humanitarian considerations be set aside, in the interests of one's own nation.

When in the aftermath of war he came to recast his *Treatise* in the more appealing form of the *Enquiries Concerning Human Understanding and Concerning the Principles of Morals* (1748, 1751), he claimed that such national partiality actually promotes 'the general interest of mankind'.[12] This and comparable statements in Hume undoubtedly support A. B Stilz's view that Hume sees liberty and political stability as dependent upon national partiality.[13] But this is only one strand of Hume's thought – a strand that aligns national partiality with reasonable self-interest rather than with illusory judgement. He seems notably reluctant to confront directly the issue of how war distorts the judgement. When he does consider how collective feeling influences our thinking, he testifies to its overwhelming power: 'he must be more or less than man, who kindles not in the common blaze'. But he refers to feelings aroused by 'popular tumults, seditions, factions, panics' (p. 275) rather than by national partiality in war. A passage in the concluding 'Dialogue' notes simply that war produces 'the greatest variations in moral sentiment, and diversifies the most our ideas of virtue and personal merit' (p. 337). Elsewhere, he carefully distinguishes between calling someone an 'enemy' (a context-bound term which derives from self-love) and calling someone 'vicious or odious or depraved' (moral terms arising from some 'universal principle', which 'touch a string to which all mankind have an accord and symphony') (p. 272). The issue is effectively disposed of, although a footnote concedes that a civilised individual may simply rationalise and disguise an animosity that appears openly in the savage (pp. 274–5). In the *Enquiries,* Hume claims that the moral philosopher treats 'The records of wars, intrigues, faction and revolutions' as 'collections of experiments', (pp. 83–84). But to some extent, he represses his knowledge of the negative moral effects of war in order to maintain his positive view of the social passions.

What is repressed in the *Enquiries* was soon to return dramatically in the *Political Discourses,* first published in 1752, in a period of uneasy peace. Here, as Emma Rothschild notes, Hume begins to take stock of the 'late wars'.[14] And more generally, he considers relations between modern nations, the balance of power and trade, and the expense and funding of modern war. In 'Of Luxury' (later entitled 'Of Refinement in the Arts'), he takes up the task of defending modern luxury against those who argue that it weakens martial virtue and corrupts morality while causing wars. He associates luxury with social virtue and humanity rather than with corruption and effeminacy and argues that commerce does not necessarily cause wars, or make them more difficult to fight. But his arguments about the civilising effect of commerce are repeatedly undermined by his observations in other essays about the disturbing effects of modern warfare. Istvan Hont, responding to J. G. A. Pocock's claim that Hume shows commerce as creating 'public debt that destroys both liberty and prosperity', rightly argues that Hume sees war rather than commerce as the source of public debt, and that Hume's problem centres on 'the conjunction of commercial society and international power politics'.[15] But this problem, I argue, exposed a more fundamental difficulty in Hume's account of moral and social development.

Much of the actual experience of war simply could not be reconciled with the more optimistic part of Hume's theory of progress – although it amply confirmed the pessimistic part of his theory of the passions. Hume's view of war was dominated by the established idea of dynastic rivalry, the threat of universal monarchy, and the need to maintain the balance of power in Europe. If war sprung ultimately from the ambitions of individual princes and ministers, it could be regarded as separate from the moderating influence of commerce. But the War of Jenkins's Ear had manifestly been caused by commercial interests, and if the War of the Austrian Succession arose from rival claims to the Hapsburg thrones, Britain's role in it had become increasingly focused on commercial rivalry with France. The capture of Cape Breton from France in 1745 marked a shift in public opinion about French ambition, which was now more widely seen as centred on the sphere of 'trade, colonial territories and maritime power'.[16] This view transcended political differences: the

Opposition, which had previously played down the French threat, now accepted it as a fact.[17] Bob Harris notes 'The principal cause of the sea-change in opposition attitudes was the growing conviction that Britain's naval forces would allow her to engross French commerce and colonies'.[18] A programme of commercial and colonial expansion was widely discussed in the press. The peace of Aix-la-Chappelle (1748) made little difference to the perceived threat from France, a perception strengthened by newspaper reports of French re-armament and military build-up in North America. A spiral of aggression seemed to be developing – even though it was hard to see what Britain had gained so far from the conflict. The commercial ambitions that had motivated the war with Spain in 1739 had not been realised. The struggle with France had led to stalemate. And yet more than £28 million had been added to the National Debt.[19] Commerce which, Hume supposed, would generate mutual dependences and so moderate international relations appeared to be stimulating ever more intense conflict.

Running through the *Political Discourses*, the optimistic view of refinement and humanity intersects with a pessimistic view of modern war, each generating a quite different view of what 'must' happen. One asserts that the socialising effects of commerce – the move towards cities, the growing appetite to receive and communicate knowledge, the rise of industry, and the refined arts – 'must' produce both an 'increase in humanity' and a refined moderation, benefits which diffuse their influence from private life to the public, and cause 'Even foreign wars [to] abate of the their cruelty'.[20] This kind of argument is supported by assertions that the wars of antiquity were 'more bloody' and fought by 'more destructive' maxims than their modern counterparts.[21]

The other view, drawn from a close observation of what has actually happened in Europe since the reign of William III, paints a quite different picture. 'According to modern policy war is attended with every destructive circumstance; loss of men, encrease of taxes, decay of commerce, dissipation of money, devastation by sea and land'.[22] The expense of modern war is staggering: since the revolution of 1688, European nations have spent 'immense treasures' in Flanders, 'in the course of three long wars' – possibly more than half of all the total money at present in Europe.[23] The wars of antiquity are dwarfed in comparison. 'The English fleet, during the late war, required as much money to support it as all the Roman legions, which kept the whole world in subjection, during the time of the emperors'.[24] What makes Britain's inflated effort possible is the invention of public credit, the colossal national debt which by

166   Part II: Developing Questions

mortgaging future wealth 'must', by 'the natural progress of things', lead to one of two outcomes: 'Either the nation must destroy public credit, or public credit must destroy the nation'. Hume implies that the latter will happen: 'The breach of national faith will be the necessary effect of wars, defeats, misfortunes, and public calamities, or even perhaps of victories and conquests'.[25]

Hume's response to this dilemma was to blame not commerce itself, but the ideology of mercantilism and the mechanisms of public credit. But how had such policies and mechanisms gained acceptance if they were, as Hume assumed, so much against the public interest? The problem resolves itself into another, of how self-interest is judged, and how conflict influences the judgement. Hume finds himself facing the problem that he had broached in the *Treatise*: war makes impartial judgement impossible, drawing us into a world of illusions; a person of reason and judgement can resist such illusions, but this seldom happens. This is the very perception he had tried to minimise in his war-time essays and in the *Enquiries*. It now returns with a vengeance.

Hume notes ruefully, 'we seem to have been more possessed with the antient Greek spirit of jealous emulation, than actuated by the prudent views of modern politics'.[26] The spectacle of modern war seems manifestly absurd: 'when I see princes and states fighting and quarrelling, amidst their debts, funds and public mortgages, it always brings to my mind a match of cudgel-playing fought in a *China* shop'.[27] But the British people seem inflamed by such a ludicrous spectacle. While Hume concedes that the balance of power in Europe must be preserved, he claims that 'above half our wars with France, are owing more to our own imprudent vehemence, than to the ambition of our neighbours'. We are 'such true combatants, we lose all concern for ourselves and our posterity'.[28] National partiality, it seems, has caused us to lose sight of reasonable self-interest. We cannot judge our enemy without distortion and we cannot arrive at a clear assessment of our true self-interest.

Hume does not allow his own observations to come to rest on such a conclusion. Instead, he develops a contradiction that he cannot resolve. The public that are described as sociable town-dwellers, peacefully exchanging information, and marked by ever 'more conspicuous humanity' are also, when Hume turns to the realities of modern war, described as immoderate, vehement, imprudent, and implicitly inhuman. The difference between the supposed historical progress of humane sociability and the passions that actually govern us in war becomes too great either to gloss with a gentle equivocation or even to acknowledge.

The History of England

When Hume engaged directly with contemporary war, the humanitarian and the historical realist were pulled apart. The *History of England* (initially published as *The History of Great Britain*) was, among other things, an opportunity to harmonise them. Hume conceived of his history as a narrative of progress, from eras of superstition and barbarism to a recent past characterised by 'the mildness and humanity of modern manners'.[29] But the development of this narrative was complicated by his treatment of war – since in describing the wars of the past, Hume was influenced by the wars of his own time. The first volume was published in 1754, when the much-anticipated conflict was breaking out between Britain and France in North America; most of the work was composed and published during the turmoil of the Seven Years War (1756–1763). The *History* provided an opportunity for Hume to emphasise two conflicting aspects of war: it allowed him to demonstrate, in a conveniently distanced form, the malign effect of war on the judgement; and it allowed him to offer models of humanitarian conduct in war. As historian, Hume addresses an audience that might contain female readers, and (as Mark Salber Phillips and others have pointed out) he shows some concern with the 'sentimental possibilities' of historical narrative.[30] Hume's positive advocacy of 'virtuous and tender sentiments', of 'female softness' and sociable humanity, could not easily be reconciled with the violence of the battlefield. But he could focus on acts of humanity that appear with the cessation of violence – when 'combatants divest themselves of the brute, and resume the man' – in the handling of peace treaties, and in the treatment of conquered civilians and prisoners of war.[31] The *History* would therefore contain both negative examples of the corrosive effects of war, and positive examples of good conduct in war – all of which might help to moderate present-day attitudes.

This twofold strategy has a general influence upon the work as a whole. In the earliest published volume, dealing with the reigns of James I and Charles I (1754), Hume presents civil and religious war as the great destroyer of humanity. But he is careful to show humanity as compatible with military courage, and as the moderator of war (as in the Earl of Manchester's attempt to promote peace during the English civil war, and in Fairfax's offer of honourable terms to the defeated royalists). In the volume which moved from the interregnum to 1688 (published 1756), he shows how faction destroys morality, and he argues that the wars with the Dutch create distress 'not for any national interests or necessity' but 'from

168   Part II: Developing Questions

vain points of honour and personal resentments'. But he also notes how, after the Battle of Bothwell Bridge, the Duke of Monmouth treats his Scottish prisoners 'with a humanity, which they had never experienced in their own countrymen'.[32] In the two volumes on the Tudors (published 1759), Hume criticises the Tudor kings' wars with France (motivated by vain dreams of glory, founded on 'little reason'), but notes that Essex treats his prisoners well in war against Spain.[33] However, it is in the last two volumes, published late in 1761, and dealing with the earliest ages of English history, that Hume's twofold strategy really comes to the fore.

Hume began work on these volumes of early history around the beginning of 1760.[34] By this time, the ongoing war had turned decisively in Britain's favour after a remarkable series of victories in the previous two years. Under the direction of Pitt, Britain's war policy had become increasingly a drive for conquest and empire, fuelled by what Hume would condemn as 'the Jealousy of Trade'.[35] From the end of 1759, discussion about peace terms intensified in the press, and during 1760 there was a growing movement in favour of imposing punitive peace terms upon France, retaining all conquests, and excluding the French entirely from North America.[36] At the same time, the theme of humanity in conquest – at least in the treatment of captives – became highly topical. There were many French prisoners of war in Britain and, when the Louis XV's 'Royal Bounty' for their upkeep suddenly stopped, subscriptions were raised in London and other towns for their relief – an action seen, by Hume among others, as a sign of national benevolence.[37] The papers were still full of the successful siege of Quebec (September 1759), which had been hailed not only as a triumph of courage but also of humanity in the treatment of French civilians.[38] Historical precedents for the siege were found – sometimes in the medieval struggles between England and France. In 1760, Drury Lane theatre staged John Home's tragedy *The Siege of Aquileia*, a work inspired by Wolfe's death at Quebec and by Edward III's siege of Berwick, but recast in a Roman setting.[39] In April, it was reported that the Society for the Encouragement of Arts, Manufactures and Commerce had awarded a premium 'for the best historical picture' to Robert Edge Pine, 'whose subject was the behaviour of Edward III to the burghers of Calais when he besieged that place'.[40] The painting showed Edward III acceding to his wife's request to have mercy on the burghers who had been delivered up for execution. The theme of British humanity in conquest was given a further boost after siege of Montreal (September 1760). The victorious Amherst was praised for this generosity to 'vanquish'd Canadians', and by the following June Francis Hayman's painting of 'The Surrender of

War and the 'Science of Man' 169

Montreal to General Amherst', showing Amherst as magnanimous conqueror feeding his starving captives, was on display in the Great Room at Vauxhall.[41]

Hume's medieval history reflects some of these developments. On the one hand, the wars of medieval England against France provided him with ideal opportunities for vigorous criticism of irrational military ambition and its destructive consequences. When Hume declares that no reign of the ancient English monarchs 'deserves more to be studied than that of Edward III', he suggests its immediate relevance to the present. He claims that Edward's foreign wars were 'neither founded in justice, nor directed to any salutary purpose'; they procured him 'no solid advantages', but ran his kingdom into debt. Despite this, Hume notes, the English consider his reign 'with peculiar fondness', since 'the glory of a Conqueror is so dazzling to the vulgar, the animosity of nations is so violent, that the fruitless desolation of so fine a part of Europe as France, is totally disregarded by us, and is never considered as a blemish in the character or conduct of this prince'.[42] Even as he is presenting the damning evidence, then, Hume begins to reflect upon the insurmountable problem inherent in the production of national history. He is writing for a national audience subject to the same national partiality when reading history that they feel when reading news. And he knows that, in this context, the negative evidence loses its power to influence either 'the vulgar' or 'us' in a morally appropriate way. This kind of truth becomes powerless.

But another kind of evidence seems to retain its power. At the same time as the historian uncovers the perils of national partiality and the spurious 'glory' that clouds the judgment in war, he also repeatedly singles out from medieval warfare acts of humanity for particular praise. He includes the scene in which Edward III pardons the burghers of Calais at his wife's request (even though he disputes its authority); it is a scene that conveniently illustrates the beneficial effect of 'female softness' upon masculine aggression. And he repeatedly emphasises the conciliatory humanity of other victorious medieval warriors, the compassionate treatment of conquered civilians and prisoners of war (by Saladin, Robert Bruce, the Earl of Leicester, the Black Prince and others), and the beneficial effect of peace treaties that are generous rather than punitive (for example, Louis IX's treaty with Henry III, and Edward III's with King John of France).[43] Conversely, he stresses how lack of humanity breeds conflict and puts a stain upon victory (as in the cases of Richard I and Louis XI). Hume is sometimes following Rapin in his treatment of these themes, but usually developing them, sometimes in a way that contrasts strikingly with the variable approach taken by Smollett in his *Complete History of England* (1758).[44] As Donald T. Sieberg has argued, in the *History* Hume gives an 'increasingly favorable estimation of chivalry's civilizing, hence moralizing, power', even while ridiculing its more extravagant notions.[45]

One consequence of this part of Hume's strategy is that his medieval history has more examples of humanity in war than all of the other volumes combined – an odd outcome for a work intended to associate humanity with modern 'science and civility', and to show the early periods of English history as eras of 'superstition and barbarism'. How, one might wonder, could such an emphasis on magnanimous victory possibly work to undermine the process of glorification that Hume seeks to oppose? What might be seen as an example of the historian's own scrupulous impartiality, in, for example, balancing damning criticism of Edward III's military ambition with an acknowledgement of his good conduct in victory, might also simply feed into national partiality. Can the process of moderating public attitudes by emphasising humanity in war really be separated from the process of glorifying irrational war?

The wider consequences of Hume's emphasis on good conduct in war were almost certainly unintended. While the *History* was to become a standard work and – with its provision of scenes designed to engage the sympathies of the reader – a key reference point for history painters later in the century, it was the medieval volumes that were particularly attractive to artists. As Roy Strong points out, the illustrations in Robert Bowyer's *Historic Gallery*, based upon Hume's history, show 'an overwhelming preoccupation with the Middle Ages'.[46] And the *History* helped to popularise scenes of medieval English warriors showing humanity in victory – which contributed to the process of glorification. The burghers of Calais scene became a favourite with history painters (it was painted by Edward Edwards, Benjamin West, Robert Smirk, Richard Westall, Edward Bird, George Jones, and Henry Holliday). Benjamin West painted it, along with the scene of the Black Prince's honourable treatment of his captive King John of France, as part of a series depicting episodes from the reign of Edward III, produced for the King's Audience Chamber at Windsor Castle (1787–9). In this way, a history intended to associate humanity with modern commerce, 'science and civility', in practice contributed to the positive re-evaluation of chivalry, and of the Middle Ages, in the later eighteenth century.[47] In this respect, as in others, Hume's progressive agenda was undermined by his need to respond to modern attitudes to war, to counteract the bellicose nationalism of the public and to reinforce hopeful signs of humanity and moderation.

Adam Smith

The origin of Adam Smith's *Theory of Moral Sentiments* (or *TMS*) may lie around 1752, when he was lecturing on moral philosophy at Glasgow.[48] But the writing of the book itself may have begun at about the same time as Hume began his *History* – that is, in 1754–5, in a period of intense public agitation about the French military build-up in North America. Much of the first edition was apparently completed during the first few years of the Seven Years' War. It was first published in April 1759 – a few months before the capture of Quebec. These were years of extreme public anxiety during which the war often seemed to be going badly, and military failures could produce harsh reactions, including calls for inquiries and for severe punishment of the military leaders involved.

The deepest crisis of this period arose from the case of Admiral Byng, which seemed to expose a profound moral malaise in the nation. In 1756, when Byng failed to stop the French taking Minorca from the British, there was public outrage, fed by a wide range of publications in which Byng was satirised as effeminate and cowardly. Some of the anti-Byng feeling was deliberately managed by the government, to deflect attention from its own role in the disaster. Ceremonies to burn and hang effigies of Byng were held in London and at more than 24 other towns across Britain. He was court-martialled and found guilty of negligence, which, under newly revised articles of war, carried a mandatory death sentence. Although the court martial described him as a 'proper object of mercy', the King did not pardon him and he was executed. Pro-Byng writers condemned the government's brutality and argued that Byng had been sacrificed to public anger.[49] In the wake of this turmoil, John Brown published his influential *Estimate of Manners* (1757–58), which gave a dire assessment of the nation's declining virtue, and even characterised feelings of 'humanity' as the natural growth of an effeminate nation.[50] Smith's *TMS* was, among other things, an intervention in response to a period of crisis, aimed at bringing moral clarity and reassurance where there was confusion and anxiety. He presents himself as a public-spirited writer, working in support of the war effort. In a period of extreme reactions, he offers models of the moral sentiments appropriate to the conduct of war, by addressing the need for violence and discipline, and by defining the role of 'humanity' in ways that steered a course between the twin dangers of brutality and effeminacy.

Smith shared Hume's ambition to produce a 'scientific' account of moral development. And like Hume, he assumed that the rise of commerce and good government worked to promote humanity and to moderate the

172 Part II: Developing Questions

conduct of war.[51] But whereas Hume saw no threat to military capacity in this development, the view of progress Smith outlined in his lectures suggested the opposite – the steady undermining of martial virtue, and a need to counteract this dangerous process.[52] Accordingly, the stoical element of Smith's theory emphasised the importance of self-command, a masculine virtue set in a complementary relation with the feminine virtue of humanity. He writes to stiffen the public's resolve, and to show that feelings of humanity can be reconciled with the tough actions needed in war. But, in the face of the unseemly public clamour, he also wants to show that a public-spirited response to war can be noble and generous. That is, he wants to base the national view of war on moral sentiments, without an appeal to the teachings of the Church or to heroic tradition. At some key moments, his argument addresses issues of principle raised by the case of Admiral Byng.

While Smith praised feelings of humanity, and saw them as characteristic of 'civilized nations', he also repeatedly qualified their value.[53] He insists that naturally our sympathy with physical pain or with the affliction of our friends is limited (p. 47). Like Hume, he shows that in conflicts, our sympathy and sense of justice are guided by partiality, and we have little sympathy for those we regard as wrong (p. 72). He notes that our partiality is also shaped by social distinctions (men are naturally indifferent 'about the misery of their inferiors' p. 52). Smith writes of 'indulgent humanity', classifies it with the 'excessive' passions and with 'weakness' and shows how it can become fanaticism (pp. 23, 306, 33, 40, 232). He associates it with 'Men of retirement and speculation' and notes that 'men of the greatest humanity' may seem 'entirely devoid of public spirit' (pp. 23, 185–186). He claims that 'The most humane actions require no self-denial, no self-command, no great exertion of the sense of propriety' (p. 191).

If Smith works to downgrade feelings of humanity as much as he can, he does this not to discount them completely, but to adapt them to a specific role in his theory. Their key role is to fight a losing battle with our feelings of revenge and our commitment to justice. As long as we can show convincingly that 'passion has not extinguished our humanity', and that 'if we yield to the dictates of revenge, it is with reluctance, from necessity' – as long as our resentment is 'guarded and qualified in this manner, it may be admitted to be even generous and noble' (p. 38). He draws a key example from military discipline: the sentinel who falls asleep on duty. Markus Elder has shown that this was the most common disciplinary offence in the navy.[54] It fell into the same category as Byng's offence, negligence, which now carried a mandatory death sentence. Smith uses the example not to

War and the 'Science of Man' 173

expose the inhumanity of the law, but to provide a detailed illustration of how, in his view, the moral sentiment of humanity operates. He is clear that the sentinel has to be executed (although we know that in practice commanders often punished offenders summarily rather than have them executed, and that clemency – by royal pardon – was often obtained for death penalties).[55] Smith notes that the safety of the multitude may justify the sacrifice of the individual, but that 'A man of humanity must recollect himself, must make an effort, and exert his whole firmness and resolution, before he can bring himself either to inflict it, or to go along with it when it is inflicted by others' (pp. 90–91). This is what distinguishes the man of humanity from the brutal man, who can perform the punishment without the emotional struggle: not the act of violence itself, but the moral sentiment attached to it. Smith, addressing the kind of dilemma that war had recently thrust into public notice – one that arises not only in the heat of battle, but in the deliberations of the court martial – provides a reassuringly sophisticated theoretical grounding to the idea that 'humanity' works not to prevent violence, but to reconcile us to it, and so to justify it.[56] It makes a virtue of acquiescence.

If humanity could be reconciled with the brutal necessities of war in this way, the national partiality generated in wartime posed a trickier problem. Like Hume, Smith identified moral judgement with impartiality. He insisted that we could develop the ability to make disinterested judgements by learning to imagine how situations would appear to an 'impartial spectator' (pp. 24–26). This was supposed to allow individuals to transcend the partiality of the group in order to acquire a viewpoint that had a kind of universal status. But like Hume, Smith was acutely aware of the power of collective feeling, and of how war could generate national partiality. And he was only too aware that such collective feelings could lead to unthinking brutality rather than impartial judgement. One function of the work was to accommodate patriotic responses by presenting them in an acceptable form.

Smith argues that a collectivised response to war is already latent within peaceable experience, ready to be aroused by military signs and symbols. So, for example, while non-combatants may find the sight of surgical instruments displeasing, they find that

> instruments of war are agreeable, though their immediate effect may seem to be in the same manner [as dissecting and amputation-knives] pain and suffering. But then it is the pain and suffering of our enemies, with whom we have no sympathy. With regard to us, they are immediately connected with the agreeable ideas of courage, victory, and honour. They are themselves,

174 Part II: Developing Questions

> therefore, supposed to make one of the noblest parts of dress, and the imitation of them one of the finest ornaments of architecture. (p. 26)

In this context, 'enemies' is simply a category term, which has meaning in peace time as well as in the concrete emergencies of war. 'We' are collectivised by the very idea of war into a hostile nation, withholding sympathy from the imagined pain and suffering of potential enemies, triumphing in our imagined victory over them. Smith imagines this collective response in terms that distance it from the noisy brutality of popular nationalism. The lack of sympathy is, typically, not seen in terms of aggression, but in terms of 'agreeable ideas' of courage. In connecting this collectivised response and national partiality with the supposedly 'noblest' and 'finest' appearances, Smith dignifies it. The national view of war is reconstituted upon a suitable psychological basis.

The attempt to present improving models of the collective response to war leads Smith to produce an extraordinary sequence on generosity and public spirit, in which he tries to align national partiality as closely as he can with impartiality, and tries to align the civilian response to war with the sacrificial heroism of the combatant. He begins with the impartial spectator, giving an example of a soldier who throws away his life to defend that of his officer: when the soldier tries to act so as 'to make the impartial spectator enter into the principles of his conduct, he feels, that to every body but himself, his own life is a trifle compared with that of his officer, and that [...] he acts quite properly and agreeably to what would be the natural apprehensions of every impartial bystander' (p. 191). This gives a clear illustration of how Smith conceives the operation of the impartial spectator and its imagined universality ('every body').

But as Smith proceeds, impartiality is unobtrusively displaced by national partiality. The next example, supposed to illustrate 'the greater exertions of public spirit', involves the self-sacrificing bravery of a young officer: 'to him his own life is of infinitely more value than the conquest of a whole kingdom for the state which he serves'; but if he doesn't view these things 'in the light in which they naturally appear to himself, but in that in which they appear to the nation he fights for', he 'immediately feels that he cannot be too prodigal of his blood' (p. 191). Here, national partiality has silently taken the place of impartial judgement; Smith shows that the moral sentiments of the reflective individual are directly bound up with ideas of national interest in the context of war, even in judgements that might resemble 'impartial' ones. The purpose of this example, it seems, is not to explain the impartial spectator, but to suggest that wars can give rise to a self-sacrificing – and reasonable – generosity.

War and the 'Science of Man' 175

In the next example, we can see where Smith is leading us. This is about the responses of the non-combatant, one who reads about war, and who imagines being in the place not of an impartial spectator – but of Admiral Byng:

> There is many an honest Englishman, who, in his private station, would be more seriously disturbed by the loss of a guinea, than by the national loss of Minorca, who yet, had it been in his power to defend that fortress, would have sacrificed his life a thousand times rather than, through his fault, have let it fall into the hands of the enemy. (p. 192)

Smith is obviously thinking of the national outrage caused by the loss of Minorca. He seeks to moderate national sentiment by re-imagining it, substituting more acceptable ideas of self-sacrifice for the historical clamour against the unfortunate Byng. The response of Smith's imaginary 'honest Englishman' is implicitly contrasted with the Admiral's failure to sacrifice his life in defence of Minorca. In this way, Smith attempts to bring national partiality closer to the 'the propriety of generosity and public spirit' it actually displaces.

The idealised images of war in the first edition of *The Theory of Moral Sentiments*, then, can be seen in relation to the conflict that was ongoing when the work was first published, an attempt to improve public ideas about war, by flattering rather than directly criticising the public, and by recasting bellicose national feeling in a more dignified and de-libidinised form. Smith's hypothetical illustrations offer models of reflective conduct that would be of little use to the soldier who has to act in the heat of battle. They are reassuring fictions designed to suggest that war might be conducted virtuously, that death in war might be noble, that a non-combatant's response to war might be generously public spirited rather than meanly nationalistic. In this way, Smith works to raise the whole tone of war, in the face of the widespread evidence of its brutalising effect.

But once the Seven Years' War was over, Smith began to reflect more critically on the public enthusiasm for war, and the indifference to suffering and injustice it entailed. Looking back at the 'late war' in his 'Lectures of Jurisprudence' (which he didn't publish), he notes how ignorant the public is about the offences actually committed in war, how little they feel for those at a distance from them, how easily they succumb to 'a blind indiscriminating faculty natural to mankind', by which [their enemies] 'become the objects of unreasonable resentment' and can be treated with the 'greatest injustice'.[57]

In *The Wealth of Nations* (1776), Smith would condemn the credit-funding of war which allowed non-combatants to regard war-news as an

Part II: Developing Questions

amusement, and he attacked the mercantile system that promoted military competition between states and empire building through conquest. But these ruinous political and economic policies shaped and were supported by the moral sentiments of the public. If war was funded through taxation, Smith notes, rather than through 'the ruinous expedient of perpetual funding':

> The people feeling, during continuance of war, the complete burden of it, would soon grow weary of it; and government, in order to humour them, would not be under the necessity of carrying it on longer than it was necessary to do so. The foresight of the heavy and unavoidable burdens of war would hinder the people from wantonly calling for it when there was no real or solid interest to fight for.[58]

We are some way here from the idea that war is caused by the ambition of princes. The public was not duped into credit funding by a government that concealed the magnitude of the accumulating debt, since this was often discussed. When it comes to war, the public was wilfully blind to real self-interest, exerting an irresponsible, and seemingly irresistible pressure upon government to adopt destructive policies. Having insulated itself from the true costs of war, both financial and human, the modern public enjoys an illusion that allows 'the animosity of national vengeance' free expression but makes responsible judgement impossible.

Smith returned to the problem of public responses to war in the major revisions he made to the last edition of *TMS*, published early in 1790, a few months before his death. By this time, the outbreak of the French Revolution had produced a reaction to national partiality that Smith would have found particularly disturbing. As Smith's editors note, some of his final revisions seem designed to deal with the arguments made by Richard Price in his notorious 'Revolution sermon' of 1789 (pp. 229, 231, nn). Price had proclaimed that a wise man would 'not suffer any partial affections to blind his understanding', and that the love of country had hitherto been only a love of conquest, domination, grandeur and glory, leading to 'plunder and massacre'.[59] Price simply judges national partiality in relation to a universal benevolence which – like Smith's impartial spectator – stands apart from self-interest.

This wholesale dismissal of self-interested nationalism would have seemed unrealistic to Smith. In his revisions in the 1790 *TMS* Smith attempted to clarify the nature of national partiality. He now makes it clear that those involved in war do not have access to a transcendent perspective from which the conflict can be judged, since 'neutral nations are the only indifferent and impartial spectators in war and negotiation'. In war, the whole ambition of an individual 'is to obtain the approbation of his fellow-citizens', which he can do by 'enraging and offending their enemies'. In war, Smith concedes, 'The partial spectator is at hand: the impartial one at great distance' (p. 154). He now openly admits that national feeling allows military outrages to be tolerated, approved, and admired. The laws of nations, supposed to moderate the conduct of war, themselves legitimise brutality, since they are 'laid down without regard to the rules of justice'. And anyway, these laws 'are frequently violated without bringing the violator into disrepute among his own countrymen' (p. 155). The public's response to such things is entirely governed by national interest. Morality and humanity seem to have little or no relevance in this account.

Smith's acknowledgement of the injustices endorsed by national partiality in war becomes part of a process of reluctant justification. We have to 'go along with' such outrages because it is natural to do so. If civilised morality is suspended in war, Smith implies, this is the responsibility of 'The wisdom which contrived the system of human affections' (p. 229). Irrational passion is quietly converted into acquiescence which implies reasonable self-interest. And praise of the hero paradoxically works to vindicate the self-interested civilian response. Smith notes that

> Foreign war and civil faction are the two situations which afford the most splendid opportunities for the display of public spirit. The hero who serves his country successfully in foreign war gratifies the wishes of the whole nation, and is, upon that account, the object of universal gratitude. [...] The glory which is acquired by foreign war is [...] always more pure and more splendid than that gained in civil faction. (p. 232)

Glory is here 'purified' of its injustice and inhumanity, just as the nation is universalised. We are no longer placed at a distance from a questionable public opinion. The partial spectator seems fully vindicated.

In retrospect, the history of Smith's attempt to moderate the public's response to war exposes a fundamental problem. He begins by providing reassuring and improving images of the moral sentiments associated with war, which in their idealising form dignify or mask war's brutal realities, and so effectively insulate the public from them. But he comes to identify the public's insulated condition, their ignorance about, and indifference to, the actual violence of war, their wanton state of denial about its real costs, as contributing to the destructiveness of modern war. A conundrum emerges: the effort to moderate the public response to war by reimagining it begins to look as if might be part of the problem, while an open

178 Part II: Developing Questions

recognition of the harsh realities of war begins to undermine Smith's assumptions about humanity and impartiality. War emerges as an anomaly that cannot be reconciled with the ideals of modern society, that cannot be effectively moderated, and that cannot be securely justified, except through appeals to what is natural.

In writing about war, then, both of these writers begin to expose a seemingly insoluble problem. The brutality and injustice that war unleashes is found most disturbingly within that public that they wish to describe as humane, moderate, and – in the best of senses – public-spirited. Indeed, war is an activity that sometimes makes the writers themselves adopt and vindicate that national partiality which, at other times, they recoil from. Their attempts to challenge the public with the unvarnished truth about its responses to war threaten to undermine their claims about progress – and, as they acknowledge, can have no real effect. In negotiating this conundrum, these writers began to map out the kind of ambivalences that modern societies who defend civil order with violence must learn to live with.

Notes

1 J. G. A. Pocock, *Virtue, Commerce and History* (Cambridge: Cambridge University Press, 1985), 60.
2 For Smith's reservations about the prospects for peace, see Maria Pia Paganelli and Reinhard Schumacher, 'Do Not Take Peace for Granted: Adam Smith's Warning on the Relation between Commerce and War', *Cambridge Journal of Economic History*, 43: 3 (2019), 785–797.
3 On the state monopoly of force, see Bruce Buchan, 'Enlightened Histories: Civilization, War and the Scottish Enlightenment' in *The European Legacy*, 10: 2 (2005), 177–192. Mark Neocleous discusses 'prerogative powers' in *Critique of Security* (Edinburgh: Edinburgh University Press, 2008), 15–30.
4 Richard B. Sher, *Church and University in the Scottish Enlightenment* (Edinburgh: Edinburgh University Press, 1985); John Robertson, *The Scottish Enlightenment and the Militia Issue* (Edinburgh: John Donald, 1985).
5 J. G. A. Pocock, *Virtue, Commerce and History*, 132–133; Istvan Hont, *Jealousy of Trade: International Competition and the Nation-State in Historical Perspective* (Cambridge, Mass.: Harvard University Press, 2005), 326.
6 David Hume, *A Treatise of Human Nature*, ed. Páll S. Árdal (London: Collins, 1962, 1972), 2 vols, I, pp. 42, 44. Further references are given after quotations in the text.
7 J. G. A. Pocock, *The Machiavellian Moment: Florentine Political Thought and the Atlantic Republican Tradition* (Princeton: Princeton University Press, 1975), 199–213, 290–92.

War and the 'Science of Man'   179

8 On the crisis of 1738–9, see P. Langford, *A Polite and Commercial People: England 1727–1783* (Oxford: Oxford University Press, 1989), 50–52; Kathleen Wilson, *The Sense of the People: Politics, Culture and Imperialism in England, 1715–1785* (Cambridge: Cambridge University Press, 1998), 140–142.

9 See James Fieser, ed., *Early Responses to Hume's Metaphysical and Epistemological Writings,* (Bristol: Thoemmes Press, 2000) 2 vols.

10 Nicholas Phillipson, *Hume* (London: Weidenfeld and Nicolson, 1989), 53–54.

11 David Hume, *Essays: Moral, Political and Literary* ed. Eugene F. Miller (Indianapolis: Liberty Classics, 1987), 538–539. Further references are given after quotations in the text.

12 *Enquiries Concerning Human Understanding and Concerning the Principles of Morals* ed. L. A. Selby-Bigge, rev. P. H. Nidditch (Oxford: Oxford University Press, 1979), 225. Further references are given after quotations in the text.

13 A. B. Stilz, 'Hume, Modern Patriotism, and Commercial Society', in David Hume, ed. Knud Haakonssen and Richard Whatmore (Farnham: Ashgate, 2013), 159–176, p. 173.

14 Emma Rothschild, 'David Hume and the Seagods of the Atlantic', in *The Atlantic Enlightenment*, ed. Susan Manning and Francis D. Cogliano (Farnham: Ashgate, 2008), 81–96.

15 Istvan Hont, *Jealousy of Trade*, 332.

16 Robert Harris, *Politics and the Nation: Britain in the Mid-Eighteenth Century* (Oxford: Oxford University Press, 2002), 120.

17 P. J. Marshall, 'Britain and the World in the Eighteenth Century: I, Reshaping the Empire', *Transactions of the Royal Historical Society*, Sixth Series, 8 (1998), 1–18, p. 8.

18 Robert Harris, *A Patriot Press: National Politics and the London Press in the 1740s* (Oxford: Oxford University Press, 1993), 222.

19 P. G. M. Dickson, *The Financial Revolution in England; A Study in the Development of Public Credit 1688–1754,* (Farnham: Gregg Revivals, 1993), 217.

20 'Of Luxury' [later, entitled, 'Of refinement in the arts'] *Political Discourses* (Edinburgh, 1752), 27, 31. All subsequent references are to this edition.

21 *Political Discourses*, 'Of the Populousness of Ancient Nations', 188–189, 193.

22 *Political Discourses*, 'Of Public Credit', 125.

23 *Political Discourses*, 'Of the Balance of Trade', 99–100.

24 *Political Discourses*, 'Of Money', 42.

25 *Political Discourses*, 'Of Public Credit', 135, 137.

26 *Political Discourses*, 'Of the Balance of Power', 110.

27 *Political Discourses*, 'Of Public Credit', 137.

28 *Political Discourses*, 'Of the Balance of Power', 110–111.

29 *The History of Great Britain. Vol. I. Containing the Reigns of James I and Charles I* (Edinburgh: 1754), 26.

30 Mark Salber Phillips, *Society and Sentiment: Genres of Historical Writing in Britain, 1740–1820* (New Jersey: Princeton University Press, 2000), 104.

31 *Political Discourses*, 'Of Luxury', 31.

180 Part II: Developing Questions

32 *The History of Great Britain. Vol. II. Containing the Commonwealth, and the Reigns of Charles II and James II* (London, 1757), 42, 309.

33 *The History of England, Under the House of Tudor* (London, 1759), 2 vols, I, 124; II, 665.

34 Letter to Andrew Millar, Edinburgh 18 December 1759: 'As soon as this Task [adding the Authorities to the Volumes of the Stuarts] is finish'd, I undertake the antient English History'. *The Letters of David Hume*, ed. J. Y. T. Greig, 2 vols (New York: Garland, 1983), I, 171.

35 See Hume, *Essays*, 327. The essay 'Of the Jealousy of Trade' first appeared in 1758.

36 Robert Donald Spector, *English Literary Periodicals and the Climate of Opinion During the Seven Years' War* (The Hague and Paris: Mouton & Co., 1966), 88–95; Marie Peters, *Pitt and Popularity: The Patriot Minister and London Opinion during the Seven Years' War* (Oxford: Oxford University Press, 1980), 124–274.

37 Francis Abell, *Prisoners of War in Britain 1756–1815* (Oxford: Oxford University Press, 1914), 8. Oliver Goldsmith, *The Citizen of the World* (London, 1762), 2 vols, Letter 23, I, 91–96. See *Letters of David Hume*, I, 373.

38 The *London Gazetter*, October 27–30 1759, for example, carried an Address of the City of Bristol, which proclaimed: 'your gallant Commanders remember the Rights of Humanity and instantly afford both Safety and Protection to the Conquered'.

39 On 22 March 1760, Hume wrote to Andrew Millar about the supposed success of John Home's play at Drury Lane Theatre. *Letters of David Hume*, I, 321–324.

40 *London Chronicle* April 3 to April 5 1760. By May a subscription was being taken for a print of the subject.

41 *London Evening Post*, January 15–17, 1761. *The St James's Chronicle* of June 9 1761 reports that Hayman's painting is on display at Vauxhall.

42 *The History of England from the Invasion of Julius Caesar to the Accession of Henry VII* (London, 1762), 2 vols, II, 240, 231, 277, 232.

43 Jeffery M. Suderman notes that the worthiest kings in Hume's *History* are 'found almost exclusively in the medieval volumes', 'Medieval Kingship and the Making of Modern Civility: Hume's Assessment of Governance in *The History of England*', in *David Hume: Historical Thinker, Historical Writer*, ed. Mark G. Spencer (Philadelphia: Pennsylvania State University Press, 2013), 121–142, p. 123.

44 Smollett's *History of England* (1758) contains, for example, nothing on the humanity of Saladin, is severely critical of Edward III's treatment of civilians at Calais, but does pay tribute to the Black Prince's generosity to the French King John.

45 Donald T. Siebert, 'Chivalry and Romance in the Age of Hume,' *Eighteenth-Century Life*, 21: 1 (1997), 62–79, p. 70.

46 Roy Strong, *And When Did You Last See Your Father?* (London: Thames and Hudson, 1978), 21.

War and the 'Science of Man'

47 Roy Strong, 25. Mark Girouard, *The Return to Camelot: Chivalry and the English Gentleman* (New Haven: Yale University Press, 1981), 19–20.

48 Nicholas Phillipson considers the origins of the work in *Adam Smith: An Enlightened Life* (London: Penguin, 2011), 137.

49 Chris Ware, *Admiral Byng, His Rise and Execution* (Barnsley: Pen and Sword, 2009), 102; M. John Cardwell, *Arts and Arms: Literature, Politics and Patriotism during the Seven Years War* (Manchester: Manchester University Press, 2004), 51–65.

50 John Brown, *An Estimate of the Manners and Principles of the Times* (London, 1758), 2 vols, II, 40.

51 Adam Smith, *Lectures on Jurisprudence*, ed. R. L. Meek, D. D. Raphael, and P. G. Stein (Indianapolis: Liberty Fund, 1978), 547–548.

52 *Lectures on Jurisprudence*, 540.

53 Adam Smith, *Theory of Moral Sentiments*, ed. D. D. Raphael and A. L. Macfie (Indianapolis: Liberty, 1982), 204. Further references are given after quotations in the text.

54 Markus Elder, *Crime and Punishment in the Royal Navy of the Seven Years' War, 1755–1753* (Farnham: Ashgate, 2004), 71.

55 Elder, 119, 128.

56 Julia Banister notes that 'Smith's enthusiasm for involuntary feeling only thinly disguises his greater investment in self-discipline', *Masculinity, Militarism and Eighteenth-Century Culture 1689–1815* (Cambridge: Cambridge University Press, 2018), 127.

57 *Lectures on Jurisprudence*, 547–48.

58 *An Inquiry Into the Nature and Causes of the Wealth of Nations*, ed. Edwin Cannan (Chicago: University of Chicago Press, 1976), V, iii, 462–63.

59 *Political Sermons of the American Founding Era: 1730–1805* (Indianapolis: Liberty Fund, 1998), 2 vols, II, 1010.

PART III

War and Peace in an Age of Revolutions

During the period of the American and French Revolutions the relationship between war, social inequality and unjust government became an important issue in radical works aimed at political demystification.[1] During the American Revolution, for example, Thomas Paine in his republican pamphlet *Common Sense* (1776) argued that wars were rooted in unjust institutions and traditions that were normalized in daily life, and that 'dazzled' and 'deceived' the people, that 'warped' their will and 'darkened' their understanding. In the *Rights of Man* (1791–92), published in the early years of the French Revolution, he declared that in approaching war 'the wisdom of a Nation should apply itself to reforming the system' rather than attacking 'the ambition of kings'. The idea that wars are rooted in unjust political and social systems that cloud the public's judgement was shared by some who did not necessarily endorse Paine's republicanism or radicalism.[2] Systemic criticism, by connecting war to established social practices, suggested the unacknowledged complicity of the public in its violence. In Chapter 7, we shall examine how two novelists consider the social causes of war and the issue of complicity, one writing at the time of the American Revolution, and one at the time of the French Revolution. As criticism of the nation's war-making increases, two related tendencies appear. Strategies are developed for insulating individuals from the guilt associated with war (examined in Chapter 8). And war is imagined as a communal activity in terms that distance it from, or defuse, contentious social issues (Chapter 9). A third response takes the form of an emergent movement to campaign for the principle of absolute non-resistance, 'pacifism', a movement related to the expanding horizons opened by Britain's imperial activities (Chapter 10).

Notes

1 Gordon S. Wood, ed. *The American Revolution: Writings from the Pamphlet Debate, Volume II: 1773–1776* (New York: Library of America, 2015), xxii.
2 Gregory Claeys, *The French Revolution Debate in Britain: The Origins of Modern Politics* (Basingstoke: Palgrave, 2007), 9.

CHAPTER 7

Complicities in the Novel

This chapter examines two novels, one published during the American war and one during the debate about the French revolution, both of which attempt to address the systemic causes of war. In the first, Samuel Jackson Pratt's *Emma Corbett* (1780), there is an attempt to imagine a young woman's conversion to a position of absolute pacifism. In the second, Charlotte Smith's *The Old Manor House*, a British soldier fighting against rebels in America is led to question the purpose of war and to see its utter futility. In both novels, the national view of war is undermined, while the moral view becomes associated with a fundamental questioning of social order.

The eighteenth-century novel had already been used to show the consequences of war as they affect those at home, with a particular emphasis on war's victims. In a period of revolutionary turbulence, the novel was adapted to explore the idea that the causes of war lie within the familiar conditions of social life itself – including the property relations that provide the basis of domestic security. The novel form allows the kind of systemic critique that appears in theoretical discussions of society to be shown emerging as a personal discovery, grounded in the experience of relatively unexceptional individuals who are driven by the impact of war to act and think in exceptional terms. In this way, the novel could work to authorise deeply critical, even extreme perspectives.

Samuel Jackson Pratt: Feminine Virtue, Property and Pacifism

Sterne's reaction to femininity and female audiences in *Tristram Shandy* indicates their growing influence in eighteenth-century culture, an influence that inevitably helped to determine approaches to war. The conception of feminine virtue that became established in the novel, and that was offered as a model for female readers and as an index of the novel's moral respectability, was potentially at odds with the national view of war.[1] The conflict between pacific feminine feeling and support for war had to be

186   Part III: War and Peace in an Age of Revolutions

negotiated or contained in some way. In Fielding's *Amelia*, the heroine's attempt to stop her husband going to war is qualified as an example of 'amiable weakness'. But as we shall see, the association between femininity and pacific feeling proved useful during the American War of Independence (1775–1783) when a significant minority of Britons were fundamentally opposed to the government's war aims. The conflict was a civil war fought across the Atlantic, in which attitudes on both sides were deeply divided. A number of British Army and Navy officers refused to serve in America, while a significant part of the British public condemned the British war effort as unjust.[2] As Wil Verhoeven points out, 'The vast majority of novels that appeared during and in the aftermath of the War of Independence were critical of Britain's role in the conflict with its American colonies'.[3]

In these circumstances, Samuel Jackson Pratt published an epistolary novel about the American war, *Emma Corbett* (1780), in which feminine virtue gives rise to pacifist feelings that are seen as a sign of personal strength rather than of weakness – while inevitably being qualified by their association with the female. Eve Tavor Bannet notes that the novel 'was universally read as a pro-American work'.[4] Jackson Pratt, a widely read writer in the 1770s, who had established a reputation as a humanitarian, undoubtedly sympathised with the American cause (he had been working with Benjamin Franklin in Paris between February and May 1778). But the anti-war sentiments expressed by his heroine Emma do not distinguish between causes. They may have been intended to resonate with a British public that, since the entry of France, Spain, and the Netherlands into the war on the rebels' side was becoming increasingly anxious to make terms with the Americans. But they represent an assault on the material and cultural causes of war in general.

There are two strands to the heroine's journey to pacifism – one is a response to ideas of military honour; the other, more radical, is a critique of property relations. Both of these are developed through Emma Corbett's relationship with her suitor, Henry Hammond, who goes to America in order to fight on the British side of the war in America, in answer to 'the call of his country'. Emma initially respects Henry's appeal to honour as a motive, but as the novel unfolds, she increasingly finds martial honour to be a masculine preoccupation destructive of natural feeling and domesticity. Emma's friend Mrs Arnold, who has been brought up among soldiers, tells her that to military men the voice of public fame speaks louder than private affection. The 'little military history' Mrs Arnold finds among her father's papers and sends to Emma is ostensibly a vindication of military honour, but actually shows its absurdity. The fragmentary account of 'The

Complicities in the Novel 187

Carbines' demonstrates how military education encourages a ludicrous repression of natural tenderness, love, and compassion and a perverse pride in disabling wounds.

The second, and more challenging strand of Emma's development entails a fundamental questioning of property relations. The Seven Years' War had brought a huge expansion of Britain's territorial empire, which had an impact on property relations at home and abroad. The return to Britain of 'Nabobs' – wealthy employees and officials of the East India Company who were able to buy up considerable estates in Britain (as Robert Clive did) – inevitably created resentment and prompted satirical attacks. Wealthy Britons who invested in North American property encountered a different problem. When the growing dispute between the British government and the American colonies turned into open conflict, property became an easy target. Loyalists in America were liable to have their estates confiscated by rebel forces with or without the authority of local American Assemblies.[5] On the other hand, British soldiers punished American rebels by plundering their property, so that Thomas Paine warned his American readers of 'the precariousness with which all American property is possessed'.[6] The conflict that at one level was about taxation, political representation and forms of government, at another level was focused bitterly upon the ownership of land – an issue that resonated across political divisions. This issue provided Samuel Jackson Pratt with a way of dealing with a highly controversial subject for a divided British readership. Rather than becoming involved in constitutional issues, the novel draws upon theories of civilisation inherited from John Locke and Jean Jacques Rousseau in order to focus on property as a fundamental cause of conflict.

The males of the Corbett family, Emma's father Charles and her brother Edward, live in Britain but have property in America. An apparently innocent origin is attributed to this land – it is said (by Charles) to have been reclaimed by the labour of his ancestors from an original wilderness (conforming to the Lockean principle that labour gives a right to property).[7] When Edward goes to fight in America his only motive is to protect this property from British aggression. His decision implicitly undermines any simple assumptions about the relationship between landownership and patriotism. His father Charles Corbett condemns the war in emotional terms as the 'assassination of America' (I, 5), but his feelings for America, and for the safety of his son, are closely bound up with his feelings for his property: 'O, my poor Edward! – my buried property! – my massacred America' (1, 135). The echo of Shylock ('My daughter, Oh my ducats', *The Merchant of Venice*, II, viii), casts an ironical reflection on Corbett's

188   Part III: War and Peace in an Age of Revolutions

sentiment at this point. His sensibility does not mask his materialistic mindset: he has tried to stop Edward marrying Emma's friend Louisa on the grounds of her lack of wealth. The loss of the American property helps to ruin Corbett, leading him to sell both his London house and the family home of Castleberry. Castleberry is bought by Sir Robert Raymond (Corbett's friend and a clumsy suitor to Corbett's daughter Emma), who makes it available once more to the Corbett family. But the subject of war brings Sir Robert's own benevolence, and its relation to property and empire, under critical observation.

Raymond is apparently a Nabob, a beneficiary of empire who has made his fortune in India having left England poor. Nabobs attracted much contemporary criticism on account of their rapidly acquired wealth and influence, a fact that needs to be born in mind here, since within the novel Raymond is seen from his own point of view and from the views of friends and beneficiaries.[8] His newly made wealth has allowed him to acquire property in both Britain and America, along with a title. He was at one time a ship's surgeon at war, but has since kept himself 'unengaged from scenes for which nature did not form [him]' (1. 143). His wealth encourages and allows him to maintain this detachment: having property on both sides of the Atlantic he 'dare not lean either way' for fear of 'unsettling that system of general loving kindness' which he sees as the basis of his happiness (1. 143). His 'predilection' (1. 138) for his native country has been tempered by his extensive travel and has none of the patriot's intense love. He claims attachment to no party but the 'human face divine', adopting a depoliticised idea of humanity which preserves the status quo and its potential for violence ('in every army characters are to be loved' 1. 140). He represents a distinctly modern, 'liberal' ideal of private, civilised enjoyment – which has none of the sense of public duty conventionally associated with the patriotic landowner in the civic humanist tradition, and in this context looks more like selfish paralysis than virtue.

In contrast to this impotent neutrality – a wealthy man's luxury – the heroine's movement towards pacifism entails a questioning of the material basis of British culture and a courageous form of action. This movement can be compared with the case of Richardson's Clarissa, whose virtue leads her to withdraw from a social world that seems fundamentally corrupt. Emma's withdrawal takes a different form. Her fears for Hammond lead her to query the need for war, and this questioning leads inexorably to an imagined renunciation of property. Writing to her friend Mrs Arnold, she denounces 'what is falsely called the property of each other', and the fact that men fight over 'acres of dirt', which will shortly cover them (1.175). In a

Complicities in the Novel

climactic scene, she comes to see that the domestic dwelling of Castleberry is not only a sanctuary of peace but also implicated in the glorification of war. The library is decorated with prints of military engagements, a reflection of the contemporary taste for such patriotic commemorations. Emma is found 'weeping over the representation of a complete victory', which she sees as 'lawful glory-crowned murder', motivated by the struggle over 'ridiculous portions of ideal property' (2.17–2.19).

In Emma's growing alienation from the domestic world and her dawning realisation of its complicity in the promotion of war, Jackson Pratt's novel sets up a dilemma which can only be resolved through a sensational fantasy involving romance conventions. While Emma's friend Louisa adopts a Clarissa-like stance of quiet Christian endurance in the face of her husband Edward's absence, Emma rejects 'the pious example of the resigned Louisa' (1. 179). Instead, she seeks relief in a form of humanitarian action. When she receives news that Hammond may have been killed, she takes flight for America, disguised as a sailor, to look for him. In America, she finds it necessary to shed the trappings of European civilisation: she disguises herself as a native American, wandering unprotected in the woods, picking her food from the hedges, entering into a condition that resembles that of Rousseau's natural man, a condition that predates the creation of private property – which, in Rousseau's view, stands at the root of inequality and war.[9] Emma finds Henry with a poisoned arrow lodged in his bosom, extricates the arrow and sucks out the poison, events which eventually lead, after she has married Henry, and given birth to a son, to her own and Henry's death. The arrow indicates the presence of those who are omitted in the Lockean account of property acquired through labour – the native Americans displaced by the arrival of colonists.

In this way, the novel calls into question the property relations upon which modern domestic life is founded and in which feminine virtue is nurtured, finding a startling relationship between the brutality of war and the sheltering spaces of the home. As the distinction between the domestic sanctum of virtue and the outer world of social corruption dissolves, the critique of war becomes a critique of civilisation; Emma recognises a problem that she cannot resolve. The epitaph with which the novel concludes pays tribute to Emma as a moral ideal, praising her combination of 'More than Roman virtue/ With more than female softness' [2. 258]. But there can be no genuine reconciliation between a masculine ideal of public virtue and Emma's feminine sensibility. The heroine's pacifist courage is in practice directed only to private interests: she only wants to protect the man she loves, and then her child. It is an ideal shaped by – and

190   Part III: War and Peace in an Age of Revolutions

made possible by – the ideal of femininity she embodies: Emma remains obscure, voiceless, powerless, and as far removed as possible from the contemporary world of political debate, petitioning, and public dissent. Her pacifism is not envisaged as a position that one might argue for in the world, but as a feeling that inspires a conscientious woman to stand by her man at all costs.

Although Jackson Pratt formally endorses the heroine's position with an epitaph, his novel tells another story. For Emma is not the only example of heroic virtue in the novel. Edward dies when he draws his sword to defend the inhabitants of an American village that is burned by a party of English soldiers. If he went to war simply to defend his own property, he dies defending others. This is the most genuinely disinterested humanitarian act in the novel, a gesture not made on behalf of someone in whom he has a personal interest, but simply an attempt to protect the defenceless. It is a moment that indicates most clearly Jackson Pratt's own pro-American views, and his own view of war. The year after *Emma Corbett* first appeared, he published *Sympathy*, a poem which announced, in the kind of poetic paradox that had become commonplace in the age of Defoe, that 'War, the scourge of human kind/ But serves more close the social links to bind'.[10]

Charlotte Smith: Compromising with War

Jackson Pratt's representation of pacifist feeling was a sign of one kind of change. In the wake of the war with America, there was an outpouring of publications in Britain opposing war and hoping for a new age of universal peace.[11] But at the same time, a growing revival of interest in chivalry and romance was helping to disseminate the view that war was compatible with feminine virtue, and to connect war-making with nobility and the defence of chastity rather than with modern commercial interests (see Chapter 9). The advent of the French Revolution in 1789 gave rise to a wide-ranging political debate in which both the chivalric idea of war and the hopes for peace took on a new significance. Edmund Burke's conservative *Reflections on the Revolution in France* (1790) attempted to enlist the sentimental appeal of chivalry in defence of aristocracy, monarchy, and long-established institutions. In response, the radical Tom Paine, in *The Rights of Man* (1791–92), mocked Burke's chivalrous sentiments, attacked war as a device used to tax and deceive the public, and claimed that an ongoing, radical demystification of corrupt government would allow people across the globe to escape from the errors of the past into a new age of republican peace.[12]

Complicities in the Novel

Charlotte Smith's novel, *The Old Manor House*, was clearly influenced by the revolution debate. It was begun in August 1792, before the outbreak of war between Britain and revolutionary France in February 1793, and finished shortly after the war had begun. The novel is set at the time of the American Revolution but responds to the growing likelihood of war with France. Setting the events of the novel at a slightly earlier period allowed some useful distance. The work is in many respects an anti-war novel, but it suggests that war exerts its power over eighteenth-century society not simply through errors that can be exploded, but through the material opportunities it provides, and through the sympathies it elicits. One of the original features of the novel is that the most powerful anti-war sentiments are attributed not to the novel's central representative of feminine virtue, Monimia, but to the male hero Orlando in his role as a soldier at war.

The complexities of Smith's approach to war can be understood in relation to her social circumstances. As the poet of *Elegiac Sonnets*, which began to appear in 1784, Smith identified herself with her family seat of Bignor Park.[13] That is, she identified herself publicly with the landed classes. She read radical authors and, on the outbreak of the French Revolution, she thought of herself as pro-Revolutionary. But as Loraine Fletcher points out, she 'had no notion of extending levelling principles into her own family'.[14] Smith's identification with Bignor Park was at odds with her actual situation: she began to compose *Elegiac Sonnets* in King's Bench prison where her husband was confined for debt. As a woman suffering the dire economic consequences of her lack of rights in law, she would have had an acute awareness of how acquiescence in what one condemns might become necessary. There was often a conflict between the moral position she avowed in her published works and the private realities of her economic position. In her writings she protested against both slavery and war, but she had derived some benefit from her father-in-law's wealth, drawn from slave plantations in the West Indies, while her husband Benjamin had profited from military contracts with the government during the American Revolution.[15] People of Charlotte Smith's social background found the militarised British state and its imperial operations an important source of opportunity. Such openings were of vital significance to Smith's own children, given her husband's profligacy and the tying up of her children's inheritance in a lawsuit. Two of her sons became civil servants in the East India Company in the wake of the second Anglo-Mysore War (1780–84); one of these (Nicholas) was eventually sent home after participating in a military action.[16] She helped three of her younger sons into careers in the army – a profession which carried a kind of social

192   Part III: War and Peace in an Age of Revolutions

respectability suitable to the ideas of family status Smith tried to retain. Her younger sister Catherine married a soldier. If this personal context is sometimes played down or ignored in critical discussions of her response to war, that is no doubt because the passionate denunciation of war in her published writings effectively works to distance her from it.

Smith must have been only too aware of the compromising conflict between her anti-war pronouncements and her desire to find socially acceptable positions for her children. This compromised position is part of the subject of her novel *The Old Manor House*. From the beginning, the hero Orlando is critical of the traditional chivalric military ethos that is admired by the wealthy estate-owner Mrs. Rayland. But although he condemns the 'sanguinary monsters' responsible for the crimes committed in war, he feels he has 'no choice' but to take an Ensigncy in the army, given his limited career options (and his dislike of 'trade' (80, 101)). In this, he is encouraged by Mrs Rayland, whose property, Rayland Hall, he wishes to inherit. Military service is from the outset linked to the prospect of gaining wealth and status.[17]

Shortly after the novel was finished, and three weeks after France had declared war on Britain, Charlotte Smith's own son Charles applied for an Ensigncy in the army, since the trustees of the family inheritance would not supply the money needed to educate him for the Church.[18] He had been living at home for at least part of the time she was writing the novel, and would have discussed his own limited career options with his mother, since she would need to help him acquire the backing of the trustees in order to purchase his commission. In a letter Smith explained 'nothing can be more distressing to him & to me than his being at home witht any plan of Life'.[19]

These personal circumstances appear to have had a significant influence upon her writing. While she is severely critical of the ideology that justifies war, and of the terrible violence produced by conflict, Smith finds it hard in this context to see the soldier simply as guilty, or as an indifferent murderer. Indeed, in *The Old Manor House* Charlotte Smith has imagined herself into the situation of a soldier in a remarkable way. The novel's critique of war is partly focalised through Orlando, a soldier-hero who is actually seen at war. This approach is highly unusual: serious novelists since the time of Defoe usually avoided representing a hero actively engaged in combat, so evading the moral problems this entailed.[20] Smith's understanding of the soldier's ambivalent position, as at once a guilty instrument of violence and a victim of it, complicates her wide-ranging critique of war. Some of this critique is represented through the hero's developing

Complicities in the Novel

awareness, as he confronts the brutal realities of war. Orlando, on surveying with wonder and disgust the chaotic preparations for the embarkation of troops to America, and on seeing the distresses of his men as they fall sick at sea, asks himself 'what all this was for?' (350, 353). Having experienced the violence of war directly, his growing disgust leads him to assent 'to some of the most gloomy aphorisms of Rousseau' (362), and to question the political justice of a war carried on 'in absolute contradiction to the wishes of the people who were taxed to support it'(363). His capture by Iroquois leads him to deplore the British policy of authorising the Indians 'to take up the hatchet' (366); he subsequently witnesses the Iroquois' horrific attacks upon the 'defenceless villages of the English Americans' (381).

Through such scenes, the traditional idea of the soldier's duty is directly called into question. When Orlando is faced with a guilty recognition of 'all the horrors and devastations of war' (360) in America, which seem 'not to be justified by any cause' (362), the good-natured lieutenant Fleming attempts to reassure him, using the orthodox argument that, having sold his sword to his king, he must use it in the King's service 'whatever and wherever it may be pointed out' (363). This resembles Dr Harrison's advice to Booth in Fielding's *Amelia*. Here, however, Orlando is not convinced. But Smith's view of the soldier's duty in the novel is far from simple. Carmel Murphy, emphasising the 'radical' critique in *The Old Manor House* of Edmund Burke's veneration of tradition, finds that 'the play on romance elements which allows Smith to present her hero in terms of a chivalric knight is consciously juxtaposed with the harsh historical reality of the American campaign'.[21] But Smith's examination of reality includes a recognition of the need for human sympathy and respect towards those who risk everything in the service of their country, a recognition that sometimes competes with the novel's political concerns.

If the critique of chivalric tradition that Murphy and other critics describe works to undermine traditional ideals of military honour and heroism, Smith's realistic portrayal of war experience sometimes works to re-establish such ideals on the basis of compassion. For example, when Lieutenant Fleming is struck down while leading a bayonet attack against American rebels, he begs his friend Orlando 'If you return to England, be a friend to my poor wife – to my poor little ones' (368). In the light of the narrator's critical perspective on war, increasingly shared by Orlando, Fleming can be seen as a dupe of the state, who has foolishly sacrificed the welfare of his own family to the cause of a thoroughly unjust and cruel war. But Orlando sees his dying friend as a 'noble spirit', and subsequently takes comfort in the idea that he 'died gloriously' like other 'brave officers' (368).

194   Part III: War and Peace in an Age of Revolutions

Seen in relation to the novel's criticism of war, this incident clearly illustrates, as Murphy notes, the 'inherent emptiness' of such military ideals (274). But it also shows that such ideals can be a source of comfort in the face of personal loss: indeed, they can be fed by the same humanitarian sympathy that gives rise to the condemnation of war. Orlando will eventually give an account of this death to Fleming's widow (465), but Smith leaves readers to imagine this scene for themselves. Are we to imagine that Orlando gives a comforting version to the unhappy widow, or that he emphasises the utter futility of her loss? I will leave readers to decide.

Smith criticises the corruption, selfishness, and cruelty entailed in war, and has little sympathy for the Commanders. But she finds it hard not to sympathise with those individuals who, as the servants of an unjust system, struggle to perform their duty, even when it is hopeless. Accordingly, she acknowledges that (367) 'a great number of brave men fell, as well English as Germans' in the action that kills Fleming, and she commends the bravery of the British officers who strive to encourage their men when faced with the prospect of defeat (368): 'The officers still endeavoured to encourage their men, and keep the spirits up of each other – they recollected other occasions in which armies, in a condition equally desperate, had broken through their enemies, and conquered those who hoped to have destroyed them: but the commander himself knew the fallacy of these hopes'. One can argue, as some critics do, that Smith is simply conceding to the expectations of her novel readers in such cases.[22] But as a mother, Smith was not immune to parental pride in a report that her son Charles had acted with 'honour' in battle.[23] It seems likely that she herself would have taken more comfort from such reports than from accounts that emphasised the senseless barbarity of his activities. The critique of British war-making as the product of a cruel, aristocratic system fed by false ideas of military glory is in conflict with the affirmation of virtues that Smith apparently admires, such as self-sacrificing duty and, paradoxically, sympathy for the afflicted. Smith's treatment of the soldier contrasts strikingly with Defoe's, whose adventuring Cavalier may have occasional pangs of conscience about the violence of his occupation but does not really question its purpose (see Chapter 5). In Smith, the fact that the soldier's troubled conscience it at odds with his duty becomes a major issue.

There is a similar conflict in Smith's treatment of the forms of patronage generated by war, which can appear as either ensnaring or enabling. The patronage provided by an old captain of a man of war appears to entrap Fleming's widow and her children in a vicious circle: the captain provides them with a cottage, takes the eldest son from Winchester College, and

Complicities in the Novel

adopts him on condition he becomes a sailor. Mrs. Fleming feels compelled to surrender her son to the 'same dreadful trade' of war in which her husband died, because her pension as lieutenant's widow is quite inadequate. The captain also supports her second son 'at an academy, intending him for the sea' (480). However, at the end of the novel, we find that the eldest son's 'gallant behaviour' (522) in a recent naval engagement has persuaded his benefactor to adopt him as heir and make a settlement upon him. In a comparable way, the naval midshipman Young Newell (whose fearless, honest, generous demeanour, like his 'rough sea language' (479) aligns him with the conventional, patriotic image of the British sailor) is able to help his parents out of their financial difficulties since 'the frigate he was on board had taken two small prizes' (478). The 'dreadful trade' has led to welcome material benefits.

Orlando, who claims to have 'no choice', chooses the army in preference to trade, a course that resembles the choices that would be made within Smith's own family; the kind of material successes described at the end of the novel are the kind Smith would have wished for her own children. The novel shows that it is not only the self-interested values and behaviour of the ruling classes that perpetuate war, but also the values of those below them, the ideas of respectability and the material aspirations that Smith herself shares, which lead to the acceptance of the material opportunities war creates.[24] The novel is in part a response to Smith's recognition of her own difficulty in dissociating herself from the system of war she condemns. After overcoming legal obstacles Orlando inherits the estate of Mrs. Rayland, whose chivalric values he deplores, and he wins the hand of Monimia, who is the embodiment of pacific feminine virtue. The outcome suggests a desire to free property from the chivalric ideology that perpetuates and glorifies war, so that it can be enjoyed, and perhaps defended, innocently – an outcome imaged, appropriately enough, in the mode of romance.

Both of these novels reflect upon a society pervaded by ideas about war, and by the effects of war. Both show how war exposes the selfish foundations of ordinary social life. But the novels do not simply criticise war. While the inset fragment about the Carbines in *Emma Corbett* mocks the ethic of sacrifice promoted by the glorification of war, Edward's readiness to sacrifice himself in defence of American villagers seems admirable. While Smith's Orlando questions the cause for which soldier's die in America, such sacrifices are sometimes viewed with some compassion. While corruption in the armed forces is satirised, the soldier on active service may be portrayed more sympathetically than other professionals,

196   Part III: War and Peace in an Age of Revolutions

such as lawyers or doctors, in these novels. The writers show the moral condemnation of war as emerging from particular social positions that are always already compromised by their complicity with a system founded on injustice and defended by violence.

Jackson Pratt's association of the claims of peace with femininity was enabling, precisely because it separated them from the realm of political action. Emma Corbett's thoroughgoing rejection of the ideological and material bases of war is possible because it is apolitical and leads only to her death. Her pacifism could be entertained in the novel as part of a tragic fantasy that might influence readers' attitude to the ongoing American crisis, but it was something the author did not share, and that most of his readers may not have shared either. The novel could accommodate such a position without forcing readers to question their own readiness to defend the national interest in a 'just' cause. Charlotte Smith's depiction of a soldier at war who questions the justice of the national cause and the morality of warfare more widely, but who continues to do his duty, is potentially more damaging: it hollows out the conventional claims about war through a witness who cannot be accused of cowardice, dereliction of duty, or unpatriotic behaviour. It presents a picture of society that is fundamentally complicit in the barbarities of war, a complicity that encompasses not only the manifestly selfish and corrupt but also the apparently good-natured and virtuous. Where Emma Corbett escapes a seemingly all-encompassing corruption through death, Smith's hero and his innocent heroine eventually make terms with it, as they take possession of a valuable estate and are united in a conclusion that is conventionally happy. The conclusion suggests that, as Smith found in her own life, there is no space in which one can live beyond the corruption generated by the violence of the modern state. The acquiescence, the 'relaxation of the morality' in relation to war, that Hume formally endorses, appears to be the basis of ordinary social life, the basis of property relations, the basis upon which peace itself is built.

Notes

1 See Chapter 8 for a view of how the emergence of the 'domestication of patriotism' in the 1770s began to address this problem.
2 Kathleen Wilson, *The Sense of the People: Politics, Culture, and Imperialism in England, 1715–1785* (Cambridge: Cambridge University, 1995), 255; Stephen Conway *The War of American Independence 1775–1783* (London: Edward Arnold, 1995), 209.

Complicities in the Novel

3 Wil Verhoeven, *Americomania and the French Revolution Debate in Britain, 1789–1802* (Cambridge: Cambridge University Press, 2013), 248.

4 Eve Tavor Bannet, ed., *Samuel Jackson Pratt, Emma Corbett* (Peterborough, Ontario: Broadview Press, 2011), 22.

5 Howard Pashman, 'The People's Property Law: A Step toward Building a New Legal Order in Revolutionary New York,' *Law and History Review*, 31: 3 (2013), 587–626; Sarah V. Kalinoski, 'Sequestration, Confiscation, and the 'Tory' in the Vermont Revolution,' *Vermont History*, 45: 4 (1977), 236–246; *Morning Post*, September 23, 1775; *London Chronicle* 25–27 April 1782.

6 Thomas Paine, *Common Sense, Thoughts on the Present State of American Affairs* (1775–76).

7 John Locke, *Second Treatise of Government*, II, Section 6.

8 See Philip Lawson and Jim Phillips, '"Our Execrable Banditti": Perceptions of Nabobs in Mid-Eighteenth-Century Britain', *Albion: A Quarterly Journal Concerned with British Studies* 16: 3 (1984), 225–241.

9 See Jean Jacques Rousseau, *A Discourse on Inequality* (1755).

10 *Sympathy; or a Sketch of the Social Passion: A Poem* (London, 1781), 34.

11 Martin Ceadel, *The Origins of War Prevention: The British Peace Movement and International Relations, 1730–1854* (Oxford: Oxford University Press, 1996), 66.

12 Kuklick, Bruce, ed., *Thomas Paine: Political Writings* (Cambridge: Cambridge University Press, 1989), 86, 154.

13 *Elegiac Sonnets, and Other Essays, by Charlotte Smith, of Bignor Park, in Sussex*, 2nd ed. (Chichester: Dennett Jacques, 1784).

14 Loraine Fletcher, *Charlotte Smith: A Critical Biography* (Basingstoke: Macmillan, 1998), 88.

15 Fletcher notes: 'Richard [Smith] gave Charlotte and Benjamin an allowance of £2000 a year' (30); 'For [...] Benjamin [...] war meant lucrative contracts for supplying the army and navy abroad' (60).

16 Judith Philips Stanton says 'it was her goal to launch them [her children] in life into the landed gentry, a station appropriate to her own birth and equal to the promise of their inheritance'. Stanton, Judith Phillips, ed. *The Collected Letters of Charlotte Smith* (Bloomington: Indiana University Press, 2003), xxiv–xxv.

17 Jacqueline M. Labbe, 'Metaphoricity and the Romance of Property in The Old Manor House',' *Novel*, 34: 2 (2001), 216–231.

18 France declared war on 1 February 1793. On 12 February, Charlotte sent the whole of *The Old Manor House* off for publication. On 21 February, Charles went to London to speak to his Trustees about the Ensigncy.

19 Letter to Joseph Cooper Walker, Feb 20, 1793, 'My Son Charles goes to London tomorrow to see if he can prevail on the Trustees to let him have three hundred pounds to purchase an Ensigncy in some new raisd companies as nothing can be more distressing to him & to me than his being at home witht any plan of Life'. *Letters*, 62.

20 Tobias Smollett's hero Roderick Random becomes a ship's surgeon, for example, rather than a combatant. His brief appearance on the French side at the

198   Part III: War and Peace in an Age of Revolutions

battle of Dettingen is hardly described. *The Adventures of Roderick Random* (London: J. Osborn, 1748).

21 Carmel Murphy, 'Jacobin History: Charlotte Smith's *Old Manor House* and the French Revolution Debate', *Romanticism*, 20: 3 (2014), 271–281, 274.

22 See especially Joseph F. Bartolomeo, 'Subversion of Romance in *The Old Manor House*', *SEL*, 33 (1993), 645–658.

23 On 15 October 1793 Smith wrote to Charles Burney that her son Charles had 'acquitted himself with so much honour that if I had much of the Spartan or the Roman about me might make me proud rather than miserable', *Letters*, 83.

24 Katharina Rennhak argues that Smith, like her contemporary Fanny Burney, criticizes the 'humiliating treatment the poor and impoverished are exposed to' rather than 'the unequal distribution of property or the class system as such'. 'Tropes of Exile in the 1790s: English Women Writers and French Emigrants,' *European Romantic Review*, 17:5,(2006), 575–592, 580. Derek T. Leuenberger notes 'Smith's acknowledgment of a conundrum in which security and comfort in Britain demand adherence to the cults of property and inheritance even though they produce immense suffering', '"Their Only Protector and Support": Protection and Dependency in Charlotte Smith's *The Old Manor House*', *European Romantic Review*, 28:2 (2017), 139–161, 157.

CHAPTER 8

Saving Individual Virtue

Moral Insulation

As public dissatisfaction with Britain's wars became more vocal and more searching, there were corresponding moves to allow some moral distancing of the public from the nation's war-making. The process of moral disconnection is now a familiar topic in some twenty-first-century approaches to the morality of war.[1] Some writers, for example, use the term 'moral insulation' to identify the adjustments combatants may need to make in order to cope with the violence of their occupation – such as the 'compartmentalization of roles' and learning to follow orders without seeing themselves 'as morally responsible for policy outcomes'.[2] These adjustments, which are sometimes described with some distaste, are deemed necessary because a moral threshold is supposedly crossed, one that separates the peace-oriented domain of civilian life from the specialised realm of the armed forces in which violence is a professional practice. The term 'moral insulation' is not usually applied to 'civilians' in the same way because they are assumed to be insulated already. William F. Felice, for example, in *How do I Save my Honor?*, makes a clear distinction between those working for the armed forces, who are expected to pursue the public good, and 'private individuals' who are not. Including himself in the latter category he writes:

> Our major moral duty is primarily to ourselves and our families and not the overall public good. Liberal capitalism encourages the individual pursuit of self-interest. Each of us has a personal duty to act with integrity and protect our individual moral autonomy.

The claim to 'individual moral autonomy' implies some freedom from responsibility for the actions of one's nation when it engages in war, an exemption that arises from lack of direct involvement and – even in the age of universal adult suffrage – lack of direct influence. In Felice's account, responsibility is directly related to power:

199

200   Part III: War and Peace in an Age of Revolutions

> Our ability to impact the government's policies during a time of war is circumscribed. We can express our displeasure with the occupation of Iraq [by USA and UK in 2003] with our votes. It is true that as private individuals we have more freedom than government employees and military personnel to speak up and publicly oppose policies that seem unjust or immoral. Such acts of protest are often critical for an individual to save his or her honor and moral integrity.[3]

Such acts of protest are not 'critical' as far as the progress of the war is concerned since their influence is circumscribed. In this respect, a protest may have much the same weight, or lack of weight, as a declaration of support for war. But protest is critical 'for an individual' because it is an outward sign of the individual's moral integrity, helping to maintain this both in his or her own eyes and in the eyes of others.

Here, thinking about moral responses to war is not simply concerned with humanitarian objections to violence, or with worries about the aims and methods of war, but has become bound up more specifically with the problem of maintaining an appropriate sense of self in relation to moral difficulty. The civilian here is not deemed responsible for the public good but assumes a self-directed responsibility in the act of protest. The combatant formally takes on responsibility for the public good but, in performing an allotted role, may not assume responsibility for policy outcomes. The central problem in both cases is how to take responsibility without taking responsibility.

Felice's concept of moral autonomy shares some features with the liberal understanding of the individual that gradually consolidated during the eighteenth century. As we have already seen, the term 'civilian' did not begin to assume its current meaning until the Romantic period, even though the non-combatant status to which it became attached had long been familiar in Britain. The influential theories of moral development that emerged in the Scottish Enlightenment were inevitably based primarily upon the model of the non-combatant male. Adam Smith's account of moral responses in his *Theory of Moral Sentiments* are based on the idea of impartial judgement, an approach which suits the non-combatant more than the combatant precisely because it suggests moral autonomy. Nevertheless, Smith includes examples designed to suggest that both non-combatants and combatants could make appropriate moral judgements when faced with the dilemmas posed by war; both could preserve their moral autonomy.

Smith's reflections first appeared during a wartime crisis when the reactions of the nation often seemed far from impartial. His work was in some

Saving Individual Virtue 201

ways symptomatic of a growing concern in British culture with the instrumental role of non-combatants in the waging of war. The nation at large had always been granted a role to play through its prayers and repentance, since patriotic support for war was actively encouraged by the Church. But there was increasing awareness of the influence of public opinion on the nation's war-making.

When Smith turned from the theoretical models of the *Theory of Moral Sentiments* to the critical observations of the *Wealth of Nations*, he gave less reassuring views which reflected a growing disquiet. Here he claims that modern non-combatants, living 'remote from the scene of action', enjoy the 'amusement' of reading war news which inspires 'a thousand visionary hopes of conquest and national glory' and compensates for the extra taxes they have to pay – taxes lessened by the system of credit funding. This enjoyment makes them 'wantonly' call for war when there is 'no real or solid interest to fight for'.[4] At the same time, he shares with other Scottish enlighteners, including Adam Ferguson, William Robertson, Lord Kames, and John Millar, a developing unease about the moral condition of the professional combatant.[5] Smith, who saw modern standing armies as superior to militias, nevertheless conceived professional soldiering as 'a trade' subject to the same division of labour that led to a potentially debilitating specialisation in other trades. According to Smith, a modern soldier needs merely 'regularity, order, and prompt obedience to command' to fulfil his duties and has every aspect of his daily routine determined by his officers' orders. Smith continued to speak of the soldier's 'valour', but in this context, the word seemed to mean little more than passionless, slavish obedience.[6] The soldier seems to have lost his moral autonomy.

Like other historians of progress, Smith finds that the individual responses of non-combatants and combatants to war are caught up in larger systems characteristic of modern civilisations – international and imperial relations, complex financial arrangements, technological and disciplinary systems, and the news industry – that threaten to erode the basis of individual moral judgement and so undermine moral responsibility. At the same time, Smith's positioning of the non-combatant 'remote from the scene of action' allows him to leave out of account war-related activities closer to home that might require a moral response. The public had reason to know that the barbarity of war began long before the warzone was encountered – in the processes of recruitment, the press gangs and deceptive practices used to get men into the lower ranks of the forces, in the brutal corporal punishments used to enforce what Smith terms 'regular discipline', in the neglect of demobilised war veterans and other disturbing abuses. It was well known

202   Part III: War and Peace in an Age of Revolutions

that the conditions of service in both the army and navy often seriously disrupted family life. Regulations discouraged married men from taking their wives with them on service (although there were some exceptions, as we shall see).[7] Wives left behind could face poverty and be forced into prostitution. The movement of men around the country at home or on service abroad inevitably encouraged promiscuity. Prostitutes were allowed on board naval ships when the fleet had anchored since captains found this preferable to granting shore leave (which tempted men to desert).[8] Army and navy officers acquired a reputation for using their powers of patronage to seduce the wives of their juniors, or for living openly with their mistresses. As criticism of such practices became louder, those seeking to reconcile the national view of war with moral virtue had to visualise that reconciliation in a form divorced not only from the selfish material interests and vengeful bellicosity that Smith condemned but also from the sexual corruption associated with the armed forces. In this context, support for war became closely associated with feminine virtue. As Mary Favret notes, in the later eighteenth century, a 'particular correspondence between war and domesticity' appears, which works to 'filter the destructive impact of war through invoking the traditionally "private" images of women (especially mothers) and children'. Favret is particularly concerned with bodily violence, which she finds evoked by the body of the war widow or wife left at home by the soldier, in a way that undermines the fiction that 'war will keep violence from coming home'.[9] I shall be more concerned with how feminine virtue is used to handle the issue of moral responsibility – a process that sometimes connected the virtuous wife closely with the warzone.

Feminine Virtue and War

The middle-class ideal of the pure domestic woman, who had no separate legal status when married, who was notionally separated from the realm of commerce, who could not vote and was formally excluded from the realm of politics, and who did not fight in wars, has – for all her differences – some features in common with the present-day civilians among whom Felice places himself. Felice's civilians, like the virtuous woman, are conceived as individuals whose moral duty is primarily to themselves and their families and not the overall public good. The ideal of feminine virtue that emerged in educational writings, sermons, novels, and other works, offered a form of insulation when the subject turned to war since it was clearly set apart from the abuses and aggression associated with warmaking. As a peaceful domestic ideal, it was dissociated from a range of

Saving Individual Virtue 203

other, less pacific, roles performed by contemporary women. In practice, women's work both inside and outside the home contributed significantly to the nation's war efforts, and some women worked in battle-zones – as nurses, spies, and sometimes even as combatants.[10] Indeed, the female warrior was a familiar figure in popular ballads, heroic poems, in the theatre, and in real life, drawing attention to the capacity of women to take on roles traditionally reserved for men, including martial roles.[11] The biography of Hannah Snell, a cross-dressing female soldier who had served in the army on both sides of the Atlantic, and who performed a popular onstage military routine, presented her as an example of 'genuine Heroism' to an age sunk in 'Effeminacy and Debauchery'.[12] When Richard Glover published a revised version of *Leonidas* in 1770, he included a dignified and heroic female warrior, Queen Artemisia, perhaps to appeal to the established interest in martial women.

Such possibilities for women were firmly held at bay by the domestic ideal, an ideal strengthened by the publication of works such as Rousseau's highly influential *Emile* (1762), and James Fordyce's *Sermons to Young Women* (1765). The insulated condition of this ideal allowed it to become associated with a purified or domesticated form of patriotism. Harriet Guest has attributed the emergence of the 'domestication of patriotism' to a sense of disillusionment shared by many writers, male and female, during the 1770s, a reaction in part to the government's handling of the dispute with the American colonies and its treatment of Ireland (180). She notes that in a range of writings, including the letters of Elizabeth Carter, Henry Mackenzie's Edinburgh periodical *The Lounger*, and poems by Hannah More, patriotism becomes associated with private sympathy, sentimental affections, sensibility, and a sense of place, rather than with a direct responsibility for the public good conceived in political terms.[13]

Among other examples of the conjunction of domestic and patriotic feeling, Guest cites Hannah More's poem 'Sensibility' (1782), addressed to the widow of Admiral Boscowan, whose only remaining son was currently at the battle of Lexington:

> Hereditary valour you deplore,
> And dread, yet wish to find one hero more.[14]

At this time, 'deplore' meant 'lament', but this maternal lamenting of the son's commitment to war still suggests an element of impotent protest, which is joined directly to patriotic support for that commitment. A patriotism grounded in such conflicted feelings offered a striking contrast to the aggressive patriotism promoted by Bolingbroke in the 1730s, and to

204   Part III: War and Peace in an Age of Revolutions

the coarse war-mongering and vengefulness sometimes attributed to the public at large. This expression of concern for the safety of the son differs from many of the examples of humanitarian sympathy for the victims of war that we have already considered, since it is not deployed to counterbalance a particular act of violence witnessed in the warzone. Its primary function is to characterise an appropriate sense of responsibility – or balance of responsibilities. The mother left behind shares not only the potential victimhood of her soldier son but also his hopes for glory. The kind of fear and dread that Fielding attributes to the heroine of *Amelia* when her husband is called to war is here linked to martial aspiration. The domestication of patriotism allowed support for the war to be unified with an ideal feminine virtue – the very unification that some eighteenth-century novelists had tended to avoid. While John Brown's influential *Estimate of Manners* had disparaged feelings of humanity by associating them with effeminacy, the domestication of patriotism associated feminine gentleness with a principled support for war.[15] In this development, patriotism is not necessarily detached from those sources of power and authority that formally authorise the national view of war – the sovereign, the church, law, the nation – but the individual's duty to such authorities is understood in relation to personal feelings, particular sympathies, and individual attachments.

The Wife-at-War

Dror Wahrman has noted that after the outbreak of the American Revolution female warriors rapidly fell out of fashion, as public expectations about conventional gender boundaries began to harden.[16] However, while the female warrior became less popular, the previously neglected figure of the wife-at-war started to become visible. Women had been a normal part of European armies since at least the fourteenth century. In the eighteenth century, British wives sometimes accompanied their soldier-husbands to war, although they were discouraged by the army and were rarely mentioned in campaign reports.[17] And in spite of Admiralty regulations, some naval officers, and especially warrant officers, sometimes took their wives to war with them.[18] In the last decades of the eighteenth century, such women began tentatively to find a place, and sometimes a voice, in writings about war. As non-combatants, they represented a view of war quite unlike that of the bold female warrior. They brought the domestic perspective of respectable wives and mothers into the warzone. Such women were well placed to voice protests against the misrepresentations and social abuses that arose

Saving Individual Virtue

from war. What surer sign of disinterested patriotism could there be than their willingness to accompany their husbands to war?

Catherine Upton's journal, for example, published as *The Siege of Gibraltar*, 1781, gives a harrowing account of how she, with two small children, endured the daily horrors of living under siege with her soldier-husband. Upton's account, as she points out, is not the usual combatant's war journal and makes no attempt to give 'the exact number of men killed and wounded each day'.[19] It focuses instead on the impressions of a mother who takes no part in the fighting, but who is still exposed to its violence, and has young children to protect. Part of its function is to counter press reports of '*Writers, Printers* and MINISTERS' about the abundant provisions on Gibraltar, where dire scarcity brings astronomical prices (p. 2). But while it includes anguished accounts of the conditions she and her family endured, it is not offered as a work of anti-war protest. The book's dedication to the Queen links Upton's suffering directly to pro-war loyalty:

> The partner of my heart is now serving his King and Country at the *Siege of Gibraltar*; and though I have gone through every scene of distress which the wife of an officer could be subject to in that place, yet I am returned to England with a firm resolution to educate my son to arms. (iii-iv)

Her distresses become a form of moral credit, which she hopes will pay dividends: the rest of the dedication indirectly solicits a commission on her son's behalf, while the Preface declares the work is published from a '*truly maternal*' motive, 'an anxious desire to benefit my little family' (vi). Upton presents her suffering not simply as a personal misfortune, but as a form of patriotic virtue – implicitly, a kind of sacrifice. The figure of the mourning widow that had begun to appear on the monuments of eminent soldiers and sailors earlier in the century was a recognition of this kind of domestic sacrifice – but one that was firmly subordinated to the heroic sacrifice attributed to the male warrior. Now middle-class women were beginning to draw attention to the sacrifices made in the warzone by less eminent figures like themselves, who loyally supported the nation's war-making – indeed, in Upton's journal, the role of the soldier-husband is minimised.

Maria Barrell's poem *British Liberty Vindicated, or, a Delineation of the King's Bench* (1788) sympathises with, and protests against, the fate of veterans of the war with America who have been imprisoned for debt, and laments the suffering of their families, but the poet describes herself as an 'unfortunate loyalist' who, while she condemns the severity of the law at home, praises the bravery of British soldiers and sailors.[20] Her poem includes the sentimental tale of Maria – her namesake – another 'female loyalist' who sails to America during the War of Independence in answer to 'the calls of love and duty', implicitly accompanying, or hoping to join, her soldier-husband, who is effectively displaced from the poem's narrative (p. 16, ll. 197, 200). In America, she is apparently widowed, captured, and imprisoned with her two children, and when she is released returns to Britain only to be imprisoned for debt. Barrell presents her own compassionate protest against such treatment as a patriotic gesture in support of British liberty.

The wife-at-war did not become a dominant figure in contemporary culture, but her appearance was symptomatic of wider developments. She illustrates how the domestication of patriotism works, paradoxically, to insulate domestic virtue from complicity in the violence of war. Her physical proximity to that violence indicates that this insulation depends upon her moral status, rather than upon geographical distance; she is not, like the newspaper readers condemned by Adam Smith, 'remote from the scene of action'. While she is loyal to the Crown, her support for the war effort is expressed primarily through her care for her husband and family, rather than through direct support for the political causes at stake in the hostilities or for the conduct of the war. Her concern for the price of provisions, or for the unhappy fate of families torn apart by debt, is compatible with her domestic role and her humanitarian sympathies. But since her moral responsibilities are defined primarily in relation to that domestic role, she bears little or no responsibility for the violence committed directly by her nation, or by her soldier-husband, in the warzone.

This combination of humanitarian engagement with moral insulation was the obverse of the view, found in Adam Smith and others, that modern war encouraged public indifference to the suffering of others and stimulated gross nationalistic ambition. It showed that one could express loyal support for war and sympathy with its victims without necessarily condoning or condemning the war's particular aims or methods. In this respect, it blurred the boundaries between patriotic support for the nation's war-making and protest against that war-making – between the national view and the moral view.

War and Revolution

The outbreak of the war with revolutionary France in February 1793, in the context of a debate that had polarised political opinion in Britain, brought into focus with particular urgency the issue of moral responsibility for war. While the Church, as usual, urged support for war by presenting it as a divine punishment for the nation's sins, there was vigorous opposition to the war by critics who saw it as unjust, unnecessary, or as against peaceful Christian doctrine. Some of these critics were associated with the self-styled 'Friends of Peace', liberal groups and individuals united by, as J. E. Cookson notes, an anti-aristocratic orientation and by 'the values and beliefs of rational Christianity'.[21] Although France had declared war upon Britain, the Friends of Peace regarded the British response as an act of aggression because it was directed against the right of the people of France to choose how they were governed. Thus, they opposed the national view promoted by Pitt's government on political as well as moral grounds. When, after the Peace of Amiens (1802–1803), Britain renewed its war against France, they opposed the resumption of hostilities as unnecessary, and proposed diplomacy instead. Such opposition did not imply a non-resisting pacifism: when invasion threatened, they were mostly willing to support the nation's effort of defence.

In opposing the war against revolutionary France, they followed the example of the campaign for the abolition of the slave trade, appealing to the public's conscience by emphasising their guilt. Some of them argued that the nation had been thoroughly 'impregnated' with bellicose principles and by 'the diffusion of military taste among all ranks' or claimed that the people were lost in a 'dream of glory and vengeance'.[22] Such collectivising arguments spread moral responsibility to all parts of society. Lack of power brought no exemption: most Britons could not vote, but 'all ranks' were said to have been subject to corruption. In the teaching of the Church, the nation's sins had to be atoned for by prayer, repentance, and obedience to God and the Sovereign. In contrast, the reformers' arguments made unthinking obedience to government policy itself a form of sinful behaviour. The criticism raised, in other words, a fundamental question about the responsibility of those who, unlike professional soldiers and sailors, were not ordered to fight, but who had to pay taxes and obey the laws – the responsibility of non-combatants in relation to a government at war. In such a situation, how could those who opposed the war save their moral integrity?

This problem was brought into focus in one of the earliest critical responses to the war. Soon after hostilities were declared in 1793, the Dissenter Anna Barbauld published a Fast Day sermon, *Sins of Government, Sins of the Nation,* written in a masculine voice, and signed 'A Volunteer' (presumably to suggest that the writer was a patriot).[23] Here Barbauld denounces the casual willingness of both the government and the people

208   Part III: War and Peace in an Age of Revolutions

to accept war as an instrument of state policy. However, given the volatility of the times she is keen to discourage a 'spirit of insubordination', and argues that reluctant acquiescence in 'iniquitous' state policy, including the current war she condemned, is 'a necessary condition of political union', the price of maintaining social order. The moderate protest she recommends is therefore accompanied by a message of acceptance. Unlike Felice, who takes for granted the right to vote, Barbauld was disenfranchised as a Dissenter and as a woman and was writing at a time when most adults could not vote. But she nevertheless implies that private individuals have a duty to the public good, because their acquiescence helps to maintain social order. This is a minimal conception of public duty, a duty of obedience rather than of participation, what would now be classified as a liberal conception rather than a civic humanist one (the later placing more emphasis on active participation).

In this part of her argument, then, she both condemns and endorses acquiescence in the war, and so the distinction between moral corruption and moral integrity becomes blurred. But elsewhere this distinction is maintained as a choice between alternative modes of feeling. As an antidote to the emotional indifference and resentful bellicosity she attributes to the public, she recommends humanitarian sympathy for the ordinary victims of war: 'We must fix our eyes not on the hero returning with conquest, nor yet on the gallant officer dying in the bed of honour, the subject of picture and song, but on the private soldier, forced into the service, exhausted by camp-sickness' or on the bereaved woman, and the distress and anxiety caused by war (313). In evoking the sentimental response to war that was already well established, Barbauld gives it a twofold remedial function: to counteract a public response that is either too cold (the emotionally deadening effects of militarism) or too warm (bellicose passion, 'proud defiance and sanguinary revenge').[24] At a time when the government was beginning to clamp down on oppositional writing, this imagined democratisation of sympathy demanded an emotional change in 'us' rather than an immediate change in the policies or system of government. In the face of what is deemed a necessary acquiescence in guilt, Barbauld's recommended response to the suffering caused by war is a way of reclaiming an uncontaminated virtue, a virtue that was supposedly realised in the spontaneous expression of compassion. Having argued in favour of moral compromise, she proclaims: 'let us keep our hearts pure, and our hands clean' and 'act with simplicity and singleness of intention' (42). The expression of sympathy may have little impact on the conduct of the war, but it is, like Felice's protest, critical for the individuals who produce it,

Saving Individual Virtue 209

since it saves or restores their moral integrity. It is an outward sign of that integrity.

In this respect, the non-combatant is addressed as one whose responsibility to the public good is minimised – and does not amount to more than obeying the law, and moderate protest against state iniquity. This individual's acquiescence is both a form of evil and a form of virtue. This is like the condition we saw Cowper adopt in *The Task* (see the Introduction), where acquiescence in war is seen as unwise in one sense and as compatible with virtue in another. The civilian, like that conceived by Felice, is beginning to appear, an individual who is compromised by a duty to uphold the law, and who saves virtue through moderate protest and private benevolence.

The turn to principles of benevolence was a common response to the war among artists and writers, who were keen to dissociate themselves from brutal war-mongering or indifference to suffering. While the revolution polarised political opinion and led to a sharp contrast between the ideal of universal benevolence (advocated by radicals in order to moderate nationalist aggression) and the ideal of local benevolence (advocated by Edmund Burke and other conservatives), a sympathetic response to the victims of war could transcend this opposition.[25] The numerous poems about ruined cottages, returning veterans, widows, bereaved lovers, and dead soldiers published during the years of the Revolutionary and Napoleonic wars often give vivid expression to the suffering caused to ordinary individuals by war, and to its disruption of domestic life. The enactments of sympathy sometimes imply the author's personal dissociation from the guilt of war and may entail an implicit claim to a moral high ground. This claim sometimes breaks into a startlingly overt self-justification, as in Robert Southey's 'The Soldier's Funeral', in which the poet sets himself apart from 'Reverend lip-comforters', preachers who easily reconcile the violence of war with the Christian Gospel:

> O my God!
> I thank thee that I am not such as these
> I thank thee for the eye that sees, the heart
> That feels, the voice that in these evil days
> That amid evil tongues, exalts itself
> And cries aloud against the iniquity.[26]

In their sympathetic focus on the miseries of ordinary victims, anti-war protests could resemble loyalist works. Mark Rawlinson has noted how pro- and anti-war sentiments converge in 'representations of alarm' in times of invasion.[27] But the convergence seems more fundamental than this, and arises in part from the domestication of patriotism, which may

210   Part III: War and Peace in an Age of Revolutions

align patriotic sentiment with a protesting concern for suffering. While loyalist Catherine Upton had earlier described her terror at having to flee with her children in a blazing town while being shelled from Spanish batteries (11), Charlotte Smith – protesting against the current war in her poem *The Emigrants* (1793) – now imagined the 'frantic Fear' of a French woman attempting to escape with her child while under a comparable bombardment (Book II). Maria Barrell's descriptions of Maria's trials on both sides of the Atlantic during the American war form a precedent for William Wordsworth's anti-war poem about a wife-at-war, 'The Female Vagrant', first published in *Lyrical Ballads* (1798). Poems designed to evoke sympathy for the victims of war could be a way of protesting against the war without directly attacking government policy, but their expressions of sympathy could also perform the traditional role of reconciling audiences to the unfortunate necessities of conflict and encouraging sad acquiescence. Indeed, the emphasis on the pathos of suffering could make it difficult to distinguish between protest and regretful acceptance.[28] Some of Mary Robinson's *Lyrical Tales* (1800), for example, focus on socially marginalised victims of war – the poor widow, the obscure soldier, the bereaved parent – in terms that can be read either way because readers are invited to empathise rather than to protest. The 'Deserted Cottage', which describes how war leads to the destruction of a family, ends with the exhortation to the reader: 'Smile, and be contented'.[29] Wordsworth's famous poem 'The Ruined Cottage', eventually published as the first book of *The Excursion* in 1814, includes an intensely moving tale of the slow decline of a young mother whose unemployed husband joins a troop of soldiers going to fight in a distant land; at the conclusion, the tale's narrator describes how he himself is comforted – even made happy – by an image of natural tranquillity. The appeals to feeling offer a kind of indemnification to both the poet and the reader from the charge of unfeeling complicity in the suffering produced by war.

It is not always easy to determine whether a writer supports the war or not from their poetry, since individuals who hate war, and who complain about its horrors and its futility, may at the same time loyally support their nation's war effort. Moreover, as Cookson points out, although the Friends of Peace protested against the war, they were sometimes ready to celebrate naval victories (168–69). In 1798, Elizabeth Moody published a volume entitled *Poetic Trifles* which included several poems that protest about the futility of war and express sympathy for its victims ('The widow's tears, the orphan's ruin'd state' 4), and one about Napoleon's invasion of Egypt that hails 'our Hero, brave Nelson' (162).[30] An expression of sympathy for the victims of conflict could provide a form of moral insulation, which separated sensitive patriotism from nationalistic aggression.

Christian Doctrine

The charge that war was against Christian principle gained considerable currency during the debates of the 1790s; it was made in sermons, pamphlets, and by the popular prophet Richard Brothers.[31] In response to such claims, some loyalist Christian theorists tried formally to separate private morality from the business of war. In *Evidences of Christianity* (1794) William Paley, an Anglican Archdeacon and utilitarian philosopher, accepted the literal meaning of Christ's words about not resisting evil and turning the other cheek, but insisted they 'relate to personal conduct from personal views' – and that when public issues are considered 'it comes to a case to which the rules do not belong'.[32] Conversely, the Evangelical Thomas Gisborne in his *Enquiry into the Duties of Men in the Higher and Middle Classes of Society in Great Britain* (1795) simply rejected the literal meaning of Christ's pacific statements, but treated war largely as a professional matter, effectively separating the moral problems associated with it from the rest of society which, he argued, had a duty of obedience to law and loyalty to the sovereign.[33] Gisborne's Evangelical view of society as a divinely ordained hierarchy, with the sovereign as God's appointed representative, lent itself to what twenty-first-century writers term 'compartmentalization', the subordination of individuals to specific roles, and the non-acceptance of responsibility for actions belonging to other roles elsewhere in the hierarchy. Gisborne defines duties strictly in relation to a man's allotted 'station' in life. While critics of the war condemned the effects of modern discipline which, they claimed, led combatants to fight with blind obedience and a dehumanising indifference to brutality, Gisborne's class-based survey, limiting its view of combatants to officers, insisted on their moral autonomy.[34] In line with a regulation of 1749 which supposedly limited the combatant's duty of obedience to 'lawful' orders, he argued that officers should 'resign their employment' rather than engage in an unjust war, and face death rather than obey an illegal command (189, 191).[35] He was writing at a time when anti-war critics spoke out not only against the violence of the battlefield but also about the brutal means used to acquire and discipline men in the lower ranks – the crimping, press gangs, floggings, and other routine forms of violence.[36] The compartmentalised nature of Gisborne's approach allowed him to circumvent such difficulties. He simply declined to extend his enquiry to the conscience of combatants lower down the social scale,

212   Part III: War and Peace in an Age of Revolutions

who might be subject to, or involved directly in, 'objectionable', 'knavish', and 'illegal' methods of recruiting, or brutal disciplinary activities – and who did not have the option of resigning (199). In this way, he effectively insulated the professional conduct of the higher social ranks from that of the lower ranks who were more directly affected by the most disreputable practices of modern war. This allowed him to preserve the idea promoted by Addison and other earlier eighteenth-century writers that war could be judged largely as a matter of gentlemanly conduct, requiring benevolence, charity, and humanity – and to evade the issues of institutionalised brutality raised by critics.

Gisborne went on to define the moral responsibilities of upper- and middle-class women in his *Enquiry into the Duties of the Female Sex* (London, 1797), which takes 'The sphere of domestic life' as the centre of female action. The outbreak of the war with revolutionary France had intensified well-established fears about the role of women in British society.[37] Anxieties about female sexuality had been deepened by claims that the French Revolution arose from a dangerous loosening of morality.[38] Katherine Binhammer argues that a 'sex panic' took hold in 1790s Britain, a panic which ran in parallel with an alarmed reaction to the signs of women's political activism in France and Britain, and was fed by a rise in the number of divorce and 'crim. con'. cases, fears about the dangers of seduction and the incidence of prostitution.[39] Gisborne's *Enquiry* is part of a wider reaction to the fears of the moment, a reaction in which the virtues of domesticity and feminine chastity were extolled as a foundation of patriotism, across the political spectrum, by those keen to promote the education of women (on this issue, radical Mary Wollstonecraft, who criticised 'the present system of war' in her *Rights of Woman*, 1792, and who subsequently opposed the war with France, agreed with more conservative writers).[40] Gisborne from the outset presents the defence of feminine virtue as analogous to the military defence of a threatened territory, and therefore makes feminine virtue a keystone of national security (14–15). His discussion includes an account of the wife-at-war, who provides a useful example of extreme vulnerability, not only on account of her proximity to the violent business of warfare but also by her inevitable exposure to the sexual attentions of other officers. In Gisborne's account, this figure remains uncompromised by the threats that surround her if she retains the exemplary virtues of 'female diffidence' and 'purity of heart'.[41]

Such affirmations of moral purity could apparently coexist with an emphasis on human sinfulness in Evangelical thought. In *Strictures on the Modern System of Female Education* (1799), the Evangelical reformer

Hannah More had no difficulty in finding a salutary moral purpose in the violence of war: she argued along traditional lines that God used violent means (including the 'bloody and unjust conqueror') to 'punish or purify his offending children'.[42] But in her account, a virtuous domestic woman did not appear to need this kind of purification. Such a woman embodied the true Christian and feminine quality of 'gentleness' and could there-fore support war patriotically and appreciate the higher justice entailed in its cruelty, while exercising pity for those who suffer and offering prayers for the enemy (I, 143, ii, 325). While Shaftesbury's advocacy of a polite humanitarianism had been part of a programme that sought to moderate the intimidating aspect of Church doctrine, Evangelicals like More were more at home with that aspect.[43] In her view, the virtuous domestic female remains unsullied by the human sinfulness that justifies war.

The debate stimulated by the war with revolutionary France worked to clarify moral positions relating to war, and to put into formal state-ments of doctrine assumptions that may have seemed unexceptional to some contemporaries. Both critics and supporters had to live with the war, and to find ways of reconciling themselves to its costs and horrors without losing faith in their own moral values. They may have been 'remote from the scene of action', but the distance that made a virtuous life possible was provided by various forms of moral insulation.

Jane Austen

Jane Austen's fiction inevitably depends upon this kind of insulation. She was influenced by Evangelical writings and read Gisborne's *Enquiry into the Duties of the Female Sex* with pleasure in 1805.[44] Mary Favret, in her pioneering study *War at a Distance*, questions the common idea that in the romantic period 'The home front had been insulated, as if in childlike innocence, from the horrors of war'. She notes that 'For many later war-time readers, the village life of Jane Austen's novels typified this privileged insulation and her wars an outmoded possibility'.[45] In contrast, Favret shows how deeply the experience of war penetrated ordinary experience in the romantic period, and how this penetration is registered, for example, in Austen's sensitive portrait of Anne Elliot in the novel *Persuasion*. But I would argue that this kind of penetration is made possible in Austen's fic-tion by the moral insulation – neither especially privileged nor outmoded – that preserves the integrity of her virtuous characters.

In Austen's novels, the conflict between peaceful feminine virtue and the corrupting influence of war does not operate as it does in the novels

214 Part III: War and Peace in an Age of Revolutions

of Richardson and Fielding. Austen includes morally disreputable figures associated with war, such as the militiaman George Wickham in *Pride and Prejudice* (1813), Admiral Crawford in *Mansfield Park* (1814), and General Tilney in *Northanger Abbey* (1817), but these characters are amply matched by army and navy officers who are, or become, models of virtue and good sense. Whereas Fielding's Amelia struggles to accept that her soldier-husband must go to serve his country, in Austen's *Persuasion* (published after the author's death in 1817), Anne Elliot's willingness to 'pay the tax of quick alarm' as a naval officer's wife is a sign of her admirable maturity and patriotism. Austen, unlike her contemporary Charlotte Smith, is quite at ease with such support for the nation's war-making. She can connect a gentle heroine like Anne to the violent and often disreputable business of war and at the same disconnect her thoroughly from its compromising influence, just as she distances the admirable naval officer Frederick Wentworth from the brutal violence of his occupation. We can explain her position, of course, by referring to Austen's own family connections to the armed forces, and her remoteness from Smith's kind of radicalism.[46] But such explanations do not in themselves deal with the moral adjustments needed to sustain the kind of fictional worldview Austen presents. These adjustments involve moral insulation.

However, in adopting such insulation to preserve the virtue of her heroines, she demonstrates a keen and quizzical awareness of its relation to class and sexuality. In her novels, the violence of war is carefully excluded from the realm of the gentry home – however, much its effects may impinge upon the characters' consciousness. The army and navy officers and the militia men who appear are judged primarily in terms of individual social and moral conduct. Their bravery in action may be reflected in their social behaviour and status – as the example of Captain Wentworth demonstrates in *Persuasion*. But the violence of battle is not to be mentioned. The sensible Mrs Croft is an example of the wife-at-war, now safely returned to the domestic world, a model of affable and virtuous good sense. The heroine Anne Elliot exemplifies the domestication of patriotism, as she combines feminine gentleness, purity, and a moderate sensibility with a readiness to face the personal sacrifices demanded by war when she marries the naval officer Wentworth. In Austen's novels, the separation of the physical brutality of war from the domestic realm that supports it is almost, but not quite, complete. An exception appears in *Mansfield Park* (1814), where the class-basis and sexual implications of the moral vision are partially exposed: we are shown that the conventions maintained within the polite atmosphere of Mansfield Park have less currency in the humbler

Saving Individual Virtue 215

domain of Fanny's family home at Portsmouth. Here we are allowed to see that the violence of war is not simply a distant threat but one that is already latent within the home, as an attitude conditioned by the brutal discipline of service at sea, a potential ready to meet the perceived threat of female transgression. When Fanny's father, a lieutenant of marines, reads in the newspaper of Julia Bertram's liaison with Henry Crawford, his reaction has none of the refinement of Austen's more gentlemanly naval officers:

> Then, there's the devil to pay among them, that's all! There' (holding out the paper to her); 'much good may such fine relations do you. I don't know what Sir Thomas may think of such matters; he may be too much of the courtier and fine gentleman to like his daughter the less. But, by G—! if she belonged to *me*, I'd give her the rope's end as long as I could stand over her. A little flogging for man and woman too would be the best way of preventing such things'.[47]

This not only tells us something about domestic relations but also about war. The violence Mr Price threatens is useful, even necessary, for maintaining order at sea.[48] It comes with his occupation and rank (and can be related without too much difficulty to the brutality of the contemporary slave trade, to which this novel makes a notorious allusion). Austen allows us to see what Gisborne would evade: that Lieutenant Price has his place within a larger cultural system which included fine gentlemen and courtiers, who did not have to manifest such violence directly, since men of lower rank were employed to use the rope's end and perform other brutal tasks. The fine gentlemen, conditioned by the kind of feminine gentleness represented by Fanny herself, would be critical of the brutality of the lieutenant's sentiments when applied to an erring daughter, just as the lieutenant is critical of the gentleman's 'fine' leniency at a time when 'so many fine ladies were going to the devil'. But both seek in their own way to control female sexuality and both are essential components of the kind of civilisation Mansfield Park represents. The feminine gentleness exemplified in the heroine, a gentleness that tames masculine desire and deplores masculine brutality, is related to the masculine brutality exemplified in the heroine's father, a brutality that would punish female desire and deplores effeminacy.

War quite obviously depends upon the systematic violation of the peaceful norms that govern civil society. Moral insulation does not completely conceal this scandal, to which civilians are connected by a complex web of social and economic relations. But it keeps the scandal at bay, allowing those at home to focus instead on forms of behaviour that are easier to reconcile with their ideas of moral integrity, and that give them a sense of their

216   Part III: War and Peace in an Age of Revolutions

own moral autonomy – a sense that they are free to make unconditioned choices between right and wrong. The compassionate wife-at-war who performs her domestic role as a victim of terror within the warzone takes the reader's attention away from the violence her husband is employed to enact. Barbauld's sympathy for victims restores the possibility of virtue after her grim lesson of moral compromise. The gentleness of Hannah More's pitying, virtuous female upstages the uncompromising brutality of her war-like, punishing god. The concept of the civilian, emerging into distinct form at a time when the nation's collective complicity in war was being proclaimed by protestors, distances non-combatants in moral terms from the violence enacted on their behalf. Gisborne's gentlemanly officer, who can preserve his moral integrity by always acting on his conscience, is a close relation of the civilian. His work may depend upon behaviour that Gisborne finds 'objectionable', 'knavish', and 'illegal'. But by distancing him from such behaviour, Gisborne can present him as an instructive moral ideal. Austen is unusual in that she openly acknowledges what the others tend to slide over – that the modern virtue associated with refined feminine gentleness teaches us to recoil from an encounter with the undisguised brutality needed in war, not because we want to dispense with its services, but because we want to preserve a more compassionate image of our own social existence.

Notes

1 Samuel P. Huntington, *The Soldier and the State* (Cambridge, Mass: Belknap Press, 1957); William F. Felice, *How Do I Save My Honor?: War, Moral Integrity and Principled Resignation* (Lansham: Rowman and Littlefield, 2009); Nancy Sherman, *Heroism and the Changing Character of War: Towards Post-Heroic Warfare* (London: Palgrave, 2014), 12–13; Thomas Nagel, *Moral Questions* (Cambridge: Cambridge University Press, 1979); Cheyney Ryan, *The Chickenhawk Syndrome* (Lanham: Rowman and Littlefield, 2009).
2 Nancy Sherman, 285; Felice, 12–13; Nagel, 76.
3 Felice, 13–14.
4 *An Inquiry into the Nature and Causes of the Wealth of Nations*, ed. Edwin Cannan (Chicago: University of Chicago Press, 1976), V, iii, 463.
5 Adam Ferguson, *Essay on the History of Civil Society*, 5th ed. (London, 1782), 235; William Robertson, *History of Scotland*, iii, 249–60; Lord Kames, *Sketches in the History of Man* (2 vols), ii, 4–5; John Millar, *The Origin of the Distinction of Ranks*, 3rd edn., (London, 1781), 271, 275.
6 *The Wealth of Nations*, V, I, 219, 222–223.
7 Barton C. Hacker, 'Women and Military Institutions in Early Modern Europe: A Reconnaissance', *Signs* 6 (1981), 659.

Saving Individual Virtue

8 Margarette Lincoln, *Naval Wives and Mistresses*, (London: National Maritime Museum, 2007), 142.

9 Mary Favret, 'Coming Home: The Public Spaces of Romantic War', *Studies in Romanticism* 33: 4 (1999), 539–548, 539, 547.

10 Margarette Lincoln, *Naval Wives and Mistresses*, 73–7; Kathleen Wilson, 'Nelson's Women: Female Masculinity and Body Politics in the French and Napoleonic Wars', *European History Quarterly* 37: 4 (2007), 562–581.

11 Dianne Dugaw, *Warrior Women and Popular Balladry 1650–1850* (Chicago: University of Chicago Press, 1989, 1996).

12 *The Female Soldier; Or, The Surprising Life and Adventures of Hanna Snell* (London, 1750), 9.

13 Harriet Guest, *Small Change, Women Learning, Patriotism, 1750–1810*, (Chicago: Chicago University Press, 2000), 176–192.

14 Guest, 189.

15 John Brown, *An Estimate of the Manners and Principles of the Times* (London, 1758), 2 vols, II, 40.

16 Dror Wahrman, 'Percy's Prologue: From Gender Play to Gender Panic in Eighteenth-Century England', *Past & Present*, 159 (1998), 113–160, pp. 155–156.

17 Barton C. Hacker, 'Women and Military Institutions in Early Modern Europe: A Reconnaissance,' *Signs* 6 (1981), 643–671.

18 Margarette Lincoln, *Naval Wives and Mistresses*, 37–39.

19 Catherine Upton, *The Siege of Gibraltar* (London, 1781), vi.

20 Maria Barrell, *British Liberty Vindicated, or, A Delineation of the King's Bench* (London, 1788), iii; 19 (ll. 268–272); 20 (ll. 290–295).

21 J. E. Cookson, *The Friends of Peace: Anti-war liberalism in England, 1793–1815* (Cambridge: Cambridge University, 1982), 5.

22 William Fox, *Defence of the War against France* (1794), 2; Vicesimus Knox, *The Spirit of Despotism* (London, 1795), 153; Christopher Wyvill, *A Letter to the Right Hon. WILLIAM PITT* (York: W. Blanchard, 1793) 3rd edn., 29, 36.

23 McCarthy, William and Elizabeth Craft, eds., *Anna Letitia Barbauld: Selected Poetry and Prose* (Peterborough, Ont: Broadview, 2001), 297–320.

24 Philip Shaw notes that 'by the late 1780s depictions of fallen soldiers, forlorn mothers and orphaned children had become something of a stock images for writers and artists seeking to capitalize on the vogue for sentimental depictions of the effects of war', *Suffering and Sentiment in Romantic Military Art* (Farnham: Ashgate, 2013), 82. John Richardson considers the presence of sensibility and sympathy for the victims of war in English poetry from the 1740s onwards: 'War, Lyric Poetry and Politics in the Eighteenth Century', *Eighteenth-Century Studies*, 50 (2017), 381–399. For a discussion of Barbauld's radicalism, see Anne Janowitz, *Women Romantic Poets: Anna Barbauld and Mary Robinson* (Horndon, Northcote House, 2004), 62–70.

25 Evan Radcliffe, 'Revolutionary Writing, Moral Philosophy, and Universal Benevolence in the Eighteenth Century', *Journal of the History of Ideas*, 54 (2), 1993, 221–240.

218   Part III: War and Peace in an Age of Revolutions

26 Robert Southey, 'The Soldier's Funeral', *The Annual Anthology*, I (1799), 269–271, from Betty T. Bennett, *British War Poetry in the Age of Romanticism, 1793–1815, Digital Text edited by Orianne Smith*, tiny.one/2p8n6782.

27 Mark Rawlinson, 'Invasion! Coleridge, the Defence of Britain and the Cultivation of the Public's Fear', in *Romantic Wars: Studies in Culture and Conflict, 1793–1822*, ed. Philip Shaw (London: Routedge, 2017), 110–137.

28 R. S. White has argued that poets and other writers could influence government policy by 'stirring popular revulsion against the inhumane practices' of war – but does not consider how humanitarian sentiments could be used to justify violence, 'Victims of War: Battlefield Casualties and Literary Sensibility' in *Tracing War in British Enlightenment and Romantic Culture*, ed. Neil Ramsey and Gillian Russell (Basingstoke: Palgrave, 2015), 61–76, 72.

29 Mary Robinson, *Lyrical Tales*, (London, 1800), 128.

30 Elizabeth Moody, 'On Hearing That Buonaparte Was Landed in Egypt,' *Poetic Trifles* (London 1798), 162–163.

31 Richard Brothers, *A Revealed Knowledge of the Prophecies of the Times* (London, 1794), 10; Gilbert Wakefield *The Spirit of Christianity compared with the Spirit of the Times* (London, 1794), rev. edn., 11; Vicesimus Knox, *Antipolemus: or the Plea of Reason, Religion, and Humanity against War* (London 1794); Thomas Broadhurst, *Obedience to God, rather than men*, (Taunton, 1795); J. H. Williams, *War the Stumbling-Block of a Christian; or, The Absurdity of Defending Religion by the Sword* (London, 1795).

32 *A View of the Evidence of Christianity*, 2 vols, 2nd edn., (London, 1794), I, 36.

33 Thomas Gisborne, *An Enquiry into the Duties of Men in the Higher and Middle Classes of Great Britain*, 2 vols, 4th edn (London 1797), I, 57, 61.

34 Critics of the impersonal nature of modern war include William Godwin, *An Enquiry Concerning Political Justice*, 2 vols (London: G. G. J. and J. Robinson, 1793), II, 516; Gilbert Wakefield, *The Spirit of Christianity*, 11, 13, 26–27; Joseph Fawcett, *The Art of War: A Poem* (London: J. Johnson, 1795), 20–21.

35 *Rules and Articles For the Better Government of his Majesty's Horse and Foot Guards, And all Other His Forces in Great Britain and Ireland, Dominions beyond the Seas, and Foreign Parts. Anno 1749* (London, 1749), 5–6.

36 J. R. Dinwiddy, 'The Early Nineteenth-Century Campaign against Flogging in the Army', *The English Historical Review*, 97 (1982), 308–331; E. E. Steiner, 'Separating the Soldier from the Citizen: Ideology and Criticism of Corporal Punishment in the British Armies, 1790–1815', *Social History* 8: 1 (1983), 19–35; Patrick Underwood, Steven Pfaff, Michael Hechter, 'Threat, Deterrence, and Penal Severity: An Analysis of Flogging in the Royal Navy, 1740–1820', *Social Science History*, 42: 3 (2018), 411–439.

37 See Linda Colley, *Britons*, 253.

38 As Kathleen Wilson notes, the threat of political disorder and its remedy were often 'figured in terms of female sexual license and its suppression' ('Nelson's Women,' 566).

39 Katherine Binhammer, 'The Sex Panic of the 1790s', *Journal of the History of Sexuality* 6: 3 (1996), 409–434.

Saving Individual Virtue

40 *Rights of Woman*, Chapter 9.

41 Thomas Gisborne, *An Enquiry into the Duties of the Female Sex* (London 1797), 2, 354.

42 Hannah More, *Strictures on the Modern System of Female Education* 2 vols (London, 1799) I, 178–179.

43 Lawrence E. Klein, *Shaftesbury and the Culture of Politeness*, (Cambridge: Cambridge University Press, 1994), 154.

44 Friday 30 August 1805, to Cassandra Austen, *Jane Austen's Letters*, ed. Deirdre Le Faye, 3rd edn. (Oxford: Oxford University Press, 1997), 112.

45 Mary A. Favret, *War at a Distance: Romanticism and the Making of Modern Wartime* (Princeton University Press, 2010), 9, 44–45.

46 For an account of Austen's conservatism, see Marilyn Butler, *Jane Austen and the War of Ideas* (Oxford: Oxford University Press, 1975, 1987).

47 Jane Austen, *Mansfield Park*, ed. Kathryn Sutherland, (Harmondsworth: Penguin, 2003), 408.

48 Brian Southam points out that Marines were disliked by ordinary seamen 'for the part they played in enforcing the Captain's authority', *Jane Austen and the Navy* (London: National Maritime Museum, 2005), 209.

CHAPTER 9

Saving Communal Virtue

The Melancholy Call-to-Arms

The moral insulation we have considered in the previous chapter is primarily concerned with the integrity of individuals. Although it may depend upon the domestication of patriotism involving intensely personal feelings and attachments, it nevertheless appears within the context of a preordained order. It involves loyalty to the crown, or obedience to law or to gospel teaching or to spiritual power, or conformity to an established gender or social hierarchy. It assumes limits which are morally protective because they are taken to be authorised and independent of the individual will, aspects of a permanent order beyond the vicissitudes of history. This kind of insulation works best when the active violence of the warzone is avoided, and war is approached more passively as something to be endured and made the best of, rather than as something to be advocated.

However, in a period of revolutionary change and invasion threats, when constituted authorities of all kinds were being challenged from without and from within, the moral integrity of communities was also at issue. The collective willingness to fight could itself become a test of legitimacy, independent of the usual institutional frameworks that authorise the national view of war. A communal war effort could be evoked to suggest the nation as a unified people rather than as an established state, and so to transcend divisive material interests and political issues. It could be evoked by those who supported the national war effort against revolutionary France and by liberals who opposed it (and who preferred to imagine communities overseas in Europe or further afield rising against oppressive regimes). When threats of invasion intensified, it could be evoked to suggest a common interest among politically divided groups. In all such cases, the community at war is authorised by the martial responsibilities imposed by the urgent historical moment rather than by the established norms of a peaceful society; the collective interest appears to override particular social interests.

220

Saving Communal Virtue 221

There was a revolutionary potential in this vision of communal militancy which made it attractive to radicals as well as to liberals and conservatives – William Blake's 'Prophecy' *America* (1793), for example, portrays the American rebels at the time of War of Independence as unified by an inspiring revolutionary energy personified in the fiery figure of Orc. But for those who feared the prospect of radical change, the end point of such a collective effort had to be imagined in terms that allowed an indefinite, melancholy postponement, or in terms that distanced militancy from the divisive realities and injustices that threatened society from within, or through a turn to ideas of common humanity, often evoked through sorrowful feeling. In this chapter, we shall consider some contemporary examples of this process.

By the end of the eighteenth century, a modern war fought by professional combatants was often condemned on the grounds that its violence was unfeeling and impersonal. Julia Banister has traced in detail the relationship between civic humanist assumptions about military masculinity and contrasting assumptions reflecting the 'revolution' in military practices since the medieval period. Unlike the soldier of civic humanist tradition, the 'modern' soldier does not express his natural 'masculine' identity in his martial actions; he performs martial actions that are conditioned by his professional discipline and training.[1] Scottish Enlightenment historians looked back with admiration and a sense of loss on the martial vigour displayed in the feudal era, and claimed that the modern professionalisation of war had produced highly disciplined soldiers who fought, as Adam Ferguson put it, 'from habit, and from the fear of punishment' rather than from 'love of the public, or a national spirit'. Ferguson was a militia advocate, but Adam Smith, who favoured the standing army, had similar views. In the *Wealth of Nations,* he described professional soldiering as a 'trade', a term that linked it to the unheroic realm of economic calculation and self-interest rather than to fervent heroism and patriotic sacrifice.[2] Such views of modern war placed it at odds with the idea that a just war was driven by patriotic emotion, by love of family, of community, and of liberty, undermining the national view of war. There was an implicit tension between the impersonal means available to fight a just war, and the deeply personal feelings that justified it.

The contrast between passionless violence driven by calculating self-interest and ardent violence driven by patriotic feeling influenced views across a spectrum of political opinion. It played in various ways through the debate that erupted in Britain in response to the French revolution. Conservative Edmund Burke famously compared the generous 'manly

222 Part III: War and Peace in an Age of Revolutions

sentiment' of the age of chivalry, in which men would readily fight to defend their queen, with the modern age of self-interested 'sophisters, economists and calculators', whose revolutionary doctrines were generating chaotic violence in France.[3] Radical Thomas Paine viewed professional soldiers and sailors as unheroic victims of modern state oppression, but admired the Parisians who attacked the Bastille 'with an enthusiasm of heroism, such only as the highest animation of liberty could inspire'.[4]

When war broke out between Britain and Revolutionary France in 1793, the contrast was used both to condemn and endorse the British war effort. It allowed critics of the war to voice their condemnation in terms suggesting intense moral horror while reserving a space for a virtuous defensive war. Among those Britons who opposed the war were liberals whose hopes for peace were linked to political reform: the self-styled 'Friends of Peace and Reform' who campaigned in pamphlets, sermons, and petitions.[5] The Unitarian Gilbert Wakefield, in condemning the war, observed that soldiers 'hew into pieces' enemy soldiers 'without one impulse of private animosity, at the mere instigation of their superiors'; yet he admired 'the magnanimous struggles of the Poles for life and liberty against two of the most profligate tyrants' (i.e. Prussia and Russia).[6] Some of those who supported the war against France also found this kind of distinction useful, since it allowed them to adopt the language of patriotic feeling – sometimes used in earlier decades by opponents of the government. The prowar propagandist John Bowles, for example, condemned France – which had decreed its *levée en masse* on 23 August 1793 – as a 'Military Republic' whose martial aggression depended on 'the compulsory efforts extorted by cruelty, oppression and terror'. He argued that the campaign against the French was not, as critics declared, a conflict foisted upon a British public already habituated to the horrors of war and with a greedy appetite for conquest, but one requiring 'Energy inspired by a genuine attachment to one's country, and heightened by every benevolent and social feeling'.[7]

In an age wracked by violent revolutionary turmoil abroad and unsettling political agitation at home, the positive valuation of military 'ardour' was not without risk. Faced with the possibility of a French invasion during the mid-1790s, the British government had to make plans to expand the militia and to call for volunteers. There had been invasion scares earlier in the century, but the political uncertainty generated by the revolution, and the rapid militarisation of France, made the current situation seem exceptionally perilous. Linda Colley, in her study of British attempts to expand the armed forces at this time, observes that in the early years of the war the government 'was as afraid of its

Saving Communal Virtue 223

own people as it was of the enemy'. While there was often resistance to militia recruitment, 'labouring men were neither welcome nor very much trusted in the less structured world of the volunteers'.[8] But as the war continued, the governing classes were obliged to accommodate what they feared. The Defence of the Realm Act of 1798 worked to broaden the social base of the volunteer groups that were being organised across the country. Some former members of Corresponding Societies – radical groups that had campaigned for Parliamentary reform – joined the volunteers, while some volunteer groups became active in seeking to protect their members' interests, some resisting press gangs or prompting food riots. Colley notes that 'the more industrialised and urbanised a region was, the more likely it was to produce a high level of volunteers' (293). As such regions were also becoming sites of industrial and political agitation, their mobilisation in the cause of national defence could potentially help to foster demands for political change while providing training in organised violence.

Those liberals who opposed the war with France were not blind to the dangers of unruly violence breaking out at home. The Dissenting members of the Friends of Peace, for example, had some reason to feel especially vulnerable in times of unrest. The Gordon Riots of 1780, aimed in the first instance against Roman Catholics, had unleashed devastation on London more spectacular than anything inflicted on mainland Britain by wars during the eighteenth century. And in July 1791, in response to Dissenters' sympathy for the French Revolution and their attempts to get the Test and Corporation Acts repealed, a loyalist mob in Birmingham had destroyed the house and laboratory of Barbauld's friend Joseph Priestley, and the homes and chapels of other Dissenters, over four days of rioting. The Friends of Peace had no wish to excite violent resistance to government authority. As Cookson points out, they were anxious that 'the "deprived" classes should not [...] become discontented enough to contemplate or exact some form of vengeance'.[9]

In response to this seemingly unprecedented crisis, then, writers across a range of political opinion had to reconcile their approval of genuine martial ardour with their dread of spontaneous violence and political turmoil. Their attempts to imagine virtuous patriotic emotion often coexisted with, and even coalesced with, calming measures designed to encourage more peaceful responses. Ardour was simultaneously evoked and disposed of – defused by mourning, by conciliation, or by an insistence on its obsolescence. The result was often a decidedly melancholy, and muted, call to arms.

224   Part III: War and Peace in an Age of Revolutions

Communal Mourning

In this period, mourning begins to assume more clearly the role of con-flict resolution in writings about war. The imagined act of public mourn-ing, already extended in the poems of Collins into an inclusive response to all of the 'brave' who fall (see Chapter 4), is now seen as a method of healing divisions between and within groups. It is not only the feelings of the bereaved that are at issue, or the sense of national pride and indebt-edness to an honoured martyr, but the feeling of unity and tranquillity generated by a shared feeling of grief, a feeling that can cross national and social divisions, and bring peace out of potential discord. In a way that parallels the call to arms, the appeal to mourning allowed writers to find the basis of social unity not in divisive material interests but in a common humanity.

Robert Southey captures this function precisely in his poem 'The Soldier's Funeral', published in 1799, when Southey still considered him-self a radical. Here the poet, even as he protests against the human cost of war, finds something to admire in the funeral march: it 'awes the very rabble multitude' who, in his view, are impressed not by the pomp and pageantry of the procession but simply by the measured sounds. It is, he claims, a 'universal language' which speaks to the heart and 'compels one feeling'.[10]

This view of the compelling, unifying effect of mourning, so attractive in a period threatened with the possibility of violent social unrest, proved as useful to those who recommended war as to those who opposed it. As we saw in the previous chapter, Anna Barbauld opposed Britain's war against revolutionary France. But she was not a pacifist, and during her career as a poet she wrote a number of works that encouraged armed patri-otic resistance (including, notoriously, *Eighteen Hundred and Thirteen*, a poem that begins with a powerful condemnation of the ongoing war in Europe but ends with an endorsement of South American groups ris-ing to 'noble strife' against the forces that oppress them – which in 1806 and 1807, included British forces that had attempted to occupy Buenos Aires).[11] When the Duke of Brunswick threatened to invade revolutionary France in the summer of 1792, she wrote a poem that argued both for and against violence: 'On the Expected General Rising of the French Nation in 1792'. On the one hand, the poet urges the French to rise up in collective defence of their nation:

> Let thy great spirit rous'd at length,
> Strike hordes of Despots to the ground.

Like many in Britain, she sympathised with the early aims of the French revolution but was alarmed by the effects of its violence. Her encouragement of French resistance was therefore qualified by her fear that unleashed violence might run shamefully out of control (the poet dreads 'Each deed that clouds thy glory's page'). The poem concludes with a model of peaceful conflict resolution that shuns triumphalism in favour of sympathy and understanding for the enemy, whose dead should be included in the mourning process:

> Then build the tomb–O not alone,
> Of him who bled in freedom's cause;
> With equal eye the martyr own,
> Of faith revered and antient laws.

Peace involves a generous recognition that both sides in the conflict will have their martyrs.[12]

Amelia Alderson (later Amelia Opie) adopts a comparable approach in her 'Ode On the Present Times, 27th January 1795', but takes it further. Alderson, who like Barbauld moved in radical and Dissenting circles, claims to be inspired by the 'matchless victories' of Freedom as she surveys the struggles across continental Europe, but is also saddened by them:

> Yet I thy *triumphs* too must weep,
> And in my tears thy bloody laurels steep.

She not only declares that one should mourn for slaughtered enemies, but also that Victory should 'wear the sombrous aspect of *defeat*'.[13] The idea that victories should be mourned as defeats may in part be a reflection upon contemporary victory celebrations, which were not only occasions of raucous, chauvinistic triumphalism, but which could become violent, since householders who failed to illuminate their windows could have them broken, and drunken revellers could turn ugly. Faced with such a prospect, a funeral march which, in Southey's phrase, 'awes the very rabble multitude' could seem a safer as well as a more dignified and humane option.

Some Dissenting ministers formally justified their approval of war by appeals to mourning. The Baptist minister Joseph Hughes, in a Fast Day sermon on the resumption of war after the Peace of Amiens, declared 'if I concede the necessity of arming, I call upon the friends of religion and virtue to mourn over it as a *fearful* necessity'.[14] The imagined act of mourning could provide a basis on which a range of different attitudes to war, both favourable and unfavourable, could unite. Mourning signified acquiescence, but without the sense of guilt implied by the fast and humiliation.

226   Part III: War and Peace in an Age of Revolutions

The Congregationalist Thomas Cloutt went further: he recommended weeping in sympathy with victims of war as a beneficial contribution to the national campaign. Evoking the carnage of a battlefield, Cloutt proclaims in a Fast Day sermon of 1806:

> There the Angel of Christian Sympathy has taken her stand, and mingles her tears with the living, with the dying, and with the dead. [...] no sooner is her work accomplished on the gory plain, than she spreads her wings, and visits every country [and] with soothing aspect enters alike the cottages of the peasant, and the palaces of kings [...] to administer the consolations of religion.

The rhetorical work of this fantasy is to disavow any sense of hostility towards national enemies, while defusing political rancour by suggesting an equality of need between peasants and kings. But its ultimate purpose, as Cloutt eventually reveals, is to 'make us better soldiers and defenders of our country', to prepare for an attempt to rouse 'all the feelings of the husband, the father, the patriot, with tenfold ardour' against Bonaparte.[15] This belief in the efficacy of tears has a kind of precedent in earlier Fast Day sermons which implied that the nation's tears of repentance would speed the war effort. For Cloutt, tears of sympathy perform a comparable function, but in a way that suggests virtue rather than guilt. The traditional role of the Fast Day in supporting the national view of war is at once maintained and transformed by ideas of benevolence. The moral integrity of the community is imagined, rather than its sinfulness.

Obsolescence

The need to moderate the call-to-arms was also met by a turn to obsolete modes of warfare. In such cases, the fact of obsolescence was itself an occasion of mourning. Burke's famous lament for the age of chivalry was prophetic in this sense. While in his *Reflections on the Revolution in France* (1790), he evoked the leaping of a thousand swords from their scabbards in imagined vengeance for the mistreatment of the French Queen, the reality of people impulsively laying hold of weapons in order to take the law into their own hands was something he dreaded, as the rest of *Reflections* makes abundantly clear. He could safely evoke the violence of the age of chivalry precisely because it was gone. The irrecoverable loss of chivalry was part of its value; it allowed a call to action to be combined with a melancholy sense of belatedness.

Writers, artists, and musicians had always turned to the distant past for models of martial heroism, but the distance between the martial virtue of the past and the impersonal discipline of the present was increasingly conceived in relation to cultural and material progress that seemed beyond the control of any individual. Changes in the understanding of time had given rise to ideas of evolution and to the recognition that some species might become extinct. The idea of cultural extinction had become fashionable: the defiant hero of Thomas Gray's Ode 'The Bard' (1757) and the courageous warriors and bards of James Macpherson's Ossianic epics (1760–65) were presented as the last of their race, remnants of a heroic way of life about to disappear.[16] Such figures were intended to inspire both patriotic ardour and feelings of pathos. Katie Trumpener's study *Bardic Nationalism* shows how nationalist antiquaries in eighteenth-century Ireland, Scotland, and Wales see the bard as a figure who mourns the 'inconsolable tragedy' of the collapse of their respective cultural traditions in the face of subjugation and English hegemony.[17] I would add that bardic figures and the collapse of cultural tradition were thematically important not only within the context of such cultural nationalism but also within the context of Britain's war against France. In relation to the crisis of war, they were useful precisely because they evoked both the desire for, and the annulment of, patriotic martial ardour.

James Boaden's play *The Cambro-Britons*, which was staged with some success at the Haymarket theatre in the summer of July 1798, and twice reviewed the *Anti-Jacobin Review*, is an instructive example of this. Loosely based upon Edward I's invasion of Wales, it premiered in the wake of the French invasion of Switzerland and the defeat of Swiss resistance, when invasion fears were rife in Britain – and when reports of the Irish rebellion were at their height. In his preface, Boaden argues that the noblest duty of the stage is to inspire ardour against an invading enemy. At the climax of his play, a Welsh bard appears amid sublime mountain scenery to confront King Edward and his forces, reciting lines from Thomas Gray's Ode *The Bard* ('Ruin seize thee, ruthless king…',) and even imagining the king's death, before enacting the suicidal leap described in that poem, and dying as the last of the bards.[18] This heroic, self-sacrificial gesture inspires a Welsh victory and stands in contrast to the self-interested actions of some Welshmen who are bribed to join Edward. But in 1798, such a violent challenge to monarchical power had to be carefully circumscribed (some of Boaden's audience may have known that a source for Gray's Ode, Thomas Carte, had described the Bards as stirring 'the people to sedition').[19] The bardic figure is useful here precisely because, as the last of his race, he represents an inspiring, passionate resistance in the moment of its own demise. After his disappearance, the play becomes less concerned

228   Part III: War and Peace in an Age of Revolutions

with invasion, more concerned with the politics of conciliation: following a Welsh victory, Edward and the Welsh prince Llewellyn reach a peaceful accommodation in a way that looks forward to the modern British Union. The heroic bard is survived by a comic Irish minstrel, who sings for money, a reassuring counter-image of the violent Irish rebel who was currently challenging British rule in Ireland. In this way, the play attempts to rally patriotic resistance to the French while justifying the suppression of the Irish rebellion and encouraging a spirit of peaceful co-operation that transcends divisive interests.[20]

The year after Boaden's play appeared, the pattern of stirring and moderating war-like feelings was created in a comparable way by Sheridan's play about the conquest of Peru, *Pizarro* (1799), the most popular play of the period. This includes in the second act a rousing speech of patriotic resistance by the Inca hero, Rolla, a speech which resonates with political allusions to British violence in India and Ireland – issues which Sheridan had spoken about in Parliament as a Whig politician.[21] The speech inspires Inca victories, but the defiant martial passions it generates are eventually displaced as the play concludes with sombre funeral preparations for both Rolla and his adversary Pizarro, levelled in death. The stage directions make clear that 'the Triumph of the Day is lost, in mourning for the fallen Hero' (148). As audiences knew, the death of Rolla figured the imminent collapse of the Inca empire.

The idea of cultural obsolescence helped to make representations of brutal violence more acceptable to polite readers. It could make the act of representation itself a form of reclamation, which signified the careful stewardship of antiquity rather than a love of brutality. In this respect, it appealed to a shared, civilised standard of taste while making the issues at stake in the violence seem distant. Historical footnotes and other antiquarian apparatus reinforced this sense, helping to separate the text from the realm of public action, placing it in the world of culture, as an object of private but sociable appreciation. The concept of 'taste' was often invoked by eighteenth-century antiquarians when recommending supposedly 'primitive' or 'vulgar' antiquities to a wider audience.[22] Taste was thought to allow readers to enter into feelings that had no place in, and might conflict with, the norms of modern life. As David Hume explained, taste could function as an antidote to 'rougher and more boisterous emotions'; it promoted empathy, countered prejudice, and evoked feelings that drew 'the mind off from the hurry of business and interest'. In this way, it disposed us towards tranquillity, agreeable melancholy, love, and friendship.[23] Such a concept might seem to have little to do with the violent turmoil of war,

Saving Communal Virtue 229

but effectively provided a form of moral insulation from it. If, as some maintained, reading about ongoing wars in the newspapers made people indifferent to suffering and encouraged unseemly nationalistic aggression, reading about ancient wars in romances or other antiquities that appealed to the reader's taste could be thought of as morally edifying, as encouraging emotional sensitivity, and as promoting access to a civilised community of shared values remote from divisive material interests.

The link between chivalry and romance reinforced such thinking. Thomas Percy's essay 'On the Ancient Metrical Romances' (1765) compared romance favourably with classical epic, since he found in chivalry a 'respectful compliance to the fair sex, (so different from the manners of the Greeks and Romans)'.[24] Clara Reeve in her *Progress of Romance* (1785) took a comparable view.[25] Like Richard Hurd, author of an influential study of chivalry (1762), these writers appealed to the idea of taste in recommending the works they surveyed. Romances, disdained by Richardson's Clarissa, and condemned by conduct books written for young women, could now be seen more favourably. The chaste ideals of the chivalric code, like the domestication of patriotism, allowed war to be seen as compatible with feminine virtue – but without displacing the business of fighting. As we saw in the previous chapter, the figure of the patriotic wife-at-war tended to displace the figure of the warrior and the violence in which he engages. The re-evaluation of chivalry and romance, on the other hand, allowed vivid descriptions of martial violence to be reintroduced into prose fiction and modern poetic romances aimed at polite readers. In James White's *The adventures of John of Gaunt, Duke of Lancaster* (1790), which celebrates the exploits of the Black Prince, the warrior-narrator gives matter-of-fact descriptions of his own acts of violence, including beheadings, and the slaughter of sleeping Irish soldiers in their camp, descriptions that could hardly be attributed to a modern narrator without discrediting him.[26] Clara Reeve's *Memoirs of Sir Roger de Clarendon* (1793), which appeared when Britain was at war with France, also celebrates the violent exploits of the Black Prince, who is described as 'terrible in war' but as possessing 'all the social and domestic virtues'.[27] Robert Southey reacted against such bellicose nationalism and its aristocratic basis in his epic poem *Joan of Arc* (first published in 1796). But he admired Glover's *Leonidas*, and shared Glover's interest in portraying the horrific violence of war. Unlike Glover, he underpinned his poem with historical footnotes and made abundant use of humanitarian sentiment to guide the reader's response to combat. As a result, violence is simultaneously condemned and authorised in the poem, since the poet attempts to distinguish between the heartless aggression of

230   Part III: War and Peace in an Age of Revolutions

the English, and the admirable patriotic resistance of the French, the latter inspired by the saintly Joan's example.

A key advantage of the turn to chivalry was that, in returning to a medieval era, it avoided modern commercial and industrial relations, eliminated the grounds of modern social and political agitation, and avoided the worries associated with a volunteer force that included large numbers of working men from manufacturing areas. The problems of modernity were only too apparent in the attempts of the poet laureate, Henry James Pye, to celebrate war in the 1790s. In *Naucratica: Naval Dominion* (1798), Pye's account of the progress of society culminates in reflections on the importance of naval power to the rise of modern Britain. The idea of a prosperous modern nation united by commerce and industry, which had served earlier patriotic poets such as James Thomson, was becoming more problematic in an age of rapid change. Pye finds that the development of canals, for example, has bred a 'vile inglorious race' of bargees that threatens to replace the vigorous merchant 'tars' who can be recruited by the navy. In an age of revolution, the navy itself has been rocked by 'Faction' and mutiny.[28] Britain's naval dominion seems to be threatened by the nation's own modernisation. Such contentious issues could be avoided by turning towards a safely distant past.

Walter Scott, writing after Peace of Amiens and the resumption of the war, captivated the public with a series of poetic romances featuring obsolete forms of combat. He began to publish these works at a time when the revolutionary turmoil in France had given way to Napoleonic rule, and there was a renewed threat of French invasion. There were also continuing fears of unrest at home, especially in the developing industrial regions, where workers were beginning to organise protests against the war, rising food prices, taxes, and for political and social reform.[29] Scott was a Tory who sought to moderate political opinion, attempting, in William Hazlitt's phrase, to 'conciliate all the suffrages', although his works were expensive, aimed primarily at a polite readership.[30] The immediate popularity of his romances depended to some extent on their ability to transport readers away from contentious modern problems and from 'civilized war' into an archaic chivalric world in which martial virtue flourished. Like Boaden's play, they pushed problems of internal division into the past, so that history could be seen as moving towards resolution. Scott included animated descriptions of fighting in his poems but avoided gory details in deference to women readers. And the war-like passions he evokes are checked by more tranquilising emotions.

The Lay of the Last Minstrel (1805) is set mainly in the age of Henry VIII, which allows Scott to reflect upon a feudal world about to disappear. Much of

Saving Communal Virtue

the *Lay* is narrated by an aged minstrel who has survived into a more modern age in which the localised feudal loyalties of the Scottish Border have been replaced by a sense of nationhood, a process the minstrel associates with alienation. This alienation can be related to contemporary understandings of history as linear progress, the product of an age of rapid modernisation that seemed to be eradicating traditional ways of life and which turned history into, as Ira Ferris says, 'a mode of connection' with the past 'posited on the historian's own alienation'.[31] In Scott's romance, this alienation determines the emotional context in which the action is presented. The minstrel does not simply evoke a heroic past (as Glover does in *Leonidas*) but a world he has personally lost, and whose loss he laments. The war-like events within the narrative are therefore introduced by, and sometimes permeated by, elegiac feeling. Scott shows how news of war (relayed by beacons, not newspapers) impinges upon a noble medieval household, where all have accustomed roles to play, and it is the Seneschal, the steward of the house, who gives the orders as part of his household duties. At a time when, in modern Britain, barrack-building had separated professional troops from civilians, Scott depicts the medieval house itself as accommodating the equipment and specialised skills needed to launch an immediate response to the threat of attack, and to tend to the wounded (a role taken by the Lady of Branksome). In contrast to the modern reliance on militia laws, crimping, and elaborate war propaganda to secure national defence, Scott evokes a habitual readiness for war rooted in a whole way of life:

> Fair Margaret, from the turret head,
> Heard, far below, the coursers' tread,
> While loud the harness rung,
> As to their seats, with clamour dread,
> The ready horsemen sprung;
> And trampling hoofs, and iron coats,
> And leaders' voices, mingled notes,
> And out! and out!
> In hasty route,
> The horsemen galloped forth;
> Dispersing to the south to scout,
> And east, and west, and north,
> To view their coming enemies,
> And warn their vassals and allies. (III, xxviii)[32]

The Marxist critic Georg Lukács argues that the French Revolution, the revolutionary wars and the rise of Napoleon 'for the first time made history a *mass experience*' and gave rise to the sense of war as involving a people as a

232 Part III: War and Peace in an Age of Revolutions

whole.[33] He finds this sense exemplified in Scott's historical novels, but it is already clearly present in this poetic romance. Scott seems to have enjoyed imagining groups of people rising to arms with a shared purpose (when he worked on this poem, Scott was personally engaged in military training as an enthusiastic volunteer in the Royal Edinburgh Light Dragoons). The subject evoked a longed-for social unity and national unity. But it also evoked what he most feared: as his account of the feast at Branksome Hall shows later in the poem, ardent group passions can soon produce discord. The design of the work therefore counterbalances rousing warlike ardour with the pathos of loss. While the landscape becomes busily peopled in the tale, in the minstrel's comments and the poet's own commentary the landscape is emptied out, leaving only ghostly memories:

> His legendary song could tell—
> Of ancient deeds, so long forgot;
> Of feuds, whose memory was not;
> Of forests, now laid waste and bare;
> Of towers, which harbour now the hare;
> Of manners, long since chang'd and gone;
> Of chiefs, who under their grey stone
> So long had slept, that fickle Fame
> Had blotted from her rolls their name,
> And twined round some new minion's head
> The fading wreath for which they bled—
> In sooth, 'twas strange, this old man's verse
> Could call them from their marble hearse. (IV, 124)

Such restorative remembering provides for Scott's readers the basis of a national feeling grounded not in divisive material and political interests but in a haunted and mournful sense of place, a domesticated patriotism. The poem might have ended with the celebrations at the end of canto 5, but ends instead, after a Canto of songs, with a funeral dirge.

The Losing Hero

The turbulent age of chivalry provided distant analogies for the conflicts of the present age, which writers could invest with noble passions and sharply drawn moral choices free from the complications and uncertainties found in press reports and commentaries. Events in modern Spain would lead many writers to seek such analogies. In 1808, after France had invaded Spain and attempted to remove members of the Spanish royal family from Madrid, a popular Spanish rising produced a sharp clash of

Saving Communal Virtue 233

views in Britain. After the Tory government decided to send troops in aid of the Spanish, the Whig *Edinburgh Review* took an oppositional stance, claiming that the rising had little chance of immediate success.[34] The Tory *Quarterly Review* backed the government, arguing that the Spanish people did not rise against the constituted authorities but were 'docile and submissive, though prompt and ardent, instruments of their leaders' and were fighting for the defence of church and state against innovation. In this top-down view, the rising was inspired by 'the undaunted spirit of the universal nation'. Having classified the rising as patriotic resistance rather than revolutionary insurrection, the *Quarterly* had little difficulty in finding parallels between Edward I's interventions in Scotland and Napoleon's in Spain, and looked forward to some 'Future Bannockburn' in which the Spanish would take their vengeance on the French.[35]

Jane Porter, who had already written a novel on the doomed Polish struggle against Russian invasion in *Thaddeus of Warsaw* (1803), took up the story of Edward's I invasion of Scotland in order to present a topical, conservative view of a successful national rising in her historical novel *The Scottish Chiefs* (1810).[36] But although this presents an encouraging story of Scottish triumph, it also places much emphasis on Scottish loss, highlighting the betrayal and defeat that lie behind the triumphant Scottish victory over the English.[37] Porter's top-down view of patriotic resistance required an ideal chivalric hero. She might have chosen for this role Robert Bruce, who as king of Scotland would defeat the English at Bannockburn and assert Scottish national independence with the Declaration of Arbroath. But while Bruce appears in the novel, the hero is William Wallace, who would eventually be defeated and die in English custody. As Graeme Morton points out, this emphasis served Porter's 'constitutional narrative for Britain'.[38] Wallace's great military successes as unifier and liberator of his country are followed by his betrayal at the hands of corrupt Scottish nobles. Porter contrives to circumvent the final indignity of Wallace's execution – just as Boaden omits the grisly end of Llewellyn at English hands in *The Cambro-Britons*. But Bruce's final triumph at Bannockburn is merely summarised in the context of mourning for Wallace. It is news of Wallace's death that reunifies his nation ('the whole country rose as one man').[39] By putting that unity upon a firmer basis, Wallace's death enables Bruce's victory. The sequence emphasises that without a foundational national myth of sacrifice Scotland falls into self-interested division. The novel ends with 'honourable terms of pacification' (lxxxix, 775) with the English, a process of sober reconciliation that portents the constitutional arrangements of modern Britain.

234   Part III: War and Peace in an Age of Revolutions

Throughout the novel, Porter combines rousing appeals to martial feeling with chastening lessons about loyalty, duty, and sacrifice. The Scottish people who respond to Wallace's leadership resemble the *Quarterly's* view of the Spanish: 'Docile and submissive, though prompt and ardent'. By placing a violent martial hero at the centre of the novel, Porter not only insists on the sacrifices required in domestic life but also to some extent sacrifices the domestic values she ostensibly endorses. At the beginning, the newly wed Wallace, living in a Scotland dominated by Edward I, forgets 'Scotland and its wrongs' in his marital bliss (ii, 18). It is the murder of his wife that transforms Wallace into a patriotic leader, wedded to his nation (and so freed from ordinary domestic obligations, vi, 60). When peasant mothers hold up their children to show their willingness to sacrifice them for their country (xx, 170), there is none of the maternal deploring we saw in Hannah More's poem 'Sensibility' (see Chapter 8). Porter, who never married, presents Lady Mar's overtly sexual passion for Wallace (which leads her to become a cross-dressing female warrior) as a dangerous evil, but sympathises with the repressed passion of Helen, the prime exemplar of feminine virtue in the novel, whose own cross-dressing as a page boy can be approved since her desire for Wallace is sublimated into chaste and modest adoration. Wallace himself emerges not only as the antithesis of Napoleonic imperial ambition but also as a national hero quite unlike Nelson, whose sexual liaison with Emma Hamilton and eager accumulation of personal honours set him at odds with the kind of heroic purity Porter celebrates.[40]

The tension between the martial and social themes in the novel leads to a striking contrast between tones. The historical context licenses the portrayal of violence as explicit as anything in Glover – beheadings, burnings, mass slaughter – moderated by a Christian warrior ethic which respects pleas for quarter and shows concern for the burial of the dead. But scenes of martial violence appear in a narrative that repeatedly dwells upon tender feeling, and in which patriotism is shown to be founded on a deeply personal sense of loss. In adapting medieval history Porter, like Scott, sets the events of her novel in picturesque or sublime locations within the Scottish landscape, sometimes describing large gatherings and giving the sense of a whole people engaged in the struggle for their country. What the *Quarterly* defines as 'the undaunted spirit of the universal nation' is here not grounded in particular material or political interests so much as in shared popular memories.[41] The English invaders are shown to be destroying public records (xvi, 132), but they cannot destroy popular memory, rooted in the sense of place, and perpetuated by bardic tradition. That tradition feeds upon mourning, in a way that recalls Macpherson's Ossianic poems. When Wallace dons the minstrel's garb, he sings of 'King Arthur's Death in Glory' (lvii, 506). To Bruce, he plays 'The Death of Cathullin' (lvii, 512). Near the end of the novel, a sublime Bard foresees Wallace's own death (lxxiv, 666). Wallace is a sombre character who never knows 'buoyant mirth' (lxvi, 598). In this version of history, the restored nation must have melancholy foundations (the Scottish regalia finally emerges from an iron box placed on Wallace's coffin, lxxxix, 774).

The Byronic Hero and His Poet

The Byronic hero who first emerged to public view in *Childe Harold's Pilgrimage* represented, among other things, perplexity in the face of the challenge of war. The young Byron contemplated a career as a Whig politician, and his hero's despondency puts into dramatic, personal form a Whig response to the ongoing Peninsular War. The Tory government's military intervention in Spain created a dilemma for Whig politicians. While the Whigs opposed the French invasion of Spain, and initially welcomed the Spanish rising, they were divided over the prospects of Spanish success and generally had little enthusiasm for a struggle to restore what they saw as a despotic monarchy. The dilemma can be seen in the *Edinburgh Review*'s response to the uprising in an article of July 1808. In discussing a letter from the Whig Samuel Whitbread, which gave a pro-war view of 'the present situation in Spain', the reviewers offer tortuous reasons for taking 'the desponding view of things', explaining their 'unhappy' and 'melancholy' apprehension that the Spanish patriots would be defeated, and urging the British government to seek 'pacific measures'. While in principle the writers support 'active resistance to all sorts of oppression', which they 'openly avow and glory in', they will not feed upon false hopes – 'nor is even an excess of incredulity altogether inexcusable in those who have drunk deeply of disappointment'.[42] They see their position, then, as at once eagerly idealistic and profoundly disillusioned. The *Edinburgh Review* elaborated upon this view later in the year, when it speculated upon the consequences of a longer-term victory of the 'revolution' in Spain – the liberalising of the Spanish constitution and the spread of 'revolutionary movements' across Europe. But this provocative vision was introduced and licensed by the same 'melancholy forebodings' of imminent Spanish defeat.[43] This acute Whig dilemma provides a context for approaching Byron's *Childe Harold's Pilgrimage*. As Richard Cronin

236   Part III: War and Peace in an Age of Revolutions

argues, the poem recognises that Whig principles could not be applied to contemporary Europe.[44]

The first two cantos (published in 1812) were conceived as, among other things, a riposte to Scott's Tory conception of the chivalric minstrel patriot.[45] Byron, like Scott, shows the poet turning away from classical tradition to romance: he 'dares not' invoke the classical Muse but adopts the stanza form Edmund Spenser used in his chivalric epic *The Fairy Queen*, and frames the poem loosely as a minstrel's lay.[46] He sings of a 'shameless wight' who has no patriotic feelings for his 'native land' and who plays his harp simply for the secret relief of his own private feelings (I: 2, 14, p. 23; I: 13, 110–114, p. 26). This hero's disillusionment is therefore personalised, rooted in individual excess. But the poet's own pilgrimage is nevertheless a search for a heritage of song and landscape that will sustain a heroic form of national memory and a war of liberation – a heritage that would be, as Malcolm Kelsall puts it, 'freed (for Byron) from the class and party complexities of Britain'.[47] When Childe Harold is in Portugal and Spain, which were currently close allies of Britain, disillusionment eclipses most forms of hope: for the poet, the landscape provides only 'memorials frail of murderous wrath' (I: 21, 264, p. 31), while the songs that celebrate recent military actions are transient 'worthless lays' (I: 43, 467, p.37). Where Scott, in his poetic romance *Marmion* (1808), distributed praise for heroic loyalty widely through a plethora of family names, Byron identifies a modern reality in which thousands of 'hirelings' 'fall to deck some single name' (I: 44, 471–73, p. 37). In the realm of gender, however, values are reversed: where Scott's romance works to promote a conventional ideal of feminine virtue, the Byronic poet sings the praises of young Spanish women who take up arms and fight. The poem is not only concerned with 'anti-war sentiment', as is sometimes claimed.[48] In the second Canto, as Harold gets beyond Western Europe, the mood begins to change. The Albanian soldiers he meets – shepherds who leave their flocks in order to fight – have a sturdy, warlike independence, not unlike the feudal borderers in Scott's *Lay*. Their war song, which erupts into the poem in a different meter, is performed with a 'barbarous, yet not indecent, glee' (II: 72, 644, p.73). The song is vengeful, rapacious and merciless, with no chivalric concern for humanity and honour, and no equivocation about the cruelty unleashed in war:

> Remember the moment when Previsa fell,
> The shrieks of the conquer'd, the conquerors' yell;
> The roofs that we fir'd, and the plunder we shar'd,
> The wealthy we slaughter'd, the lovely we spar'd. (II: 8, 677–680, p. 74)

Saving Communal Virtue

At Previsa Ali Pasha's Ottoman-Albanian troops defeated French republican forces on 23 October 1798. The poet sees in this warlike spirit a contrast with the modern-day Greeks, languishing under Ottoman rule:

Fair Greece! sad relic of departed worth!
Immortal, though no more; though fallen, great!
Who now shall lead thy scattered children forth,
And long accustomed bondage uncreate?
Not such thy sons who whilome did await,
The hopeless warriors of a willing doom,
In bleak Thermopylae's sepulchral strait—
Oh, who that gallant spirit shall resume,
Leap from Eurotas' banks, and call thee from the tomb? (II, 73, 693–701, p. 75).

Bernard Beattie notes the striking contrast in tones between the fiery war song and this lamenting stanza that follows it, but sees no 'opposition of values' between them: the poet implies that 'if the modern Greeks wish to emulate their forbears, they must have a chief, a gallant spirit, and dare to strike the blow like the Albanians'.[49] But while the Albanians certainly form a stirring example to the supine modern Greeks, there is a crucial opposition of values here. The Spartan example of patriotic self-sacrifice in 'bleak Thermopylae' is quite unlike the 'gleeful', barbarous, self-serving ethic of the war song. Byron, that is, assigns true heroism to the lost classical past of which the contemporary world, whether civilised or barbarous, seems unworthy. In its context, the Albanian war song presents an ambivalence typical of a radical Romantic Orientalism which, as Gerard Cohen-Vrignaud explains, offered readers the 'thrill' of 'violations', but at the same time 'reinforced liberal faith in procedural safeguards' and served 'liberalism's project to more fully humanize humanity'.[50]

In Greece, the view of landscape changes, as the poet comes to see it as 'consecrated land' (II: 93, 873, p. 81) congenial to his own melancholy

When wandering slow by Delphi's sacred side
Or gazing o'er plains where Greek and Persian died. (II: 92, 871–872, p. 81)

Here we can see the seeds of an interest in the cause of Greek independence to which Byron would eventually commit himself. In the meantime, Greece provided a standard of heroism by which the ideals of the modern world could be judged and found wanting. While he has earlier claimed to take no interest in 'scenes of vanish'd war' (II: 40, 355, p. 64), here his response is quite different. The poet does not finally reject war. Sometimes, as Philip Shaw notes, he treats it as 'a passion, perhaps even an antidote to

238   Part III: War and Peace in an Age of Revolutions

depression that Byron and his audience cannot easily forgo'.[51] But Byron also suggests that, given the right conditions and the right cause, war can and should inspire a truly 'gallant spirit'; he may claim that such conditions and causes are temporarily defeated in the modern world, but he wants his readers to recognise and feel that spirit.

In Canto III of the poem, published in 1816 after the Napoleonic wars had ended, Byron reflects critically upon the victory at Waterloo and assures his reader that true patriotic heroism has a 'civic' dimension not found in the corrupt monarchical powers that have now been restored across Europe:

> While Waterloo with Cannae's carnage vies,
> Morat and Marathon twin names shall stand;
> They were true Glory's stainless victories,
> Won by the unambitious heart and hand
> Of a proud, brotherly, and civic band,
> All unbought champions in no princely cause
> Of vice-entailed Corruption; they no land
> Doom'd to bewail the blasphemy of laws
> Making king's rights divine, by some Draconic clause. (III: 64, 608- 616, p. 123)

As Shaw points out, Byron twice condemns Napoleon as a 'despot' in this Canto.[52] Nevertheless, the monarchical victory of Waterloo is, for the Whig hoping for European liberalisation, a kind of defeat, and a violation of the civic ideal of the ancient Greeks. Readers are encouraged to feel the worth of this 'stainless', inspirational example, and are counselled against 'despair'. Rousseau, Voltaire, and Gibbon are evoked as figures whose intellectual challenge has helped to loosen the power of oppressive authority (III: 77–82, pp. 127–128). The poet insists that the repressive post-Waterloo settlement 'will not endure, nor be endured!' because 'Mankind have felt their strength, and made it felt' (III: 83, 779–780, p. 129). But he does not envisage positive action; instead, he depicts a hopeful passivity, which is, after all, a form of endurance:

>   in his lair
> Fix'd Passion holds his breath, until the hour
> Which shall atone for years; none need despair:
> It came, it cometh, and will come,--the power
> To punish or forgive—in *one* we shall be slower. (III: 84, 792–796, p. 129)

While the poem's hero is consumed with a singular melancholy, the poet aligns himself with a like-minded community, a 'we' of whom 'none need despair', a community whose moral integrity is defined by its 'Fix'd

Passion' rather than by its place within the restored political order of contemporary Europe.

Byron would eventually come to favour, as Kelsall says, 'direct-action anti-colonial politics in Italy and then in Greece' which were attractive to him precisely because they freed him from the complexities of British politics.[53] The complexities included the growing militancy of British working people, towards which Byron had shown mixed sympathies during his brief parliamentary career.[54] The direct action would include involvement in the Greek War of Independence. But in the meantime, resistance to oppression remained a matter of words rather than of action. In the final canto of *Childe Harold*, published in 1818, the famous lines addressed to 'Freedom' voice a qualified hope that in future 'a better spring' will bring forth 'less bitter fruit' (IV: 98, 882, p. 176). But this is another image of deferral. The sense of loss which for Scott's minstrel provides the ground for a unifying national spirit, for Byron provides the ground for the communal hopes of like-minded critics of the status quo. The alienated pose which allows Scott to push his call to arms into the past allows Byron to push his into the future. He is linked to concurring liberals not by a programme of specific political action but by a feeling that insulates them from such action, and puts them morally on the right side of a Whig version of history.

In the exceptional years of crisis produced by the Revolutionary and Napoleonic wars, the needs of the modern patriot, whether rebellious or conservative, were often served more appropriately by a melancholy call-to-arms than by a genuinely rousing one. Scott sees this need clearly in his first historical novel *Waverley* (1814), where he associates it with an earlier crisis: the Jacobite enthusiast Flora Macdonald translates a Scottish bard's fiery Gaelic war-song (which leads clansmen to reach for their swords) into a melancholy ballad that leaves the young Hanoverian soldier Waverley in a state of emotional paralysis. The rebellious figure of Fergus MacIvor is finally transformed into an acceptable symbol of patriotic resistance when, after he has been executed by the victorious Hanoverians, he appears in a heroic portrait with the turncoat Waverley, as part the capacious realm of British national heritage. This war-like portrait enhances the pleasure of a sociable moment before dinner, when it 'drew tears'; the subjects are going down to defeat. It's over.[55]

In an age of revolution, rapid industrialisation and growing social divisions, of organised opposition to war, of increasing criticism of the role of the Church in sanctifying war, the idea of war as a unified and unifying endeavour was often evoked in ways that distanced it from the troubling

240   Part III: War and Peace in an Age of Revolutions

realities of modern life and quietened the ardent passions it aroused. The melancholy call-to-arms was directed primarily at non-combatants rather than professional combatants governed by modern forms of training and discipline. Its prevalence in British writings during the French and Napoleonic wars may presage the emergence of the civilian, as a distinct and designated identity. The critique of 'civilized war' that developed in the eighteenth century was largely concerned with the professionalisation of warfare, which eventually created the civilian by default. This critique encouraged writers to turn with qualified admiration to the unrefined ardour of those whose way of life preceded, or still continued outside of, the constraints of civil society. But such ardour was feared as well as desired. Writers usually preferred to imagine it in distant forms because they did not want to find it irrupting on the streets of modern Britain. The obsolete and the exotic provided forms of insulation; contemplating their unrecoverable otherness gave rise to tranquilising melancholy and mourning designed to create a reassuring sense of communal justification. At the beginning of the eighteenth century, the promotion of gentler manners often worked in the service of the nation's commitment to military aggression. By the end of the century, the complementary relationship between the encouragement and restraint of warlike feeling had taken a new form, based upon a unifying sense of loss.

Notes

1 Julia Banister, *Masculinity, Militarism and Eighteenth-Century Culture, 1689–1815* (Cambridge: Cambridge University Press, 2018), 7–10.
2 Adam Ferguson, *Essay on the History of Civil Society* (Edinburgh, 1767), 232. Adam Smith, *The Wealth of Nations*, ed. Edwin Cannan (Chicago: University of Chicago Press, 1976), V, i, 219, 222–223.
3 Edmund Burke, *Reflections on the Revolution in France, Select Works of Edmund Burke, Vol 2* (Indianapolis: Liberty Fund, 1999), 89.
4 Thomas Paine, *Rights of Man: Part the Second* (London: J.S. Jordan, 1792), 167; *Rights of Man*, (London: J.S. Jordan, 1791), 33.
5 Jenny Graham, 'The Friends of Peace' *The Eighteenth Century* 26: 1 (1985), 104–111, 106.
6 Gilbert Wakefield *The Spirit of Christianity Compared with the Spirit of the Times*, (London, 1794) rev. edn., 11, 13, 26.
7 John Bowles, *Reflections Submitted to the Consideration of the Combined Powers* (London, 1794), 9.
8 Colley, *Britons*, 289.
9 Cookson, *Friends of Peace*, 42.

Saving Communal Virtue 241

10 Robert Southey, 'The Soldier's Funeral,' *The Annual Anthology* 1 (Bristol, 1799), 269–271.

11 E. J. Clery, *Eighteen Hundred and Eleven: Poetry, Protest and Economic Crisis* (Cambridge: Cambridge University Press, 2017), 157–159.

12 The poem was not published until 2 November 1793, by which time Britain was at war with France (it appeared in the *Cambridge Intelligencer* under the title: 'To A Great Nation', 'Written by a Lady'). William McCarthy and Elizabeth Kraft, eds., *Anna Letitia Barbauld: Selected Poetry and Prose* (Peterborough, Canada: Broadview, 2001), 133–134.

13 *The Cabinet*, II (Norwich, 1795), 92–95.

14 Joseph Hughes, *Britain's Defence* (London, 1803), 15.

15 Thomas Cloutt, *Christian Sympathy Weeping over the Calamities of War* (London, 1806), 15–16, 31.

16 Fiona Stafford, *The Last of the Race: The Growth of a Myth from Milton to Darwin* (Oxford: Oxford University Press, 1994), 55.

17 Katie Trumpener, *Bardic Nationalism: The Romantic Novel and the British Empire* (New Jersey: Princeton University Press, 1997), 6.

18 See John Barrell on the contemporary significance of imagining the king's death: *Imagining the King's Death: Figurative Treason, Fantasies of Regicide* (Oxford: Oxford University Press, 2000).

19 Thomas Carte, *A General History of England* (1744–55), 4 vols, 2 (1750), 196; See Sarah Prescott, '"Gray's Pale Spectre": Evan Evans, Thomas Gray, and the Rise of Welsh Bardic Nationalism', *Modern Philology* 104:1 (2006), 72–95, 74–5.

20 James Boaden, *Cambro-Britons* (London, 1798), iii, 76–77, 8.

21 Selena Couture and Alexander Dick, eds., *Pizarro: A Tragedy in Five Acts, Richard Brinsley Sheridan* (Peterborough, Ontario: Broadview, 2017), 40–49.

22 It had been invoked by Addison in the *Spectator*, when recommending the violent ballad of Chevy Chase:*The Spectator* 70 (21 May 1711) 1, 297–303. Rosemary Sweet, *Antiquaries:The Discovery of the Past in the Eighteenth Century* (London: Hambledon, 2004), 73–77.

23 David Hume, *Essays Moral, Political and Literary* ed. Eugene F. Miller (Indianapolis: Liberty, 1987): 'Of the Standard of Taste' 226–249, 239; 'Of the Delicacy of Taste and Passion', 3–8, 7.

24 Thomas Percy, *Reliques of Ancient English Poetry* (London, 1765), 3 vols., 3, iii.

25 Clara Reeve, *The Progress of Romance* (Colchester, 1785), 2 vols., I, 67–68.

26 James White, *The Adventures of John of Gault* (London, 1790), 3 vols., III, 82–4, 146–47.

27 Clara Reeve, *Memoirs of Sir Roger de Clarendon* (London, 1793), 3 vols, I, 3.

28 Henry James Pye, *Naucratica: Naval Dominion* (London, 1798), III, 383–84, 69.

29 Frank Munger, 'Suppression of Popular Gatherings in England, 1800–1830', *The American Journal of Legal History*, 25:2 (1981), 111–140; E. P. Thompson, 'The Moral Economy of the English Crowd in the Eighteenth Century', *Past & Present* 50 (1971), 76–136; Cookson, *Friends of Peace*, 203, 215.

242 Part III: War and Peace in an Age of Revolutions

30 William Hazlitt, 'Why the Heroes of Romance Are Insipid,' in P. P. Howe (ed.), *The Complete Works of William Hazlitt*, 21 vols (London: Dent, 1930–3), vol. xvii, 246–254, 252.

31 Ina Ferris, 'Melancholy, Memory, and the "Narrative Situation" of History in Post-Enlightenment Scotland', in Leith Davis, Ian Duncan and Janet Sorenson (eds.), *Scotland and the Borders of Romanticism* (Cambridge: Cambridge University Press, 2004), 77–93, 84.

32 Walter Scott, *The Lay of the Last Minstrel* (Edinburgh, 1805), 86.

33 Georg Lukács, *The Historical Novel*, translated from the German by Hannah and Stanley Mitchell, (London: Merlin Press, 1962), 23.

34 *Edinburgh Review* vol 12 (1808), 443; Godfrey Davies, 'The Whigs and the Peninsular War, 1808–1814,' *Transactions of the Royal Historical Society*, 2 (1919), 113–131. See Ian Haywood, 'The Spanish Revolution in Print and Image', in *Spain in British Romanticism 1800–1840*, ed. Diego Saglia and Ian Heywood, (London: Palgrave, 2017) 215–240.

35 *Quarterly Review*, (1809) vol 1, 7, 15, 19.

36 Her brother Robert, a history and panorama painter, was with the British army in Spain during the retreat to Corunna.

37 As Fiona Price points out, Porter's 'Constructs patriotism as defensive rather than expansionist'. 'Resisting "The Spirit of Innovation": The Other Historical Novel and Jane Porter', *Modern Language Review* 101 (2006), 638–651, 644.

38 Graeme Morton, 'Bruce, Wallace, and the Diminished Present 1800–1964', in *Scotland and the First World War: Myth, Memory, and the Legacy of Bannockburn*, ed. Gill Plain (Lanham: Bucknell University Press, 2017), 27–45.

39 Jane Porter, *The Scottish Chiefs* (Windsor, Colorado: Elerslie, 2017), ch. LXXXVI, 748.

40 Devoney Looser argues that Porter's conception of military heroism was influenced by her friendship with contemporary war hero Sir Sidney Smith, 'The Great Man and Women's Historical Fiction: Jane Porter and Sir Sidney Smith', *Women's Writing*, 19:3 293–314.

41 Graeme Morton, 'The Social Memory of Jane Porter and Her Scottish Chiefs', *The Scottish Historical Review* XCI: 2 (2012), 311–335.

42 *Edinburgh Review*, 12 (1808), 444. See Godfrey Davies, 'The Whigs and the Peninsular War, 1808–1814', *Transactions of the Royal Historical Society, 1919*, 2 (1919), 113–131; Richard Cronin, *The Politics of Romantic Poetry: in Search of the Pure Commonwealth* (Basingstoke: Macmillan, 2000), 128–144.

43 *Edinburgh Review*, 13, (1808–09), 219–205.

44 Richard Cronin, *The Politics of Romantic Poetry*, 140, 143.

45 Ronald A. Schroeder, 'Ellis, Sainte-Palaye, and Byron's "Addition" to the "Preface" of Childe Harold's Pilgrimage I–II', *Keats-Shelley Journal* 32 (1983), 25–30.

46 Lord Byron, *Childe Harold's Pilgrimage: A Romaunt* (London, 1812), I, I, 3.

47 Malcolm Kelsall, 'Byron's Politics', *The Cambridge Companion to Byron*, ed. Drummond Bone (Cambridge: Cambridge University Press, 2004), 44–55, 51–52.

48 See Bainbridge, *British Poetry and the Revolutionary and Napoleonic Wars,* 171.
49 Bernard Beattie 'Childe Harold's Pilgrimage Cantos I and II in 1812', *The Byron Journal* 41 (2), 2013, 101–114, 105.
50 Gerard Cohen-Vrignaud *Radical Orientalism: Rights, Reform, and Romanticism* (Cambridge: Cambridge University Press, 2015), 61.
51 'Byron's *Childe Harold* and War: Sketches of Spain', *Palgrave Advances in Byron Studies*, edited by Jane Stabler (Basingstoke: Palgrave, 2007), 213–233, 229.
52 Philp Shaw, *Waterloo and the Romantic Imagination* (Basingstoke: Palgrave, 2002), 184.
53 Kelsall, 'Byron's Politics', 52. See also Kelsall, *Byron's Politics* (Brighton: Harvester, 1987), 64–65.
54 See Kelsall *Byron's Politics*, 38–52.
55 Walter Scott, *Waverley*, ed. Andrew Hook (Harmondsworth: Penguin, 1985), 498.

CHAPTER 10

Thomas Clarkson and the Ideal of Non-resistance

In this chapter, I will consider some aspects of the process that led, in the wake of the Napoleonic wars, to the founding of peace societies dedicated to promoting what would now be termed 'pacifism', a doctrine of absolute non-resistance.

During the 1780s, there was much to feed public criticism of war: the divisive American conflict; unease about British military operations in Mysore; the trial of Warren Hastings (1788–1795), which publicised a horrifying range of abuses inflicted upon Indians; the campaign to abolish the slave trade (officially founded in May 1787) which brought to light the terrible practices that had flourished under British military protection. If such developments gave grounds for pessimism about the violence promoted by the modern British state, doubt was often counterbalanced by the idea of progress. Some who condemned Britain's aggression nevertheless saw themselves as living in an age of improvement, discovery, and enlightenment, which created extraordinary opportunities for global peace – opportunities conceived in political or religious terms, or in both. The possibility of achieving unprecedented global change inspired millenarian hopes across a spectrum of Christian believers. The idea that the kingdom of Christ, a kingdom of universal peace, was dawning, preoccupied a number of writers in the 1780s.[1]

In the political debate that erupted in Britain in 1789 in response to the French revolution, optimism about the prospects for peace assumed a dramatic political form. In the second part of *The Rights of Man* (1792), for example, Thomas Paine claimed that an ongoing, radical demystification of corrupt government would allow people across the world to escape from the errors of the past into a new age of peace.[2] Christians of various denominations and convictions, including some who opposed the war with France that began in 1793, and some who loyally supported it, shared millenarian hopes of a peaceful transformation of the world. For many, perhaps most, there was no essential contradiction between the hopes for

244

Thomas Clarkson and the Ideal of Non-resistance

peace and the acceptance of war. The process of global expansion that fed the anticipations of millennial peace was manifestly enabled by military power. The relationship between the brutal realities of warfare and the hopes for peace was often understood within the framework of providence. One could condemn the human destructiveness unleashed by war while accepting the opportunities for peaceful change that arose from it as part of a divine plan.[3]

During the Revolutionary and Napoleonic wars, therefore – when Christian nations across modern Europe were embroiled in the devastating conflict, when Britain was troubled with the threat of internal disorder and rebellion in Ireland, when the proportion of men of military age in Britain and Ireland serving in army, navy, volunteer and militia forces rose to about 1 in 6 – religious groups in Britain laid plans to spread the gospel of peace to nations beyond Europe, while philanthropists aspired to spread the arts of 'civilization' abroad.[4] All were apparently convinced that these efforts would contribute to their aim of global peace. In the terminology of present-day Democratic Peace Theory, they were proposing 'norm externalization', on the assumption that shared pacific values would reduce incentives to war.[5] But whereas there is some (disputed) evidence that war is less likely to occur between modern democracies than between authoritarian states, the evidence of relations between eighteenth-century Christian nations gave little grounds for optimism. Nevertheless, the very condition of war-torn Europe may have made it easier to imagine the diffusion of peace in distant lands, and within asymmetrical relations between the 'civilized' and those supposedly in dire need of improvement.

It was in the context of this optimism for change that absolute non-resistance began to assume more prominence in discussions of war. Martin Ceadel has defined the 'phases' by which a British peace movement arose during the revolutionary and Napoleonic wars and notes the appearance of several non-Quaker tracts urging a non-resistant view of war during the 1790s.[6] In the campaigns of the self-styled 'Friends of Peace', opposition to war was initially linked to demands for political reform, but during the war with Napoleonic France, the link between peace and reform loosened. J. E. Cookson notes that anti-war petitions were linked to trade depressions, and that after the petitions of 1797, the protest was concentrated in the rapidly developing manufacturing districts of the Midlands and the North. But after 1808, Lancashire cotton towns did not renew their demands for peace because they adopted the view of the political campaigner Major Cartwright, 'that any social good awaited the purification of the state by a radical reform'. In a complementary movement, 'the

246   Part III: War and Peace in an Age of Revolutions

Christian sources of the protest tended to become more explicit, culminating in the petitions of 1812–13 raised in the name of "The Friends of Peace and Christianity"'.[7]

The peace movement that eventually gave rise to the Society for the Promotion of Permanent and Universal Peace in 1816 was led not by those groups who had favoured constitutional reform, but by Evangelical Christians who put their faith in gradual moral and spiritual reform guiding material progress.[8] Among the leading lights were Thomas Clarkson and the Quaker William Allen, who had played prominent roles in the successful campaign against the slave trade. The society they founded, after the war with Napoleon had ended, was committed to absolute non-resistance. Cookson finds that the object of this Society 'had little to do with the predicaments of the present'.[9] But the case of Thomas Clarkson, a founder member of this society, will show that for some activists in the period the goal of non-resistance was intimately bound up with such predicaments.

Clarkson and Empire

Clarkson, an Anglican by upbringing and ordained as a deacon, had developed close relations with Quakers through his interest in abolishing the slave trade. The British public's acquiescence in slavery helped to convince him of the difference between 'true' Christian principles and the beliefs currently held by most Christians. In *An Essay of the Slavery and Commerce of the Human Species Particularly the African* (1786), he denounced the perverse cultural habituation to cruelty and violence which made murder honourable in the so-called Christian nations.[10] The origins of his later commitment to a non-resisting version of Christianity lay in such protests. We should note that this view was not shared by all who wrote against slavery. The ex-slave Olaudah Equiano, in his *Interesting Narrative of the Life of Olaudah Equiano, Or Gustavus Vassa, The African* (1789) described his own war service during the Seven Years' War, which helped to establish his credentials.

From the beginning, Clarkson's thinking about peace and war was concerned less with relations between modern states than with relations between 'civilized' and 'barbarous nations'. The sense of superiority felt by the civilised towards other peoples, he argued, gave rise to 'inhuman' attitudes: he cited, for example, Aristotle's advice to Alexander on his Asiatic expedition, to treat non-Greeks or 'Barbarians' 'as it became a master', that is, 'as brutes and plants'.[11] However, for Clarkson, the sense of superiority was

Thomas Clarkson and the Ideal of Non-resistance 247

not itself at issue: he shared common assumptions about the pre-eminence of European culture. But this superiority, he thought, should motivate an attempt to improve the lot of others. Peace would come initially from a fundamental change in the attitude of the civilised – who should relinquish their prejudicial contempt, suspicion, and hostility towards the barbarous, and practice instead the brotherhood preached in the Gospel.

The terrible legacy of slavery led him to call for new, entirely peaceful relations with Africa, based upon mutual respect, trade, and investment rather than on violent exploitation. He pursued this interest in part through his personal involvement with Sierra Leone, a new colony founded in 1787 by the abolitionist Granville Sharp to resettle liberated slaves. Clarkson and some of his abolitionist associates took up this project after its early collapse, seeking to re-establish the colony and to develop its economy by founding the Sierra Leone Company, and bringing loyalist ex-slaves from Nova Scotia to settle the land. The early history of the venture was far from peaceful, since the arrival of settlers provoked indigenous peoples to violence, and there was internal unrest. But Clarkson was not deterred by the setbacks, which he regarded as in part the legacy of slavery.[12]

Clarkson's thinking about peace was clearly influenced by his hopes for Sierra Leone and for Africa more generally. When, having renounced his Anglicanism, he began to advocate non-resistance while Britain was still at war, the example of William Penn, the Quaker founder of Pennsylvania, assumed an important place in his writing. Penn was already famed as a peaceful coloniser. Voltaire had described Penn's celebrated treaty with Native Americans as 'the only treaty between those people and the Christians that was not ratified by an oath, and was never infring'd'.[13] Benjamin West's painting, *Penn's Treaty with the Indians* (1771–72), commissioned by Penn's son Thomas, and reproduced in print form by John Boydell (1775), had helped to promote the image of Penn as a benevolent man of peace. This example proved vitally important to Clarkson (Figure 4).

His first account of Penn appeared in his *Portraiture of Quakerism* (1806). This was, as Gibson Wilson notes, 'the first book to explain the principles and peculiarities of the sect to the world at large'.[14] In giving a comprehensive account of the history and beliefs of a marginalised group, the *Portraiture* brought before the public a full and carefully considered discussion of the principle of non-resistance. In Clarkson's account, Quaker principles suggest the ultimate displacement of civic humanist virtue by the 'peaceful' morality associated with commerce: an austere, self-denying ethic, opposed to luxury, is found among those largely excluded from public office, who engage diligently and profitably in trade but refuse to

Figure 4   John Hall, engraved after Benjamin West, *The Treaty of Penn with the Indians 1771–1772* (1775). Penn offers a roll of white cloth to a native American chief and his tribe as part of his 'treaty' with them.
[© Granger Historical Picture Archive / Alamy]

fight in any circumstances. Using a detailed history of early Christianity as evidence, Clarkson argued that this Quaker principle was true to Christ's own pacific statements. And he firmly endorsed, and recommended, this principle himself.

Clarkson never joined the Society of Quakers or submitted to its discipline, but the Quakers were particularly useful to his attempt to challenge customary opinion in a period of crisis. They were well known for their rejection of war, but they had an established record of loyalty (a loyalty demonstrated in the American Quakers' refusal to condone armed resistance against the government of George III during the War of Independence, or to participate in revolutionary affairs). The historical approach of the *Portraiture* allowed Clarkson to challenge accepted thinking about hostilities without attacking government policy directly or resorting to the kind of bitter indignation he had used so effectively in his writing about slavery. His initial enthusiasm for the French revolution had led his associates William Wilberforce and Archdeacon Joseph

Thomas Clarkson and the Ideal of Non-resistance 249

Plymley to advise him to 'keep clear' of divisive party politics in the abolition campaign; Plymley insisted 'Our object is quite abstracted from all political parties'.[15] Clarkson followed this advice carefully when discussing war. Whereas the Dissenter Anna Barbauld regarded paying taxes for an unjust war as a shameful necessity, to be accompanied by 'remonstration', Clarkson's Quakers in the *Portraiture* apparently feel no guilt about paying such taxes: they follow the recommendation of Jesus, to 'render unto Caesar the things which are Caesar's', leaving the application of the taxes to Caesar himself.[16] They simply accept, that is, the gap between their own peaceful principles and the warlike 'policy of the world' (III, 87). But the very quietism of the Quakers, so useful to Clarkson in some respects, threatened to limit their usefulness in others. Their refusal to participate in warfare or to obey the legal requirement to serve in the militia had no significant influence on the nation's war-making. They might 'bear patiently all the penalties annexed to such a refusal' (III, 3), but in doing so they protected only their own moral purity.

Clarkson needed to show how the Quakers' peace doctrine could have a transformative effect in the world outside of their own secluded groups, and here the example of William Penn seemed to provide vital empirical evidence. In the *Portraiture,* Clarkson includes an account of interactions between European settlers and Native Americans. He represents the latter as a baseline case: as more 'barbarous' (III 99) than Africans or Asians, and characteristically war-prone. Penn's Quakers, unlike other colonial settlers (including those in Sierra Leone) used no weapons or fortifications, spoke 'the language of peace to the native' (III, 103) and were prepared to bear whatever injuries were offered to them. As a result, Clarkson claims, 'the harmonious intercourse between the Quakers and the Indians continues uninterrupted to the present day' (III 104). The example appeared to support his assertions about the peaceful, civilising effects of non-resistance: under the Quaker influence, he notes, some native Americans have 'laid aside the toilsome occupations of the chase' and adopted agriculture. 'They have houses, barns, and saw-mills among them. They have schools also, and civilisation is taking place of the grossest barbarism' (III 105).

Soon after the bill to abolish the slave trade had been passed by parliament in early 1807, Clarkson helped to set up the Africa Institution, which was dedicated to introducing by peaceful means 'the blessings of civilized society among people sunk in ignorance and barbarism'.[17] Its primary focus was to be on Sierra Leone, which at that time was becoming a Crown colony. The Institution's first report (1807, published 1811) cited the activities of contemporary Quakers in civilising Native

250 Part III: War and Peace in an Age of Revolutions

Americans as a model for their own plans (27). In his highly successful *History* of the Abolition campaign (1808), Clarkson claimed that Sierra Leone would be a gateway to the peaceful civilising of Africa as a whole.[18] This imagined project stood in marked contrast to the actualities of the developing British empire. As P. J. Marshall points out, the empire now included large numbers of people 'who were not British in origin, who had been incorporated into empire by conquest and who were ruled without representation'. It was sustained not just by the Royal Navy but 'by the deployment of British troops across the world in a way that was to last until the 1960s'.[19] The mounting activities of missionary groups were directed in part at complementing these military forces by spreading the gospel of peace and encouraging cultural assimilation.[20] In 1813, the government finally gave formal permission for missionaries to operate in India. The move, championed by William Wilberforce, had been resisted by the East India Company, who feared that missionaries might provoke violence (the mutiny of Sepoys at Vellore in 1806 had been sparked by fears of an attempt at enforced conversion to Christianity).[21] In this context, the example of William Penn's non-violent transformation of Pennsylvania offered a model that could be used to address the problems of resistance that were endemic throughout the empire. In the same year that missionaries gained formal access to India, 1813, Clarkson published his two-volume *Memoirs* of Penn, in which the coloniser is said to prove 'the possibility, of a nation maintaining its own internal police amidst a mixture of persons of different nations and different civil and religious opinions, and of maintaining its foreign relations also, without the aid of a soldier or man in arms'.[22]

In this more detailed account of Penn as governor, Clarkson's hero is a benign paternalist who regards good citizenship rather than faith as the basis of liberty. For Penn, the civilising process is a step towards religious conversion, in contrast to missionary groups for whom conversion is the priority. While the Anglican abolitionist Granville Sharp, the original founder of Sierra Leone, thought that 'Pagans, Papists, Mohametans, Infidels, etc' should not be admitted to the colony, Penn the Quaker believes in freedom of conscience and so practices toleration: 'Jews, Turks, Catholics, Presbyterians, and people of all persuasions in religion, were to be entirely free both as to their Faith and Worship'.[23] However, it later becomes clear that 'all persuasions' includes only those who believe in one God, and that only Christians can hold offices.[24] It is a model that might liberalise Christian attitudes while keeping administrative control of imperial possessions firmly in Christian hands. Penn is said to regard the Native

Americans Indians as brothers who need his fatherly care, a care which includes extending justice to them – by placing them under the system of laws and property rights he brings from England (he insists on buying land from the Native Americans rather than relying on his royal patent or legal right, I, 263). In a comparable way, he comes to regulate the morals and manners of the slaves at work in Pennsylvania, the 'vilest' of the 'class of aliens' living under his jurisdiction, who are fitted 'by degrees' for a state of freedom (II, 473).

As 'evidence' of peaceful practice, then, Clarkson's Penn illustrates colonial relations rather than relations between European states. Although Clarkson, like Penn, offers the principle of arbitration between nations as a vitally important goal for maintaining peace between states and allowing a renunciation of war, in practice, he finds little to support the principle in the realm of international politics. In the *Portraiture,* he can imagine arbitration working between Quaker leaders (II, 96–97), but not between modern nations in their present unreformed condition (he imagines instead a unilateral renunciation of war, and simply refuses to consider the dire consequences that could result, II, 113). As Clarkson shows, within Quakerism, the principle of non-resistance is embedded in, and sustained by, a highly disciplined lifestyle. He confirms that when disputes arise within the Quaker world, they are settled internally without recourse to violence or law. But arbitration works in these circumstances because the habitual restraint of the passions required by the Quaker regimen allows the disputants 'to conduct themselves with temper and decorum in exasperating cases' (II, 184). This implies that arbitration can only be expected to settle disputes between nations if those in power have already acquired the necessary habitual restraint.[25]

The emulation of Penn as a moral example required a long-term strategy to cultivate the appropriate disciplined lifestyle and character in those in power, as in those they governed. The organised action that Clarkson envisages in his *Portraiture*, therefore, is not a campaign against the ongoing war but an educational strategy aimed at producing 'future Penns' (II, 360). While he criticises the narrowness of Quaker education, he recommends its moral aims and suggests the setting-up of public seminaries 'for the children of the rich', or large private seminaries which might be placed 'under the visiting discipline' of the Quakers (II, 359). The future Penns formed under such supervision will, it seems, be able to spread peace from above as the paternal supervisors of a benign civilising process. Clarkson envisages a form of peace education in the interests of what is now termed 'peace leadership'.[26]

252   Part III: War and Peace in an Age of Revolutions

The benign paternalism that Clarkson saw in Penn is seen quite differently by modern historians. James O'Neil Spady, for example, points out
that one purpose of Penn's description of his own friendly relations with
the native Lenapes living within Pennsylvania was to encourage 'the confidence of potential colonists' (just as Clarkson issued glowing accounts
of the commercial prospects of Sierra Leone aimed at potential investors
in London). In fact, Spady argues, Penn was seeking to 'extinguish' the
'Indian encumbrance' on the land through English property law, while the
Lenapes had no conception or expectation of 'absolute' property rights.[27]
Susan A. E. Klepp also concludes that 'in reality the Lenapes were being
dispossessed' and claims that Penn was able to maintain peaceful relations
with Native American people in part 'because of the dislocations throughout the territory at the end of the beaver wars' and because of 'western military and diplomatic developments over which he had little control' and of
which he had little knowledge.[28] Clarkson, drawing heavily on Penn's own
account of his actions in Pennsylvania, finds no such evidence to challenge his admiring account (although he ruefully admits that no historical
account of Penn's famous treaty with the Indians survives).[29]

On both sides of the Atlantic, the influence of Clarkson and the example of Penn were highly important in the foundation of Peace Societies.
The American Quaker Noah Worcester cited Penn as an example to be
imitated in his *Solemn Review of the Custom of War* (Boston, Mass., 1814), a
work in which he called for the formation of American peace societies. He
printed a lengthy extract from Clarkson's *Portraiture of Quakerism* – the
section dealing with Penn – in his work *The Friend of Peace*.[30] In Britain,
Clarkson played a leading role in the foundation of The Society for the
Promotion of Permanent and Universal Peace, which was established in
1816. Although the Society was based on the principle of non-resistance, it
came to admit auxiliary societies for members who endorsed strictly defensive war. Its journal, *The Herald of Peace*, began to appear in 1819. This had
a broad educational agenda: it included articles urging the advantages of
arbitration over conflict, poems on peace, illustrations of the horrors of
war, and letters addressed to royalty or other dignitaries recommending
peace. The first issue included a dialogue between Lycurgus and William
Penn (March 1819, 6–9). The journal reprinted the same extract from
the *Portraiture* that Noah Worcester had used, as well as lengthy extracts
from Clarkson's *Memoirs* of Penn (and a version of his early history of
Christianity).[31] William Penn and Pennsylvania became frequent points
of reference in the journal – in verse, correspondence, and articles – as
proof of the possibility of non-resisting government. The influence of this

Thomas Clarkson and the Ideal of Non-resistance

example is hardly surprising, given the lack of alternative sources of evidence concerning non-resisting governance, and given that on both sides of the Atlantic the prospects of an expanding arena for the 'civilizing' process beckoned. In America, the creation of the new Republic had removed the Proclamation Line that supposedly limited colonial incursions into territories occupied by Native Americans, and ushered in a new era of Westward expansion in which Quakers became involved.[32] In Britain, the period of the revolutionary and Napoleonic wars had seen the greatest expansion of British imperial sway power since the seventeenth century, and the pacification of imperial territories was a major preoccupation.[33] *The Herald of Peace* included articles reflecting upon relations between civilised and uncivilised peoples, sometimes to illustrate the natural peacefulness of peoples untouched by European corruption, sometimes to deplore the corrupting effects of European violence upon previously non-violent communities, sometimes to condemn the war-like habits of 'imperfectly civilized tribes' in order to suggest that the arrival of Christianity will lead to peace.[34] The Peace Societies were of course concerned with relations between modern nation-states, and took some comfort from the Congress of Vienna, which brought European leaders together in the hope of establishing a lasting political settlement. Clarkson met privately with Tzar Alexander of Russia to discuss abolition and peace.[35] But they were also inevitably concerned with the new possibilities and challenges opening up in an age of empire.

Peace by Peaceful Means

The case of Clarkson and the Society he helped to found illustrates some of the problems entailed in seeking peace by peaceful means. The need to avoid government suppression and the risk of provoking violent agitation at home led him towards treating war as a long-term moral issue rather than an immediate political one. He sought to promote changes in feeling or moral disposition in the public at large or in future generations – changes that might eventually provide the conditions in which arbitration could replace armed conflict. The Society saw itself as a religious rather than a political organisation, whose function was to support rather than to criticise governments – although this did not render it immune from attack as a potentially subversive body.[36] The *Herald*, launched in the year of the Peterloo Massacre, was largely silent upon the issue of contemporary civil disorder, just as it refrained from condemning specific military operations. Instead, it endorsed a quiet refusal to comply with the demand to fight – as the Quakers had traditionally refused – insisting that this was a

254   Part III: War and Peace in an Age of Revolutions

truly Christian position that did not constitute rebellion.[37] Eric W. Sager argues that the organised peace movement that developed in nineteenth-century Britain was 'really directed at domestic issues'.[38] This claim should be modified, but we do need to recognise the close relationship between the desire for peace abroad and the desire for peace at home.

Where the Friends of Peace in the 1790s had painted a picture of a nation corrupted by the militarism of the state, the *Herald of Peace,* while interested in peace leadership, promoted a bottom-up view of influence, seeking to encourage 'the universal adoption of the principles of peace' in the nation at large rather than expecting the government to become 'absolutely' pacific first (I, 34, 130). Its faith in gradual enlightenment – at home and abroad – was the necessary foundation of the Society's moral position. While the *Herald* quoted Cowper's lines about wresting the truncheon from the hero, it advocated no such dramatic intervention. Enlightenment depended upon the setting up of other societies, the exchange of information, the dissemination of the Christian message of peace, and the spread of peace education – things that all members could help with quietly, if only through their pockets.

From its inception, the *Herald* attacked the national view of war and redefined love of country in entirely peaceful terms, as 'love to the lives, the privileges, the virtue, the peace, the prosperity, and the happiness of the community of which we are members' (I, 191). The privileges and prosperity enjoyed by comfortable Britons, of course, had some violent foundations, as the slavery campaign had amply demonstrated. But such evidence could be folded into a progressive view of history in which humanity would eventually free itself from its own violent practices. Contributors to the *Herald of Peace* often deplored the military nationalism they found in their fellow compatriots; but when they looked abroad, they saw distant opportunities to bring the advantages of their Christian civilisation to those who lived by other standards. The knowledge that these opportunities had often been opened up by violence strengthened their duty to bestow their message of peace. They inherited the global ambitions visible in the foundational establishments of Britain's military-fiscal state at Chelsea and Greenwich, while attempting to separate themselves from, and benefit from, the state's power. They did not see their acceptance of this inheritance, or their avoidance of direct criticism of government war policy, as forms of acquiescence in war, because they were actively engaged in the cause of peace, a cause they embraced absolutely, and in the name of Christian benevolence. Their progressive view of history rested upon a sense of divine will that made universal peace seem ultimately inevitable.

Thomas Clarkson and the Ideal of Non-resistance 255

Clarkson's desire to separate the civilising process from the manifest violence of empire can be compared with that 'great longing' that Marie Louise Pratt attributes to the natural historian who records the flora and fauna made accessible by the imperial penetration of distant lands in the later eighteenth century and through the nineteenth century: 'for a way of taking possession without subjugation and violence'. Pratt is referring to the strategies of representation adopted by naturalists, which she classes as examples of 'anti-conquest', in which 'European bourgeois subjects seek to secure their innocence in the same moment as they assert their hegemony'.[39] But Clarkson sought a much more direct and active influence than the naturalist. And in practice, the kind of influence he sought to promote could not be divorced from the political and economic control at the heart of empire. His assumption of cultural superiority delegitimised other cultures and underwrote a policy of implanting European patterns of property ownership, work practices and religious belief which tended to create long-term dependencies. From the perspective of a present-day peace researcher such as John Galtung, Clarkson's appeal to civilisation would look like a form of 'cultural violence', which 'makes direct and structural violence look, even feel, right – or at least not wrong'.[40] In seeking to replace the hard power of guns and chains with the soft power of law, commercial investment, and cultural influence, Clarkson makes territorial dispossession, and the destruction of indigenous traditions look like positive benefits. When he first became involved with Sierra Leone Clarkson personally invested in it, as did his associates, hoping to establish the basis of a thriving trade there but, as Wilson notes 'to attract investors the government of the colony was taken out of the settlers' hands' and placed in the hand of the Sierra Leone Company in London'.[41] When the Africa Institution became involved, it disavowed any intention to colonise Sierra Leone, seeing itself instead as 'assisting the endeavours of others' – but in practice it chose the first Crown Governor of the colony, and its members arranged for that Governor's dismissal when he criticised the colony's apprenticeship system as another form of slavery.[42] Clarkson might have wished for a regime based upon non-resistance, but in fact, the colony had to be fortified, defended, and assisted by the Royal Navy and, as we have already noted, it was embroiled in violence.

In her searching critique of peace studies, Vanessa Pupavac argues that 'peace education is now part of the arsenal of western foreign policy, in a form that complements rather than opposes military campaigns'.[43] Present-day advocates of peace education would vigorously refute this claim, as no doubt would those who formulate western foreign policy. But as this

256   Part III: War and Peace in an Age of Revolutions

study has shown, the desire for peace has often existed in a complementary relationship with the drive for war, and if members of the first British peace movement to embrace non-resistance recoiled from the aggression entailed in the expansion of empire, they were inspired by the consequent prospects for 'peaceful' intervention. The 'civilizing process' continues to exist in an uneasy relationship with the heritage of past conflicts, the ongoing expense of defence, and the urge to settle disputes by force. To regard ourselves as 'civilized' often appears to entail adopting a conflicted view of our own status as the beneficiaries of violence.

Notes

1 See, for example, Joseph Cornish, *The Miseries of War, and the Hope of Final and Universal Peace* (Taunton, 1784); Richard Price, *Observations on the Importance of the American Revolution and the Means of Making It a Benefit to the World* (London, 1784).

2 Thomas Paine, *The Rights of Man, Part the Second* (London, 1792), 2.

3 For example Joseph Priestley, *A Sermon Preached at the Gravel Pit Meeting in Hackney, April 19th 1793* (London, 1793); James Bicheno, *The Signs of the Times* (London, 1793).

4 Clive Emsley, *British Society and the French Wars, 1793–1815* (London : Macmillan, 1979), 33, 189.

5 Sebastian Rosato, 'The Flawed Logic of Democratic Peace Theory,' *Political Science Review* 97: 4 (2003), 585–602, 586; Anna Geis, Lothar Brock, and Harald Müller, *Democratic Wars: Looking at the Dark Side of Democratic Peace* (Basingstoke: Palgrave, 2006).

6 Martin Ceadel, *The Origins of War Prevention: The British Peace Movement and International Relations, 1730–1854* (Oxford: Oxford University Press, 1996), 171–221.

7 J. E. Cookson, *The Friends of Peace: Anti-War Liberalism in England, 1793–1815* (Cambridge: Cambridge University Press, 1982), 214, 5.

8 Eric W. Sager, 'Religious Sources of English Pacifism from the Enlightenment to the Industrial Revolution', *Canadian Journal of History*, 17: 1 (2017), 1–26; 'The Social Origins of Victorian pacifism', *Victorian Studies* 23: 2 (1979/80), 211–236.

9 *Friends of Peace*, 2.

10 Thomas Clarkson, *An Essay on the Slavery and Commerce of the Human Species*, (London: J. Phillips, 1786), 256.

11 *An Essay on the Slavery and Commerce of the Human Species*, 24–25.

12 Ellen Gibson Wilson, *Thomas Clarkson: A Biography* (York: William Sessions, 1996); Adam Hochschild, *Bury the Chains: The British Struggle to Abolish Slavery* (London: Pan, 2010), 177, 201–202, 248–249.

13 Sandra Gross and Jeffrey P. Roberts, *William Penn: Visionary and Proprietor* (Philadelphia: Arwater Kent Museum, 1983), 21; Voltaire, *Letters Concerning the English Nation* (London, 1733), 29.

14 Wilson, 103–104.

15 Wilson, 71.

16 [Anna Barbauld], *Sins of Government, Sins of the Nation* (London, 1793), 316–317; Thomas Clarkson, *A Portaiture of Quakerism*, 3 vols. (London, 1803), III, 26.

17 *Report of the Committee of the Africa Institution Read to the General Meeting on 15th July, 1807* (London, 1811), 11.

18 Thomas Clarkson, *The History of the Abolition of the Slave Trade*, 2 vols. (London, 1808), II, 344.

19 P. J. Marshall, 'Empire and Authority in the Later Eighteenth Century', *Journal of Imperial & Commonwealth History*, 25: 2 (1987), 105–122, 115.

20 Javed Majeed, *Ungoverned Imaginings: James Mill's 'The History of British India' and Orientalism* (Oxford: Oxford University Press, 1992), 16, 27.

21 Laurence Kitzan, 'The London Missionary Society and the Problem of Authority in India, 1798–1833', *Church History* 40 (1971), 457–473, 457, 459.

22 Thomas Clarkson, *Memoirs of the Private and Public Life of William Penn*, 2 vols. (London 1813), II, 479–480.

23 Hochschild, *Bury the Chains*, 150. Clarkson, *Life of Penn*, II, 420.

24 Clarkson, *Life of Penn*, II, 425.

25 Clarkson may have heard from his Quaker friends of the contemporary activities of the Quaker Indian Committee in its attempts to 'civilize' Native Americans without violence.

26 *Peace Leadership: The Quest for Connectedness*, ed. Stan Amalada and Sean Byrne (Abingdon: Routledge, 2017); E. J. Brantmeier, 'Toward a Critical Peace Education for Sustainability', *Journal of Peace Education*, 10: 3 (2013), 242–258; D. A. Gruenewald, 'The Best of Both Worlds: A Critical Pedagogy of Place', *Educational Researcher*, 32: 4 (2003), 3–12.

27 James O'Neil Spady, 'Colonialism and the Discursive Antecendets of Penn's Treaty with the Indians', in *Friends and Enemies in Penn's Woods: Indians, Colonists and the Racial Construction of Pennsylvania*, ed. William A. Pencak and Daniel K. Richter (Pennsylvania: Penn State University Press, 2004), 18–40, pp. 35–37.

28 Susan E. Klepp, 'Encounter and Experiment: The Colonial Period,' in *Pennsylvania: A History of the Commonwealth*, ed. Randall M. Miller and William Pencak (Pennsylvania: Penn State University Press, 2002), 47–100, pp. 64–5.

29 *Life of Penn*, I, 264.

30 *The Friend of Peace*, III, 35–39 (Boston, n.d.). The *Solemn Review* was the first publication to be issued by the Society for Abolishing War, founded in 1816.

31 The *Portraiture* was extracted in Vol. 2 (1820), 277, 297, 328, 355 and Vol. 3 (1821), 19–21, 37–40, 77–79. Extracts from the *Life of Penn* appeared in Vol. 4 (1822), 91–96.

32 Kari Elizabeth Rose Thompson, *Inconsistent Friends: Philadelphia Quakers and the Development of Native American Missions in the Long Eighteenth Century*, University of Iowa, PhD (2013).

258   Part III: War and Peace in an Age of Revolutions

33 C. A. Bayley, *Imperial Meridian: The British Empire and the World 1789–1830* (London: Routledge, 1989), 100.

34 See, for example, Vol. I (1819), 35, 65, 78–79, 91.

35 P. H. Peckover, *Thomas Clarkson's Interview with the Emperor Alexander I of Russia at Aix-la-Chapelle, as Told by Himself* (Wisbech: Poyser, 1930).

36 See Martin Ceadel, *The Origins of War Prevention* (Oxford: Oxford University Press, 1996), 211.

37 *The Herald of Peace*, I (1819), 130.

38 Eric W. Sager, 'The Social Origins of Victorian pacifism', *Victorian Studies*, 23: 2 (1979/80), 211–236, p. 232; 'Religious Sources of English Pacifism from the Enlightenment to the Industrial Revolution,' *Canadian Journal of History* 17:1 (1982), 1–26.

39 Marie Louise Pratt, *Imperial Eyes: Travel Writing and Transculturation* (London: Routledge, 2003), 57, 7.

40 John Galtung, 'Cultural Violence', *Journal of Peace Research* 27: 3 (1990), 291–305, p. 291.

41 Wilson, 64.

42 Michael J. Turner, 'The Limits of Abolition: Government, Saints and the "African Question" c1780–1820', *English Historical Review*, 112 (1997), 319–357.

43 Vanessa Pupavac, *Culture of Violence: Theories and Cultures of Peace Programmes: A Critique* (Sheffield: Sheffield Hallam University Press, 2001), 35.

PART IV

The Landscape of Conquest

The ideal of global peace, arising in an age of exploration and imperial conquest, inspired in Thomas Clarkson a plan to establish cultural and commercial influence over other territories and other peoples in the name of Christian civilisation, without using violence. This, of course, was not the model of operations that prevailed in the nineteenth century, a century during which the British empire dramatically expanded. Instead, military power maintained an essential role in imperial expansion, although empire building was usually represented by its agents as a civilising process. The association between empire building and civilisation was reinforced by a variety of means. Holger Hoock has emphasised the importance of official commemorations of martial heroes and victories in the development of empire, and notes that 'the gathering of knowledge became a key ambition for the nineteenth-century British imperial state'.[1] A wide range of activities such as surveying, mapping, collecting, conducting archaeological investigations and, of course, representing landscape and peoples in drawings and paintings, helped to support claims about the civilising effect of British influence. During the second half of the eighteenth century, such activities gained increasing support and authority from the founding of officially sponsored institutions such as the British Museum and the Royal Academy. But well before such institutions appeared, the process of reconciling the conquest of territory with the idea of civilisation was under way. Some key aspects of the development of this process can be traced conveniently in relation to a single place of modest size but growing significance – the rock of Gibraltar.

Note

[1] Holger Hoock, *Empires of Imagination: Politics, War, and the Arts in the British World, 1750–1850* (London: Profile Books, 2010), 315.

CHAPTER II

A Case Study
Gibraltar

The history of Gibraltar in the eighteenth century includes typical reversals. On the one hand, a conquered Spanish territory becomes a British territory that must be protected against Spanish aggression, illustrating the general tendency of the national view of war to assume defensive form. On the other hand, as the process of observation becomes more clearly organised, and authorised by institutional developments in Britain, a fashionable movement away from the material signs of modernity encourages an emphasis upon natural landscape rather than upon civilised improvements. This appeal to the sensitivity of the observer, rather than directly to ideas of national self-interest or achievement, is understood within the framework on an unspoken history, once the visual appearance of Gibraltar has acquired an iconic status and its history is well-known. Under these conditions, the national view of war could be articulated without an explicit appeal to sovereignty, religion, national destiny or, indeed, war.

Gibraltar was a special case in the history of Britain's developing empire, not least because during the eighteenth century this distant outcrop acquired an iconic status, its outline becoming instantly recognisable to the British public (so that it could function as a trademark in advertising material).[1] Its stark rocky landscape, which offered so little potential for colonisation, became an important part of its mythical value, in a process made possible by cultural developments in Britain – and by warfare. The scene of repeated contention with Spain, its landscape gradually became 'British', and became firmly associated with the defence of liberty rather than with conquest.

The transformation of British views of Gibraltar was part of a wider change in Britain's imperial self-image. Historians have traced the emergence of a 'cosmopolitan' vision of Britain's place within a 'global fraternity of nations' to the era of the Protectorate in the seventeenth century, and the attempt of writers loyal to Cromwell to celebrate a Protestant 'empire of the sea', based upon trade and natural productivity rather than

262   Part IV: The Landscape of Conquest

on territorial domination – an idea of empire that Royalist poets, including Edmund Waller and John Dryden, also adopted.[2] As we shall see, the British acquisition of Gibraltar did not sit easily with such a vision of empire. But in the course of the eighteenth century, as Britain emerged as undeniably an empire of conquest with huge and expanding territories in Canada and India, Gibraltar became the focus of well-publicised defensive struggles, which helped to counterbalance the reports of British aggression further afield, and to support the idea of British imperial expansion as a civilising project.

Acquisition

The capture of Gibraltar during the War of the Spanish Succession was announced in an edition of the *London Gazette* that also brought news of the Duke of Marlborough's dazzling victory over the French at Blenheim.[3] Marlborough's triumph, in August 1704, became the subject of euphoric public celebrations and a huge number of poetic tributes. Gibraltar attracted far less attention. The poorly defended Spanish stronghold was taken by a combined British and Dutch fleet in the name of Archduke Charles, the Austrian contender for the Spanish throne. It was not captured for the British. The advantages of Gibraltar as a naval base had been noted by Cromwell, and certainly featured in the strategic thinking of British ministers. But the government seems to have had no settled intention to acquire Gibraltar for Britain at this stage, and some British observers doubted the value of the capture.[4]

Soon, disquieting accounts of the military operation at Gibraltar appeared in the British press, describing how the invading forces had plundered the Church of Notre Dame, 'rifled' the women taking shelter there and then pillaged other churches in the town – in spite of reassurances given in the articles of capitulation.[5] Such outrages were not of course unusual in the wars of the time. Marlborough had ravaged Bavarian villages as part of his Blenheim campaign. But the violations at Gibraltar undermined any attempt to portray the conquest as a liberation from tyranny – after the outrages most of the surviving Spanish inhabitants had fled.[6]

This unhappy history no doubt helps to explain the relative neglect of Gibraltar by contemporary observers. The Whig writer John Dennis, who penned elaborate poems celebrating Marlborough's victories, did write a comedy about the capture of Gibraltar, in which the British violence upon the Spanish inhabitants was transmuted into scenes of rakish courtship of coy Senoritas. But when the play appeared in 1705 it had only two performances. At the time Dennis was writing, Gibraltar could not yet be seen as a British territory – between September 1704 and May 1705 it was besieged by Bourbon forces trying to recapture it, and after this siege was abandoned Gibraltar's future was still bound up with the outcome of the wider European conflict. British possession of Gibraltar was only confirmed in 1713 by the negotiations of the Treaty of Utrecht, at which the new Tory ministry abandoned Archduke Charles as would-be King of Spain, and accepted Phillip of Anjou instead. Ironically, British possession had come through peace talks rather than through the act of war itself, but the acquisition of this territory marked a significant new stage in the development of a British empire. How should this new piece of empire be represented for a British public?

In relation to the myth of an empire of productive liberty, Gibraltar looked decidedly anomalous – a barren rock largely devoid of natural resources, a stronghold attached to the European mainland whose significance was primarily naval and strategic, a town whose population had fled in the wake of brutal invasion. Gibraltar posed a severe challenge to the image of the developing British empire as founded upon liberty, agricultural plenty and commerce.

Most poets simply ignored the challenge. Those poets who celebrated the outcome of the Utrecht Treaty, as Alexander Pope did in his poem *Windsor Forest*, preferred to remain in the realm of celebratory fantasy at a safe distance from actualities. But the challenge was taken up by John Breval, whose poem *Calpe, or Gibraltar*, although dated 1708, was first published in 1717 (it includes a tribute to the newly installed George I). Breval, unlike Dennis, had actually been to Gibraltar, probably during his brief military service. He could assess local attitudes, examine the physical damage, observe the geographical features, and reflect upon the relationship between the past and present condition of the place. His Gibraltar poem connects different contemporary views of the landscape in ways that bring into focus fundamental conflicts between them.

Breval was the son of a French immigrant, and was, like John Dennis, a Whig and a professional writer of verse and dramatic entertainments, making a living from the expanding commercial market for the arts in Britain. He wrote satires, farces, a mock-opera, all calculated to sell by their topicality and sometimes licentious humour. His poem *The Art of Dress* (1707), for example, is described on the title page as a 'heroi-comical poem' which, like Pope's *Rape of the Lock*, reflects ironically upon modern urban society, playing with the idea that female consumption is the driving force of global commerce, a force which pulls in banal consumer

264   Part IV: The Landscape of Conquest

goods from all around the world ('Some Toy from ev'ry Part the Sailor brings'), and which consequently destabilises traditional values (the dome of Wren's St Paul's is said to provide the model of the petticoat).[7] In the *Art of Dress* Breval suggests that the civilising effect of empire cannot be distinguished from its corrupting influence.[8] His poem on Gibraltar, while generally more serious than his satires, also includes some ironical reflections on modern urban society. But it makes a serious attempt to assess the value of Gibraltar as an addition to the empire, and to celebrate it in patriotic terms.

The poem sets out to describe the most distinctive features of the Gibraltar landscape, and in doing so it brings together, and connects, two quite different topographical modes, which provide contrasting ways of justifying empire. One is the mode of topographical poetry that descends from John Denham's highly influential poem *Cooper's Hill* (1642), and which is influenced in turn by Virgil's *Georgics*. This kind of poem typically reflects upon a distant view or prospect of a British rural landscape, often *from* the top of a hill, and while it may reflect on the political divisions and disorders of recent history, it typically presents the prospect of a harmonious national order. The sense of harmony depends upon the distance between the poet and the landscape he observes, since this allows the urban world and its associated divisions and corruptions to be obscured or partially buried in the landscape. It celebrates the prospects of a peaceful libertarian British empire, seen as a providential development, and it gestures towards distant parts of the empire from what it takes to be the symbolic centre. The other mode is a new colonial discourse, influenced by the scientific interests of the Royal Society, dedicated to reporting back on the local characteristics and history of particular territories within the empire to a British readership. Hans Sloane's *History of Jamaica*, the first part of which appeared in 1707, is a key example.[9] Sloane was clearly aware of the violence entailed in imperial control, including the violence of slavery. But he wrote as a scientist, as a supposedly innocent observer and collector, exemplifying what Marie Louise Pratt terms the idea of 'anti-conquest'.[10] And his science still belongs to the age of the cabinet of curiosities, in which enticing 'curiosities' and 'strange things' lie beside detailed observations on history, meteorology, local customs and natural history – all offered for the instruction of those back home. While the poetic topographical mode, then, conventionally gestures towards a distant empire from the symbolic centre, the newer colonial mode reports back to the centre from the imperial territory itself. Breval's poem connects these two modes.

A Case Study: Gibraltar 265

He adapts the conventions of the topographical poem to reflect directly, at first hand, upon the landscape of Gibraltar rather than the landscape of home. But the hill itself becomes the subject, rather than the vantage point, and Gibraltar is a rock upon which the commonplaces of topographical poetry have no purchase. If Denham and his successors offer a distant view of the expanding British empire as a benign realm of liberty and plenty driven by commerce, Breval presents instead a close encounter with the devastating effects of conquest in a landscape largely devoid of commercial resources. Reflecting upon the violence in which British forces were involved, Breval acknowledges that the attacking fleets were not seen as liberators by the local peasants, who 'call'd on Saints to sink the Hostile Keels'.[11] The town, usually obscured in a topographical poem, is here clearly visible, exposed as a ruin. While he discreetly ignores the evidence of plunder and sexual violence, he frankly acknowledges the resulting devastation of the town:

> Now if from Calpe, down we cast our Eyes
> Where low in Dust the sumptuous Rubbish lies
> The splendid Ruins we survey with Pain,
> And o'er the Carcass of a Town complain (7)

If the topographical mode of Denham and his successors views British landscape as 'a representative image of the national order,' the rocky landscape of Gibraltar must serve a quite different function. It becomes instead a palimpsest upon which the evidence of successive conquests can be traced: each an attempt to establish a permanent social order, each one doomed to be replaced by another.[12]

This landscape, while it exposes the *im*permanence of human order and the recurrence of war, offers no sense of continuity in the realm of agriculture. In the Virgilian Georgic which influenced British topographical poetry, agriculture has a central place, as a peaceful, enduring activity that contrasts with the disruptive violence of war. The key reference point in this tradition is Virgil's description of a ploughing peasant turning up rusty weapons, the relicts of some forgotten conflict.[13] But on Gibraltar, this contrast no longer functions as it should. Although Breval does make passing references to distant fruitful vales and pleasing medicinal herbs, in his poem agriculture appears not upon the rock of Gibraltar itself, but in Cartea, a nearby Spanish village, at one time a Roman settlement (a poetic excursion for which Breval asks to be excused). There, the ploughing hind turns up not rusty weapons, but the warlike image of Hercules upon a 'rude Coin'. Hercules is said to have

266   Part IV: The Landscape of Conquest

Rais'd his proud Pillars on the conquer'd Shore,
And rul'd the Nations which he free'd before. (9)

Here, then, is an archetypal myth of the liberating conqueror, the founder of a benign empire. But the heroic image appears in a debased form: Hercules is rendered an 'imperfect hero' through time's defacement of the coin--his 'lines worn away' (9). This, we are to understand, is the fate of all conquerors: the image encapsulates the history of Gibraltar as the object of successive invasions. The 'unwieldy' power exercised by Rome 'o'er the conquered West' (10) is shown to be a precedent for the imperial ambitions of the Islamic hosts who conquer Spain, and of Ferdinand, who retakes Gibraltar for Christian Spain and dreams that his own sons 'Shall rule the West alone' (13). When, in the final lines, Breval includes the patriotic hope that British rule, by 'Fates decree'd' (15), will be permanent, the hope is tempered by his recognition of its inevitable transience, since Gibraltar must be destroyed in the Last Judgement.

So Breval transforms the topographical poem into a reflection upon the recurrence and transience of imperial conquest. The process of reflection becomes, paradoxically, a form of justification. The current devastation of the town is seen as part of a larger, repeated process that seems historically inevitable. And the poet's sensitive and enlightened response to the process implicitly validates his own presence in Gibraltar. Indeed, this is how Breval connects his poetic moralising of the landscape with the new colonial mode of reporting back epitomised by Sloane's *History of Jamaica*. The history of these successive, doomed attempts to establish permanent empires through conquest can be read in the fragmentary relicts, ruins and legends that survive in Gibraltar, which become, under the reflective gaze of the poet, resources that can be offered for the instruction and enchantment of readers back home.

Accordingly, in the Preface Breval presents himself as an 'idle' tourist musing with detachment upon a landscape that 'is Remarkable for its Height, Figure, and Curiosities of Art and Nature'. In recording its 'Curiosities,' Breval appeals to the interests of the same modern readership that Sloane addresses. The imperial project can now be judged as a form of cultural stewardship: the appreciation of the conquered territory by a refined, attentive, inclusive observer, whose enlightened observations set him apart from the evidence of superstition and barbarism he observes, can be the measure of the fitness for possession.

Here, however, we encounter a problem. This kind of cultural stewardship entails a transfer of authority from the official, mythicized sources of power and stewardship – the monarch, a symbol of divinely sanctioned

A Case Study: Gibraltar 267

national sovereignty, or the nation itself, as bearer of providential destiny – to those mere functionaries like Sloane and Breval, who represent the curiosities of art and nature to a modern society. Breval's poetry more usually satirizes modern society. In his heroi-comical poem *The Art of Dress*, he sees the values of modern society as undermined by the flow of trivialities from abroad. Breval was writing at a time when the activities of men like Sloane were viewed not only with admiration but also with suspicion and derision. As Barbara Benedict and others have shown, Sloane was a figure who brought into focus anxieties about the destabilising effect of new discoveries, and about the social power that could be gained by new forms of cultural stewardship.[14] The poet William King attacked Sloane for elevating trifles with mystifying language, for endowing the commonplace and banal with false importance in the process of advancing himself.[15] Copies of curiosities from Sloane's extensive collection were displayed in Saltero's coffee house in Chelsea, where they were seen by Richard Steele, who described them in *The Tatler* as an attempt, 'under the specious pretence of learning and antiquities, to impose upon the world'.[16] Breval, writing in the shadow of Sloane's work, contributes to, and at the same time ironises, the idea of such modern stewardship. The curiosities Breval finds on Gibraltar are not resources with the potential for useful development, but relics of barbarous ages which have the power to charm the modern visitor or reader. The most alluring is a cave, presented in terms of gothic horror, in which bald hermits and dreaming monks once performed their superstitious devotions, where the treasures of Vandals and later Moors are said to be hidden, and where the petrified remains of those adventurous misers who perished hunting the treasure can still be seen. The hardened remains of these 'undissolving Dead' are said to be

> Wonders more strange than Kings in pickle shown
> Or Dynasties transmitted down to Sloan. (5)

These lines echo Addison's satire on the Royal Society in *The Tatler*, where 'The Will of a Virtuoso' is said to include, among other exotic items, the mummy of an Egyptian king (No. 216. Saturday, August 26, 1710); and they allude directly to Sloane's collection of curiosities, which is said to have included a mummy and human remains preserved in spirit. There may also be a sly allusion here to Sloane's role as 'physician extraordinary' to Queen Anne: soon after the Queen's death Abel Boyer published a *Life of Queen Anne* which gave a detailed account of her final days, including voyeuristic details of her physical symptoms and medical treatment, and of the supervisory role played by her doctors.[17] Breval evokes a world in

268 Part IV: The Landscape of Conquest

which the traditional, sacred aura of dynasties is dispersed as royal bodies – or what are passed off as royal remains – become subject to a new class of custodians and are exposed to the curiosity of a credulous public. Breval implies that the wonders he is describing on Gibraltar might be seen in comparable terms. He mocks the taste of a public that responds to such enticing curiosities, even as he is engaged in recommending such curiosities to the public.

Breval, then, finally connects in his poem three different ways of thinking about empire, which conflict with and illuminate each other: an idealising topographical mode, a descriptive colonial mode, and a satirical mode that reflects upon, and reproduces, the confusion of values arising in an age of expanding horizons. The final impression he creates is of a paradoxical continuity with an unenlightened past. Just as the savage violence of barbaric ages has been replaced by the terrible destructive power of modern war's 'dire Engines' (7), so the superstitious credulity of past ages has been replaced by the detached wonder of the modern observer, which may be a new form of credulity, one that hallows the trivial and banal, while undermining the sacred. The language of divine destiny and regal glory, traditionally used to justify empire, coexists with a recognition that empire now serves the leisure interests and trivial curiosity of an unheroic public.

Consolidation

Once the possession of Gibraltar had been settled by treaty, British public interest in the place was fitful and determined primarily by crises arising from conflict. In 1727 Spain, determined to reclaim this strategic stronghold, mounted a siege which caused British interest in the place to flare. Geoffrey Plank notes that Parliament received over 50 addresses from across England, Scotland and Ireland insisting that Gibraltar be retained.[18] The *Craftsman*, journal of the newly organised opposition to the ministry of Robert Walpole and Charles Townshend, insisted on the right of British possession to the 'Invaluable Fortress' granted by Treaty and that 'the united voice of the whole People' was against giving it up.[19] However, it seems unlikely that, when the siege began, many Britons knew much about the place. A poem on the conflict described a war at sea with little sense of the land mass at issue.[20] But maps and descriptions were soon published.[21] A plan of the town appeared in a pamphlet anticipating war with Spain, and in an 'Impartial Account' of the siege, both of which have been attributed to Daniel Defoe.[22] *The right draft of the town of Gibraltar*

A Case Study: Gibraltar 269

(Dublin, 1727?) offered a crude woodcut of the headland and Bay, seen from off shore, with an account of the settlement. Breval's poem was republished twice under two different titles.[23] An advertisement for 'The Temple of the Arts, at Fawkes's Booth, in Upper Moorfields' promised viewers two moving pictures with automated figures: the first presenting a musical concert, the second a view of the town and bay of Gibraltar, with warships, transports and 'Spanish Troops marching through Old Gibraltar'. The advertisement includes an illustration of the machine and a view of Gibraltar with warships, and indicates one of the chief advantages of Gibraltar as an object of publicity – its whole outline could be represented in a small space and taken in at a glance; it was easy to recognise.[24]

The 1727 siege fizzled out after five months, having inflicted costly damage upon the town and fortifications. But as the scene of more than one successful conflict, the outpost had begun to acquire an emotive place in British history. In the later 1730s, when the opposition to Walpole's ministry encouraged a belligerent outcry against the 'depredations' suffered by British merchants at the hands of the Spanish in trans-Atlantic waters, the *Craftsman* used the possibility of Gibraltar reverting to Spain to rally readers to the cause of war.[25] A satirical print dated 8 October 1739 (that is, shortly before the War of Jenkins's Ear began) includes a scene in which the Spanish navy blockades the British fleet at Gibraltar.[26] During the war that followed, William Rayner published a series of prints under the title *England's Glory* (1739–40), depicting illustrious British victories, including Vernon's recent triumph at Portobello, the battlefield of Oudenard in 1708 (where Marlborough and Prince Eugene had prevailed over the French), and 'The Raising of the Siege of Gibraltar & Destroying Mons's Ponti's Squadron by Sir John Leake, March 20, 1705'.[27] These representations of Gibraltar showed no direct knowledge of its landscape, but they helped to cement the outpost into a canon of venerable British triumphs in a way calculated to make it difficult for a government to give the place up. Tindall's continuation of Rapin's *History of England* (1743–47) has a plan of the town and fortifications of Gibraltar, suggesting the importance of Gibraltar in Britain's history. A print of the taking of Gibraltar by the Anglo-Dutch fleet under Sir George Rooke, showing the outline of the rock, was included among the illustrations of Conyers Harrison's *History of the Life and Reign of Her Late Majesty Queen Anne* (1744).[28]

Britain and Spain were on opposing sides during both the War of the Austrian Succession (1740–48) and the Seven Years War (1756–63), and although Spain made no serious attempt to recover Gibraltar by force during these years the conflicts helped to keep the place in the mind of the

270   Part IV: The Landscape of Conquest

British public. During the negotiations for the Peace of Aix la Chappelle in 1748, the possibility of exchanging Gibraltar for Elba or Cape Breton Island was considered but rejected.[29] The possibility of losing Gibraltar inevitably stirred a reaction. A ballad published in 1749, for example, *England's Alarum-Bell, Or, Give not up Gibraltar,* claimed that giving up the outpost would allow French and Spanish fleets to block Britain's access to the Mediterranean, leading to, among other things, the loss of the British stronghold at Minorca and of trade with Italy and Turkey.[30] The sense of Gibraltar's strategic importance to Britain increased when, at the beginning of the Seven Years War, Britain did lose Minorca. By the end of that war Britain had major new territorial acquisitions in India and Canada. The importance of Gibraltar's position at the mouth of the Mediterranean was now well-established and its value as a port for the re-export of goods was rising.[31]

When Francis Carter published his *Journey from Gibraltar to Malaga* (1777), his view of Gibraltar's importance to Britain was much more confident than Breval's had been, and was influenced by cultural developments that had transformed Britain in the intervening years. Carter, unlike Breval, was not a soldier on a posting to Gibraltar, and has none of the defensive irony that covers Breval's uncertainty about the value of what he presents to his readers. His book is representative of the era of scientific travel and exploration that developed in the second half of the eighteenth century, in which travellers engaged in observing, collecting, and classifying artefacts and natural objects with a clear sense of the importance of what they found.[32] In Britain, a whole series of developments had created a cultural environment more favourable to the reception of traveller's findings, including the establishment of the British Museum (initially based largely around Sloane's own collection), officially sponsored voyages of discovery, and the extension of Royal patronage to public organisations such as the Royal Academy (whose exhibitions sometimes included scenes derived from voyages of discovery). These developments helped to establish a new authority for the observations of travellers and gave a reassuring promise of value to the public reader or viewer. They also helped to establish a link between the expansion of empire and the civilising process.

In his *Journey* Carter based his authority not only upon his deep personal knowledge of the localities he describes but also upon his credentials as an antiquarian. He dedicates his *Journey* to the President and members of the Society of Antiquaries, a Society which had gained its Royal Charter in 1751. While Breval had described the random discovery of a Roman coin, Carter presents himself as a dedicated exponent of the 'numismatick

A Case Study: Gibraltar

science' helping Britain to catch up in a field of study it has tended to neglect, and including illustrated tables of ancient coins and medals found in the area he explores (ix, 140–141). But his observations go far beyond such things, taking in the history and topography of Gibraltar, including the buildings and caves, as well as surrounding areas along the Spanish coast. Whereas Breval sees a parallel between the British occupation of Gibraltar and the successive, earlier possessors whose traces are found across the area, Carter has a more confident sense of the enlightened superiority expressed in Britain's global presence, and tells a tale of recovery after long decline. He praises the culture of the ancient Romans but finds little of value in the Moorish occupation. Under the British, Gibraltar has 'regained its ancient consequence,' the fortifications have been 'improved and perfected,' and it is now 'the seat of British dominion in the Mediterranean sea' (187).

His sense of Britain's tenure of the place is, like Breval's, bound up with a particular vision of the landscape. Carter's assertion of British dominion appears most strikingly when he invites his readers to join 'a very agreeable party' on a walk to take 'a view of the Southward part of the rock' (187). Here we begin to see the influence of another cultural change since the time of Breval. The Seven Years' War, by preventing travel across mainland Europe, had encouraged the growth of internal tourism in Britain. From the late 1760s tours to the more remote areas of the kingdom, including the Lake District, North Wales and the Scottish Highlands became fashionable among the wealthy, stimulating a taste for unimproved and mountainous landscapes. Carter's walk, from a modernised town to a dramatic hill-top encounter with unadorned nature, reflects this fashion. The presence of ladies emphasises the peaceful, sociable nature of this excursion, but there is no hiding the fact that possession of the rock depends upon military and naval power. The sequence is preceded by an allusion to a failed attempt of Spanish engineers during the 1727 siege to blow up 'the head of the hill' with a mine (186). Carter does not dwell on the violence of war, but instead emphasises British consideration for its victims: the view of an asylum erected in the king's name for sick sailors prompts him to praise the 'care and attention which are extended all over the British dominions'; such hospitals are seen as 'so many monuments of humanity and benevolence that distinguish the English among the nations'. What is seen from the top of the rock is nothing akin to the 'wanton vallies' of the Thames that appear in Denham's *Cooper's Hill*. Instead, Carter describes a scene of 'romantic' wildness, with vast masses of stone projecting overhead in 'horrid attitudes,' towering eagles, and a 'fathomless depth' underneath – a description informed by Edmund Burke's fashionable theory

Part IV: The Landscape of Conquest

of the sublime, which stresses the pleasurable effect of sensations of terror.[33] The figure of a miner is discerned far below – evidence, after all, of resources that can be peacefully exploited (a counterpoint to the Spanish engineers mentioned earlier). But the echo of the miner's hammer, though 'louder than thunder,' 'expires' in the expanse, while 'the fearful distance dwindles him to a pigmy' (191). Human industry is trumped by a sense of overwhelming natural power, which the viewers' elevated vantage point and aesthetic sensitivity allow them to appreciate. At this point, then, the grand is decisively privileged over the useful, to establish the disinterested taste of the viewers. Carter is engaged in what Pratt terms 'anti-conquest', by which 'European bourgeois subjects seek to secure their innocence' in the same moment as they assert their dominance (7). The commanding view becomes a correlative of British dominion, and helps to naturalise the right of conquest. When the party observes passing ships hoisting their flags 'in homage to the fort' 191, Carter supplies a couplet adapted from Popes' *Windsor Forest:*

> Where high in air Britannia's standard flies,
> Her crimson cross exalted to the skies

In Pope, the first line is preceded by words that cast a critical light upon British conquest: 'Sudden they seize th' amaz'd, defenceless prize' (line 109). Such hints of disapproval have no place in Carter's exultant view of British dominion.

The Monument of its Protectors

During the war of American Independence Spanish forces engaged in what is now known as the Great Siege of Gibraltar (1779–1783), which provided a focus for British patriotic fervour during a conflict that in other respects brought division and resounding defeat. The Spanish blockade, which lasted for three years and seven months, helped to keep Gibraltar in the news, while its eventual lifting brought widespread jubilation. The events of the siege were represented through a wide range of cultural forms suitable for different audiences, including broadsides, paintings, prints, and theatrical events. Bermondsey Spa regularly hosted a spectacular re-enactment of the siege, with 'a vast picture model,' fireworks and 'fictitious water'. Astley's circus acquired a horse from the Gibraltar Governor General George Augustus Eliott, and advertised acrobatics on 'The Gibraltar Charger'. Peter Harrington notes that the siege was the first military event to be dealt with by both history painters and maritime artists.[34] There was no culminating

A Case Study: Gibraltar

battle in the siege, but a series of incidents that artists could choose from. The burning of a flotilla of Spanish floating batteries was popular because it was a defensive triumph involving an illuminated night scene and British attempts to rescue drowning Spaniards. Following the modernising of history painting by West in the *Death of Wolfe* (1770), some of these works included an element of portraiture. In George Carter's painting, *The Siege of Gibraltar* (1782) the right-hand side of the canvas is filled with a group portrait of officers (Carter had sailed to Gibraltar to take the likeness of several officers stationed there). The American artist John Singleton Copley's huge painting *The Defeat of the Floating Batteries at Gibraltar*, produced for the City of London Corporation, shows the governor of Gibraltar, General George Augustus Elliot, with other officers, overseeing the rescue of Spanish sailors as the floating batteries burn. Copley claimed that the painting, displayed in 1791, was seen by over 60,000 visitors.[35] Another American painter, John Trumbull, in *The Sortie Made by the Garrison of Gibraltar* (1789), showed victorious British forces, led by Elliot, attending the death of the Spanish officer Don Hose Barboza, whose fate recalls that of Colonel Gardiner, deserted by his own troops and left to die – except that the Spaniard is treated with compassion by his British enemies who respect his last wishes to die at his post. Such images, focusing primarily upon defensive and humanitarian action in the face of Spanish aggression, worked to associate the British occupation of Gibraltar with the heroic preservation of liberty and decency.

Paintings on the siege appeared at the Royal Academy's annual exhibition, in other exhibition spaces in London, and, thanks to the burgeoning print industry, through relatively inexpensive reproductions. The paintings usually did not leave room for, or require, a detailed representation of the place itself – a slope of craggy rocks was enough to set the scene. But they helped to establish Gibraltar as the site of an extraordinary moral triumph, and to give it a resonant symbolic value. An anonymous poem boasted that in Gibraltar

> Victorious Britain sits enshrined in stone;
> Herself a *rock*, and not to be o'erthrown.[36]

Whereas Breval had seen Gibraltar as a challenge to transient civilising powers, here it has become the symbol of an immovable British identity.[37] In a farce performed at Covent Garden while the siege was still in progress, a soldier claims that Gibraltar is 'a pillar of the British empire, and therefore should be defended 'till made the monument of its protectors'.[38] The idea that Gibraltar could itself become 'the monument of its

274   Part IV: The Landscape of Conquest

protectors' indicates the growing importance of the sentiments associated with particular landscapes: the farce includes a climactic scene set before a view of the Rock and Strait of Gibraltar after a victorious sea battle. Earlier in the century the Duke of Marlborough had built Blenheim Palace in the Oxfordshire countryside as a monument to his own famous victory in distant Bavaria. Now the landscape of Gibraltar, the first imperial landscape to achieve a high level of visual recognition, could itself be thought of as an iconic memorial to national achievement and sacrifice.

Gibraltar was not like Blenheim, the site of a passing victory, abandoned as soon as won. It had been a recurrent presence in the news over eight decades, a small place with an accumulating history of famous events. In the 1790s Robert Southey, writing as a radical, could pen a scathing poem about Blenheim as a once famous battlefield – but Gibraltar could not be dismissed in this way (the place would later play a significant role in Southey's *Life of Nelson*, 1813).[39] History painters could commemorate a single incident and some of the prominent officers involved in it, but the rock itself commemorated a longer history leading up to the current triumph. The siege gave a new incentive to recount this history in patriotic terms. The *European Magazine* of 1st October 1782 listed the thirteen sieges that Gibraltar had endured since the fourteenth century and assured its readers that it was now 'Indubitably the strongest fortification in the universe'. The article appeared with a 'Perspective View' of Gibraltar with the British fleet arriving to relieve the garrison besieged by Spanish forces, created from a drawing 'by an Officer, taken on the spot' (177–178). The *Geographical Magazine* included a substantial entry on Gibraltar, with a history of the British acquisition and defence of the garrison which maintained that the government of the Rock was now compatible with the liberty of British subjects, and noted that curiosities from the place had been deposited in the British Museum. An accompanying print showed the landmass with its fortifications and harbour, and soldiers at peace – signs of secure possession.[40]

The cultural developments that had influenced Carter's response to landscape had encouraged a growing interest in places of wild natural beauty or historical interest. Relatively inexpensive collections of prints, such as Paul Sandby's pioneering *Virtuosi's Museum* (1778–81), which showed landscapes and historical buildings from across Britain and Ireland accompanied by brief notes explaining their historical significance, worked to establish a sense of nation constituted not in its political, economic, or social institutions, but in

A Case Study: Gibraltar

particular locations – an example of the domestication of patriotism. At a time of political divisions caused by the American War of Independence, Sandby's collection presented landscape as a unifying influence.[41] Sandby's prints had originally grown out of his experience as a military topographer employed to survey and map the Scottish Highlands in the wake of the '45 rebellion.[42] He became a drawing master at the Royal Woolwich Military Academy in 1768, the same year as he became a member of the Royal Academy. Several generations of military topographers trained under his influence at Woolwich, some of whom would subsequently help to shape the British public's appreciation of imperial landscape. Unlike history paintings, topographical studies tended to use human figures primarily to give a sense of scale to the landscape – or to exclude them completely. In such studies, the historical interest of a place was registered primarily by association; the landscape was not a background setting, but it could have a commemorative function. The *Virtuosi* collection, from the beginning of its serialised publication, included studies of craggy mountains and mountaintop castles (such as *North East View of the Rock of Cashell, County Tipperary, Ireland*; *View of Craig Toraphen and the Lin of Tumel*; and *Dunemace Castle, Queen's County, Ireland*). Visually, it was a short step from such scenery to the stony outcrop of Gibraltar. And it was also a short step from appreciating homeland scenes as part of the kingdom's heritage, to seeing the landscape of Gibraltar in comparable terms.

In the wake of the siege the most complete representation of Gibraltar was provided in a set of six aquatints produced by John William Edy in 1797, using drawings by George Bulteel Fisher, who had trained in military draftsmanship in the Woolwich Academy under Paul Sandby, and was posted to Gibraltar in 1790. Edy had previously worked on a set of views of Canada by Fisher, and on *Twelve Views of Places in the Kingdom of Mysore* (1793) by Robert Colebrooke, who had also trained under Sandby at Woolwich (Figure 5b). These works fed into a growing market for imperial landscape, from which military draftsmen were well placed to profit. The Gibraltar set shows the rock from the four different viewpoints and includes two views of what may be the North African coast nearby. In the prints, some dramatic touches have been added to the skies, but these do not really soften the stark features of the rocky outcrop with its skirt of fortifications (Figure 5a). Gibraltar is shown at peace, but nobody could view these scenes in the 1790s without recalling the events of the siege. In an age when the invention of the panorama would soon provide a sensational, immersive recreation of the violence of battle, these landscapes show that war could be commemorated without being represented or even mentioned, through an evocation of peace.[43]

276   Part IV: The Landscape of Conquest

The work of celebrating Gibraltar, as it went on through the 1780s and 1790s, overlapped with the second and third Anglo-Mysore wars in India (1780–84, 1790–92) and with the trial of Warren Hastings (1788–1795), the Governor-General of Bengal who was accused of corruption and cruelty. Compared with Gibraltar, India presented an immensely rich and varied cultural landscape for artists to engage with. But, as has often been noted, among the sets of views produced in this period there were many studies of gaunt Indian hill forts or 'droogs,' some of which had been the scene of recent fighting. Some of the fort paintings created by the artist William Hodges, who had gone to India in 1780, were commissioned by those with a personal interest in the action, as a form of commemoration.[44] Some droogs were drawn by military draughtsmen like Colebrooke as part of an 'on the spot' record of the terrain and places of interest observed during the Mysore campaigns (Alexander Allan, who produced *Views in the Mysore Country* in 1794, was, like Colebrooke, trained under the influence of Sandby at Woolwich). Colebrooke's images were accompanied by a historical narrative that refers to British military operations and includes an account of the inhuman treatment of British Officers captured in the previous Anglo-Mysore war, but unlike history paintings, they are free of, or minimise, the events themselves (Figure 5b). Recent commentators have been able to find special meanings within these landscapes, but the most significant feature of them may be that war is commemorated but not celebrated by them.[45] Such studies began the process of transforming the spaces of India – which could appear exotic and strange in its palaces, tombs and cultural customs – into something more familiar. When the artist Charles Gold explained in his *Oriental Drawings* that the Indian droogs scattered across the landscape of Mysore looked like 'so many Gibraltars in miniature,' he indicated that Gibraltar had become a familiar reference point by which British territorial conquest could be understood as part of a story of defence and civilised liberation.[46] Viewers could be reconciled to the fruits of conquest not only through representations of the material effects of civilisation but through the implicit appeal to the aesthetic taste of the observer, whose capacity to appreciate the landscape is in itself a form of justification. Such views satisfy the 'great longing' identified by Pratt, to take possession of territory 'innocently' – a longing that was felt not only by the naturalists that she describes, but – in different ways – by pacifists and by those who assumed that violence was, unfortunately, necessary to the progress and defence of 'civilisation'.[47]

Figure 5a John William Edy, after George Bulteel Fisher, *Water Port Gate, Gibraltar* (1796) [© British Museum]

Figure 5b Robert Hyde Colebrook, *South-Western View of Ootra-Durgum* (1793) [© British Library]

Part IV: The Landscape of Conquest

Notes

1 E.g. advertisement for B. Benjamin & Co, shipping agents based at Gibraltar. A stylised view from the North; John Phillips, late eighteenth century, early nineteenth century (British Museum, 1982,U.290).

2 Karen O'Brien, 'Poetry against Empire: Milton to Shelley', *Proceedings of the British Academy*, 117 (2002), 269–296, pp. 273–276; Steven Pincus, *Protestantism and Patriotism: Ideologies and the Making of English Foreign Policy, 1650–1668* (Cambridge: Cambridge University Press, 1996); David Armitage, *The Ideological Origins of the British Empire* (Cambridge: Cambridge University Press, 2000); Karen O'Brien, 'Protestantism and the Poetry of Empire, 1660–1800,' in *Culture and Society in Britain, 1660–1800*, ed. Jeremy Black (Manchester: Manchester University Press, 1997), 146–162.

3 *The London Gazette,* No. 4046, Monday August 14 to Thursday August 17, 1704.

4 For example, John Tutchen in *The Observator*, Wednesday 16th to Saturday 19th August, 1704.

5 For example, on 4 September the *Daily Courant* published a report from Paris, which gave details of the violence.

6 George Hills, *Rock of Contention: A History of Gibraltar* (London: Robert Hale, 1974), 175–177.

7 John Breval, *The Art of Dress: A Poem* (London, 1717), 17.

8 Pope mocks him in the *Dunciad* book 2.

9 See Kay Dian Kriz, 'Commodities, and Transplanted Bodies in Hans Sloane's "Natural History of Jamaica"', *The William and Mary Quarterly*, Third Series, 57 (1), 2000, 35–78.

10 Marie Louise Pratt, *Imperial Eyes: Travel Writing and Transculturation* (London: Routledge, 2003), 7.

11 John Breval, *Calpe, or Gibraltar: A Poem* (London: 1708, i.e. 1717), 14.

12 John Guillory, 'The English Common Place: Lineages of the Topographical Genre', *Critical Quarterly*, 33 (1991), 3–27, p. 6.

13 See John Chalker, *The English Georgic: A Study in the Development of a Form* (London: Routledge and Kegan Paul, 1969), 3.

14 Barbara M. Benedict, 'Collecting Trouble: Sir Hans Sloane's Literary Reputation in Eighteenth-Century Britain', *Eighteenth-Century Life*, 36: 2 (2012), 111–142.

15 Benedict, 121–22.

16 *The Tatler* 34, Tuesday 28 June, 1709.

17 Abel Bowyer, *The Life of Queen Anne* (London, 1714), 409.

18 Geoffrey Plank, 'Making Gibraltar British in the Eighteenth Century', *History*, 98 (2013), 346–369, p. 353.

19 *The Craftsman*, no. XXXIII, Friday, March 31, 1731, 307.

20 J. Mawer, *Liberty Asserted: Or, the Siege of Gibraltar. A Poem* (London, 1727)

21 G. Risk, G. Ewing and W. Smith advertised a *Map of Gibraltar* for 6 shillings.

22 *The Evident Approach of a War* (London, 1727); *An Impartial Account of the Late Famous Siege of Gibraltar* (London, 1728).

A Case Study: Gibraltar 279

23 It was published as *Gibraltar, a Poem*, and as *Calpe, or Gibraltar, a Poem*.

24 Advertisement for 'The Temple of the Arts' (London, 1727). British Museum Y,5.260.

25 E.g. *The Craftsman*, XII, no. 480 Sept 13, 1735, 113.

26 *Hocus Pocus or the Political Jugglers*, by Edward Ryland, 8 Oct. 1739. Another satirical print about the outbreak of the War of Jenkins's Ear, *The European Race* by Charles Mosely (1740), shows, among other figures, the Queen of Spain as hoping to give birth to Gibraltar.

27 See Timothy Clayton, *The English Print 1688–1802* (New Haven: Yale University Press, 1997), 150–151.

28 Conyers Harrison, *An Impartial History of the Life and Reign of Queen Anne* (London, 1744), 208–209.

29 Plank, 359.

30 *England's Alarum-Bell, Or, Give Not up Gibraltar* (London, 1749), 5.

31 Stephen Constantine, *Community and Identity: The Making of Modern Gibraltar Since 1704* (Manchester: Manchester University Press, 2009), 51.

32 Francis Carter, *A Journey from Gibraltar to Malaga* (London, 1777). See Mary Louise Pratt on the Cultural Influence of the Linnean System of Plant Classification: *Imperial Eyes* (London: Routledge, 1992), 24–35.

33 Edmund Burke, *A Philosophical Enquiry into the Origin of Our Ideas of the Sublime and Beautiful* (London, 1757).

34 Peter Harrington, *British Artists and War: The Face of Battle in Paintings and Prints, 1700–1914* (London: Greenhill Books, 1993), 45.

35 Harrington, 51.

36 *Arx Herculea Servata [...] Or, Gibraltar Delivered* (London, 1783), 9.

37 Geoffrey Plank notes, in these lines Gibraltar has become 'an emblem of the [British] nation itself', 368.

38 F. Pilon, *The Siege of Gibraltar: A Musical Farce in Two Acts* (London, 1780), 2.

39 Southey's poem 'The Battle of Blenheim' was written in 1796 and published in *Metrical Tales* (London, 1805)

40 *The Geographical Magazine, or, New System of Geography*, by William Frederick Martyn, 2 vols. (London 1785–87), I: 295–97. The print is by James Heath after Conrad Martine Metz (1785).

41 See Andrew Kennedy, 'Representing Three Kingdoms: Hanoverianism and the Virtuosi's Museum', in *Deterritorialisations: Revisioning Landscapes and Politics*, ed. Mark Dorrian and Gilliam Rose (London: Black Dog, 2003), 272–283.

42 Helen Wyld, 'Framing Britain's Past: Paul Sandby and the Picturesque Tour of Scotland', *The British Art Journal* 12 (2011), 29–36.

43 See Markman Ellis, '"Spectacles within Doors": Panoramas of London in the 1790s', *Romanticism*, 14: 2 (2008), 133–148.

44 For example, the views of the forts at Pateeta 1781–2 and Bidjegur and the fortress of Chunargarh (c1785). Giles Tillotson, *The Artificial Empire: The Indian Landscapes of William Hodges* (Richmond: Curzon Press, 2000), 87.

280   Part IV: The Landscape of Conquest

Geoff Quilley, 'Hodges and India' in *William Hodges, 1744–1797: The Art of Exploration*, ed. Geoff Quilley and John Bonehill (Greenwich: National Maritime Museum, 2004), 137–186, 162–63, 164, 160.

45 For more detailed interpretations, see Mary A. Favret, *War at a Distance* (Princeton, NJ: Princeton University Press, 2010), 192–210; Rosie Dias, 'Memory and the Aesthetics of Military Experience: Viewing the Landscape of the Anglo-Mysore Wars', in *Tate Papers*, no. 19, Spring 2013.

46 Charles Gold, *Oriental Drawings* (London, 1806) note to Amboor Fort, plate 34.

47 *Imperial Eyes*, 7.

Further Reading

This list is for readers who want a broad guide to the subject of this book. It is selective, and there is some overlap between categories.

General

Banister, Julia, *Masculinity, Militarism and Eighteenth-Century Culture, 1689–1815* (Cambridge: Cambridge University Press, 2018).

Brewer, John, *The Sinews of Power: War, Money and the English State 1688–1783* (London: Routledge, 1989).

Colley, Linda, *Britons: Forging the Nation 1707–1837* (New Haven: Yale University Press, 1992).

Dickson, P. G. M., *The Financial Revolution in England* (London: Macmillan, 1967).

Downes, Stephanie, Andrew Lynch, Katrina O'Loughlin, eds., *Writing war in Britain and France, 1370–1854: a History of Emotions* (London: Routledge, 2018).

Elias, Norbert, *The Civilizing Process*, tr. Edmund Jephcott, ed. Eric Dunning, Johan Goudsblom, and Stephen Mennell, rev. edn. (Oxford: Blackwell, 2000).

Forrest, Alan, Karen Hagemann, and Michael Rowe, eds., *War, Demobilization and Memory : The Legacy of War in the Era of Atlantic Revolutions* (New York: Palgrave, 2016).

Fortescue, J. W. *A History of the British Army* (London: Macmillan, 1899), vols. 2, 3.

Harari, Yuval, *The Ultimate Experience: Battlefield Revelations and the Making of Modern War Culture, 1450–2000* (Basingstoke: Palgrave, 2008).

Kennedy, Catriona, and Matthew McCormack, *Soldiering in Britain and Ireland, 1750–1850* (New York: Palgrave, 2013).

Kuijpers, Erika and Cornelis van der Haven, eds., *Battlefield Emotions, 1500–1800* (London: Palgrave, 2016).

Langford, Paul, *A Polite and Commercial People* (Oxford: Oxford University Press, 1989).

Linch, Kevin, and Matthew McCormack, eds., *Britain's Soldiers: Rethinking War and Society: 1715–1815* (Liverpool: Liverpool University Press, 2014).

Lincoln, Margarette, *Representing the Royal Navy: British Sea Power 1750–1815* (London: Routledge, 2002).

Further Reading

Lincoln, Margarette, *Trading in War: London's Maritime World in the Age of Cook and Nelson* (New Haven: Yale University Press, 2018).

McCormack, Matthew, *Embodying the Militia in Georgian England* (Oxford: Oxford University Press, 2015).

Neff, Stephen C., *War and the Law of Nations: A General History* (Cambridge: Cambridge University Press, 2005).

Newman, Gerald, *The Rise of English Nationalism: A Cultural History* (London: Weidenfeld & Nicolson, 1987).

Pocock, J. G. A., *The Machiavellian Moment* (Princeton, NJ: Princeton University Press, 1975).

Pocock, J. G. A., *Virtue, Commerce and History* (Cambridge: Cambridge University Press., 1985).

Ramsey, Neil, *The Military Memoir and Romantic Military Culture* (London: Routledge, 2016).

Ramsey, Neil, and Gillian Russell, eds., *Tracing War in British Enlightenment and Romantic Culture* (Houndmills: Palgrave, 2015).

Richardson, John, 'Literature and War in the Eighteenth Century', *Oxford Handbooks Online*, July 2014, tiny.one/5n76hdam.

Roger, N. A. M., *The Wooden World: An Anatomy of the Georgian Navy* (Glasgow: Collins, 1986).

Roger, N. A. M., *The Command of the Ocean: A Naval History of Britain, 1649–1815* (London: Allen Lane, 2004).

Starkey, Armstrong, *War in the Age of Enlightenment, 1700–1789* (London: Praeger, 2003).

Major Wars

War of the Spanish Succession, 1701–1713

Francis, David, *The First Peninsular War, 1702–1713* (London: Benn, 1975).

Hattendorf, John B., *England in the War of the Spanish Succession* (New York: Garland, 1987).

Matthias, Pohlig, and Michael Schaich, eds., *The War of the Spanish Succession: New Perspectives* (Oxford: Oxford University Press, 2018).

Trevelyan, George Macaulay., *England under Queen Anne* (3 vols) (London: Longman, 1930).

War of Jenkins's Ear and War of the Austrian Succession, 1739–1748

Browning, Reed, *The War of the Austrian Succession* (New York: St. Martin's Press, 1993).

Gaudi, Robert, *The War of Jenkins's Ear* (New York: Pegasus, 2022).

Harris, Robert, *A Patriot Press: National Politics and the London Press in the 1740s* (Oxford: Oxford University Press, 1993).

Further Reading

Pittock, Murray, *The Myth of the Jacobite Clans* (Edinburgh: Edinburgh University Press, 2009).

Plank, Geoffrey, *Rebellion and Savagery : The Jacobite Rising of 1745 and the British Empire* (Philadelphia: University of Pennsylvania Press, 2006).

Riding, Jacqueline, *Jacobites: A New History of the '45 Rebellion* (London: Bloomsbury, 2017).

Speck, W.A., *The Butcher: The Duke of Cumberland and the Suppression of the '45* (Caernarfon: Welsh Academic Press, 1995).

Seven Years' War, 1756–63

Baugh, Daniel, *The Global Seven Years' War, 1757–73* (Abingdon: Routledge, 2011).

Buckner, Phillip, and John G. Reid, eds., *Remembering 1759: The Conquest of Canada in Historical Memory* (Toronto: University of Toronto Press, 2012).

Cardwell, John, *Arts and Arms: Literature, Politics and Patriotism during the Seven Years' War* (Manchester: Manchester University Press, 2004).

Charters, Erica, *Disease, War, and the Imperial State: The Welfare of the British Armed Forces during the Seven Years' War* (Chicago: University of Chicago Press, 2014).

De Bruyn, Frans, and Shaun Regan, eds., *The Culture of the Seven Years' War: Empire, Identity, and the Arts in the Eighteenth-Century Atlantic World* (Toronto: University of Toronto Press, 2014).

McNairn, Alan, *Behold the Hero: General Wolfe and the Arts in the Eighteenth Century* (Liverpool: Liverpool University Press, 1997).

Robson, Martin, *A History of the Royal Navy: The Seven Years War* (London: I.B. Tauris, 2015).

Spector, Robert Donald, *English Literary Periodicals and the Climate of Opinion during the Seven Years' War* (The Hague and Paris: Mouton & Co., 1966).

American Revolutionary War, 1775–1783

Bickham, Troy, *Making Headlines: The American Revolution as Seen through the British Press* (DeKalb: University of Illinois, 2009).

Black, Jeremy, *The War for American Independence, 1775–1783* (Cheltenham: History Press, 2021).

Bradley, James, *Popular Politics and the American Revolution* (Macon, GA: Mercer University Press, 1986).

Carté, Katherine, *Religion and the American Revolution* (Chapel Hill: University of North Carolina Press, 2021).

Conway, Stephen, *The War of American Independence 1775–1783* (London: Edward Arnold, 1995).

Wood, Gordon S., ed., *The American Revolution: Writings from the Pamphlet Debate* (New York: Library of America, 2015).

284 *Further Reading*

Revolutionary and Napoleonic Wars, 1793–1815

Black, Jeremy, *The French Revolutionary and Napoleonic Wars* (Lanham: Rowman and Littlefield, 2022).

Blanning, T. C. W., *The French Revolutionary Wars, 1787–1802* (London: Arnold, 1996).

Chamberlain, Paul, *Hell upon Water: Prisoners of War in Britain, 1793–1815* (Stroud: Spellmount, 2016).

Cookson, J. E., *The British Armed Nation, 1793–1815* (Oxford: Oxford University Press, 1997).

Emsley, Clive, *British Society and the French Wars, 1793–1815* (London: Macmillan, 1979).

Fremont-Barnes, Gregory, *The French Revolutionary Wars* (Oxford: Osprey, 2014).

Kennedy, Catriona, *Narratives of the Revolutionary and Napoleonic Wars: Military and Civilian Experience in Britain and Ireland* (Basingstoke: Palgrave, 2013).

Knight, Roger, *Britain against Napoleon: The Organisation of Victory, 1793–1815* (London: Penguin, 2013).

Macleod, Emma, *War of Ideas: British Attitudes to the Wars against Revolutionary France, 1792–1802* (London: Routledge, 2018).

Robson, Martin, *The Napoleonic Wars* (London: I.B. Tauris, 2014).

Saglia, Diego and Ian Heywood, eds., *Spain in British Romanticism 1800–1840* (London: Palgrave, 2017).

Schneid, Frederick C., *Napoleonic Wars* (Washington DC.: Potomac, 2012).

Verhoeven, Wil, *Americomania and the French Revolution Debate in Britain, 1789–1802* (Cambridge: Cambridge University Press, 2013).

Empire

Armitage, David, *The Ideological Origins of the British Empire* (Cambridge: Cambridge University Press, 2000).

Barringer, Tim, Geoff Quilley, and Douglas Fordham, eds., *Art and the British Empire* (Manchester: Manchester University Press, 2007).

Bayly, Christopher Alan, *Imperial Meridian: The British Empire and the World 1789–1830* (London: Routledge, 1989).

Beaumont, Roger, *Sword of the Raj: The British Army in India, 1747–1947* (Indianapolis: Bobbs-Merrill, 1977).

Constantine, Stephen, *Community and Identity: The Making of Modern Gibraltar Since 1704* (Manchester: Manchester University Press, 2009).

Coutu, Joan, *Persuasion and Propaganda: Monuments and the Eighteenth-Century British Empire* (Montreal: McGill-Queens University Press, 2006).

Dorrian, Mark, and Gilliam Rose, eds., *Deterritorialisations: Revisioning Landscapes and Politics* (London: Black Dog, 2003).

Hills, George, *Rock of Contention: A History of Gibraltar* (London: Robert Hale, 1974).

Page, Anthony, *Britain and the Seventy Years War, 1744–1815* (Basingstoke: Palgrave, 2014).

Pratt, Marie Louise, *Imperial Eyes: Travel Writing and Transculturation* (London: Routledge, 2003).

Quilley, Geoff, and John Bonehill, eds., *William Hodges, 1744–1797: The Art of Exploration* (Greenwich: National Maritime Museum, 2004).

Simms, Brendan, *Three Victories and a Defeat* (London: Penguin, 2007).

Stone, Lawrence, ed., *An Imperial State at War. Britain from 1689 to 1815* (London: Routledge, 1993).

Tillotson, Giles, *The Artificial Empire: The Indian Landscapes of William Hodges* (Richmond: Curzon Press, 2000).

Tritton, Alan, *Scotland and the Indian Empire* (London: Bloomsbury, 2019).

Tuck, Patrick, ed., *East India Company, Vol 5, Warfare, Expansion, and Resistance* (London: Routledge, 2021).

Wilson, Kathleen, ed., *A New Imperial History: Culture, Identity and Modernity in Britain and the Empire 1660–1840* (Cambridge: Cambridge University Press, 2004).

Moral Responsibility

Felice, William F., *How Do I Save My Honor?: War, Moral Integrity and Principled Resignation* (Lansham: Rowman and Littlefield, 2009).

Gross, Michael L., *Moral Dilemmas of Modern War: Torture, Assassination, and Blackmail in an Age of Asymmetric Conflict* (Cambridge: Cambridge University Press, 2010).

Huntington, Samuel P., *The Soldier and the State* (Cambridge, MA: Belknap Press, 1957).

Lazar, Seth, ed., *Oxford Handbook of the Ethics of War* (Oxford: Oxford University Press, 2020).

Nagel, Thomas, *Moral Questions* (Cambridge: Cambridge University Press, 1979).

Orend, Brian, *The Morality of War* (London: Broadview, 2013).

Reichberg, Gregory M., Henrike Syse, and Endre Begby, *The Ethics of War: Classic and Contemporary Readings* (Oxford: Blackwell, 2006).

Ryan, Cheyney, *The Chickenhawk Syndrome* (Lanham: Rowman and Littlefield, 2009).

Sherman, Nancy, *Heroism and the Changing Character of War: Towards Post-Heroic Warfare* (Basingstoke: Palgrave, 2014).

Religion

Bartel, Roland, 'The Story of Public Fast Days in England', *Anglican Theological Review* 37 (1955), 190–200.

Blake, Richard, *Evangelicals in the Royal Navy, 1775–1815* (Woodbridge: Boydell, 2008).

Blinn, Arnaud, *War and Religion* (Berkeley: University of California Press, 2019).

Claydon, Tony, *William III and the Godly Revolution* (Cambridge: Cambridge University Press, 1996).

286   *Further Reading*

Halbertal, Moshe, *On Sacrifice* (Princeton, NJ: Princeton University Press, 2012).
Mitchell, Jolyon, and Joshua Rey, *War and Religion: A Very Short Introduction* (Oxford: Oxford University Press, 2021).
Morris, David B., *The Religious Sublime* (Lexington: University Press of Kentucky, 2014).
Rivers, Isabel, *Reason, Grace, and Sentiment, vol I, Whichcote to Wesley* (Cambridge: Cambridge University Press, 1991).

Mourning

Garganigo, Alex, 'William without Mary: Mourning Sensibility in the Public Sphere', *The Seventeenth Century* 23 (2008), 105–141.
Harrison, Robert Pogue, *The Dominion of the Dead* (Chicago: Chicago University Press, 2003).
Houldbrooke, Ralph, *Death, Religion and the Family in England* (Oxford: Oxford University Press, 1998).
Newby, Zahra, and Ruth Toulson, *The Materiality of Mourning* (London: Routledge, 2018).
Schor, Elizabeth, *Bearing the Dead: The British Culture of Mourning from the Enlightenment to Victoria* (Princeton NJ: Princeton University Press, 1994).

Politics

Barrell, John, *Imagining the King's Death: Figurative Treason, Fantasies of Regicide* (Oxford: Oxford University Press, 2000).
Brewer, John, 'Commercialization and Politics', in Neil McKendrick, John Brewer, and H. Plumb, eds., *The Birth of a Consumer Society* (Bloomington: Indiana University Press, 1982), 239–252.
Claeys, Gregory, *The French Revolution Debate in Britain: The Origins of Modern Politics* (Basingstoke: Palgrave, 2007).
Cohen-Vrignaud, Gerard, *Radical Orientalism: Rights, Reform, and Romanticism* (Cambridge: Cambridge University Press, 2015).
Gilmour, Ian, *Riot, Risings and Revolution* (London: Hutchinson, 1992).
Harris, Bob, *Politics and the Nation: Britain in the Mid-Eighteenth Century* (Oxford: Oxford University Press, 2002).
Jordan, Gerald, and Nicholas Rogers, 'Admirals as Heroes: Patriotism and Liberty in Hanoverian England', *Journal of British Studies* xxviii (1989), 201–224.
Kinkel, Sarah, 'Saving Admiral Byng: Imperial Debates, Military Governance and Popular Politics at the Outbreak of the Seven Years War', *Journal for Maritime Research* 13 (1), (2011), 3–19.
Kramnick, Isaac, *Bolingbroke and His Circle: The Politics of Nostalgia in the Age of Walpole* (Ithaca, New York: Cornell University Press, 1968).
Peters, Marie, *Pitt and Popularity: The Patriot Minister and London Opinion during the Seven Years' War* (Oxford: Oxford University Press, 1980).

Further Reading

Rogers, Nicholas, *Whigs and Cities: Popular Politics in the Age of Walpole and Pitt* (Oxford: Oxford University Press, 1989).

Rogers, Nicholas, *Crowds, Culture, and Politics in Georgian Britain* (Oxford: Oxford University Press, 1998).

Rogers, Nicholas, *Mayhem: Post-War Crime and Violence in Britain, 1748–53* (New Haven: Yale University Press, 2012).

Smith, Hannah, *Georgian Monarchy: Politics and Culture, 1714–1760* (Cambridge: Cambridge University Press, 2006).

Stevenson, John, *Popular Disturbances in England 1700–1870* (London: Routledge, 1992).

Thompson, E. P., 'The Moral Economy of the English Crowd in the Eighteenth Century,' *Past & Present* 50 (1971), 76–136.

Wilson, Kathleen, *The Sense of the People: Politics, Culture and Imperialism in England, 1715–1785* (Cambridge: Cambridge University Press, 1995).

Women

Binhammer, Katherine, 'The Sex Panic of the 1790s', *Journal of the History of Sexuality* 6 (3) (1996), 409–434.

Clery, E. J., *The Feminization Debate in Eighteenth-Century England* (Basingstoke: Palgrave, 2004).

Dugaw, Dianne, *Warrior Women and Popular Balladry 1650–1850* (Chicago: Chicago University Press, 1989, 1996).

Füssel, Marian, 'Between Dissimulation and Sensation: Female Soldiers in Eighteenth-Century Warfare', *Journal for Eighteenth-Century Studies* 41 (4) (2018), 527–542.

Guest, Harriet, *Small Change, Women Learning, Patriotism, 1750–1810* (Chicago: Chicago University Press, 2000).

Hacker, Barton C., 'Women and Military Institutions in Early Modern Europe: A Reconnaissance', *Signs* 6 (1981), 643–671.

Hagemann, Gisella Mettele, and Jane Rendall, eds., *Gender, War and Politics: Transatlantic Perspectives, 1775–1830* (Basingstoke: Palgrave, 2010).

Jones, Vivienne, ed., *Women in the Eighteenth Century: Constructions of Femininity* (London: Routledge, 1990).

Lincoln, Margarette, *Naval Wives & Mistresses* (London: National Maritime Museum, 2007).

MacKay, Lynne, and Jennine Hurl-Eamon, *Women, Families and the British Army, 1700–1880*, vol 1 (London: Routledge, 2020).

O'Brien, Karen, *Women and Enlightenment in Eighteenth-Century Britain* (Cambridge: Cambridge University Press, 2009).

Wahrman, Dror, 'Percy's Prologue: From Gender Play to Gender Panic in Eighteenth-Century England', *Past & Present*, 159 (1998), 113–160.

Wilson, Kathleen, 'Nelson's Women: Female Masculinity and Body Politics in the French and Napoleonic Wars', *European History Quarterly* 37 (4) (2007), 562–581.

288 *Further Reading*

Culture of Reform and Enlightenment

Barker-Benfield, G. J., *The Culture of Sensibility* (Chicago: Chicago University Press, 1992).

Barnett, Michael, *Empire of Humanity: A History of Humanitarianism* (Ithaca, NY: Cornell University Press, 2011).

Barnett, Michael, and Thomas G. Weiss, eds., *Humanitarianism in Question* (Ithaca, NY: Cornell University Press, 2008).

Buchan, Bruce, 'Enlightened Histories: Civilization, War and the Scottish Enlightenment', *The European Legacy*, 10 (2) (2005), 177–192.

Carey, Daniel, *Locke, Shaftesbury and Hutcheson* (Cambridge: Cambridge University Press, 2006).

Fleischacker, Samuel, *Adam Smith* (London: Routledge, 2021).

Herman, Arthur, *The Scottish Enlightenment* (London: Fourth Estate, 2003).

Klein, Lawrence E., *Shaftesbury and the Culture of Politeness* (Cambridge: Cambridge University Press, 1994).

McClure, Ruth K., *Coram's Children: The London Foundling Hospital in the Eighteenth Century* (New Haven: Yale University Press, 1981).

Phillipson, Nicholas, *Hume* (London: Weidenfeld and Nicolson, 1989).

Phillipson, Nicholas, *Adam Smith: An Enlightened Life* (London: Penguin, 2011).

Ramsey, Neil, and Gillian Russell, eds., *Tracing War in British Enlightenment and Romantic Culture* (Basingstoke: Palgrave, 2015).

Robertson, John, *The Scottish Enlightenment and the Militia Issue* (Edinburgh: John Donald, 1985).

Smith, Craig, *Adam Smith* (London: Polity, 2020).

Spencer, Mark G., ed., *David Hume: Historical Thinker, Historical Writer* (Pennsylvania: The Pennsylvania State University Press, 2013).

Stamatov, Peter, *The Origins of Global Humanitarianism* (Cambridge: Cambridge University Press, 2013).

Whelan, Frederick G., *Hume and Machiavelli: Political Realism and Liberal Thought* (Lanham: Maryland: Lexington Books, 2004).

Peace

Amalada, Stan and Sean Byrne, eds., *Peace Leadership: The Quest for Connectedness* (London: Routledge, 2017).

Ceadel, Martin, *The Origins of War Prevention: The British Peace Movement and International Relations, 1730–1854* (Oxford: 1996).

Cookson, J. E., *The Friends of Peace: Anti-War Liberalism in England, 1793–1815* (Cambridge: Cambridge University Press, 1982).

Galtung, John, 'Cultural Violence,' *Journal of Peace Research*, 27 (3) (1990), 291–305.

Geis, Anna, Lothar Brock, and Harald Müller, *Democratic Wars: Looking at the Dark Side of Democratic Peace* (Houndmills: Palgrave Macmillan, 2006).

Gross, Sandra, and Jeffrey P. Roberts, *William Penn: Visionary and Proprietor* (Philadelphia: Atwater Kent Museum, 1983).

Further Reading

Hirst, Margaret E., *The Quakers in Peace and War* (New York: Swarthmore Press, 1923).

Pencak, William A., and Daniel K. Richter, eds. *Friends and Enemies in Penn's Woods: Indians, Colonists and the Racial Construction of Pennsylvania* (Philadelphia: Pennsylvania State University Press, 2004).

Pupavac, Vanessa, *Culture of Violence: Theories and Cultures of Peace Programmes: A Critique* (Sheffield: Sheffield Hallam University Press, 2001).

Rosato, Sebastian, 'The Flawed Logic of Democratic Peace Theory', *Political Science Review*, 97 (4) (2003), 585–602.

Sager, Eric W., 'The Social Origins of Victorian pacifism', *Victorian Studies*, 23 (2) (1979), 80.

Sager, Eric W., 'Religious Sources of English Pacifism from the Enlightenment to the Industrial Revolution', *Canadian Journal of History*, 17 (1) (2017), 1–26.

Wilson, Ellen Gibson, *Thomas Clarkson: A Biography* (York: William Sessions, 1996).

Visual Arts

Barrell, John, *The Political History of Painting from Reynolds to Hazlitt* (New Haven: Yale University Press, 1986).

Bindman, David, and Malcolm Baker, *Roubiliac and the Eighteenth-Century Monument: Sculpture as Theatre* (New Haven: Yale University Press, 1995).

Clayton, Timothy, *The English Print 1688–1802* (New Haven: Yale University Press, 1997).

De Almeida, Hermione, and George H. Gilpin, *Indian Renaissance: British Romantic Art and the Prospect of India* (Aldershot: Ashgate, 2005).

Ellis, Markman, '"Spectacles within doors": Panoramas of London in the 1790s', *Romanticism*, 14 (2) (2009), 133–148.

Harrington, Peter, *British Artists and War: The Face of Battle in Paintings and Prints, 1700–1914* (London: Greenhill Books, 1993).

Hoock, Holger, *Empires of Imagination: Politics, War, and the Arts in the British World, 1750–1850* (London: Profile Books, 2010).

Roscoe, Ingrid, *Peter Scheemakers, 'The Famous Statuary' 1691–1781* (Leeds: Henry Moore Institute, 1996).

Shaw, Philip, *Suffering and Sentiment in Romantic Military Art* (Farnham: Ashgate, 2013).

Solkin, David, *Painting for Money: Visual Arts and the Public Sphere in Eighteenth-Century England* (New Haven: Yale University Press, 1993).

Theatre

O'Quinn, Daniel, *Staging Governance: Theatrical Imperialism in London, 1770–1800* (Baltimore: The Johns Hopkins University Press, 2005).

O'Quinn, Daniel, 'Theatre and Empire', in Jane Moody and Daniel O'Quinn, eds., *The Cambridge Companion to British Theatre, 1730–1830* (Cambridge: Cambridge University Press, 2007), 233–246.

290 *Further Reading*

O'Quinn, Daniel, *Entertaining Crisis in the Atlantic Imperium 1770–1790* (Baltimore: The John Hopkins University Press, 2011).

Orr, Bridget, *Empire on the English Stage 1660–1714* (Cambridge: Cambridge University Press, 2001).

Orr, Bridget, *British Enlightenment Theatre* (Cambridge: Cambridge University Press, 2020).

Russell, Gillian, *The Theatres of War: Performance, Politics, and Society: 1793–1815* (Oxford: Oxford University Press, 1995).

Schechter, Joel, *Eighteenth-Century Brechtians: Theatrical Satire in the Age of Walpole* (Exeter: Exeter University Press, 2015).

Valladares, Susan, *Staging the Peninsular War: English Theatres 1807–1815* (London: Routledge, 2016).

Van Kooy, Dana, *Shelley's Radical Stages: Romantic Drama in Wartime* (London: Routledge, 2016).

Wilson, Brett D., *A Race of Female Patriots: Women and Public Spirit on the British Stage 1688–1745* (Lewisburg: Bucknell University Press, 2012).

Novel

Davis, Lennard J., *Factual Fictions: The Origins of the English Novel* (New York: Columbia University Press, 1983).

Downie, James Alan, *A Political Biography of Henry Fielding* (London: Pickering and Chatto, 2009).

Fletcher, Loraine, *Charlotte Smith: A Critical Biography* (Basingstoke: Macmillan, 1998).

Keymer, Thomas, *Sterne, the Moderns, and the Novel* (Oxford: Oxford University Press, 2002).

Lukács, Georg, *The Historical Novel*, translated by Hannah and Stanley Mitchell, (London: Merlin Press, 1962).

Maslen, Keith, *Samuel Richardson of London, Printer* (Christchurch NZ: University of Otago, 2001).

McKeon, Michael, *The Origins of the English Novel, 1600–1740* (Baltimore: John Hopkins University Press, 1987).

McKeon, Michael, 'Generic Transformation and Social Change: Rethinking the Rise of the Novel', in Michael McKeon, ed., *Theory of the Novel: A Historical Approach* (Baltimore: Johns Hopkins University Press, 2000), 382–399.

Novak, Maximillian E., 'Warfare and Its Discontents in Eighteenth-Century Fiction: Or, Why Eighteenth-Century Fiction Failed to Produce a *War and Peace*', *Eighteenth-Century Fiction* 4 (3) (1992), 185–206.

Novak, Maximillian E., 'Defoe and the Art of War', *Philological Quarterly* 75 (2) (1996), 197–213.

Southam, Brian, *Jane Austen and the Navy* (London: National Maritime Museum, 2005).

Further Reading

Trumpener, Katie, *Bardic Nationalism: The Romantic Novel and the British Empire* (Princeton NJ: Princeton University Press, 1997).

Warner, William B., *Licensing Entertainment: The Elevation of Novel Reding in Britain, 1684–1750* (Berkeley: University of California Press, 1998).

Watts, Carol, *The Cultural Work of Empire: The Seven Years' War and the Imagining of the Shandean State* (Toronto: Toronto University Press, 2007).

Woodworth, Megan A., *Eighteenth-Century Women Writers and the Gentleman's Liberation Movement: Independence, War, Masculinity and the Novel, 1778–1818* (Burlington: Ashgate, 2011).

Poetry

Bainbridge, Simon, *Napoleon and English Romanticism* (Cambridge: Cambridge University Press, 1995).

Bainbridge, Simon, *British Poetry and the Revolutionary and Napoleonic Wars: Visions of Conflict* (Oxford: Oxford University Press, 2003).

Bainbridge, Simon, 'Romanticism and War', (2016), tiny.one/mryuh9ev

Bennett, Betty T., *British War Poetry in the Age of Romanticism, 1793–1815*, Digital Text edited by Orianne Smith, tiny.one/2p8n6782

Broich, Ulrich, *The Eighteenth-Century Mock-Heroic Poem* (Cambridge: Cambridge University Press, 1990).

Clery, E. J., *Eighteen Hundred and Eleven: Poetry, Protest and Economic Crisis* (Cambridge: Cambridge University Press, 2017).

Favret, Mary, *War at a Distance: Romanticism and the Making of Modern Wartime* (Princeton, NJ: Princeton University Press, 2009).

Gerrard, Christine, *The Patriot Opposition to Walpole: Politics, Poetry and National Myth, 1725–1742* (Oxford: Oxford University Press, 1994).

Griffin, Dustin, *Patriotism and Poetry in Eighteenth-Century Britain* (Cambridge: Cambridge University Press, 2002).

Hahn, H. George, *The Ocean Bards: British Poetry and the War at Sea, 1793–1815* (Oxford: Lang, 2008).

Kelsall, Malcolm, *Byron's Politics* (Brighton: Harvester, 1987).

Keymer, Thomas, 'Civil Rage: Poetry and War in the 1740s', *Eighteenth-Century Life*, 44 (2020), 8–29.

Lincoln, Andrew, *Walter Scott and Modernity* (Edinburgh: Edinburgh University Press, 2007).

O'Brien, Karen, 'Protestantism and the Poetry of Empire, 1660–1800', in Jeremy Black, ed., *Culture and Society in Britain, 1660–1800* (Manchester: Manchester University Press, 1997), 146–162.

O'Brien, Karen, 'Poetry against Empire: Milton to Shelley', *Proceedings of the British Academy*, 117 (2002) 269–296.

Rawson, Claude, 'War and the Epic Mania in England and France: Milton, Boileau, Prior and the English Mock-Heroic', *Review of English Studies*, 64 (2012).

292 *Further Reading*

Richardson, John, 'Modern Warfare in Early-Eighteenth-Century Poetry', *Studies in English Literature 1500–1900*, 45 (3) (2005), 557–577.

Richardson, John, 'War, Lyric Poetry and Politics in the Eighteenth Century', *Eighteenth-Century Studies*, 50 (2017), 381–399.

Shaw, Philip, *Waterloo and the Romantic Imagination* (Basingstoke: Palgrave, 2002).

Terry, Richard, *Mock-Heroic from Butler to Cowper: An English Genre and Discourse* (Aldershot: Ashgate, 2005).

Watson, J. R., *Romanticism and War* (Basingstoke: Palgrave, 2003).

Williams, Abigail, *Poetry and the Creation of a Whig Culture 1681–1714* (Oxford: Oxford University Press, 2005).

Index

acquiescence, 8, 15, 159, 161, 173, 177, 196, 208
Addison, Joseph
  The Campaign, 7–8, 79–81
  Cato, 83
  'A Poem to His Majesty', 34, 41
  The Spectator, 40, 49, 57–75
Africa, 247
  Africa Institution, 249
  Sierra Leone, 247, 249
  Sierra Leone Company, 255
Akenside, Mark
  British Philippic, 93
Alexander, Tsar of Russia, 253
Alexander the Great, 6, 66, 132, 246
Allan, Alexander, 276
Allen, William, 246
America. *See also* wars: American War
    of Independence, Penn, William,
    Pennsylvania
  American Revolution, 183, 204
  Braddock, Colonel Edward, 109–112
  native Americans, 9, 100, 108, 110, 112, 115,
    189, 193, 247, 249–251
  Proclamation Line, 253
Amherst, General Jeffery, 168
Anderson, Benedict, 46, 92
anti-heroic discourse, 3, 123–124, 126, 146
Aristotle, 246
army, 11, 33, 35, 58, 62, 201
Augustine, 5, 6
Austen, Jane, 213–215
  Mansfield Park, 214–215
  Northanger Abbey, 214
  Persuasion, 213, 214
  Pride and Prejudice, 214

balance of power, 77, 164, 166
ballads, 13, 37, 38, 40, 42, 129, 203, 210, 239, 270
  Chevy Chase, 69
Banister, Julia, 63, 221
Bank of England, 33, 60, 70

Barbauld, Anna, 2
  Eighteen Hundred and Thirteen, 224
  On the Expected General Rising, 224–225
  Sins of Government, Sins of the Nation, 207–209
bard, 227
barracks, 231
Barrell, Maria
  British Liberty Vindicated, 205–206, 210
Barry, James, 115
battles
  Blenheim, 76, 262
  Cartagena, 162
  Culloden, 100, 101, 103, 109
  Dettingen, 133
  Falkirk Muir, 96, 109
  Fontenoy, 94
  Malplaquet, 59, 62, 76
  Minden, 114
  Minorca, 144, 145, 171, 175, 270
  Montreal, 168
  Portobello, 101, 129, 130, 162
  Prestonpans, 103, 109
  Waterloo, 238
Beattie, Bernard, 237
Benedict, Barbara, 151, 267
benevolence, 5, 8, 18, 32, 176, 188, 209
Bentham, Jeremy, 3
bereavement, 75
Bermonsey Spa, 272
Bird, Edward, 170
Black Prince, 170
Blake, William, 16
  America, 221
  The Four Zoas, 19
Boaden, James
  Cambro-Britons, 227–228
Boileau-Despréaux, Nicholas, 6, 76
Bolingbroke, 1st Viscount, 83, 162, 203
  Idea of a Patriot King, 85
  Letters on the Spirit of Patriotism, 83
Bowles, John, 222

Index

Bowyer, Robert
  Historic Gallery, 170
Boyer, Abel, 39, 267
Breval, John
  The Art of Dress, 263, 267
  Calpe, or Gibraltar, 263–268
Brewer, John, 15, 32
British Museum, 259, 270, 274
Brown, John
  Estimate of Manners, 143, 171
Bruce, Robert the, 233–234
brutality, 6, 7, 35, 63, 67, 88, 126, 129, 173, 177,
  189, 212, 215, 228
Buckingham, Duke of
  funeral monument, 91
Budgell, Eustace, 65
Burke, Edmund, 222
  Reflections on the Revolution in France, 190, 226
  the sublime, 272
Burnet, Gilbert, 44
Byng, Admiral John, 171, 175
Byron, Lord
  Childe Harold's Pilgrimage, 235–239

Caesar, Julius, 6
  Commentaries, 6, 144
Canada, 100, 112–117, 262. *See also* Quebec
Carter, Francis
  Journey from Gibraltar to Malaga, 270–272
Carter, George
  painting, *The Siege of Gibraltar*, 273
Cartwright, Major John, 245
casualties hypothesis, 76
Catholicism, Roman, 128
Ceadel, Martin, 245
Cervantes
  Don Quixote, 124
chapbooks, 66, 138
Chelsea Hospital, 32
chivalry, 190, 192, 193, 195, 226, 229–230,
  232–236
Christianity, 100, 211, 246, 248, 250, 253.
  See also evangelical
Chudleigh, Lady Mary, 35
Church of England
  Communion, 88
  Fast Day and Thanksgiving services, 12, 44–47
civic humanism, 11, 17, 20, 36, 144, 188, 208, 247
civilian, 11, 18, 20, 200, 209, 240
civilized, 10, 101, 111, 172, 228, 245, 246
civilizing process, 20, 157, 170, 253, 256. *See also*
  Elias, Norbert
Clarke, Samuel, 6
Clarkson, Thomas, 246–252
  *Essay of the Slavery and Commerce of the
    Human Species*, 246

History of the Abolition of the Slave Trade,
  250
Memoirs of William Penn, 250–251
Portrait of Quakerism, 249
Clery, E. J., 34, 130, 134
Clive, Robert, 187
coffee houses, 61
  Saltero's, 267
Colebrook, Robert
  Twelve Views of Mysoor, 275
Colley, Linda, 14, 222
Collins, William, 145
  'How Sleep the Brave', 95–97
  'Ode to a Lady', 94–95
commerce, 36, 65, 69, 157, 161, 171, 263
Cookson, J. E., 207, 210, 223, 245, 246
Copley, John Singleton
  Defeat of the Floating Batteries at Gibraltar,
    273
corruption, 144, 145, 151
courts martial, 135
Cowper, William, 4, 254
  The Task, 2–5
Cromwell, Oliver, 261
Cronin, Richard, 235
Cumberland, Duke of, 101–103, 107

D'Avenant, Charles, 15
De Hondt, Lambert, the Younger, 38
De Scudéry, Madeleine, 6, 124
Defoe, Daniel, 126–129, 132, 268
  Colonel Jack, 126–128
  The Double Welcome, 126
  Essay on Literature, 126
  Essay on Projects, 126
  Hymn to the Mob, 128
  Memoirs of a Cavalier, 126–129
demobilization, 138, 147
Denham, John
  Cooper's Hill, 264
Denne, Henry, 43
Dennis, John, 47–49, 68
  The Advancement of Modern Poetry, 47
  The Battle of Ramillia, 42
  Britannia Triumphans, 47, 77
  Gibraltar, or the Spanish Adventure, 262
  The Grounds of Criticism in Poetry, 48
Dissent, 126, 208–209, 223, 225–226, 247–249
Doddridge, Philip
  Life of Gardiner, 103–108
  Rise and Progress of Religion in the Soul, 105
Drake, Sir Francis, 84
Dryden, John, 262

East India Company, 16, 70, 191, 250
Edwards, Edward, 170

Index

295

Edy, John William, 275
effeminacy, 19, 34, 143, 171, 215
elegy, 42, 80, 231
Elias, Norbert, 31–32, 157
Elstob, Elizabeth, 35
empire, 2, 16, 111, 168, 246–248, 255, 259–281
epic, 6, 81, 84–89, 108, 140, 227, 229
epitaphs, 91
Equiano, Olaudah, 246
evangelical Christianity, 9, 19, 211, 213

Farquhar, George
  The Recruiting Officer, 63
Favret, Mary, 20, 202, 213
Felice, William F., 199–200
feminine, 12, 34, 35, 40, 41, 75, 90, 115.
  See also virtue
feminization, 61, 150
Fénelon, François de la Mothe-, 3
  Telemachus, 125
Ferguson, Adam, 158, 221
Fielding, Henry, 6, 12, 130–132
  Amelia, 139–142, 186, 193, 214
  The Champion, 130
  Enquiry into the Causes of the Late Increase of Robbers etc., 139
  Joseph Andrews, 125, 130
  Miscellanies, 131
  Shamela, 130
  Tom Jones, 123
  Of True Greatness, 130
  The True Patriot, 139
  Vernoniad, 131
Fisher, George Bulteel, 275
Fordyce, James
  Sermons to Young Women, 203
Foucault, Michel, 70
Foundling Hospital, 14, 135
Franklin, Benjamin, 186
French Revolution, 18, 176, 190, 206–209, 231, 244
Fulford, Tim, 20
funerals, 91

Galt, John
  Life of West, 112, 117
Gardiner, Colonel. James, 103–108
Gerrard, Christine, 82
Gibbon, Edmund, 238
Gibraltar, 140, 205, 261–278
  Great Siege, 272
  Siege of 1727, 269
Gisborne, Thomas
  Enquiry into the Duties of Men, 211
  Enquiry into the Duties of the Female Sex, 212, 213

Glover, Richard
  Admiral Hosier's Ghost, 110
  Leonidas, 84–91, 203
  London, or the Progress of Commerce, 88
Gordon Riots, 223
Gray, Thomas
  'The Bard', 227
Greece, 84–89, 166, 237, 239
Greenwich Hospital, 32
Guest, Harriet, 203

Halbertal, Moshe, 78
Harrington, Peter, 272
Hastings, Warren, 244
Hayman, Francis
  The Surrender of Montreal, 168
Hazlitt, William, 13, 230
Hemans, Felicia, 13
Herald of Peace, 20, 252–254
histories, xi, 6, 13, 36, 132
Hobbes, Thomas, 81
Hodges, William, 276
Holliday, Henry, 170
Home, John
  Siege of Aquileia, 168
Homer, 66, 68
  Aeneid, 140
  Iliad, 86, 89, 108, 132
Hoock, Holger, 14
humanitarianism, 6, 8, 32, 163, 172, 229
humanity, 10, 12, 172–173
Hume, David, 11, 136, 148, 158–170
  Enquiries, 164
  Essays, 162–163
  History of England, 167–170
  Political Discourses, 166
  sympathy, 160
  Treatise of Human Nature, 158–161
Hurd, Richard, 229
Hutcheson, Francis, 84
Huxham, John, 136

India, 14, 15, 19, 228, 250, 262
  Nabob, 187, 188
  Second Mysore War, 191, 244, 276
  Third Mysore War, 276
  Trial of Warren Hastings, 276
invasion, 220, 222, 230
Ireland, 203, 227, 228, 245, 275
Italy, 239

Jacobite rebellion (1745), 100, 123, 135, 143
  Culloden, 100–103, 109
  Falkirk Muir, 109
  Prestonpans, 103, 109

296 Index

Johnson, Samuel, 123
Jones, George, 170
Jones, Vivienne, 12
journals, campaign, 4, 13, 38, 124

Kant, Immanuel, 3
Kelsall, Malcolm, 236, 239
Keymer, Thomas, 101, 147
King, William, 267
Klepp, Susan A., 252

Lamb, Jonathan, 149
landownership, 144, 148, 187, 189
law of nations, 77
Le Bossu, 67
liberalism, 11, 157, 188, 200, 208, 220, 237
licensing laws, 34
Life and Memoirs of Ephraim Tristram Bates,
   143–146
Locke, John, 11, 32, 81, 187
   Some Thoughts Concerning Education, 6, 36, 65
Lucan, Marcus Annaeus Lucanus, 38
Lukács, Georg, 231
luxury, 34, 75, 86, 87, 90, 139, 164, 247
Lyttleton, George, 84

Maas, Dirk, 37
Machiavelli, Niccolò, 11
Macpherson, James, 235
   Ossian, 227
magazines, 13
   European Magazine, 274
   Gentleman's Magazine, 10, 85, 93, 111, 123
   Geographical Magazine, 274
   London Magazine, 9
   Universal Magazine, 9
Mallett, David
   Alfred the Great, 96
Mandeville, Bernard, 77
   The Fable of the Bees, 2
manners, 1, 31, 39, 48, 63–64
   societies for reforming, 35
Marlborough, Duke of, 6, 62, 77, 262
Marshall, P. J., 250
masculinity, 11, 32, 34, 40, 63, 134, 215, 221
Mead, Richard, 136
medicine, 135, 136, 141, 149, 267
memoirs, 13, 125, 127
mercantilism, 166
military dictionaries, 13
military-fiscal state, 16
militia, 11, 19, 34, 65, 231
   militia debate, 158
millenarianism, 21, 244
Milton, John
   Paradise Lost, 81, 86

minstrel, 228
missionaries, 250
mock heroic, 38, 124
monarchs
   Alfred the Great, 84
   Charles I, 167
   Edward I, 233
   Edward III, 84, 168–170
   Elizabeth I, 84
   George II, 85
   Henry V, 84
   James I, 38, 167
   Louis XIV, 32, 37, 57, 61
   Louis XV, 168
   Queen Anne, 35, 44, 78, 267
   Queen Mary, 40, 42
   William III, 35, 37, 42, 44
Monck, General George, 41
Monmouth, Duke of, 126, 168
Montagu, Charles, 41
monuments, 13, 90–96, 106
Moody, Elizabeth
   Poetic Trifles, 210
morality of war. *See also* acquiescence
   moral dualism, 2, 5
   moral insulation, 17, 199–200
   moral view, 3, 19, 123, 125, 135
   national view, 3, 19, 123, 146, 158–161,
      172–174, 185, 254, 261
More, Hannah
   'Sensibility', 203
   *Strictures on the Modern System of Female
      Education*, 213
mourning, 18, 90–97, 224–226, 233, 235
Murray, General James, 10
music, 14
   concerts, 14
   popular songs, 14, 37

Napoleon, 16, 231, 233
national debt, 15, 164, 165
navy, 32, 35, 202, 230, 250, 255
   mutiny, 230
Nelson, Horatio, 16, 80, 210, 234, 274
newspapers, 38–40, 59–60, 138
Newton, Isaac, 11
non-combatant, 11, 143
Novak, Maximillian, 123
novel, 9, 123–151, 185–196, 213–215, 232–235, 239

obsolescence, 18, 226–232
Oglethorpe, James, 110
Opie, Amelia, 13
   'Ode on the Present Times', 225
orientalism, 237
Owen, Wilfred, 4

Index 297

pacifism, 18, 186, 188, 189, 196, 245. *See also*
  Herald of Peace
  commercial, 157, 161
Paine, Thomas, 19, 222
  Common Sense, 183, 187
  Rights of Man, 3, 183, 190, 244
painting, 14, 33, 37, 66, 113, 137, 168, 259, 273
Paley, William
  Evidences of Christianity, 211
panorama, 14, 275
patriotism, 3, 14, 144, 234
  domestication of, 17, 204, 214, 232, 275
Patriots, 82–89
patronage, 13, 16, 22, 37, 38, 124, 127, 136, 147,
  151, 194, 202, 270
peace, 196
  Aix la Chappelle, 270
  Amiens, 230
  anti-conquest, 255, 264, 272
  arbitration, 251
  Congress of Vienna, 253
  cultural violence, 255
  Democratic Peace Theory, 245
  Friends of Peace, 207, 222, 223, 245
  Friends of Peace and Christianity, 246
  global, 244
  pacification, 37, 233
  peace education, 1, 251, 255
  peace leadership, 251
  Peace of Paris, 147
  peace societies, 1, 14, 20
  Society for the Promotion of Permanent
    and Universal Peace, 246
Penn, William, 247, 249–252
  relations with Lenapes, 252
Pennsylvania, 250–252
Penny, Edward, 115
Percy, Thomas
  'on the Ancient Metrical Romances', 229
periodicals
  The Craftsman, 82, 268
  The Spectator, 60–75
  The Tatler, 58–69, 267
Peterloo Massacre, 253
petitioning, 17, 190, 222, 245
philanthropy, 5, 13, 32, 70
Phillips, Mark Salber, 167
picketing (military punishment), 130, 150
Pine, Robert Edge, 168
Pitt, William
  Pitt the Elder, Earl of Chatham, 19, 113, 147
  Pitt the Younger, 16
Plank, Geoffrey, 112, 268
Pocock, John, 11, 157
politeness, 12, 33, 35, 57–71
Pope, Alexander, 6

Homer, 124
  Windsor Forest, 263
Porter, Jane
  The Scottish Chiefs, 233–235
  Thaddeus of Warsaw, 233
Pratt, Marie Louise, 255, 264, 272, 276
Pratt, Samuel Jackson
  Emma Corbett, 17, 191–196
  Sympathy, 190
Price, Richard
  Discourse on the Love of Our Country, 176
Priestley, Joseph, 223
Pringle, James, 136
  Life of Wolfe, 115
  Observations on the Diseases of the Army, 150
prints, 13, 101, 129, 189, 269, 274
Prior, Matthew, 76
prisoners of war, 135, 168
prize money, 135
progress, 157, 160, 172, 227, 231, 244
promotion, 135
providence, 21, 46, 76, 245
public opinion, 58, 76–77, 158, 164, 201
Pye, Henry James
  Naucratica, 230

Quakers, 14, 16, 247–249, 253
  Penn, William, 247, 249–252
  Worcester, Noah, 252
Quebec, 112–117, 171

radicalism, 19, 183, 190, 191, 209, 212, 221, 223,
  237, 244
Raleigh, Sir Walter, 84
Rapin de Thoyras, Paul, 169
recruitment, 63, 103, 135, 136, 201, 211, 223, 230
Reeve, Clara
  Memoirs of Sir Roger de Clarendon, 229
  Progress of Romance, 229
Reviews
  Edinburgh Review, 233, 235
  Quarterly Review, 233
Richardson, John, 38
Richardson, Samuel, 12
  Clarissa, 105, 125, 135, 188, 189
  Daily Gazeteer, 133
  House of Commons Journal, 133
  Pamela, 129
  Sir Charles Grandison, 134
Rivers, Isabel, 108
Robinson, Mary
  'The Deserted Cottage', 210
romance, 124–126, 131, 134, 138, 190, 229–232,
  236
Romney, George, 115
Roubiliac, Louis François, 91

Index

Rousseau, Jean Jacques, 3, 17, 187, 189, 193, 238
  A Discourse on Inequality, 3
  Emile, 203
Rowe, Nicholas, 42
Royal Academy, 14, 115, 270

Sacheverell crisis, 59
sacrifice, 7, 87, 108, 205, 234
  atonement, 77, 80, 88, 111, 116
  sacrificing for, 80
  sacrificing to, 78
Sager, Eric W., 254
sailors, 4, 9, 91, 138, 222, 271
Saint-Pierre, Abbé de, 3
Sandby, Paul, 275
  Virtuosi's Museum, 274
Sandwich, First Earl of, Edward Montagu, 42
savagery, 6, 100–101, 106–112, 115–117, 246
Science of Man, 11, 157
Scotland, 100–108, 230–235, 239
Scott, Walter
  Lay of the Last Minstrel, 230–232
  Marmion, 236
  Waverley, 108, 123, 239
Scottish Enlightenment, 9, 158, 221
sermons, 3, 44, 105, 202, 226
sex panic, 212
Shaftesbury, 3rd Earl of, 5, 32
  Characteristics, 63, 81–82
Sharp, Granville, 247, 250
Shaw, Philip, 7
Shelley, Percy Bysshe, 19
Sheridan, Richard
  Pizarro, 228
Shovell, Admiral Cloudesly, 42, 91
Sieberg, Donald T., 170
sin, 12, 44, 47
slavery, 15, 19, 191, 207, 215, 244, 246, 247, 249, 251
Sloane, Hans
  History of Jamaica, 264
Smirk, Robert, 170
Smith, Adam, 11, 191–196
  impartial spectator, 174
  'Lectures on Jurisprudence', 175
  Theory of Moral Sentiments, 171–178, 200
  Wealth of Nations, 175–176, 201, 221
Smith, Charlotte, 20
  The Emigrants, 210
  The Old Manor House, 16, 191–196
Smollett, Tobias, 125, 136
  Complete History of England, 138
  Roderick Random, 136–138, 149
  Tears of Scotland, 102, 138
Snell, Hannah, 203
Society for the Encouragement of Arts,
  Manufactures and Commerce, 168

Society of Antiquaries, 270
Society of Artists, 14
soldiers, 42, 58, 63, 91, 96, 138, 143, 144, 221
South Sea Bubble, 82
Southey, Robert
  'The Battle of Blenheim', 274
  Joan of Arc, 229
  Life of Nelson, 274
  'The Soldier's Funeral', 209, 224
Spady, James O'Neil, 252
Spain, 232–233, 235, 261, 266, 268
Spragge, Sir Edward, 42
Steele, Richard, 103
  London Gazette, 58
  The Lover, 33
  The Tatler, 58–65, 267
Stepney, George, 41
Sterne, Laurence
  Tristram Shandy, 143, 146–151
Strong, Roy, 170
sublime, 47–49, 67, 68, 272
Swift, Jonathan
  Gulliver's Travels, 3
Switzerland, 227
symmetrical warfare, 77

tapestries, 37, 38
taste, 228–229
taxation, 15, 58, 83, 148, 165, 176, 190, 249
Temple, William, 6
theatre, 2, 14, 75, 88, 123, 168, 203, 227–228
Thomson, James, 230
  Alfred the Great, 96
  Britannia, 83, 110
  Castle of Indolence, 83
  Liberty, 83
Toland, John, 64
Tolstoy, Leo
  War and Peace, 123
Tories, 42, 58, 62, 69, 101, 159, 230, 233, 235
Treaty of Aix la Chappell, 143
Treaty of Utrecht, 263
Trotter, Thomas, 136
Trumbull, John,
  Sortie Made by the Garrison of Gibraltar,
  273
Trumpener, Katie, 227
Tutchin, John, 39

unrest, 18, 128, 138, 223, 224, 230
Upton, Catherine, 210
  Siege of Gibraltar, 205

Vauxhall Gardens, 14, 137, 169
Vernon, Admiral, 101, 107, 129, 130, 162
victories, 13, 14, 37, 66, 123, 225

Index

Virgil, 68
Georgics, 264, 265
virtue
  feminine, 134–135, 141–142, 145, 150, 185, 186,
    189, 195, 202–206, 212–215, 229, 234, 236
  martial, 11, 144–146, 172, 223, 230
  social, 7, 32, 33, 41, 79, 131, 164
Voltaire, 238, 247

Wahrman, Dror, 204
Wakefield, Gilbert, 222
Wallace, William, 233–235
Waller, Edmund, 262
Ward, Ned, 62
Warner, Michael, 125
wars
  American War of Independence, 16, 18, 186,
    206, 248, 272
  Anglo-Spanish War, 139, 269
  French Revolutionary Wars, 222, 245
  Napoleonic, 238, 245
  Nine Years' War, 58, 148
  Second Mysore War, 191, 244, 276
  Seven Years' War, 9, 16, 19, 143, 167, 171,
    187, 246, 269
  Third Mysore War, 276
  War of Jenkins's Ear, 129, 161, 164
  War of the Austrian Succession, 100, 138,
    147, 148, 161, 164, 269
  War of the Spanish Succession, 13, 58,
    148, 262

West, Benjamin, 170
The Death of General Wolfe, 115–117
Penn's Treaty with the Indians, 247
Westall, Richard, 170
Westminster Abbey, 92, 113
Whigs, 19, 34, 64, 69, 159, 233, 235–236, 263
  Robert Walpole, 82–84, 130–132, 269
White, James, 229
Wilberforce, William, 248, 250
Williams, Abigail, 38, 40, 57
Williams, Raymond, 134
Wilton, Joseph, 113, 115
Wolfe, General James, 19, 80, 112–117
Wollstonecraft, Mary
Rights of Woman, 212
women
  army wives, 202
  domestic, 1, 17, 61, 130, 189, 202, 206,
    212, 213
  female warrior, 203, 204, 234
  investors, 33
  mistresses, 202
  prostitutes, 202
  readers, 9, 230
  wife-at-war, 204–206, 214, 216
  writers, 35
Woolwich Military Academy, 275
Wordsworth, William
  'The Female Vagrant', 210
  'The Ruined Cottage', 210
Wyck, Jan, 37